"Too Much to Grasp"

Journal of Theological Interpretation Supplements

MURRAY RAE
University of Otago, New Zealand
Editor-in-Chief

1. Thomas Holsinger-Friesen, *Irenaeus and Genesis: A Study of Competition in Early Christian Hermeneutics*
2. Douglas S. Earl, *Reading Joshua as Christian Scripture*
3. Joshua N. Moon, *Jeremiah's New Covenant: An Augustinian Reading*
4. Csilla Saysell, *"According to the Law": Reading Ezra 9–10 as Christian Scripture*
5. Joshua Marshall Strahan, *The Limits of a Text: Luke 23:34a as a Case Study in Theological Interpretation*
6. Seth B. Tarrer, *Reading with the Faithful: Interpretation of True and False Prophecy in the Book of Jeremiah from Ancient Times to Modern*
7. Zoltán S. Schwáb, *Toward an Interpretation of the Book of Proverbs: Selfishness and Secularity Reconsidered*
8. Steven Joe Koskie, Jr., *Reading the Way to Heaven: A Wesleyan Theological Hermeneutic of Scripture*
9. Hubert James Keener, *A Canonical Exegesis of the Eighth Psalm: Yhwh's Maintenance of the Created Order through Divine Intervention*
10. Vincent K. H. Ooi, *Scripture and Its Readers: Readings of Israel's Story in Nehemiah 9, Ezekiel 20, and Acts 7*
11. Andrea D. Saner, *"Too Much to Grasp": Exodus 3:13–15 and the Reality of God*
12. Jonathan Douglas Hicks, *Trinity, Economy, and Scripture: Recovering Didymus the Blind*

"Too Much to Grasp"

*Exodus 3:13–15 and the
Reality of God*

ANDREA D. SANER

Winona Lake, Indiana
EISENBRAUNS
2015

Copyright © 2015 Eisenbrauns
All rights reserved.

Printed in the United States of America

www.eisenbrauns.com

Library of Congress Cataloging-in-Publication Data

Saner, Andrea D.
   Too much to grasp : Exodus 3:13–15 and the reality of God / Andrea D. Saner.
      pages cm. — (Journal of theological interpretation supplements ; 11)
   Includes bibliographical references and index.
   ISBN 978-1-57506-397-3 (pbk. : alk. paper)
   1. God—Name—Biblical teaching. 2. Bible. Exodus—Criticism, interpretation, etc. I. Title.
   BS1192.6.S26 2015
   222′.1206—dc23
                                                           2015028992

The paper used in this publication meets the minimum requirements of the American National Standard for Information Sciences—Permanence of Paper for Printed Library Materials, ANSI Z39.48-1984.♾™

For Eric

Table of Contents

Introduction 1

Part 1. Clearing the Ground for Theological Interpretation of Exodus 3:13–15 11

Chapter 1. Reading Exodus 3:13–15 from von Rad to Childs and Beyond 13

    1. Etymology, Religio-historical Approaches 13

        1.1. Etymology 14

            1.1.1 Storm god 15

            1.1.2. To be 17

            1.1.3. Conclusion 19

        1.2. Historical Reconstruction 20

        1.3. Conclusions 27

    2. Brevard Childs, The Book of Exodus 31

        2.1. Diachronic Analysis and the Final Form 33

        2.2. New Testament, History of Interpretation,
        and Theological Reflection 35

            2.2.1. New Testament 35

            2.2.2. History of interpretation 37

            2.2.3. Theological reflection 39

        2.3. Childs's Multilevel Reading and Ontological Interpretation 39

    3. The Literal Sense 45

        3.1. The Literal Sense According to Hans Frei 46

3.2. Childs and the Literal Sense 52

3.3. Critiquing Frei's Christological Literal Sense 55

Chapter 2. Augustine's Literal-Sense Reading of Exodus 3:14–15 59

1. The Literal Sense in Augustine 60

2. Confessions Book 7 69

3. Augustine's Characteristic Reading of Exodus 3:14 76

3.1. Expositions of the Psalms 121 76

3.2. Sermon 6 and Sermon 7 80

3.3. Christ the Mediator 85

4. Divine Being 88

4.1. Idipsum, Est, and the Nature of Divine Being 89

4.2. Divine Being, Holy Trinity 94

4.3. Trinity and Exodus 3:14–15 102

5. Summary 104

Part 2. Rebuilding Theological Interpretation of Exodus 3:13–15 107

Chapter 3. The Divine Name in the Book of Exodus 109

1. Call of Moses (Exod 3–4) 110

1.1. Paronomasia and Translation (Exod 3:14) 110

1.2. Exodus 3:13–15 in Its Immediate Literary Context 117

2. The Name in Exodus 5–40 129

2.1. Plagues and Exodus (Exod 5–15) 129

2.1.1. "Who is YHWH?" (Exod 5:2) 130

2.1.2. "I [am] YHWH" (Exod 6:2) 131

2.1.3. "So you will know that I [am] YHWH" (Exod 7–14) 138

2.1.4. "YHWH is a warrior" (Exod 15:3) 146

2.2. Decalogue (Exod 20) 149

  2.3. Threatening the Presence of God (Exod 32–34) 153

    2.3.1. Setting the scene: the tent of meeting (Exod 25–31) 153

    2.3.2. Golden calf (Exod 32–34) 155

  2.4. Summary 163

 3. Conclusion 164

Chapter 4. Moses as Covenant Mediator 165

 1. "Never Since Has There Arisen a Prophet in Israel Like Moses" 167

 2. "Whom the Lord Knew Face to Face" 172

  2.1. Moses as Covenant Mediator 173

  2.2. Risk and Intercession 176

  2.3. "Face to Face" 178

  2.4. Numbers 12:6–8 179

 3. "Signs and Wonders," "Mighty Deeds," "Awesome Displays of Power" 187

  3.1. Prophets and "Signs and Wonders" 188

  3.2. The Incomparability of YHWH, Israel, and Moses (Deut 4:32–40) 189

  3.3. Dual Agency 192

 4. Moses Sees and Hears His Prophetic Call (Exod 3: 3:1–4:17) 194

 5. Implications for Reading Exodus 3:13–15 199

  5.1. The Nature of the Question 200

  5.2. Divine Self-Reference in Exodus 3:14a 202

  5.3. Sight and Action 203

  5.4. Perception and Knowledge of God 204

  5.5. "Face to Face" in the New Testament 204

Chapter 5. Exodus 3:13–15 and Trinitarian Doctrine 206

 1. Old Testament "Monotheism" and Divine Unity: Nathan MacDonald 207

 2. Naming God in Three Patterns: R. Kendall Soulen 219

3. The Triune God and the Literal Sense of Exodus 3:13–15 228

Conclusion 231

Bibliography 237

Index of Scripture 255

Index of Authors and Subjects 261

Acknowledgments

This book is a revised version of my PhD dissertation, which was submitted to Durham University in 2013. Thus the first of many thanks goes to my supervisor, Prof. Walter Moberly. Prof. Moberly's careful attention to the nuances of biblical texts is matched only by the integrity with which he reads them. If either virtue is even partially evident in my own work, then I have succeeded. My hearty gratitude extends next to Prof. Lewis Ayres, my secondary supervisor, for his patience in working with a biblical scholar who dabbles in patristics and his help in conceptualizing and organizing the project as a whole. I would also like to thank my examiners Profs. Richard Briggs and Brent Strawn, whose feedback influenced many of the revisions evident in this work.

I would also like to thank my many conversation partners, who have shaped this in countless ways over the years, including study residents of Dun Cow Cottage and those who attended Prof. Moberly's informal seminar, especially Josh Furnal, Angie Harvey, Ben Johnson, Paul Jones, Thomas Lynch, Jon Parker, Zoltán Schwáb, and Charlie Shepherd; and my colleagues and students at Eastern Mennonite Seminary, Eastern Mennonite University.

Finally, my thanks is due to Prof. Murray Rae and the Editorial Board of the JTI Supplement Series for accepting the manuscript for publication, to Andrew Knapp for his formatting expertise, and to Jim Eisenbraun for guiding the process.

This book is dedicated to my husband, Eric Saner, whose support would take another book to adequately characterize. Thank you for your unfailing confidence and encouragement. Here's to our next adventure.

Andrea D. Saner
Ascension Day 2015

Abbreviations

Biblical Texts, Translations, and Versions

LXX	Septuagint
MT	Masoretic Text
NETS	*New English Translation of the Septuagint*
NJPS	*Tanakh: The Holy Scriptures: The New JPS Translation according to the Traditional Hebrew Text*
NRSV	New Revised Standard Version
Sam. Pent.	Samaritan Pentateuch
Syr.	Syriac
Vulg.	Vulgate

Targumic Texts

Tg. Neof.	*Targum Neofiti*
Tg. Onq.	*Targum Onqelos*
Tg. Ps-J.	*Targum Pseudo-Jonathan*
Tg. Yer. I	*Targum Yerušalmi*
Tg. Yer. II	*Targum Yerušalmi I*

Works of Ambrose

Exp. Luc.	*Expositio Evangelii secundum Lucam*	Ambrose

Works of Augustine

Civ.	*De civitate Dei*	*City of God*
Conf.	*Confessionum libri XIII*	*Confessions*
Doctr. chr.	*De doctrina christiana*	*Christian Instruction*

Enarrat. Ps.	Enarrationes in Psalmos	Expositions of the Psalms
Trin.	De Trinitate	The Trinity
Serm.	Sermones	Sermons
Tract. Ev. Jo.	In Evangelium Johannis tractatus	Tractates on the Gospel of John

Works of Philo

Mos. 1	De vita Mosis I	On the Life of Moses 1

Secondary Sources

AB	Anchor Bible
AfO	Archiv für Orientforschung
AOTC	Abingdon Old Testament Commentaries
ASTI	Annual of the Swedish Theological Institute
AThR	Anglican Theological Review
AugStud	Augustinian Studies
BBB	Bonner biblische Beiträge
BBR	Bulletin for Biblical Research
BCBC	Believers Church Bible Commentary
BETL	Bibliotheca ephemeridum theologicarum lovaniensium
BIOSCS	Bulletin of the International Organization for Septuagint and Cognate Studies
BTCB	Brazos Theological Commentary on the Bible
BZAW	Beihefte zur Zeitschrift für die alttestamentliche Wissenschaft
CBQ	Catholic Biblical Quarterly
CJA	Christianity and Judaism in Antiquity
CSCD	Cambridge Studies in Christian Doctrine
CTHPT	Cambridge Texts in the History of Political Thought
DDD	Dictionary of Deities and Demons in the Bible
Enc	Encounter
ErIsr	Eretz-Israel
ETL	Ephemerides theologicae lovanienses
ExAud	Ex auditu
ExpTim	Expository Times
FAT	Forschungen zum Alten Testament

FOTL	Forms of the Old Testament Literature
FRLANT	Forschungen zur Religion und Literatur des Alten und Neuen Testaments
HALOT	*The Hebrew and Aramaic Lexicon of the Old Testament*
HBM	Hebrew Bible Monographs
HBT	*Horizons in Biblical Theology*
HSS	Harvard Semitic Studies
HTR	*Harvard Theological Review*
HUCA	*Hebrew Union College Annual*
IB	Interpreter's Bible
IBC	Interpretation: A Bible Commentary for Teaching and Preaching
Int	*Interpretation*
IJST	*International Journal of Systematic Theology*
JBL	*Journal of Biblical Literature*
JECS	*Journal of Early Christian Studies*
JETS	*Journal of the Evangelical Theological Society*
JPS	Jerusalem Publication Society
JRASGBI	*Journal of the Royal Asiatic Society of Great Britain and Ireland*
JSNT	*Journal for the Study of the New Testament*
JSOT	*Journal for the Study of the Old Testament*
JSOTSup	Journal for the Study of the Old Testament: Supplement Series
JSS	*Journal of Semitic Studies*
JTI	*Journal of Theological Interpretation*
JTS	*Journal of Theological Studies*
JQR	*Jewish Quarterly Review*
Int	*Interpretation*
MT	*Modern Theology*
NCB	New Century Bible
NICOT	New International Commentary on the Old Testament
NIDOTTE	*New International Dictionary of Old Testament Theology and Exegesis*
NovT	*Novum Testamentum*
NPNF	Nicene and Post-Nicene Fathers
OBT	Overtures to Biblical Theology
OLZ	*Orientalistische Literaturzeitung*
OTL	Old Testament Library
OTS	Old Testament Studies

OtSt	*Oudtestamentische Studiën*
POS	Pretoria Oriental Series
ProEccl	*Pro Ecclesia*
Proof	*Prooftexts: A Journal of Jewish Literary History*
PRS	Prospectives in Religious Studies
RB	*Revue biblique*
RechAug	*Recherches augustiniennes*
RES	*Revue des Études Sémitiques*
RTL	*Revue théologique de Louvain*
SBLDS	Society of Biblical Literature Dissertation Series
StBL	Studies in Biblical Literature
SubBi	*Subsidia Biblica*
SJOT	*Scandinavian Journal of the Old Testament*
TDOT	*Theological Dictionary of the Old Testament*
ThTo	*Theology Today*
TJ	*Trinity Journal*
TS	*Theological Studies*
TynBul	*Tyndale Bulletin*
UF	*Ugarit-Forschungen*
VT	*Vetus Testamentum*
VT.S	Vetus Testamentum Supplements
WBC	Word Biblical Commentary
WUNT	Wissenschaftliche Untersuchungen zum Neuen Testament
WO	*Die Welt des Orients*
WS	Word and Spirit
WTJ	*Westminster Theological Journal*
ZAW	*Zeitschrift für die alttestamentliche Wissenschaft*

Introduction

The text of Exod 3 tells a dramatic story. Moses has seen the bush; burning but not consumed, it is a peculiar sight and a memorable image. Though God has appeared to him, it is not yet clear whether Moses will accept the call to Egypt. In this context, Moses asks the well-known, if convoluted, question:

> הִנֵּה אָנֹכִי בָא אֶל־בְּנֵי יִשְׂרָאֵל וְאָמַרְתִּי לָהֶם אֱלֹהֵי אֲבוֹתֵיכֶם שְׁלָחַנִי אֲלֵיכֶם וְאָמְרוּ־לִי מַה־שְּׁמוֹ מָה אֹמַר אֲלֵהֶם

> "If I come to the Israelites and say to them, 'The God of your ancestors has sent me to you,' and they ask me, 'What is his name?' what shall I say to them?" (Exod 3:13)[1]

The question raises several interpretive questions. Does Moses genuinely think that the Israelites will ask him this? If so, why? Is Moses trying to avoid asking the question for himself? If so, why? Why does such a profound theological question arise in the midst of Moses' tarrying?

The response follows in equally bewildering fashion:

> וַיֹּאמֶר אֱלֹהִים אֶל־מֹשֶׁה אֶהְיֶה אֲשֶׁר אֶהְיֶה וַיֹּאמֶר כֹּה תֹאמַר לִבְנֵי יִשְׂרָאֵל אֶהְיֶה שְׁלָחַנִי אֲלֵיכֶם: וַיֹּאמֶר עוֹד אֱלֹהִים אֶל־מֹשֶׁה כֹּה־תֹאמַר אֶל־בְּנֵי יִשְׂרָאֵל יְהוָה אֱלֹהֵי אֲבֹתֵיכֶם אֱלֹהֵי אַבְרָהָם אֱלֹהֵי יִצְחָק וֵאלֹהֵי יַעֲקֹב שְׁלָחַנִי אֲלֵיכֶם זֶה־שְּׁמִי לְעֹלָם וְזֶה זִכְרִי לְדֹר דֹּר:

> God said to Moses, "I Am Who I Am." He said further, "Thus you shall say to the Israelites, 'I Am has sent me to you.'" God also said to Moses, "Thus you shall say to the Israelites, the Lord, the God of your ancestors, the God of Abraham, the God of Isaac, and the God of Jacob, has sent me to you':

---

1. Translations of biblical texts are from the NRSV unless otherwise indicated. For discussion of translation of Exod 3:14, see chapter 3, pp. 113–16.

> This is my name forever,
> and this my title for all generations." (Exod 3:14-15)

Still more questions arise. Does the text of verse 14a answer Moses' question? What does the phrase אֶהְיֶה אֲשֶׁר אֶהְיֶה mean? What is the relationship between this phrase and the name "YHWH" in verse 15?

For a variety of reasons (not least of which is the perplexing nature of the passage), few biblical texts have received as much attention as has Exod 3:13-15. Already within the twenty-first century, a number of important articles, monographs and portions of monographs, in theology and biblical studies, have included substantial attention to this text.[2] Particularly in Christian tradition, these verses have had great importance; Gilson famously observed the "metaphysics of Exodus" with increasing clarity through the tradition from Philo and Justin Martyr to its fullest representation in Thomas Aquinas.[3] Augustine alone references Exod 3:14 forty-six times

---

2. Michael Allen, "Exodus 3 After the Hellenization Thesis," *JTI* 3, no. 2 (2009): 179-96; Michael Allen, "Exodus 3," in *Theological Commentary: Evangelical Perspectives*, ed. R. Michael Allen (London: T&T Clark, 2011), 25-40; Nissim Amzallag, "Yahweh, the Canaanite God of Metallurgy?" *JSOT* 33, no. 4 (2009): 387-404; Kathy Beach-Verhey, "Exodus 3:1-12," *Int* (2005): 180-82; C. Clifton Black, "Trinity and Exegesis," *ProEccl* 19, no. 2 (2010): 151-80; Joseph Blenkinsopp, "The Midianite-Kenite Hypothesis Revisited and the Origins of Judah," *JSOT* 33, no. 2 (2008): 131-53; Graham I. Davies, "The Exegesis of the Divine Name in Exodus," in *The God of Israel*, ed. Robert P. Gordon (Cambridge: Cambridge University, 2007), 139-53; Cornelis den Hertog, *The Other Face of God: "I Am That I Am" Reconsidered*, HBM 32 (Sheffield: Sheffield Phoenix, 2012); J. G. Janzen, "And the Bush Was Not Consumed," *Encounter* 63, no. 1/2 (2002): 119-28; R. Kearney, *The God Who May Be* (Indianapolis: Indiana University, 2001); Fergus Kerr, *After Aquinas: Versions of Thomism* (Oxford: Wiley-Blackwell, 2002), esp. 72-96; George H. van Kooten, *The Revelation of the Name YHWH to Moses: Perspectives From Judaism, the Pagan Graeco-Roman World, and Early Christianity* (Leiden; Boston: Brill, 2006); Matthew Levering, *Scripture and Metaphysics: Aquinas and the Renewal of Trinitarian Theology* (Malden, MA: Wiley-Blackwell, 2004), esp. 47-74; R. J. Pannell, "I Would Be Who I Would Be! A Proposal for Reading Exodus 3:11-14," *BBR* 16, no. 2 (2006): 351; George Pattison, *God and Being: An Enquiry* (Oxford: Oxford University, 2011), esp. 17-55; R. Kendall Soulen, *The Divine Name(s) and the Holy Trinity: Distinguishing the Voices* (Louisville: Westminster John Knox, 2011); M. Westphal, "The God Who Will Be: Hermeneutics and the God of Promise," *Faith and Philosophy* 20, no. 3 (2003): 328-44.

3. Etienne Gilson, *The Spirit of Mediæval Philosophy* (Gifford Lectures 1931-1932), trans. A. H. C. Downes (London: Sheed & Ward, 1936), 51, 433-34 fn. 9.

across his many works.⁴ Within a different tradition of study, that of Old Testament studies in the late-nineteenth century, Exod 6:2-3 became a foundational text for source criticism, as two of the sources were discerned based on their distinct views of when the Israelites learned the name "YHWH." As a result, the historical import of Exod 3:13-15 was increasingly emphasized as many viewed the name of God as foundational for historical reconstructions of the development of Israelite religion.⁵

It would seem that this text has received ample consideration. So why yet *another* study? I argue that, within Old Testament studies, the current consensus of how to read these verses disparages traditional Christian readings and offers a thin account of God's identity and work. In contrast, I argue that the literal sense of Exod 3:13-15, understood within the literary context of the received form of the book of Exodus and the wider Pentateuch, witnesses, in its own idiom, to the identity and action of the living God, known to Christians as Father, Son and Holy Spirit. Furthermore, in a Christian

---

4. According to the Benedictines of Beuron. Emilie zum Brunn, *St. Augustine: Being and Nothingness*, trans. Ruth Namad (New York: Paragon House, 1988), 119.

5. To choose a few examples: W. F. Albright, *From the Stone Age to Christianity: Monotheism and the Historical Process* (Garden City, NY: Anchor Books, 1957); Albrecht Alt, "The God of the Fathers," in *Essays on Old Testament History and Religion*, trans. R. A. Wilson (Oxford: Basil Blackwell, 1966); Frank Moore Cross, Jr., "Yahweh and the God of the Patriarchs," *HTR* 55, no. 4 (1962): 225-59; Johannes C. de Moor, *The Rise of Yahwism: The Roots of Israelite Monotheism* (Leuven: Leuven University, 1997); W. O. E. Oesterley and T. H. Robinson, *Hebrew Religion, Its Origin and Development*, 2nd ed. (London: Society for Promoting Christian Knowledge, 1937). More recently, interest in Exod 3:13-15 and 6:2-3 as important for historical reconstruction of the role of the divine name in Israelite religion has decreased significantly. For example, the role of the divine name in the documentary hypothesis receives but passing reference in the *T&T Clark Handbook of the Old Testament*; in the context of discussing the documentary hypothesis, Gertz does not even mention these two biblical texts. Jan Christian Gertz, "The Overall Context of Genesis-2 Kings," trans. Peter Altmann, in *T&T Clark Handbook of the Old Testament: An Introduction to the Literature, Religion and History of the Old Testament*, Jan Christian Gertz et al. (New York: T&T Clark, 2012), 252-54. Schmid still gives some attention to Exod 3 and 6 for understanding the prehistory of the Pentateuch, but the issues have been considerably reframed, so that he can argue that Exod 3:13-15 antedates 6:2-3. Konrad Schmid, *Genesis and the Moses Story: Israel's Dual Origins in the Hebrew Bible*, trans. James Nogalski (Winona Lake, IN: Eisenbrauns, 2010), esp. 172-93.

context, dialogue with premodern readings can assist the reader in perceiving the subject matter of the text, the self-revelation of God to Israel, and to the reader by extension.

My argument stands within the contemporary approach of theological interpretation of Christian Scripture. The proponents of theological interpretation of Scripture include openness to premodern interpretation (as long as this does not mean a "retreat from the rigors of critical analysis")[6] as one of the characteristic marks of the approach they advocate.[7] Yet, to my knowledge, there has been no *sustained* discussion of Exod 3:13-15 firmly rooted within Old Testament studies but interested in reading the text in dialogue with Christian tradition, though there have been some more brief or partial discussions.[8] For example, Michael Allen's insightful article, in which he draws on Augustine's reading of Exod 3:14-15 to critique the "Hellenization Thesis," is a launching point for my own study.[9] Paul Ricoeur's essay, "From Interpretation to Translation," primarily provides a straightforward account of the history of interpretation of Exod 3:14, though he also makes

---

6. Richard Briggs and Joel N. Lohr, eds., *A Theological Introduction to the Pentateuch: Interpreting the Torah as Christian Scripture* (Grand Rapids: Baker, 2012), 4.

7. See several essays in Ellen F. Davis and Richard B. Hays, eds., *The Art of Reading Scripture*, (Grand Rapids: Eerdmans, 2003); Henri de Lubac, SJ, "Spiritual Understanding," in *The Theological Interpretation of Scripture: Classic and Contemporary Readings*, ed. Stephen E. Fowl, trans. Luke O'Neill, *Blackwell Readings in Modern Theology* (Malden, MA; Oxford: Blackwell, 1997); the *regula fidei* and theological interpretation, e.g., George R. Sumner and Ephraim Radner, eds., *The Rule of Faith: Scripture, Canon, and Creed in a Critical Age* (New York: Church Publishing, 1998); R. R. Reno, "'You Who Once Were Far Off Have Been Brought Near': Reflections in the Aid of Theological Exegesis," *ExAud* (2000): 169-82; Christopher R. Seitz, ed., *Nicene Christianity: The Future for a New Ecumenism* (Grand Rapids: Brazos, 2001).

8. Two Old Testament scholars who self-identify as part of this loose movement have struck an impasse on one issue of concern for theological interpretation: the legacy of source criticism. See R. W. L. Moberly, *The Old Testament of the Old Testament: Patriarchal Narratives and Mosaic Yahwism*, OBT (Minneapolis: Fortress, 1992), and, contra Moberly, Christopher Seitz, "The Call of Moses and the 'Revelation' of the Divine Name: Source-Critical Logic and Its Legacy," in *Theological Exegesis: Essays in Honor of Brevard S. Childs*, ed. Christopher Seitz and Kathryn Greene-McCreight (Grand Rapids: Eerdmans, 1999), 145-61.

9. Allen, "Hellenization Thesis," 179-96. Cf. Allen, "Exodus 3," 25-40.

two points which are particularly helpful for my thesis.[10] Ricoeur claims that there are no translations of Exod 3:14 which have been made outside of the history of interpretation of the passage; to translate is already to interpret. He also observes features of the text that "give rise to a perplexity of such a nature as to make, if not legitimate, at least plausible, the so-called ontological reading."[11] This is quite similar to my own approach in chapters 2, 4 and 5, though I am able to linger at greater length on these points than was Ricoeur in his brief essay. Another important work is Cornelis den Hertog's recent collection of essays.[12] Den Hertog's essays, though published as a monograph, retain a somewhat disconnected quality. Moreover, though den Hertog's reading of the Masoretic Text of Exod 3:14 resonates with my own, he argues that Philo's interpretation is unsubstantiated by a careful reading of the Septuagint of Exod 3:14, and so he agrees with the consensus interpretation of Exod 3:13–15 in Old Testament studies (which I discuss below) that traditional readings move away from the sense of the text on its own terms. Thus though I have learned much from den Hertog's work, my project is distinguishable from his both in its conclusions as well as its structure, as I am striving to produce a sustained, monograph-length argument, drawing on both Old Testament studies as well as traditional Christian readings.

Though the approach of theological interpretation is open to premodern readings, the consensus interpretation of Exod 3:13–15 within Old Testament studies distances itself from this tradition. To demonstrate how this is the case, I must explain the apparent consensus. Telling the story from the beginning might require, for instance, beginning with de Wette or Wellhausen, or Harnack's *History of Dogma*,[13] which would lead to questions such as, what

---

10. In *Thinking Biblically: Exegetical and Hermeneutical Studies*, ed. André LaCocque and Paul Ricoeur, trans. David Pellauer (Chicago; London: University of Chicago, 1998), 331–61.

11. Ibid., 332.

12. Den Hertog, *Other Face*.

13. Wilhelm M. L. de Wette, *Beiträge zur Einleitung in das Alte Testament*, 2 vols. (Hildesheim; New York: G. Olms, 1971; 1st ed. 1806–1807); Wilhelm M. L. de Wette, *Über Religion und Theologie: Erläuterungen zu seinem Lehrbuche der Dogmatik* (Berlin: Realschulbuchhandlung, 1815); Julius Wellhausen, *Prolegomena to the History of Israel*, trans. J. Sutherland Black and Allan Menzies (Edinburgh: A. & C. Black, 1885); Julius Wellhausen, *Israelitische und Jüdische Geschichte*, 8th ed. (Berlin; Leipzig: de Gruyter, 1921); Adolph Harnack, *History of Dogma*, 3rd ed., trans. N. Buchanan, J. Millar, E. B. Speirs and W. M'Gilchrist, 7 vols. (London: Williams & Norgate, 1894).

theological and philosophical influences have shaped Old Testament studies from the nineteenth century to the present? A shorter, but nonetheless apt, route begins in the mid-twentieth century, with Gerhard von Rad, a major figure in his own time and since. In the following passage, he identifies the two aspects of early-twentieth century Old Testament readings of Exod 3:14:

> Nothing is farther from what is envisaged in this etymology of the name of Jahweh than a definition of his nature in the sense of a philosophical statement about his being (LXX Ἐγώ εἰμι ὁ ὤν)—a suggestion, for example, of his absoluteness, aseity, etc. Such a thing would be altogether out of keeping with the Old Testament. The whole narrative context leads right away to the expectation that Jahweh intends to impart something—but this is not what he is, but what he will show himself to be to Israel.[14]

According to von Rad, verse 14 supplies an etymology of the divine name "YHWH," and it is not a statement about the nature or being of God. Von Rad then makes a theological distinction involving the final form of the text; he claims that the narrative is trying to disclose something about YHWH, "but this is not what he is, but what he will show himself to be to Israel."

The present consensus interpretation of Exod 3:13–15, based on the Masoretic Text, agrees with von Rad's claim that verse 14 discloses something about God, but this is not about "what he is, but what he will show himself to be to Israel." The Hebrew text suggests the presence of God with Israel,[15] or what God will be or do in the life of Israel, perhaps particularly in the exodus.[16] Dozeman argues that "the verbal character of the name Yahweh places the focus of God's name on actions for the Israelites and not on God's independent being or essence."[17] As Larsson brusquely writes, "God is what

---

14. Gerhard von Rad, *Old Testament Theology: The Theology of Israel's Historical Traditions*, trans. D. M. G. Stalker, vol. 1 (London: SCM, 1966), 180.

15. John H. Sailhamer, *The Pentateuch as Narrative: A Biblical Theological Commentary* (Grand Rapids: Zondervan, 1992), 246–47; John I. Durham, *Exodus*, WBC 3 (Nashville: Thomas Nelson, 1987); Victor P. Hamilton, *Exodus: An Exegetical Commentary* (Grand Rapids: Baker, 2011), 66; cf. Umberto Cassuto, *A Commentary on the Book of Exodus* (Jerusalem: Magnes, 1967).

16. Moberly, *Old Testament*, 22; Seitz, "Call of Moses." Cf. Kearney's argument that Exod 3:14 should be understood in terms of possibility. Kearney, *The God Who May Be*, 20–38.

17. Thomas B. Dozeman, *Commentary on Exodus* (Grand Rapids: Eerdmans, 2009), 135.

God does."[18] In short, the Masoretic Text suggests a description of the divine name "YHWH," the meaning and nature of which is only available to the reader through study of the actions of God in Israel's history. Thus Old Testament commentators, not necessarily with explicit reference to Christian tradition of reading the passage or the Septuagint, avoid discussion of God's identity or being and focus instead on God's action in Israel.[19]

Put briefly, a theological difficulty with the consensus interpretation is that if all statements about God are replaced with statements about God's action, then interpreters may lose the subject matter of the text. Under such interpretation, it can no longer be said that the biblical text witnesses to the identity of God, but only to how God has appeared in history. The church has maintained that these two are related, but their relationship should not reduce God to God's works, or God's works to God.

Moreover, there are several reasons why one might have expected this consensus interpretation to have been challenged before now. First, as already stated, the rise of theological interpretation has given birth to arguments for seeing continuity between the biblical text, and Christian tradition and doctrine.[20] Second, the rise in prominence of Septuagint studies has deepened understanding of the changing context of biblical interpretation from the times of the Old Testament's authorship through Hellenistic and Roman periods. With increased ability to describe the cultural and philosophical factors that contributed to the development of biblical interpretation, one might also expect increased sympathy for Septuagint translators and readers. Third, the Biblical Theology Movement, and its emphasis on the distinct Hebrew mentality, in contrast with the Greek, has been toppled

---

18. Göran Larsson, *Bound for Freedom: The Book of Exodus in Jewish and Christian Traditions* (Peabody, MA: Hendrickson, 1999), 33.

19. I avoid, as much as possible, language of "immanent" and "economic" Trinity, or of God "in himself" and God "for us." Though these are terms traditionally used to distinguish between God and God's appearance to humanity, or God's works, they do not clarify the matters at hand. Instead, I use "God" to mean who God is, the identity of God, to be distinguished from how God appears to humanity, God's actions in history.

20. E.g., C. Kavin Rowe, "Biblical Pressure and Trinitarian Hermeneutics," *ProEccl* 11, no. 3 (2002): 295–312; Seitz, ed., *Nicene Christianity*, passim; Thomas G. Weinandy, *Does God Suffer?* (Edinburgh: T&T Clark, 2000); David S. Yeago, "The New Testament and the Nicene Dogma: A Contribution to the Recovery of Theological Exegesis," *ProEccl* 3, no. 2 (1994): 152–64.

almost single-handedly by James Barr, with his critique of how semantics had been used to justify biblical theology.[21] Therefore the time has come for substantial reconsideration of this text.

My argument will proceed as follows. In Part 1 of this work, I clear the ground for a fresh reading of Exod 3:13-15 and critique von Rad's claim that this passage concerns an etymology of the divine name and not an account of the being of God. Chapter 1 contains three parts. First, I describe religio-historical approaches to the text and argue that these verses are not well understood through etymology. Second, I address Childs's monumental Exodus commentary.[22] Childs broke new ground in Old Testament studies by bringing a variety of concerns to bear on the text, including attention to the prehistory of the text, its received, canonical form, and its history of interpretation. Though my interests are similar to Childs's and this project would not be possible without his work, the structure and approach of my project differs somewhat from Childs's commentary and proposal for multilevel reading. Third, I build on Frei's understanding of the literal sense of Scripture to articulate how Old Testament texts can legitimately be read, in a Christian context, as witnessing to the one God, whom Christians know as Father, Son, and Holy Spirit.

In chapter 2, I address Augustine's reading of Exod 3:14-15 as an example of the understanding in Christian tradition that verse 14 refers to the nature of God as being. I argue that Augustine's reading of these verses does not suggest an unbiblical, static, abstract God who is removed from the lives

---

21. James Barr, *The Semantics of Biblical Language* (Oxford: Oxford University, 1961). See Thorleif Boman, *Hebrew Thought Compared with Greek*, trans. Jules L. Moreau, Library of History and Doctrine (Westminster, 1960; 1st ed. 1954). Boman in many ways exemplifies the claims of the Biblical Theology Movement on this subject. Yet Boman goes beyond the movement by arguing that these two distinct mentalities are finally complementary; the two mutually exclusive categories are both true of reality, a paradox. See also Childs's classic account of this aspect of the Biblical Theology Movement and its demise: Brevard S. Childs, *Biblical Theology in Crisis* (Philadelphia: Westminster, 1970), esp. 44-47, 70-72.

Perhaps the consensus interpretation, once dependent on a Greek/Hebrew mentality polarity, has found a foothold within narrative interpretation, since God's self-disclosure in narrative form requires that God be portrayed in a dynamic fashion. See Sailhamer, *The Pentateuch as Narrative*, passim.

22. Brevard S. Childs, *The Book of Exodus: A Critical, Theological Commentary* (Louisville: Westminster, 1974).

of God's people. Rather, the terms that Augustine uses to describe God's being are grounded in Scripture, and they identify God's immateriality, supporting the character of God as steadfast, the eternally living God for us. Thus, in the first instance, both historical-critical and history-of-interpretation concerns are brought to bear in the discussion of the text. In organizing the monograph in this manner, I hope to achieve as integrated a reading of Exod 3:13–15 as possible. At the same time, I want to do justice to the contexts in which this text has been read, and so have devoted a full chapter to Augustine's reading. My account of Augustine's reading of Exod 3:14–15 grounds my references to Christian tradition throughout this study and provides substantial attention to Trinitarian concerns early on, so that I try to avoid Childs's problems of stereotyped reference to tradition and failure to develop more fully an account of how Christians might read this Old Testament text as witness to God, who is Father, Son, and Holy Spirit.

In Part 2, I move to the constructive task: exegesis of Exod 3:13–15. In chapter 3, I address the literary contexts of the book of Exodus and the divine name in this book. In chapter 4, I discuss the narrative context of the call and vocation of Moses in the Pentateuch, asking, if Exod 3:1–4:17 is to be understood as the narrative of the call of Moses, how might greater attention to the role of Moses as covenant mediator in the Pentateuch influence one's reading of Exod 3:13–15? In both exegetical chapters, I start from the received form of the text and address the text's prehistory only as it serves the purpose of illuminating the final form. In chapter 5, I consider the theological implications of the proposed exegesis: how does Exod 3:13–15 witness to the Triune God that Christians confess? Furthermore, in all three constructive chapters, I argue that the literal sense of Exod 3:13–15 in its literary context is patient of an ontological interpretation that is fruitful for the Christian church because such an interpretation is fitting to the living, Triune, Creator God, who continually offers himself to creation for its redemption.[23] Put differently, my hermeneutical point is that the Old Testament, as the church reads it, witnesses to the Triune God in its own idiom; my exegetical point is that, for the Christian, reading Exod 3:13–15 well includes attention to God's self-revelation to Israel and to the church in the names that

---

23. I mean "ontological" in the broadest possible sense: referring to what truly is, to what is real. Furthermore, I am not claiming that God is a being, a different sort of being, or beyond being.

God gives his people in order that they can call upon him, and to God, the only one who can name God.

PART 1

Clearing the Ground for Theological Interpretation of Exodus 3:13–15

CHAPTER 1

Reading Exodus 3:13–15 from von Rad to Childs and Beyond

In the Introduction, I argue that von Rad's interpretation of Exod 3:13–15 in his *Old Testament Theology* is indicative of much twentieth-century interpretation of this text. In the current chapter, I address the direction of interpretation of Exod 3:13–15 during and since the time of von Rad, on three accounts. First, I discuss etymology of the divine name and find that in the twenty-first century, religio-historical investigations are no longer concerned, as they once were, with the historical origins of the divine name "YHWH," and that questions of Israel's earliest religious experiences and knowledge are currently framed differently than they were in prior generations. Second, I discuss a major forerunner of the approach to Exod 3:13–15 that I am advocating, namely Brevard Childs and particularly his *The Book of Exodus*. In what follows, I discuss Childs's contributions to reading this text and some of the shortcomings of his commentary. A look at Childs will help to support the structure of this study and my claim that there remains more work to be done in theological interpretation of Exod 3:13–15. Third, I build on Frei's discussion of the literal sense of Scripture, which is at once a confessional claim about the ascriptive subject of biblical texts and a statement about their self-referential, realistic character, in order to articulate how Old Testament texts witness to the one God, whom Christians know as Father, Son, and Holy Spirit.

1. Etymology and Religio-historical Approaches

The late-nineteenth and twentieth centuries saw two distinctly modern approaches to searching for the origin of the divine name "YHWH": the philological study of the word's etymology, and the related task of religio-historical reconstruction of the history of Israelite religion, including how Israel came to know God by the name "YHWH." This chapter presents a survey of these approaches.[1]

Because they seek to peer "behind the text" of Exod 3:13–15 and related Old Testament texts to see what the divine name meant in its earliest uses, and because all proposals regarding the earliest origins of Israelite religion are inherently speculative, scholarship must proceed with caution in both instances. Furthermore, identifying the root of "YHWH" will not necessarily assist the reader in understanding the text of Exod 3:14–15 in its literary and communal contexts. Toward the end of this section, I address more recent trends in historical reconstruction of Israelite religion. Recently, with emphasis on congruence between Israelite and Canaanite religions and unease with historical investigation of pre-monarchic Israel, scholars have changed the landscape of religio-historical approaches. In this new situation, scholars are either uninterested in the historical origins of the name "YHWH" and the biblical texts previously emphasized in investigation of that name (Exod 3:13–15; 6:2–3), or they frame the questions differently.

While I suggest that one root (namely היה/הוה meaning "to be") should be preferred over others, etymological study of the name has significant limits. Seeking the original name often results in neglect of the explanation presented in Exod 3:14, which is considered vague, purposefully elusive, or meaningless. Interpretation that seeks to take seriously both historical investigation as well as the received form of the biblical text will need to find a different approach for understanding of the relationship between אֶהְיֶה אֲשֶׁר אֶהְיֶה and יְהוָה in the received form of the text.

1.1. Etymology

Proposals for the etymology of the Tetragrammaton have covered a vast range, including Semitic and non-Semitic, nominal and verbal roots. This has largely been the work of a previous generation of scholars, and excellent, critical summaries of etymological research into the name "YHWH" are

---

1. The etymological proposals surveyed in this chapter are likely not what von Rad had in mind when he wrote that Exod 3:14 is an etymology of the divine name; von Rad more likely meant that Exod 3:14 could be taken as a folk or scribal, rather than scientific, etymology. Heuristically, I contrast strongly between etymological approaches and those that consider the text to be wordplay.

available, notably those of Kinyongo, Murtonen and de Vaux.[2] Thus, I will only address the two most prominent types of proposals: those suggesting that YHWH was originally a storm god, and those that suggest a root meaning "to be."

1.1.1. Storm god Scholars have proposed two senses of the Arabic root *"hwy,"* meaning "to blow" or "to fall," either of which could indicate an original understanding of YHWH as a storm god. Knauf gives several examples from North Arabian inscriptions of divine epithets of similar imperfect forms: *"yaḥrr,"* "He glows"; *"yaʾūq,"* "He protects"; *"yaʾbūb"*; *"yaġidd,"* "He is in bloom"; *"yaġūṯ,"* "He helps"; *"yumayyit"* or *"yumit,"* "he kills." Then Knauf presents the three meanings of the root *"hwy,"* "to desire," "to fall," and "to blow," choosing the last option because of the lack of a Hebrew root with equivalent meaning, which may be the result of a taboo against using the word which had become a name. The lack of Hebrew etymology is evident in the *Schriftgelehrtenetymologie* presented in Exod 3:14.[3]

The Arabic root *"hwy"* can also be understood in the sense of "to fall." Moreover, הוה in Aramaic developed from "to fall," into "to become," "to be,"[4] so this etymology takes as credible the description given in Exod 3:14–15 while also positing a different original meaning. MacLaurin suggests that the reference to falling could make sense either in terms of "the Tablets of Stone falling from heaven, or to a fertility deity who causes rain to fall, or to a warrior-god who causes his foes to fall."[5]

---

2. Jean Kinyongo, *Origine et signification du nom divin Yahvé à la lumière de récents travaux et de traditions Sémitico-bibliques (Ex 3,13-15 Et 6,2-8)*, BBB (Bonn: P. Hanstein, 1970), 1–90; A. Murtonen, *A Philological and Literary Treatise on the Old Testament Divine Names* (Helsinki: Soumalaisen Kirjallisuuden Seuran Kirjapainon Oy, 1952), 61–90; Roland de Vaux, "The Revelation of the Divine Name YHWH," in *Proclamation and Presence: Old Testament Essays in Honour of Gwynne Henton Davies*, eds. John I. Durham and J. Roy Porter (London: SCM, 1970), 48–75.

3. Ernst A. Knauf, "Yahwe," VT 34, no. 4 (1984): 468–69. See Wellhausen, *Israelitische und jüdische Geschichte*, 25, fn. 1; Oesterley and Robinson, *Hebrew Religion*, 153; Theophile James Meek, *Hebrew Origins* (New York: Harper & Brothers, 1950), 99. Similarly, Bernhard Duhm, *Israels Propheten* (Tübingen: Mohr Seibeck, 1916), 34.

4. Hans Bauer and Pontus Leander, *Historische Grammatik der hebräischen Sprache I* (Halle: M. Niemeyer, 1922), 24.

5. E. C. B. MacLaurin, "YHWH, the Origin of the Tetragrammaton," VT 12, no. 4 (1962): 441.

Two observations must be made about arguments in favor of this Arabic root, either in the sense of "to fall" or "to blow." First, the aforementioned scholars differ considerably in the confidence they invest in this explanation. On the one hand, Knauf offers a significant philological analysis of Arabic divine epithets and the root "*hwy*."[6] On the other hand, Wellhausen simply footnotes the point that "der Name Jahve scheint zu bedeuten: er fährt durch die Lüfte, er weht,"[7] in the midst of discussing how the lives of Israel and YHWH were inextricably intertwined. The root refers to YHWH's pre-Israelite existence, of which he also writes that "ehe Israel war, war Jahve nichts."[8] If "he blows" was the name of the pre-Israelite "nothing" God, then this is of little significance for understanding Israelite religion, and likewise it does not feature prominently in his study.

Second, these perspectives were strongly influenced by some assumptions about the development of religion that now appear to be idealistic and colonial. Knauf states that the meaning "to be" would not meet the religious needs of desert farmers.[9] The tendency to believe that early Israelite and other ancient religions were not abstract, but perhaps naturalistic, plays a prominent role also in Meek's *Hebrew Origins*. In this work, Meek claims that YHWH was originally a storm god, and in support of this point, Meek includes, but does not depend on, philological argument. Throughout Meek's analysis, he clearly expresses that his interpretation relies on his own definition of religion, which is,

> man's belief that there is that in his environment which is greater than himself, and upon which he feels to some degree dependent, and with which he accordingly attempts to establish a relationship of mutual interest and goodwill. Just as soon as man developed to the point of reflective thought, just as soon as he became aware of his environment and his dependence upon it, he became religious. He sought a way of coming to terms with his environment in order to live, and later, as he developed beyond the point of satisfaction in mere physical life alone, in order to live more abundantly.[10]

---

6. Knauf, "Yahwe," 467–70.
7. Wellhausen, *Israelitische und jüdische Geschichte*, 23.
8. Ibid.
9. Knauf, "Yahwe," 469.
10. Meek, *Hebrew Origins*, 83–84.

According to Meek, אֵל, אָדוֹן, אֲדֹנִי, אֵל שַׁדַּי, אֵל עֶלְיוֹן were the Israelites' first names for God; each of these suggests strength and power (Gen 23:6; 31:29; Deut 28:32; Ezek 31:11; 32:21; Mic 2:1; Ps 36:7; Job 41:17; Prov 3:27).[11] Out of the cult of the dead and ancestor worship arose reverence for particular clan ancestors.[12] As tribes developed, each tribe "through accident or design, hit upon some one deity to be its particular tribal god."[13] YHWH must have been the tribal god of Judah, and as Judah became more powerful—first within the confederacy of southern tribes, and then within the united monarchy—its God became the national God of all Israel.[14]

While Meek notes that the derivation of "YHWH" from "*hwy*," "to blow" is not certain, he classifies it as a possibility that "many scholars" support (though he does not give any examples).[15] The derivation fits neatly into his thesis that Yahwism had naturalistic origins, but at the same time he does not need this etymology to make his point, which is largely made at the level of biblical references and history of religions.

1.1.2. To be The traditional and most commonly supported understanding of the name "YHWH" is that it comes from the root הוה/היה meaning "to be" or "to become." De Vaux, who argues that the divine name derives from this root, admits that it does not agree with the Amorite and Ugaritic root "*kwn*," or Akkadian "*ewu*"/"*emu*," which express the same meaning. On the other hand, it is found in Aramean, Aramaic (biblical and post-biblical), Nabatean, Palmyrenian, and Syriac, as "*hwh*," "*hwʾ*" and/or "*hwy*."[16]

If "YHWH" does stem from הוה/היה meaning "to be," the question regarding the precise form of the word remains open. Obermann has suggested that it is a participial form with a "*ya-*" prefix, and thus it means "the one who supports, maintains, or establishes."[17] G. R. Driver claims, against Obermann's argument, that proper names can appear in the construct state in

---

11. Ibid., 84–85.
12. Ibid., 85–91.
13. Ibid., 91–92.
14. Ibid., 111–15.
15. Ibid., 99.
16. De Vaux, "Revelation," 59–60.
17. J. Obermann, "The Divine Name YHWH in the Light of Recent Discoveries," *JBL* 68, no. 4 (1949): 301–23.

Hebrew, and that the Phoenician terms on which Obermann bases his argument are not necessarily participles.[18]

According to de Vaux, some scholars have suggested that "YHWH" may be a descriptive substantive of היה, formed with a "ya-" suffix and meaning "the one who is," and some Hebrew nouns have been cited in support.[19] Von Soden interprets this substantive in the sense of "to be present" or "to manifest oneself."[20] Though de Vaux admits that this substantive is rare, he also notes that it could be understood as a "substantified verbal imperfect," and this is the understanding that he prefers.[21]

A third possibility is that "YHWH" is a causative form.[22] Albright famously proposed this view, and furthermore, he suggests emendation of the text of Exod 3:14 to the more original liturgical formula, אֶהְיֶה אֲשֶׁר יִהְיֶה, "I cause to be what comes into existence."[23] Contrary to this proposal, היה is never used in a causative sense in Hebrew, though it could be the case that the divine name is the reason for this lacuna.[24] While divine sentence names are common in the Ancient Near East, the substitution of a verbal characteristic as the name of a deity is "unparalleled," according to van der Toorn.[25]

David Noel Freedman presents a version of Albright's reading which requires a less drastic emendation, accepting the *hipʿil* causative alteration but keeping both verbal locutions in the first person: "I cause to be what I cause to be" or simply "I create." Freedman's proposal takes seriously the Exodus

---

18. G. R. Driver, "Reflections on Recent Articles," *JBL* 73, no. 3 (1954): 125–36.

19. The list includes יַחְמוּר, the "red" antelope, and a "receptacle," which is the wallet of a shepherd, יַלְקוּט. De Vaux, "Revelation," 61. Cf. G. Beer, *Hebräische Grammatik*, ed. R. Meyer (Berlin: de Gruyter, 1952), §40, 3; "יהוה," Paul Anton de Lagarde, *Erklärung hebräischer Wörter* (Göttingen: Dieterischsche, 1880), 27–30.

20. Wolfram von Soden, "Jahwe 'Er ist, er erweist sich,'" *WO* 3, no. 3 (1966): 177–87.

21. De Vaux, "Revelation," 182.

22. De Lagarde, *Erklärung hebräischer Wörter*, 27–30; Paul von Haupt, "Der Name Jahwe," *OLZ* 12, no. 5 (1909): 212–13; W. F. Albright, "Contributions to Biblical Archaeology and Philology," *JBL* 43, no. 3/4 (1924), 363–93; Albright, *Stone Age*, 259–60; Cross, "Yahweh," 250–56.

23. Albright, "Contributions," 363–93; Albright, *Stone Age*, 259–60.

24. See Cross, "Yahweh," 250–56.

25. K. van der Toorn, "Yahweh," in *Dictionary of Deities and Demons in the Bible*, eds. K. van der Toorn, B. Becking, and P. W. van der Horst (Leiden: Brill, 1999), 915.

context of 3:14, and it follows the same *idem per idem* formula as Exod 33:19.[26] Thus the name "YHWH," as a common element of all layers of Israelite religion dating back to the patriarchs,[27] refers to God the Creator, but the original construction behind Exod 3:14 is connected to the primary theological significance of Exodus: "grace and mercy, patience, great kindness and devotion, all of which mark the action by which he delivers his afflicted people, creates a new community,—and not least the passionate zeal by which he binds Israel to himself in an exclusive relationship of privilege and obligation, of promise and threat, of judgment and mercy."[28]

1.1.3. Conclusion It would seem that the explanation from הוה/היה, meaning "to be" is preferable for several reasons. First, the two primary arguments for the senses of "to fall" and "to blow" do not hold. Albright and Kinyongo have demonstrated on the basis of Egyptian, Babylonian and Canaanite evidence that "to be" is not too abstract for an ANE religion.[29] Relatedly, Knauf's recent argument from silence is unpersuasive. He chooses the meaning of *"hwy"* as "to blow" on the basis that only this meaning lacks Hebrew equivalent, but this rationale seems rather weak and explicitly indebted to the historical disregard of the "scribal etymology" in Exod 3:14. While it is one thing to say that Exod 3:14 may be the work of a writer who is not acquainted with the true original meaning of the name, it is another to use this presupposition as evidence for a different original sense.

---

26. David Noel Freedman, "The Name of the God of Moses," *JBL* 79, no. 2 (1960): 152-53. S. R. Driver argues that the *idem per idem* construction occurs when the "means or desire to be more explicit does not exist"; S. R. Driver, *The Book of Exodus* (Cambridge: Cambridge University, 1918), 362-63; cf. S. R. Driver, *Notes on the Hebrew Text of the Books of Samuel* (Oxford: Oxford University, 1913), 185-86. Cf. Paul Joüon and T. Muraoka, *A Grammar of Biblical Hebrew*, 2nd rev. ed., SubBi 27 (Rome: Editrice Pontificio Histituto Biblico, 2006), §158o.

27. Freedman follows Albright in suggesting that the name "YHWH" was known and used by the Hebrews prior to the time of Moses. Thus, Freedman's argument for the antiquity of the name is tied to Albright's understanding of it as a liturgical formula whose original character was lost. W. F. Albright, *Yahweh and the Gods of Canaan: A Historical Analysis of Two Contrasting Faiths*, Jordan lectures in comparative religion (Winona Lake, IN: Eisenbrauns, 1968), 149. Cf. Freedman, "God of Moses," 155; Cross, "Yahweh," 250-59.

28. Freedman, "God of Moses," 155.

29. Kinyongo, *Origine et signification*, 57-58. Likewise, Albright, "Contributions," 375.

Second, de Vaux and Kinyongo's arguments against "to fall" and "to blow" have not (to my knowledge) been persuasively refuted. De Vaux writes that this philological explanation seems to depend on an "improper usage of Arabic in which the meaning of ancient roots has in fact undergone a great development and diversification."[30] As Kinyongo notes, whereas evidence for "to fall" and "to blow" can be given from Arabic and Syriac, these senses are not found in neighboring Aramaic and Akkadian.[31] Further, Kinyongo questions whether it is appropriate to single out the meaning of הוה found in Job 37:6 when the more obvious meaning of the root is clearly "to be,"[32] as in Aramaic (Gen 27:29; Isa 16:4; Eccl 2:22; 11:3; and Neh 6:6).[33] At this point, Bauer and Leander's claim that the Aramaic sense "to be, to occur" developed out of a prior sense of "to fall" could be helpful, but it is without support save much later developments in Latin and German.[34] For these reasons, it is preferable to understand "YHWH" as from הוה/היה meaning "to be, to become."

1.2. Historical Reconstruction

A brief look at religio-historical reconstruction of the history of Israelite religion will provide a general picture of the landscape of scholarship in which etymological research takes place and address whether there are religio-historical resources available to assist in the process of determining an etymology. Broadly conceived, recent proposals regarding the development of Israelite religion have attempted to show its resonance with its Canaanite surroundings and have demonstrated increasing skepticism about what can reasonably be known about pre-monarchic Israel and its religion. In this context, religio-historical scholars are less interested in pursuing the roots of the divine name "YHWH," or, at least, they frame the questions differently than their predecessors.[35]

---

30. De Vaux, "Revelation," 59.
31. Kinyongo, *Origine et signification*, 66.
32. According to Koehler et al., also in 1 Sam 1:18; 2 Sam 11:23; 1 Kgs 11:15; Prov 14:35. *HALOT*, "הוה I"; Kinyongo, *Origine et signification*, 66.
33. *HALOT*, "הוה II."
34. Bauer and Leander, *Historische Grammatik*, 24.
35. A dominant twentieth-century perspective, known as the Kenite hypothesis, held that the Kenites, a sub-group of the Midianites in Edom, worshipped a god called "YHWH," and Israel learned worship of YHWH from the Kenites, possibly through

Three trends have marked the direction of late-twentieth and early-twenty-first century scholarship on Israelite religion: increased attention on overlap between Israelite religion and that of its neighbors, skepticism regarding historical investigations of pre-monarchic Israel and Israelite religion, and skepticism regarding any use of the Old Testament as a primary historical resource. While these three trends are distinct, they are also related in important ways.

An earlier generation of scholarship (Albright, Kaufman, Tigay and others) held that Israel was always monolatrous: Israel always taught worship of only YHWH, even if Israelites believed that other gods existed generally, and this fueled Israelite monotheism proper which developed during exile.[36] In this way, Yahwism has been viewed as essentially distinct from Canaanite religion. However, more recently, the situation has changed. Scholars are increasingly suggesting that Israel had much in common with its neighbors.

Moses' connection with them. The hypothesis was first articulated in 1862 by F. W. Ghillany under the name Richard von der Alm. In 1872, Cornelis Tiele conceived the hypothesis apparently independently. Closer to the turn of the century, the hypothesis was advocated by Meyer, Stade, Budde, Greßmann, Morgenstern, and Beer as well as some English-language scholars (Barton, Cheyne, and Smith). In the twentieth century, the hypothesis became a dominant perspective, as notable scholars including Joseph Blenkinsopp, Gerhard von Rad, Martin Noth, H. H. Rowley, A. H. J. Gunneweg, Manfred Weippert, and Moshe Weinfeld supported it. Presently, Blenkinsopp is among the few who continue to advocate for this hypothesis, which has been challenged on both textual and historical grounds.

See Blenkinsopp and Parke-Taylor for bibliographic information: Blenkinsopp, "Midianite-Kenite Hypothesis," 142; Geoffrey H. Parke-Taylor, יהוה = *Yahweh: The Divine Name in the Bible* (Waterloo: Wilfrid Laurier, 1975), 20–21. For critiques of the Kenite hypothesis, see Martin Buber, *Kingship of God*, 3rd edition, Richard Scheimann, ed. (New York: Harper & Row, 1967); Martin Buber, *Moses* (Oxford; London: East & West Library, 1944); Chr. H. W. Brekelmans, "Exodus XVIII and the Origins of Yahwism in Israel," *OtSt* 10 (1954): 215–24; H. H. Rowley, *From Joseph to Joshua: Biblical Traditions in the Light of Archaeology*, The Schweich Lectures of the British Academy (Oxford: Oxford University, 1950), 133; Roland de Vaux, "Sur l'origine Kénite ou Madianite du Yahvisme," *ErIsr* 9 (1969): 30; Childs, *Book of Exodus*, 323; van der Toorn, "Yahweh," 912.

36. Albright, *Yahweh and the Gods*; Y. Kaufmann, *The Religion of Israel from its Beginning to the Babylonian Exile*, trans. M. Greenberg (New York: Schocken, 1960), 142–47; J. Tigay, *You Shall Have No Other Gods: Israelite Religion in the Light of Hebrew Inscriptions*, HSS 31 (Atlanta: Scholars, 1986).

The consensus opinion now finds that Israelites were not culturally distinct from Canaanites during the Iron I period (1200–1000 BCE). From a different understanding of the relation between Israelite and Canaanite culture has come a different understanding of the distinction (or lack thereof) of pre-monarchic Israelite religion.[37]

The majority position in Old Testament scholarship suggests that Israelite mono-Yahwism (exclusive worship of YHWH, monolatry if not monotheism) developed gradually. Propp stresses the slow, evolutionary nature of the dominant reconstruction of Israelite religious development:

> Reacting against past trends, particularly in the last century, our *Zeitgeist* finds more significance in gradual social development than in the impetus of Great Men. With appropriate if unthinking mistrust of foundational legends, the unconscious (il)logic runs something like this: since the texts about Israel's break with the past at Sinai under Moses' leadership are historically dubious, i.e., written long after the supposed events and full of anachronisms and improbable phenomena, we may be certain there was no founding movement at all.[38]

Thus historical reconstructions of Israelite religion confront at least two questions. First, there is the issue of whether the growth of Yahwism was more-or-less gradual, or whether growth and change was largely the effect of influential individuals. Second, Propp asks, what does this process of development say about Israelite religious origins? The later dating of Old Testament texts means that the scholar must look elsewhere for information about the beginnings of Israelite worship of YHWH, and such an endeavor will always require some amount of speculation.

Moreover, Propp writes that,

> Given the axiom of unidirectional change, since Yahwism slowly evolved into (more or less) monotheistic Judaism, it must have begun as something entirely its opposite: Canaanite polytheism. Is

---

37. See succinct overviews in Mark S. Smith, *The Early History of God: Yahweh and the Other Deities in Ancient Israel* (Grand Rapids: Eerdmans, 2002), 1–14; Herbert Niehr, "'Israelite' Religion and 'Canaanite' Religion," in *Religious Diversity in Ancient Israel and Judah*, ed. John Barton and Francesca Stavrakopoulou (London; New York: T&T Clark, 2010), 23–32.

38. William H. C. Propp, *Exodus 19–40: A New Translation with Introduction and Commentary*, AB (New York: Doubleday, 2006), 784.

this realistic? Too often the axiom of the "ancient Near Eastern cultural continuum" has authorized reconstructing an Israel maximally resembling its neighbors (and vice versa); then the reconstruction is cited to prove the continuum. We must rather steer between Scylla—the claim that Israelite popular religion was identical to its Northwest Semitic matrix—and Charybdis— the claim that it was identical to later Judaism. By definition, the truth lies somewhere in the middle.[39]

The consensus opinion regarding an exilic dating for Israelite monotheism leads to greater uncertainty regarding the origins of Israelite religion. One suspects that it is distinct from later Yahwism, and also that it shares similarities with its Canaanite surroundings. But how best to articulate these similarities and differences? Propp wisely pursues a middle ground, between a starkly independent Israelite religion and one that can be understood exhaustively in terms of the surrounding religious cultures.[40]

Rather than the concepts of "syncretism" and "borrowing," Miller and Mettinger prefer to speak of "inheritance."[41] Smith writes of "convergence" and "differentiation" between YHWH on the one hand and El and Baal on the other.[42] Some scholars argue that Israel was not culturally or religiously distinct from Canaanite culture and religion; even if one acknowledges that pre-monarchic Israelites perceived themselves as distinct from their neighbors, the similarities between Israelite and wider Canaanite religion are clear.[43] However the associations and divergences of Yahwism with

---

39. Ibid.

40. Ibid., 790. From this middle ground, Propp develops a decidedly syncretistic picture of early Israelite religion, summarized, "Egyptian monotheism + Midianite Yahweh + Canaanite Divine Patriarch and Battling Storm God types + Hittite Covenant form + Iron Age national god theology = Yahwism."

41. Patrick D. Miller, "Israelite Religion," in *The Hebrew Bible and Its Modern Interpreters*, ed. Douglas A. Knight and Gene M. Tucker (Minneapolis: Fortress, 1985), 211; Tryggve N. D. Mettinger, "The Elusive Essence: YHWH, El, and Baal and the Distinctiveness of Israelite Faith," in *Die hebräische Bibel und ihre zweifach Nachgeschichte (Festscrift Rendtorff)*, eds. Erhard Blum, Christian Macholz and Ekkehard W. Stegemann (Neukirchen-Vluyn: Neukirkchener Verlag, 1990), 413, forthcoming reprint in *Reports from a Scholar's Life: Select Papers on the Hebrew Bible*, edited by Andrew Knapp (Winona Lake, IN: Eisenbrauns, 2015).

42. Smith, *Early History of God*, esp. 7-9, 195-202.

43. Ibid., 19-31. Smith's position is debatable; for instance, Berlejung explains

Canaanite religion are described, it is clear that in Old Testament scholarship, the important current issue is how to account for the overlap and distinction between Yahwism and Canaanite religion. If Israelite and Canaanite religion were not as different as scholars previously believed, then the roots of Yahwism and the divine name are not likely to lead to a unique religious seed that, from an early stage, anticipated biblical faith. Rather, the history of the divine name and Yahwism is likely to be much more nuanced and have less to do with how one will understand the biblical text in its received form.

One manifestation of the growing tendency to stress the Canaanite heritage of Israel is the theory that worship of YHWH developed out of worship of El. There are various versions of this argument.[44] Cross builds on Albright's argument for seeing the divine name as a *hipʿil* imperfect from "*hwy*," meaning "to cause to be," and suggests that the name was originally an epithet for El. Drawing on Haupt's suggestion to read אֶהְיֶה אֲשֶׁר אֶהְיֶה as יַהְוֶה אֲשֶׁר יַהְוֶה, Cross further suggests in Hebrew, as in the neighboring language Ugaritic, אֲשֶׁר replaced דוּא in the Late Bronze Age.[45] Thus, a more original form of יַהְוֶה אֲשֶׁר יַהְוֶה would have been יַהְוֶה דוּא יַהְיֶה. The phrase יַהְיֶה דוּא likely would have had an object, such as צְבָאוֹת. Additionally, the phrase calls to mind El appellations found at Ugarit, namely "*dū yakāninu*," "*dū yaqniyu*," "*dū yakāninuhū*," all referring to El as creating.[46] On this basis, Cross suggests that what in the Masoretic Text appears as אֶהְיֶה אֲשֶׁר אֶהְיֶה could have originally been אֵל דוּא צְבָאוֹת. According to Cross, this would aid understanding several perplexing elements of Israelite religion, including why "El," "Elyon," "Shadday," and "Olam" continued to be used positively even while Baal worship was perceived as a threat.[47] Developing out of El-worship, Yahwism

---

her placement of the term "Israel" in quotation marks, even when dealing with monarchic history: "The history of the northern and southern kingdoms, and of the regions of Samaria and Judah/Jehud/Judea, can only be treated adequately within the larger perspective of the history of Palestine and the southern Levant." Angelika Berlejung, "History and Religion of 'Israel': Basic Information," trans. Thomas Riplinger, in Jan Christian Gertz et al., *T&T Clark Handbook of the Old Testament*, 61.

44. Mettinger and van der Toorn offer an alternative by stressing early association of YHWH with the traits of Baal. Mettinger, "The Elusive Essence," 393–413; van der Toorn, "Yahweh."

45. Cross, "Yahweh," 255.

46. Ibid.

47. Ibid., 257.

was unique to Israel but retained many of the elements of non-Israelite Semitic religious heritage.[48]

More recently, Dijkstra follows Cross's lead in suggesting that the original form of the divine name "YHWH" was "YHWH-El." Dijkstra argues on the basis of archeological evidence that Asherah was worshipped alongside YHWH, and he suggests that "the first millennium constellation of YHWH and his Asherah was the *interpretatio israelitica* immediately derived from the second millennium veneration of the Canaanite El and his partner Asherah."[49] Similarly, de Moor agrees with Cross and Dijkstra that YHWH was once known as YHWH-El, an ancestor of a proto-Israelite tribe that journeyed northwards in the mid-second millennium BCE. The southern groups of proto-Israelites became loyal to YHWH-El, and the northern groups, to Baal, in the second half of the second millennium BCE when other ANE nations chose one God over others (Amun-Re in Egypt, Marduk in Babylon). Later, wanting to distinguish their own high God from the lesser El gods of the nations, Israel abbreviated the name "YHWH-El" to "YHWH."[50]

Smith presents biblical evidence in support of the association of El and YHWH in Israel during the Judges period: the name of Israel, the fact that there is no biblical polemic against El as against Baal, and texts that associate El and YHWH (for example, Deut 32:8-9; Josh 22:22; Exod 6:2-3).[51] The use of Exod 6 in this argument is interesting; whereas this text has been used in previous generations to support a distinction between patriarchal and Mosaic religion, Smith uses it to support *convergence* of El-worship and YHWH-worship (while acknowledging that the text suggests that the ancestors did not know the name "YHWH") in a later historical period. If it is acknowledged that Israel, at least for a time, worshipped multiple gods and that the national god only slowly emerged as dominant and absorbed the characteristics of some of these other gods, then the quest for the origins of the name

---

48. Ibid., 226, 250–58.
49. Meindert Dijkstra, "El, the God of Israel—Israel, the People of YHWH: On the Origins of Ancient Israelite Yahwism," in *Only One God? Monotheism in Ancient Israel and the Veneration of the Goddess Asherah* (London: Sheffield Academic, 2001), 103.
50. Importantly, de Moor's proposal differs from the current majority position regarding the development of monotheism (or monolatry) in Israel. De Moor argues that monotheistic worship of YHWH occurred in Israel prior to the monarchy, in large part due to Mosaic reform. De Moor, *The Rise of Yahwism*, 371–72.
51. Smith, *Early History of God*, 32–43.

"YHWH" is no longer as religiously significant. The developments that make Israelite religion unique occur much later.

Decreased interest in Exod 3:13–15 and 6:2–3 as important for the history of Israelite religion can be seen in the near disappearance of these texts from indices of important works in the field. I have already mentioned that the *T&T Clark Handbook of the Old Testament* gives only passing reference to different divine names as support for distinct Pentateuchal sources, without addressing in detail these biblical texts.[52] In *The Early History of God*, Smith does not include Exod 3:13–15 at all, and he only addresses 6:2–3 once.[53] In his subsequent monograph, Smith twice addresses the latter and again ignores the former. El was the God of the exodus, who was only later associated with YHWH, and Exod 6:2–3 was written to address the transition.[54] These two biblical texts are referenced once in Grabbe's *Ancient Israel*; Grabbe acknowledges a past generation's concern with this text and its witness to a time in Israel when the Israelites did not know the name "YHWH." Grabbe admits that his is a simple (even "simplistic") reading of the biblical text, and adds an additional qualification, that in reading this text he "ignores the whole question of Moses' existence and the relationship of the biblical traditions to the actual settlement of the Israelite people in the land."[55]

Grabbe's qualification suggests a further reason why scholars no longer address Exod 3:13–15 and 6:2–3 as important to the history of Israelite religion. In part, this historical skepticism has to do with the early periods of Israelite religion and the speculative nature of any attempt to reconstruct these; in part, the skepticism has to do with decreasing confidence about the historical accuracy of biblical witnesses. So while Smith begins his history of Israel with the period of the Judges and uses biblical texts positively in his argument, the ANE historian Mario Liverani divides his history of Israel in two. His "Normal History" concentrates on the inconsequential histories of Israel and Judah in Palestine, in which these two kingdoms are portrayed as similar to other ANE kingdoms. His "Invented History" is a product of exilic and post-exilic people who had religious, cultural, and political reasons for

---

52. Gertz, "Overall Context," 253.
53. Smith, *Early History of God*, 34.
54. Mark S. Smith, *The Origins of Biblical Monotheism: Israel's Polytheistic Background and the Ugaritic Texts* (New York; Oxford: Oxford University, 2001), 141, 147.
55. Lester L. Grabbe, *Ancient Israel: What Do We Know and How Do We Know It?* (London; New York: T&T Clark, 2007), 153.

inventing historical archetypes for the institutions they sought to create.[56] While Liverani claims to attempt a new type of Israelite history, the more general point that the biblical texts should be treated cautiously as historical evidence is more-or-less widespread. According to Grabbe, "the biblical text is almost always a secondary source, written and edited long after the events ostensibly described. In some cases, the text may depend on earlier sources, but these sources were edited and adapted; in any case the source has to be dug out from the present context."[57] Since biblical texts as a whole are not necessarily reliable historical guides, and even less so, texts which purport to witness to pre-monarchic events in Israel, Exod 3:13–15 and 6:2–3 are no longer addressed as bases for understanding the historical roots of Yahwism.

In sum, it is difficult to see how historical reconstructions of Israelite religion will aid reading Exod 3:13–15. Increasingly a wedge is placed between the biblical text and the events to which it claims to witness. Furthermore, understanding the origins of the divine name is less of a priority now that Israel's Canaanite religious and cultural heritage has been determined, and since it is no longer generally held that much can reasonably be known about pre-monarchic Israel. Therefore, a reading of Exod 3:13–15 will need to look to different approaches.

1.3. Conclusions

1. I suggest that the name "YHWH" should be understood as likely related to the root היה meaning "to be." However, even if this etymology can be preferred over others, the question must be asked: what exactly is the point of determining the etymology of the name? In what sense is it a historically, and/or theologically valuable exercise? Broadly speaking, etymological research informs philological study, which provides the linguistic framework for reading Hebrew texts; in this section, I ask in what more specific sense is etymological study of the name "YHWH" helpful religio-historically, theologically, or otherwise.

The religio-historical value of this enterprise is unclear. Even if an etymology could be decided upon, this would not necessarily tell us anything about what any people group ever thought of YHWH,[58] particularly if the

---

56. Mario Liverani, *Israel's History and the History of Israel*, trans. Chiara Peri and Philip R. Davies, BibleWorld (London; Oakville: Equinox, 2005), xv–xvii.
57. Grabbe, *Ancient Israel*, 35.
58. Barr uses the English example of the linguistic connection between "holy"

proposal associates the name with a root in a language whose people never worshipped YHWH! The etymology might have linguistic-historical value, but its value for reconstructing the religious history of Israel would be rather indirect.

The theological value of etymological research is even more tenuous. Koehler rightly states,

> this philological question is not directly a theological question; indeed it is very indirectly that.... The important thing theologically in the matter of a divine name is not what its essential and original meaning is, but only what realm of ideas and confession and revelation the worshippers associate with their god's name.[59]

The etymologies proposed offer us little more than what Jewish and Christian tradition already know to be true about YHWH: that YHWH loves and speaks, or that YHWH is described as having some of the characteristics of Baal. But etymological arguments do not well support these theological claims, which are better made from biblical texts that directly address these characteristics of God.[60]

On the other hand, considering the name as originally part of an epithet, as Albright and others (including, differently, Knauf) have, may have greater historical and theological value. This approach can more positively appropriate the witness of Exod 3:14, which suggests that the name is a verbal form. Moreover, this approach is based on clear parallels from the ancient Near East and resonates with Barr's critique of etymologies, that the primary semantic locus of theological data is in the *sentence* rather than in individual words.[61] Unlike etymological roots, epithets do suggest that people recognized this God as acting a certain way or as having certain characteristics.

2. Another important question for developing an understanding of the history of the name in light of its reception is, how does this history relate to the received form of Exod 3:14? As I have argued, the storm god proposals tend to separate the origins of the name from its later explanation, because

---

and "healthy" to make this point, noting that the former term at no point in history ever meant the latter. Barr, *Semantics*, 111.

59. Ludwig Koehler, *Old Testament Theology*, trans. A. S. Todd (London: Lutterworth, 1953), 40.

60. Cf. Barr's critique of Snaith's discussion of נחם. Barr, *Semantics*, 116ff.

61. Ibid., 263ff.

this earlier meaning was lost (Knauf). If Bauer and Leander are correct in their suggestion that הוה itself developed from meaning "to fall" to "to become, to occur," then they are able to connect two seemingly distinct meanings of the name "YHWH." Further exploration could evaluate whether there are grounds to support this development, including whether the Latin and German parallels are simply too historically and geographically distant from Aramaic and Hebrew to be useful. If grounds are found, it would be worth asking what theological implications arise from this history.

Where the sense of "to be" is advocated, a connection to the explanation given in Exod 3:14 is not necessarily any more clear. Albright's proposal has again increased distance between this explanation and the received form of the text, as he argues that the text be read as an emendation and does not consider what value it may have as it stands. Though Freedman tries to bring this more original epithet back in conversation with the book of Exodus, he continues to rely on reading Exod 3:14 as emended.

Christian tradition, which has spilled much ink in the course of discussing this verse, has directed significant attention toward the received text and has found very significant theological meaning in this verse. So a theological reading that seeks to take seriously historical investigation of the divine name, the received text in its final form, and faith tradition concerning the interpretation of this text, will need to attend to the problem presented by this tendency to separate the original meaning of the name from its explanation in Exod 3:14. For clearly the text in question identifies this previously known God of the Fathers with the God who calls Moses to deliver the Hebrews from Egypt, and who so becomes the God of Israel: YHWH. Moreover, faith traditions, at their best, have understood Exod 3:14a as a tautology, but a *meaningful* tautology. The solution is not simply to say that God's essence is "to be" or not, but that God's essence is a true mystery that calls the reader into its depth.[62] Whereas biblical texts are more clear in their

---

62. The argument that the name originates in an ecstatic expression meaning, "O he!" comes closer to complementing Jewish and Christian understanding of Exod 3:14 as a meaningful tautology. "O he!" does not define or even describe God, but points to the people meeting a divine personality. In this way, this view resonates with Otto's phenomenology of religious experience of *mysterium tremendum et fascinosum*. Sigmund Mowinckel, "The Name of the God of Moses," *HUCA* 32 (1961): 131-32. But, rather than fully taking into account the theological insight that God cannot be defined, this proposal may too quickly turn attention to human experience. Likewise

proclamations about God's characteristics and actions, God's name is veiled; only in Exod 3 is a direct explanation attempted. It should come as no surprise, then, when the direct explanation is more or less opaque. For God is beyond definition and cannot be limited by one particular name. That etymological investigations turn in circles may suggest that this Judeo-Christian confession is basically true, for in this way philologists reach the boundaries of what can be known by any scientific method.[63]

3. Finally, historical reconstruction of the origins of the name "YHWH" and Yahwism in Israel offer little assistance either in the search for an etymology of "YHWH" or in aiding the reader's understanding of Exod 3:13–15. The two dominant etymological proposals—those arguing for the derivation of the name "YHWH" from a root characteristic of a "storm god" and those from a root meaning "to be"—seem feasible within the current debates about overlap and distinction between early Yahwism and Canaanite religion. In this context, there are no clear historical criteria for adjudicating between these options. Moreover, even if the origins of the name "YHWH" could be deduced, it would be unclear how this could inform one's reading of Exod 3:13–15, since the origins would be historically removed from the narrative in its received form.

In sum, religio-historical approaches to understanding the roots of the divine name "YHWH" and Yahwism will not aid the reader in understanding the text of Exod 3:13–15. The etymological approach is specifically limited because it separates the history of the name from that of those who worshipped the God so named. Approaches that attempt to reconstruct the origins of Yahwism are no more helpful, since they ask historical questions of the biblical text that the text does not answer. Moreover, recent directions in historical study of Israelite religious origins have emphasized overlap between Yahwism and Canaanite religion, skepticism regarding what can be known of pre-monarchic Israel, and historical distance between the early stages of Israelite religion and the received form of the Pentateuch.

Therefore, contra von Rad, it would be beneficial for the reader of Exod 3:13–15 to pursue other avenues of understanding how אֶהְיֶה אֲשֶׁר אֶהְיֶה re-

---

the relationship between universal religious feelings, on which Otto elaborates, and Jewish and Christian tradition is unclear.

63. On theological studies as methodologically similar to the humanities, see Andrew Louth, *Discerning the Mystery: An Essay on the Nature of Theology* (Oxford: Clarendon, 1983).

lates to יְהוָה. A canonical approach may provide resources for a way forward, precisely because it takes seriously the history of the text and its development, the received form of the biblical text, and the community of faith that reads this text as Scripture. I turn to a canonical approach next.

2. Brevard Childs, *The Book of Exodus*

Though written in 1974, Brevard Childs's *The Book of Exodus* remains an important critical and theological commentary on Exodus.[64] Childs's contribution is vast in scope, and his challenge is to bring insights from a wide variety of contexts to bear on the exegetical task. The commentary proceeds in several sections (though not every section is included for each segment of biblical text): 1. translation; 2. historical development (form-critical, religio-historical); 3. "Old Testament context";[65] 4. the New Testament's treatment of the Old Testament text; 5. history of exegesis; 6. theological reflection. Childs describes each of the elements in his introduction, and here I note only a few of the most important points. The last section provides the normative content of the commentary, as it "present[s] a model of how the Christian seeks to understand the testimony of the prophets and apostles in his own time and situation," though Childs hopes to avoid "biblical truths for all ages" and "random homiletical ruminations."[66] In contrast, the Old Testament context section supplies the heart of the commentary. This section

---

64. I have chosen to begin with Childs rather than Cornelis den Hertog's recent monograph for two related reasons. First, the influence of Childs and this commentary is already well established, whereas den Hertog's is less so. Second, den Hertog's work is similar to Childs's in that he structures it historically, moving from exegesis of Exod 3 forward into wider canonical context (vis-à-vis Hos 1:9), and then into translation history, beginning with the Septuagint. Thus, den Hertog himself may be indebted to Childs, and the ways in which my project differs from Childs's may also apply to how it differs from that of den Hertog. Childs, *Book of Exodus*; den Hertog, *Other Face*.

65. This section, as Mark Brett has rightly observed, should be called "Exodus context," for in it Childs rarely, if ever, moves beyond the book of Exodus in his discussion. Mark Brett, *Biblical Criticism in Crisis? The Impact of the Canonical Approach on Old Testament Studies* (Cambridge: Cambridge University, 1991), 39; cf. Paul R. Noble, *The Canonical Approach: A Critical Reconstruction of the Hermeneutics of Brevard S. Childs*, Biblical Interpretation Series 16 (Leiden; New York: Brill, 1995), 35.

66. Childs, *Book of Exodus*, xvi.

deals with the Old Testament in its final, canonical form, while the "historical development" sections have more subservient roles: "At times the results of the prehistory of the text have direct bearing on the interpretation of the canonical text; at other times the prehistory is quite irrelevant to understanding the synchronistic dimension of the biblical text."[67] So Childs acknowledges that, though he would *hope* for the prehistory of the text to illumine its final form, the two are not patient of a consistent method of relation, and so there is no certain method to apply diachronic analysis in aid of synchronic analysis. The New Testament context section is similar to the Old Testament context section in approach, but it extends the scope of study to include the entire two-testament canon. Finally, "the history of exegesis offers an analogy to the section on the prehistory of the text";[68] that is, it functions as *prolegomena* to the theological reflection, as the prehistory functions does to the final form of the text.

Childs succeeds in bringing a variety of contexts and concerns to bear in his interpretation of the text. The reader receives from Childs a substantial account of the issues and tensions that need to be dealt with in the interpretive process. However, the shadow side of this contribution, I argue, is that Childs is not as successful as he desires to be in relating the various sections of his commentary on Exod 3:1–4:17, and particularly Exod 3:13-15. If different approaches to reading the text can be understood as different contexts of interpretation, Childs moves through these contexts in a linear fashion, leaving the various arguments disconnected. There is no overarching context that binds these distinct contexts in a unified whole.[69]

My two critiques of Childs's reading of Exod 3:13-15 lead to a broader critique of his multilevel approach to biblical theology. First, Childs's di-

---

67. Ibid., xiv.
68. Childs, *Book of Exodus*, xv.
69. Reviews of Childs's commentary note that its vast scope makes difficult thorough attention to each of its parts. Some reviewers call for greater philological, textual-critical, and archeological attention, while Sakenfeld's disappointment with the "New Testament context" and "theological reflection" sections anticipates some of my criticisms. Katharine Doob Sakenfeld, review of *Book of Exodus: A Critical, Theological Commentary*, by Brevard S. Childs, ThTo 31, no. 3 (1974): 275-78; James A. Sanders, review of *Book of Exodus: A Critical, Theological Commentary*, by Brevard S. Childs, JBL 95, no. 2 (1976): 286-87; Edward Lipiński, review of *Book of Exodus: A Critical, Theological Commentary*, by Brevard S. Childs, VT 26, no. 3 (1976): 378-83.

achronic analysis does not substantially inform his interpretation of the text in its received form (which Childs himself recognizes), and this is the case *because* Childs uses form criticism to address narrative and theological questions that the received form of the text does not answer. Secondly, Childs's sections on the New Testament, history of interpretation, and theological reflection are dissatisfying because while Childs makes some insightful claims that challenge many readings of the text in question, these statements are either thinly supported (in the New Testament section), or they are offset by outdated claims characteristic of the Biblical Theology Movement (in regard to the history of interpretation of the text). The thinness of these sections relates to a third difficulty in Childs's work throughout his corpus: though Childs argues for the validity of ontological interpretation, or that which expressly observes the unity of the one God across the Old and New Testaments (and, by extension, the life of the church throughout the ages), his overwhelming concern with interpreting Old Testament texts within the conceptual limits of this testament subverts his ability to articulate positively what this type of interpretation entails and to carry it out in practice.

2.1. Diachronic Analysis and the Final Form

Childs addresses the prehistory of Exod 3:13–15 in terms of source and form criticisms. Neither approach significantly influences Childs's understanding of these verses. I observe that Childs's form-critical approach assumes that the name and its significance were once distinct, which is, at best, a disputed religio-historical claim. Then I argue that Childs's form-critical analysis has only minimal significance for his reading of the final form; these two sections of analysis lead in different interpretive directions.

Childs presents the standard account of sources (3:2–4a, 5, 7–8, 16–22; 4:1–16 = J; 3:6, 9–15; 4:17 = E). J and E are distinguished according to the following criteria: J speaks of Sinai, E of Horeb; J contains the divine messenger, in E, God calls Moses directly; other criteria need further refinement. Critics of this standard view fall to either one extreme or another: either they "unduly atomize the text" (Richter) or they force the text into a false unity (Buber). At the same time, Childs observes, following Habel, that "there is more unity in the present text than has been generally recognized," particularly in 3:1–6; "this suggests that the common core was considerable and explains why a precise separation is difficult."[70] The more significant tension in the

---

70. Childs, *Book of Exodus*, 53.

text is between 3:7–8//3:9–12, and for these verses "the presence of two sources seems still to be the most obvious solution."[71] Childs is trying to walk a fine line; he does not want to ignore sources in the text where and if they are apparent, but he finds more unity in the text than his predecessors.

In his form-critical comments on Exod 3:13–15, Childs unapologetically acknowledges that his diachronic analysis will not directly aid his reading of the final form; he suggests that a direct relationship would not do justice to the context of the latter:

> The literary and form-critical analysis (cf. above) confirmed the scholarly opinion that vv. 13ff. reflect the special tradition of one early witness which connected the communication of the divine name to Moses' commission. However, it is now our task to hear this testimony as it found its place within ch. 3.[72]

Childs argues that the oral tradition of the divine name being new at the time of Moses was preserved in E but augmented through a process of transmission, which was influenced by the tradition of prophecy validated by the use of the divine name. Further, the text of verse 14 was added when the question in verse 13 came to be understood as concerning the significance of the name rather than factual information.[73] In this way, Childs's diachronic analysis answers two basic questions about Exod 3:13–15. First, Moses asks for YHWH's name as though it is the obvious question for the Israelites (because the question was viewed in light of the tradition of the "child's question"). Second, verses 14 and 15 seem to give two distinct answers to the question in verse 13 because the question was first understood to be about the name, and only later, about the name's significance. As Childs recognizes, in the context of the final form, the role of the question within Moses' objections is more pronounced; moreover, that YHWH directs the explanation of his intention to Moses rather than to the Israelites suggests that "[Moses] has cloaked his own doubt as to God's intention in terms of the people's query."[74] Similarly, in the final form of the text, the significance and content of the divine name are fully intertwined, whereas Childs explains the development of the text through historical or traditional contexts in

---

71. Ibid.
72. Ibid., 75.
73. Ibid., 66–70.
74. Ibid., 76.

which the question about the name was seen *either* as a request for information (E and the oral tradition behind E), *or* as a question about the trustworthiness of the prophet, *or* as a question about the significance of the name.

Childs acknowledges that his diachronic and synchronic analyses move in different interpretive directions and that this situation is not ideal. Yet, it is unclear why Childs deems the different senses of the question as the product of accretion. If the final editor understood the name, its significance, and Moses' role as prophet as compatible and even mutually-informative senses of the question, could not these various senses be the result of accretion rather than original to the story? Neither the (albeit odd) construction of YHWH's three-fold answer, in the final form of 3:14-15, nor the perplexing question in verse 13 can bear the full weight of this theological distinction. Perhaps religio-historical reconstruction could provide a basis for believing that the divine name was once divorced from the significance suggested in the received form of Exod 3:13-15. However, as I argue earlier in this chapter, reconstruction of the origins and meaning of the name "YHWH" in Israel are fraught with difficulty and increasingly less interested in addressing this question. It remains possible that the distinction between the divine name and its significance is a modern construct. Thus, Childs's form criticism of Exod 3:13-15 is open to question and does not significantly aid reading the received form of this text.

2.2. The New Testament, History of Interpretation, and Theological Reflection

Childs's sections on the New Testament, history of interpretation, and theological reflection overlap significantly, so I will address them together. While Childs reflects in fresh ways on the history of interpretation of Exod 3:13-15 and New Testament texts that reference this passage, at other points his discussion borders on stereotype, and it lacks specificity with regard to how one might then read this text in the present.

2.2.1. New Testament Childs's account of Exod 3:1-4:17 in the New Testament covers three topics: references to the story in debates about the resurrection in the synoptic gospels (Matt 22:32; Mark 12:26; Luke 20:37), New Testament references to the call of Moses (or lack thereof), and New Testament references to the name formula in Exod 3:14. His discussion of references to the divine name formula of 3:14 in the New Testament is particularly relevant to the present argument. Childs notes the traditio-historical developments occurring between Exod 3:14 and the New Testament: 1. the twofold formula "first and last" (Isa 44:6); 2. the divine self-pronouncement אֲנִי הוּא, which the Septuagint translators have rendered ἐγώ εἰμι in Deut

32:39 and Deutero-Isaiah; 3. the Jerusalem Targum's gloss on Exod 3:14, which reads, "I am He who is, and who shall be." Each of these developments leads into the formula ὁ ὤν καὶ ὁ ἦν καὶ ὁ ἐρχόμενος, "who is, who was, and who is to come" (Rev 1:8).[75]

Childs's next paragraph is rather important for my argument:

> It remains a more difficult question to assess to what extent ontological overtones were attached to the biblical formula. (Naturally much turns on the term "ontological.") However, it is of interest to note that at least the vocabulary of the LXX's rendering of Ex. 3.14 (ἐγώ εἰμι ὁ ὤν) was picked up in Rev. 1.8. Certainly Philo developed the Greek translation further in terms of existence: "Tell them that I am He Who Is, that they may learn the difference between what is and what is not and . . . further . . . that no name at all can properly be used of Me, to Whom alone existence belongs" (*Vita Mos*. I.75). Although this vocabulary was not used in the New Testament, the note which Philo strikes has some real kinship with the witness of II Isaiah and cannot be dismissed as "alien Greek thinking."[76]

Childs discusses Philo within a brief account of references to Exod 3:14 in the New Testament; Childs may be trying to downplay the question of whether or not these references to the verse carry "ontological overtones." Certainly Philo's reading could suggest that the possibility of an ontological understanding of this verse was alive and well during the period of the New Testament's formation. Childs then defends such a reading, at least against the idea that it is an imposition of "alien Greek thinking." But not only does Childs fail to answer the question of whether the New Testament's references to Exod 3:14 are patient of ontological reading, he also does not specify the resonances he sees between Philo's interpretation of Exod 3:14 and Deutero-Isaiah. It is unclear what the point of quoting Philo is at all, except to admit the theoretical possibility that the New Testament's use of the verse could have "ontological overtones."[77]

---

75. Childs, *Book of Exodus*, 82–83. Childs adds, "John's use of the familiar formula ἐγώ εἰμι appears to have had a somewhat different history," though it is unclear from where John's phrase would have come if not from Deut 32:29 and Deutero-Isaiah.

76. Ibid., 83.

77. Childs's sudden interest in the possibility of "ontological overtones" in his New Testament section reveals the oversight of the same in his Old Testament con-

2.2.2. History of interpretation Childs raises issues of ontological interpretation and deals with them more directly in his section on the history of exegesis. He wants to differentiate himself from the Biblical Theology Movement and the sharp contrast it made between Hebrew and non-Hebrew (ANE and Greek) mentalities,[78] agreeing with James Barr that "it is not a self-evident historical fact that the ancient Hebrews had no concept of being, but only action."[79] Moreover, "once the simple contrast between Greek and Hebrew mentality is called into question, then the task of seeing the whole range of alternative interpretations throughout the history of exegesis takes on new significance."[80] Childs seems to suggest that ancient, medieval, Reformation and modern readers might have held a concept of being that overlapped with the Hebrew notion.[81]

In his brief but cogent survey of the history of exegesis of the passage, Childs achieves his purpose of "illuminating the text by showing how the questions which are brought to bear by subsequent generations of interpreters influenced the answers which they received,"[82] though at times his understanding of the questions and answers of the tradition seem more stereotyped than nuanced. For example, Childs's suggestion that whereas the patristic and medieval writers were concerned with "God's being as a philosophical problem," the reformers focussed "on the function of God's being in ruling, governing, and redeeming his world,"[83] is too harsh a contrast; it does justice neither to the theological concepts at hand nor to Christian tradition. Childs notes Augustine's understanding of God as "unchangeable

---

text section, in which Childs argues that verse 14 means that "God announces that his intentions will be revealed in his future acts, which he now refuses to explain." Ibid., 76. There is no discussion of Deutero-Isaiah, Deut 32:39 or the Jerusalem Targum in this section.

78. See Childs's discussion of the "distinctive Hebrew mentality" as a part of the Biblical Theology Movement's consensus and criticisms against it in Childs, *Biblical Theology in Crisis*, 44–47, 70–72.

79. Childs, *Book of Exodus*, 87. Cf. Barr, *Semantics*, 58ff.

80. Childs, *Book of Exodus*, 87.

81. This way of looking at the matter might be expressed better. More important than a "concept" of being at a particular time and place are the theological judgments made about the relation between God and all that is. Yeago, "Nicene Dogma," 152–64.

82. Childs, *Book of Exodus*, xv.

83. Ibid., 86.

essence," but his description lacks any sense of the pervasive apophasis in Augustine, which is surely the point of his discussion of substance and accidents in *The Trinity* Book 5.[84] Moreover, by writing of Eusebius, Augustine, and Aquinas together in the paragraph, and ending with a quote from Gilson, Childs suggests that these three are all part of an univocal tradition that "the proper name of God is being and that . . . this name denotes His very essence."[85] Yet this statement clearly is not true of Augustine, who identifies the name of God as "I Am Who I Am" and "I am the God of Abraham, the God of Isaac, and the God of Jacob," as well as *"idipsum,"* "Self-same." Childs's choice of Gilson stands in tension with his desire to move beyond the "unique Hebrew mentality" approach of the Biblical Theology Movement; of course, other options may not have been available in the late-1960s and early 1970s, particularly for one outside of the fields of patristic and medieval theology. Gilson's argument rests on the idea that there is a kind of biblical philosophy, a "metaphysics of Exodus," which was revealed to Moses, preserved by tradition and most fully expressed in the writings of Thomas Aquinas. To Gilson, this tradition and its Christian philosophy are quite distinct from surrounding and contemporaneous non-Christian philosophy, as the revealed ideas are translated into, and more fully expressed in, Greek and Latin. The stark contrast between Gilson and the Biblical Theology Movement is obvious: biblical theologians have generally argued that later philosophically-minded Greeks and Latins imposed concepts foreign to the Hebrew mentality onto the biblical text in their reading of Exod 3:14, whereas Gilson argues that this tradition is a legitimate, even necessary, elucidation of the text which is already philosophical in its own right. At the same time, Gilson may be understood as a particular Thomistic counterpart to the Biblical Theology Movement, because he agrees with this movement that the core of Hebrew-Christian philosophy or mentality is distinct from that of the surrounding pagan culture. If Childs wants to move beyond the Biblical Theology Movement toward a more nuanced understanding of the relationship between revelation and culture, he might need someone other than Gilson to guide him in understanding Christian tradition. In sum, Childs's account of the history of exegesis of the passage is confused, not least because he has two simultaneously conflicting and overlapping guides to this history—namely Gilson and the Biblical Theology Movement—and while he seems uncomfort-

---

84. Contra Childs, ibid., 85.
85. Gilson, *Spirit of Mediæval Philosophy*, 51 quoted in Childs, *Book of Exodus*, 85.

able with both of these approaches, he is unable to provide a more reasonable way forward.

2.2.3. Theological reflection Childs draws together some crucial theological points in his closing section. Both testaments witness to a God who makes himself known, rather than one who is discovered. The force of the revelation is past, present and future: God has spoken to the prophets, will be known in deeds among God's people, is present in Jesus, and will be manifest in the new creation. A central purpose of this revelation is to summon a response of obedience; revelation is "an invitation to trust in the one whose self-disclosure is a foretaste of the promised inheritance."[86] Both history and ontology are potentially dangerous if they are "divorced from the divine reality which appeared in its fullness in the incarnated Lord, who is both 'first and last.'"[87] Most important for our discussion, perhaps, is this paragraph:

> The being and activity of God are not played against each other but included within the whole reality of the divine revelation. God's nature is neither static being, nor eternal presence, nor simply dynamic activity. Rather, the God of Israel makes known his being in specific historical moments and confirms in his works his ultimate being by redeeming a covenant people.[88]

Who God is and what God does are intertwined so that neither one replaces the other. So, when Childs writes that God's "revelation of himself defines his being in terms of his redemptive work,"[89] he does not mean that God's being is "simply dynamic activity." Childs here strays from the view of the Biblical Theology Movement as well as the present consensus and so offers a rather helpful theological point.

2.3. Childs's Multilevel Reading and Ontological Interpretation

In this section, I move beyond Childs's Exodus commentary to his later proposal for biblical theology to be accomplished through what he calls "multilevel reading." This later proposal is relevant to my account of Childs for at least two reasons. First, it bears strong similarity to what he earlier accomplished in *The Book of Exodus*. Second, in articulating his proposal, Childs

---

86. Childs, *Book of Exodus*, 89.
87. Ibid., 88.
88. Ibid.
89. Ibid., 87.

addresses the place of ontological interpretation in reading Christian Scripture, which is immediately relevant to theological interpretation of Exod 3:13–15. In what follows, I also present two critiques of Childs's multilevel reading and ontological interpretation. First, Childs rarely attends to the third level of reading in practice; second, his account of the third level of reading is hermeneutically problematic. Nevertheless, the present study draws on the work of Childs in that he discusses ontological interpretation, that is, the witness of the Old Testament to the one Triune God, according to Christian confession.

In *Biblical Theology of the Old and New Testaments*, Childs advocates multilevel reading in three parts.[90] Daniel Driver has named these parts "*res*$_1$," "*res*$_2$," and "*res*$_3$."[91] Childs begins with the descriptive task, which he aligns with the *sensus literalis*. In addressing *res*$_1$ the interpreter hears "the voice of each biblical witness in its own right . . . within its historical, literary, and canonical context," and so avoids "drown[ing] out the Old Testament's own voice."[92] This stage of reading has to do with the *res*, the theological subject matter. However, Childs's definition of "theological" in this case is historically defined; it is Israel's witness to the one God *prior* to the advent of Christ. According to Childs, anything else confuses promise and fulfillment.

Driver's "*res*$_2$" is the second stage of a multilevel reading, which "does not in itself contradict the literal/historical reading, but rather extends it. This proceeds from the fact of a two-part canon, and seeks to analyse structural similarities and dissimilarities between the witness of both testaments."[93] *Res*$_2$ differs from *res*$_1$ not in nature (they both concern the descriptive task) but rather in scope; *res*$_2$ brings the entire canon into view.

The third aspect, Driver's "*res*$_3$," involves "hermeneutical movement of biblical interpretation . . . from reality to witness."[94] Childs's example of this

---

90. Brevard S. Childs, *Biblical Theology of the Old and New Testaments: Theological Reflection on the Christian Bible* (London: SCM, 1992), 379–83.

91. Daniel R. Driver, *Brevard Childs, Biblical Theologian: For the Church's One Bible*, FAT II 46 (Tübingen: Mohr Siebeck, 2010), 240.

92. Childs, *Biblical Theology*, 379.

93. Ibid., 380; cf. Driver, *Brevard Childs*, 240–41.

94. It may be symptomatic that Childs phrases much of his first paragraph on the subject of the third level rhetorically, in question form. Childs, *Biblical Theology*, 380.

Though Childs might not welcome the thought, there are at least formal analogies between the third stage of his proposal for multilevel reading and Bultmann's

type of interpretation is how the Old Testament is used in the New Testament. Gospel writers,

> consistently interpreted the life of the earthly Jesus from the perspective of his true identity, namely, as the resurrected Christ. Each evangelist did his theological redaction in different ways, but all came from an encounter with the reality of Christ and brought that understanding to bear on the scriptures. Similarly, it was fully characteristic of Paul's exegesis to use the gospel of the exalted Christ as the kerygmatic key for understanding the Hebrew scriptures. He also moved from reality to text.[95]

Thus the evangelists exemplify the third level of Childs's multilevel reading.

I argue that Childs's third stage of reading is theologically and hermeneutically problematic. Childs would benefit from greater clarity in describing what he means by "reality" and, in his analogy with the gospel writers, Jesus' "true identity." Surely what Childs means is that the evangelists, after Jesus' resurrection, could then understand his earthly ministry in the light of the bodily resurrection. However, to do so is not to move hermeneutically from Jesus' resurrected "reality" to earthly "witness," but rather from a later human perception of divine reality to a witness which, on its own terms, would not have elicited the fullness of the later human perception. One cannot move, hermeneutically, from God or the risen Christ to the text, because God/the risen Christ is not a text, or a thing, which one can "read in" to something else. What Childs must rather be asking is whether one can interpret the Bible based on what the church has come to understand since the time of the biblical writers. Childs's answer seems to be "yes," but this answer is tentative, perhaps because he himself is not sure what he means by "reality." Rather than showing the reader what it means to move "from reality to witness," Childs is much better at informing his readers of the limits of this movement: "The movement from *res* to witness dare not destroy the historical voice of the text. The substance of the text must not be construed as a static deposit or according to some philosophical schema, but must continue to be encountered within the dynamic of the

---

Sachkritik. For a discussion of the major twentieth-century hermeneutical issues and tensions that may be at work within Childs's proposal, see Karl Barth and Rudolf Bultmann, *Letters, 1922-66*, ed. Bernd Jaspert and Geoffrey W. Bromiley (London: T&T Clark, 1982).

95. Childs, *Biblical Theology*, 381.

biblical witness."[96] Christian understanding of God grows out of the biblical text, but it is informed by centuries of reading and reflecting on this text. Thus, it may be other than the historical voice of the text precisely because it is a different historical voice.

One can note that the definition of "reality" in the case of hermeneutical movement "from reality to witness" is necessarily more restricted than the definition of "reality" in the case of hermeneutical movement "from witness to reality." In the latter context, Childs might be—and probably is—actually talking about God. This is the norm for Christian reading of Scripture, especially in light of Barth who thoroughly developed the notion of witness that has come to have considerable influence. Moving "from witness to reality" is not the antithesis of moving "from reality to witness," which is an attempt to bring together two different conceptions of God from two different time periods within the history of God's people. The latter hermeneutical mode functions on a different conceptual plane.

Hesitation in Childs's account and practice of the third level of reading may be further evidence of its problems. After briefly describing and justifying the task of res_3, Childs moves on to a more pressing concern: explaining how *not* to do it:

> I think that it is important in analysing such a level of interpretation to recognize that it does not function as a rival to the historical study of the biblical text. To substitute a theological context for the historical caused a major problem for the traditional allegorical approach. Nor does an exegesis which comes to the biblical text from a larger theological grasp of God's reality function apart from the various other historical and literary readings. It is not a final step, nor does exegesis proceed in stages within a fixed sequence. Rather, it is constitutive of true interpretation to move within a circle which encompasses both the movement from text to reality as well as from reality to the text. That subtlety is required is obvious. The movement from *res* to witness dare not destroy the historical voice of the text. The substance of the text must not be construed as a static deposit or according to some philosophical schema, but must continue to be encountered within the dynamic of the biblical witness. Yet quite clearly a knowledge of the nature of the subject matter does decisively affect the

---

96. Ibid.

perception of the text and influence the questions posed and the response received in interpretation.[97]

Thus Childs states the task of the third level of reading largely in negative terms and so shows his lack of ease with it. Indeed, Childs is extremely vague in positive terms: "the interpreter's fuller grasp of God's reality which he brings to the biblical text is not a collection of right doctrine or some moral idea, but a response to a living God who graciously lets himself be known."[98]

In *Biblical Theology*, Childs offers little discussion that would be characterized as res_3 or the third stage of his multilevel approach.[99] A primary section in which one might expect to find this might be in Part 6, the chapter entitled "Christ the Lord." Under the heading "Christology in the Context of Biblical Theology," Childs simply moves through the Old Testament, describing God's reconciliation with humanity witnessed there in terms that stay within the epistemological purview of Old Testament authors: the "from above" direction of reconciliation, God's covenant with Israel, and the "from below" direction, through various offices in Israel (kingship, priesthood, prophets). Then, Childs looks to the New Testament and argues that both directions of reconciliation are united in the one person of Christ, who is also described according to the various offices of Israel. Childs concludes with the rich statement,

> The continuing task of Biblical Theology is to engage in critical theological reflection on the christological witness of both testaments to the person and work of Jesus Christ as the one reality of God towards which all scripture points. Such reflection does not consist in simply joining together various prooftexts from the Old and New Testaments, but to engage the witness of both testaments in the light of the reality made known in Jesus Christ, in the incarnate and exalted Lord.[100]

But Childs hardly has accomplished this in what precedes. Again, in the following sub-section, entitled "Biblical Theology and Dogmatic Reflection," Childs makes some substantial statements about the potential for movement from *res* to witness, including that "the major function of Biblical Theology is

---

97. Ibid., 381–82.
98. Ibid., 382.
99. Cf. Noble, *Canonical Approach*, 75–76.
100. Childs, *Biblical Theology*, 480.

to provide a bridge for two-way traffic between biblical exegesis and systematic theology's reflections on the subject matter"[101] and that "the theological question is whether ['*homoousios*'] is a faithful rendering of the biblical witness in light of proposed alternatives"[102] (though Childs does not even begin to answer this question). However, it is difficult to see that Childs's third level of reading is a substantial element of his biblical interpretation in actual practice.

Despite this critique of Childs's multilevel reading and particularly res_3, Childs does positively address the topic of ontological interpretation of the Old Testament. In his commentary on Isaiah, Childs writes that the canonical shape of Isaiah and of the suffering servant has forced the church to read the text in light of Jesus, but the movement of such interpretation is not from prophecy to fulfillment: "Rather, an analogy was drawn between the redemptive activity of the Isaianic servant and the passion and death of Jesus Christ. The relation was understood 'ontologically,' that is to say, in terms of its substance, its theological reality."[103] Driver suggests that talking "about the God of the Old and New as a unified being" is "principally what Childs means when he invokes an 'ontological' dimension."[104] In his 1997 essay, "Does the Old Testament Witness to Jesus Christ?" Childs defines "ontology" as that which "refers to a mode of speech in relation to a subject matter which disregards or transcends temporal sequence."[105] Christian doctrine may be ontological at points, but here Childs uses the term "ontology" not to define a philosophy of being, but to identify the unity of the subject matter of both testaments.

Childs's articulation of the role of allegory—that is, of beginning with the *res* and moving toward the witness—does not carry weight because at least some of the ways that Childs describes it are theologically problematic, and because he applies most of his exegetical energy toward the descriptive

---

101. Ibid., 481.

102. Ibid., 482.

103. Brevard S. Childs, *Isaiah: A Commentary*, OTL (Louisville: Westminster John Knox, 2001), 423; also quoted in Driver, *Brevard Childs*, 263.

104. Childs, *Biblical Theology*, 259.

105. Brevard S. Childs, "Does the Old Testament Witness to Jesus Christ?," in *Evangelium Schriftauslegung, Kirche: Festschrift für Peter Stuhlmacher*, ed. J. Adna et al. (Göttingen: Vandenhoeck & Ruprecht, 1997), 60; also quoted in Driver, *Brevard Childs*, 259.

task. Nevertheless, Childs's canonical approach leaves room for Trinitarian readings of Old Testament texts on ontological grounds, as the God to whom the Old Testament witnesses by the name "YHWH" is none other than the Father, Son, and Holy Spirit of Christian confession.

One of the questions Christian readers of the Old Testament need to address is how a reading that places Old Testament texts in an explicitly Christian context can nevertheless be a legitimate understanding of the witness of these texts. The closest Childs comes to addressing this concern is in the third level of his multilevel approach. However, difficulties with the theological basis of the approach problematize this part of Childs's reading proposal. Moreover, Childs's failure to offer detailed examples of the third level of reading may be a further symptom of its misconception.

In sum, Childs's work contributes to the current study of Exod 3:13-15 on at least two accounts. First, Childs brings a variety of contexts, including history of interpretation, to bear on the interpretive process. Second, to the extent that Childs challenges the Greek-versus-Hebrew philosophical diachotonomy in interpretation of these verses, he makes substantial gains over prior readings. Yet, because of problems in various stages of Childs's reading of the passage and his "multilevel approach," we will do well to turn our attention elsewhere for a framework to guide the present study.

3. The Literal Sense

In order to argue that a reading of Exod 3:13-15 in an explicitly Christian context may nevertheless be a legitimate reading of the witness of this ancient text, I will not follow Childs's multilevel approach. Instead, I use the broad Christian concept of the literal sense to draw together various elements of exegesis, from the semantics of the text to historical and contemporary theological understanding of those semantics. Hans Frei's account of the literal sense is better positioned than Childs's to show that a reading of an Old Testament text can be legitimately perceived as rendering witness to the one God, known to Christians as Father, Son and Holy Spirit. However, at points Frei's account of the literal sense is unnecessarily christological in its focus, which may misconstrue the Christian's understanding of the witness of the Old Testament as a witness to Jesus in the first instance, rather than as a witness to God, known in the life, teachings, death, resurrection and ascension of Jesus Christ.

The work of Hans Frei will assist me in describing what I mean by "literal sense."[106] In using the phrase "literal sense," following Frei, I seek to make two related points. First, "literal sense" refers to "the way the words go"[107]—that is, the basic sense of the text as self-referential—which is the primary sense of Scripture in the church. Second, "literal sense" refers to the basic ascriptive character of the biblical witness: that the identity of God is the true ascriptive subject of biblical texts about God.

3.1. The Literal Sense According to Hans Frei

Frei's account of the literal sense includes several sub-claims: 1. that the identity of Jesus Christ, the Son of God made man, is the true ascriptive subject of the gospel narratives about him; 2. that the literal sense of Scripture

---

106. The difficulty in untangling notions of various "senses" of Scripture—literal, plain, figural, typological, allegorical, anagogical, and so on—is well documented. Two good, recent accounts are John David Dawson, *Christian Figural Reading and the Fashioning of Identity* (Berkeley; Los Angeles; London: University of California, 2002), and Frances M. Young, *Biblical Exegesis and the Formation of Christian Culture* (Cambridge: Cambridge University, 1997).

Not only is the phrase "literal sense" difficult to define, but a host of uses of the phrase are quite distinct from my own. For example, Barr suggests that the meaning of "literal" is self-evident, though whether or not it is a good thing in biblical interpretation is debatable. For Barr, "literal" means something like "factually real." It might be the factuality of historical, spatial description, as in the example of Jesus' ascension, or it may be the theological factuality of God's love. Stating that something is "literal" or "literally true" communicates that what exists is most certainly one way and not another. Defining "literal" in this way leads Barr to claim that modern biblical scholarship is not so much concerned with the literal sense as it is with allegory, with the meaning of particular texts. Modern biblical scholarship is not concerned with "the facts as they happened," but with the mindset of particular authors, hearers, and/or readers in the processes of writing, reading, and hearing the Old Testament in its original contexts. James Barr, "The Literal, the Allegorical, and Modern Biblical Scholarship," *JSOT* 44 (1987): 3, 12-16.

107. Bruce Marshall uses "the way the words go" as a translation of Aquinas's *circumstantia litterae* in Bruce D. Marshall, "Absorbing the Word: Christianity and the Universe of Truths," in *Theology and Dialogue: Essays in Conversation with George Lindbeck* (Notre Dame: Notre Dame University, 1990), 93-94. The context is Aquinas's refusal to restrict Scripture to "have a single sense in such a way that other senses which have truth in them and can be adapted to Scripture by agreeing with the way the words go (*salva circumstantia litterae*) are completely excluded."

is a claim about all of Scripture's relation to Jesus Christ and to the gospel narratives; 3. that the literal sense is the most basic, and hence foundational, sense of Scripture, in distinction from the derived senses (allegorical, moral, anagogical); 4. that because the church has understood the gospel narratives in this way, the literal sense is also the "plain sense," that is, the consensus view of how Scripture should be interpreted.[108]

Frei argues that in the eighteenth and nineteenth centuries, the meaning of biblical texts and the actual words of those texts, or flow of the writing, became disjointed. The premodern church understood the literal sense as the basis of the spiritual senses (allegorical, tropological, and anagogical). According to Frei, "precritical exegesis"[109] was characterized by three elements: 1. the identification of a literal reading with actual historical events (though not as evidence of those events); 2. a coherent narrative sequence from the beginning to the end of the Bible, including both testaments, interpretively mirrored or retained by typology (which was congruent with literal meaning as a "natural extension"); 3. the text's ability to embrace or envelop the experience of the reader, regardless of time and place, because the text depicts the world truly.[110] One effect of the nature of premodern literal sense and the transformation of the literal sense in modernity is that modern readers are puzzled to discover that, as the literal sense once included typology, so the *sensus literalis* of the Old Testament, according to premodern Christian readers, includes christological readings.

Frei argues that, in the eighteenth and nineteenth centuries, there came to be "a logical distinction and a reflective distance between the stories and the 'reality' they depict."[111] In other words, meaning was understood as the reference of the text to something outside of the text. This was as true for conservatives as it was for liberals. The meaning of a story came to be something other than the story itself—either a historical event or its religious

---

108. My understanding of Frei's concept of the literal sense has been informed by Dawson's account, though any faults in my description are my own. Dawson, *Christian Figural Reading*, passim.

109. I prefer the term "premodern" to "precritical" because the latter appears to exclude the possibility that patristic and medieval Christian thinkers were critical in their own, premodern, ways.

110. Hans W. Frei, *The Eclipse of Biblical Narrative* (London: Yale University, 1980), 2–3.

111. Ibid., 5.

meaning. It is not that the "realistic character" of biblical stories was denied in the eighteenth century, but that the premodern means of identifying it were no longer deemed acceptable, so these characteristics came to be ignored. Frei asserts,

> In both affirmative and negative cases, the confusion of history-likeness (literal meaning) and history (ostensive reference), and the hermeneutical reduction of the former to an aspect of the latter, meant that one lacked the distinctive category and the appropriate interpretive procedure for understanding what one had actually recognized: the high significance of the literal, narrative shape of the stories for their meaning. And so, one might add, it has by and large remained ever since.[112]

Frei's historical description is surely critical, not only of the eighteenth and nineteenth centuries, but also of his hermeneutical contemporaries. One can anticipate that Frei would, in other works, offer a way forward, for the renewal of the literal sense has primarily to do with the flow or structure of the text itself; that meaning and text are fundamentally interrelated is a central point of the church's reading of the *sensus literalis* of the New Testament and understanding of Jesus Christ as the Son of God.

This christological point becomes increasingly clear as one seeks to understand the communal point: how it is that the literal sense became the plain sense, the church's consensus reading of Scripture. In his dense article, "The 'Literal Reading' of Biblical Narrative in Christian Tradition: Does it Stretch or will it Break?," Frei argues for an understanding of the literal sense that includes the plain sense. He claims that that if the literal reading of Scripture is built on an account of narrative that ignores the rules by which the community of faith (the church) receives the written text in actual fact, then the literal sense may not survive critical analysis. Frei summarizes his argument as follows:

> I believe that the tradition of the *sensus literalis* is the closest one can come to a consensus reading of the Bible as the sacred text in the Christian church and that current hermeneutical theory defends a revised form of it; but I also believe that the defense is a failure, so that, in the words of the essay's title, the literal reading will break apart under its ministrations.[113]

---

112. Ibid., 12.
113. Hans W. Frei, "The 'Literal Reading' of Biblical Narrative in the Christian

If hermeneutical theory's defense of the *sensus literalis* is a failure, how does Frei suggest that Christian readers use and defend it? Frei continues,

> One may well hope that the *sensus literalis*, a much more supple notion than one might at first suspect, has a future. If it does, there will be good reason to explain what it is about with a far more modest theory—more modest both in its claims about what counts as valid interpretation and in the scope of the material on which it may pertinently comment.[114]

The future of the literal sense is not in justifying it as a legitimate mode of reading, but rather in describing how it functions "in its primary and original context, a religious community's 'rule' for faithful reading."[115]

Frei argues that though all religious traditions with sacred texts have undergone a gradual process by which these texts have been expanded and the arms of the community opened to welcome hitherto unknown or unrecognized texts as sacred, "the most striking example of this kind of takeover in the history of Western culture" is the inclusion of the Old Testament—its narrative, legal texts, and prophetic, poetic, and wisdom literature—in the Christian Bible by way of typology or figuration.[116] Two features of this inclusion are particularly noteworthy to Frei. First, in contrast to the Hebrew Bible and Rabbinic tradition, in which regulations are understood vis-à-vis narrative texts,

> Christian tradition tends to derive the meaning of such regulations—for example, the sacraments, the place of the "law" in Christian life, the love commandment—directly from (or refer them directly to) its sacred story, the life, teachings, death, and resurrection of Jesus the Messiah. This narrative thus has a unifying force and a prescriptive character in both the New Testament and the Christian community that, despite the importance of the Exodus accounts, neither narrative generally nor any specific narrative has in Jewish Scripture and the Jewish community.[117]

Tradition: Does It Stretch or Will It Break?" in *Theology and Narrative: Selected Essays*, ed. George Hunsinger and William C. Placher (New York; Oxford: Oxford University, 1993), 118-19.
114. Ibid., 119.
115. Ibid., 139.
116. Ibid., 120.
117. Ibid., 120-21.

According to Frei, the coherence of the two-testament canon stems from the unifying pressure that the narrative of Jesus Christ exerts over the Old Testament. Second, Frei asserts that "it was largely by reason of this centrality of the story of Jesus that the Christian interpretive tradition in the West gradually assigned clear primacy to the literal sense in the reading of Scripture."[118] Allegorical interpretations of the Old Testament were allowed before the Reformation because they supported the literal reading of the gospels.[119] Reading the gospels literally meant that "[Jesus] was the Messiah, and the fourfold storied depiction in the gospels, especially of his passion and resurrection, was the enacted form of his identity as Messiah."[120] Because of the christological claims that the church made about Jesus, the "plain" sense of Scripture—the church's consensus interpretation—became the "literal sense." "There is no a priori reason why the 'plain' reading could not have been 'spiritual' in contrast to 'literal,' and certainly the temptation was strong."[121] Nevertheless, the literal sense was asserted "right from the beginning in the *ascriptive* even more than the *descriptive* mode. That 'Jesus'—not someone else or nobody in particular—is the subject, the agent, and patient of these stories is said to be their crucial point, and the description of events, sayings, personal qualities, and so forth, become literal by being firmly predicated of him."[122] The incarnation is not only the paradigmatic instance of, but the basis for, the claim that truth and meaning are a unity. Because of this, the *sensus literalis* is not a general theory that can be applied to all texts or even to certain categories of texts. It is a claim about Christian Scripture. As such, it may well overlap with, even bend to include, general hermeneutical theories. But a hermeneutical justification for the literal sense will render it incomprehensible. The *sensus literalis* is by definition case-specific. Moreover, the *sensus literalis* belongs to a particular socio-linguistic community, the church. "Both considerations involve lowering our theoretical sights yet further to the level of mere description rather than explanation, to the specific set of texts and the most specific context, rather

---

118. Ibid., 121.
119. Except in the case of Origen and his school who maintained an independent justification for allegorical reading. Ibid.
120. Ibid.
121. Ibid., 122.
122. Ibid., 122–23.

than to a general class of texts ('realistic narrative') and the most general context ('human experience')."[123]

While, for Frei, the literal sense is a theological claim—a christological claim about the relation between Jesus Christ and *these* texts about him—it is also a claim about the realistic character of biblical narrative (namely, gospel narratives, but by extension, all of Scripture) and a claim about the socio-linguistic context in which Christian biblical interpretation takes place. But is Frei's account helpful for speaking of the literal sense of the Old Testament? Can Frei say that the Old Testament has its own literal sense, or does it only speak literally through its typological relation to the gospels and their ascriptive subject? Does the Old Testament also have an ascriptive subject?

As already described, Frei's christological focus for Old Testament hermeneutics stems from his claim that a two-testament canon, whereby a group of later texts were added to an already established group of authoritative texts, is a unique phenomenon. Frei observes that there are difficulties with establishing the coherence of such a canonical extension, which leads Frei to argue that the gospel stories of the life, teachings, death, resurrection, and ascension of Jesus Christ provide the canonical pressure and coherence needed for the transition to a two-testament canon to take place in Christian communities. Thus, in Frei's account, it is difficult to see how both Old and New Testaments have ascriptive character, since the Old Testament does not explicitly reference "Jesus Christ" as such and under that title (though Christians may legitimately perceive Christ as figured in the Old Testament).[124] It rather seems that, according to Frei, the Old Testament does not have ascriptive character except through its relation to the New Testament; the Old Testament prefigures Christ, the ascriptive subject of the New Testament. If this is true for Frei's account of the literal sense of the Old Testament, then the realistic character of Old Testament texts would also be in anticipation of their fulfillment in the narratives of Jesus Christ.

This christological focus to understanding the literal sense of the Old Testament is problematic on several counts, not least because it stands in tension with Frei's attention to the self-referential quality of biblical texts. In reading the Old Testament, it would seem that in order to attend to this self-referential quality, one must hold that the theological subject of the Old Tes-

---

123. Ibid., 144.
124. Cf. Christopher R. Seitz, *Figured Out: Typology and Providence in Christian Scripture* (Louisville: Westminster John Knox, 2001).

tament is God, in the first instance. In a Christian context, understanding this subject matter will be informed by the person of Jesus Christ and the gospel narratives about him, but one can still understand the literal sense of Old Testament texts without explicit reference to Christ.

Frei may not have *meant* to deny the realistic character or ascriptive quality of Old Testament texts. However, Frei's proposal for how one might understand the literal sense functions better in relation to the gospel narratives that it does in relation to the Old Testament. Later in this chapter, I suggest how one might build on Frei's account of the literal sense to include a more robust understanding of the Old Testament's own literal sense as a theological claim about the Old Testament's ascriptive subject, the one God, whom Christians know as Father, Son, and Holy Spirit. First, I will address the concept of the literal sense in the work of Childs, who strives to describe it in a way that renders intelligible the Old Testament's literal sense without explicit reference to Jesus Christ. However, Child's account restricts the literal sense to a historical sense.

3.2. *Childs and the Literal Sense*

Childs's understanding of the fate of the literal sense in the modern period owes much to Frei's. Childs calls Frei's *Eclipse* "brilliant," summarizing:

> Frei's analysis has gone a long way toward demolishing the familiar thesis that the Reformers and the 19th century critics shared a similar view regarding the literal sense of the text. . . . Basic to the new approach [beginning in the 18th century] was the attack on the identity of the explicative sense and the historical reference of the text. When the coherence between the verbal sense of the text, that is the literal sense, and its real reference was shattered, a whole set of new hermeneutical options opened up for the interpreter.[125]

Yet, at points Childs restates Frei's argument with his own twist. For example, Childs places particular stress on the modern concept of the historical sense as original meaning. Thus, Childs summarizes the eighteenth- and nineteenth-century developments in this way:

---

125. Brevard S. Childs, "The *Sensus Literalis* of Scripture: An Ancient and Modern Problem," in *Beiträge zur Alttestamentlichen Theologie: Festschrift für Walther Zimmerli zum 70. Geburtstag*, Walther Zimmerli, Herbert Donner, Robert Hanhart and Rudolf Smend, ed. (Göttingen: Vandenhoeck & Ruprecht, 1977), 88.

> In the new approach the identity of the terms ["*sensus literalis*" and "*sensus historicus*"] was also continued, but the historical sense now determined its content. The historical sense of the text was construed as being the *original* meaning of the text as it emerged in its pristine situation. Therefore, the aim of the interpreter was to reconstruct the original occasion of the historical reference on the basis of which the truth of the biblical text could be determined. In sum, the *sensus literalis* had become the *sensus historicus*.[126]

The rise of modern criticism included strong emphasis on the *sensus literalis*, though this was redefined so that the original reference, the original context or even the context lying behind the words, became the goal of exegesis.[127] Childs argues that the effects of the transition can be clearly seen in Jowett's late-nineteenth century argument that the Bible should be read "like any other book," by which Jowett means that recovering the original meaning of the words—how they would have been understood to their first readers and hearers—is the goal of exegesis.[128]

Childs's slight adaptation of Frei's argument is indicative of a greater distinction between their interpretive approaches. Driver observes Frei's and Childs's similar accounts of the fate of the *sensus literalis* in modernity, but asserts that the breaking down of the literal sense can mean at least two different things for the renewal of figuration in the present: "[Figuration's] renewal can be predicated either on the Bible's narrative thrust, or, with a more historical view of the text's prehistory and a distinct take on its reference, on some unitive read of the Christian canon."[129] In this way, Driver suggests that for Frei, the renewal of figural reading hangs on a claim about the nature of biblical narrative, but for Childs, it concerns a more nuanced view of the canon's history of development, its received form, and its

---

126. Ibid., 89.
127. Childs writes of the eighteenth century: "The task of exegesis lay in working out the true historical reference since revelation no longer consisted in the words, but exclusively in the subject matter to which the words referred. Before too long, when philosophers such as Wolff equated meaning with transconceptual essence to which a concept referred, the ultimate ground for any meaning became ontology." Ibid. See Childs's statement that history and ontology are twin dangers that may threaten to overshadow the subject matter of the text in Childs, *Book of Exodus*, 88.
128. Childs, "*Sensus Literalis*," 89.
129. Driver, *Brevard Childs*, 155–56.

subject matter. Though Driver's account of Frei's understanding of biblical narrative may be somewhat reductive, the implications he draws for distinctions between Frei's and Childs's account of figural reading seem appropriate. First, they disagree on the relation between the testaments: for Frei it is linear, whereas for Childs, there is a dialectical relation that is both linear and vertical (that is, relating to the unitary subject matter of both testaments). Second, whereas Frei claims that the difference between Christian reading and *peshat* is that Christian reading engages the larger narrative (including the New Testament), Childs argues that the difference is that Christian reading moves from text to subject matter, from text to *res*. Third, Frei views figuration as fundamentally different from allegory, while Childs is content with figuration being quite similar to, even a subset of, allegory.[130]

While Driver's description may ignore important elements of Frei's understanding of the literal sense (namely that it is primarily a christological claim about Jesus Christ and the gospel narratives that tell of his life, death, and resurrection), Frei's and Childs's arguments for figural reading clearly diverge. For Childs, as Driver has shown, the *sensus literalis* of the Old Testament is explored in the first stage of the multilevel reading—the descriptive task of hearing the discrete voice of the Old Testament. Thus, the conceptuality of the *sensus literalis* of the Old Testament is historically bound to what was available prior to the advent of Jesus Christ. Reading the Old Testament becomes figural only at the point of the second stage of the multilevel reading, in which the entire canon is in view. Thus, if Driver is correct, for Childs, the *sensus literalis* can be identified with the descriptive task of exegeting a passage according to the conceptuality available within a particular historical and/or literary context—that is, according to the Old Testament without the New Testament, historically prior to the advent of Christ. Therefore, whether Childs admits it or not, he is actually rather indebted to the modern understanding of the *sensus literalis* that he critiques. To the extent that the literal sense functions in Childs's proposal for multilevel reading, its primary conceptuality seems to be literary-historical, rather than theological and socio-linguistic, as in Frei's case.

Moreover, Frei is more concerned than Childs to defend the intertwined nature of text and reality. There is no movement from text to *res* in Frei because the text and *res*, while not identical, are inseparable. Since the literal sense is a Christian theological concept, to read Scripture according to the

---

130. Ibid., 156.

literal sense is to meet the *res*, Jesus Christ. I have already suggested that Childs's claim that interpretation can move from *res* to text is christologically problematic. What Childs might mean is that one can, at one stage of interpretation, read one's knowledge of God in Christ into the Old Testament, whereas at another stage of interpretation, this knowledge can and must be bracketed out in order to expound the *sensus literalis*. Frei's understanding of the *sensus literalis* avoids the theological awkwardness of movement "from *res* to witness," because the *res* and witness are already inextricably bound. For these reasons, while Childs's account of the literal sense attends more carefully to the Old Testament's witness, it does not provide a better way forward than Frei's account.

3.3. Critiquing Frei's Christological Literal Sense

Frei's account of the literal sense provides a broad framework for understanding the inextricability of text and meaning, and the connection between confessional theological claims and the self-referential quality of biblical texts. Yet, Frei's account has not sufficiently spoken to how one might understand the literal sense of Old Testament texts, since his account seems unnecessarily reductionistic in its christological focus. Rather, Frei's account of the realistic character of biblical narrative and its *ascriptive* character vis-à-vis a subject, particularly in the Old Testament, would benefit from Trinitarian re-shaping.

In his 2004 article, Brent Strawn considers what difference Trinitarian theology might make for christological readings of the Old Testament.[131] In such consideration, Strawn raises the concern that christological readings might become theologically reductionistic, and Strawn's concern is similar to the theological concerns I raise in critique of Frei's reading. Thus Strawn's discussion will form a basis for my own nuancing of Frei's approach and subsequent understanding of the literal sense.

Strawn argues that in a Christian context where the Trinitarian doctrines of either *perichoresis/circuminsession* (mutual indwelling) or inseparable operations is in view (or where both of them are), a christological approach is certainly permissible, but only one that affirms the interrelation of Christology and Trinity in Christian grammar. Both of these doctrines are central to Christian affirmation that while the Father is God, the Son is God,

---

131. Brent A. Strawn, "And These Three Are One: A Trinitarian Critique of Christological Approaches to the Old Testament," *PRS* 31, no. 2 (2004): 191–210.

and the Spirit is God, these three are one God. I will focus on Strawn's account of inseparable operations, a doctrine well articulated by Augustine.[132]

Simply put, the doctrine of inseparable operations is the claim that any action predicated of a person of the Trinity can be predicated of all three; in all of the actions predicated of the Trinity, the Father, Son and Spirit are "inseparable." Strawn summarizes Barnes's and Ayres's description of Augustine's articulation of inseparable operations as having three points: inseparable activity is central to divine unity; this unity and inseparable activity are revealed fully in the incarnation; and "faith or a certain type of life obedience leads to greater understanding of the Trinity and doctrinal insight into it."[133] Though Strawn draws on the example of Augustine, he notes that this doctrine was present in the works of Augustine's eastern and western predecessors and thus that it is "a rather central point in trinitarian doctrine."[134] Strawn concludes the section with a beautiful quote from *De Trinitate*:

> They are indeed one, as he tells us, *I and the Father are one* (Jn 10:30). In a word, because of this inseparability, it makes no difference whether sometimes the Father alone or sometimes the Son alone is mentioned as the one who is to fill us with delight at his countenance. Nor is the Spirit of each separable from this unity.... The actual truth is that *I and the Father are one* (Jn 10:30), and therefore when the Father is shown, the Son who is in him is shown also, and when the Son is shown, the Father who is in him is shown too.[135]

Whatever the Father does, so also does the Son and the Spirit.

What the doctrine of inseparable operations means for christological readings of the Old Testament is that Christ, as God, does whatever God the Father or the Spirit does in the Old Testament. Therefore,

---

132. Ibid., 203.

133. Ibid., 204. See Michel René Barnes, "Rereading Augustine's Theology of the Trinity," in *The Trinity: An Interdisciplinary Symposium on the Trinity*, eds. Stephen T. Davis, Daniel Kendall, and Gerald O'Collins (Oxford: Oxford University, 1999), 154, 158; Lewis Ayres, "'Remember That You Are Catholic' (serm. 52.2): Augustine on the Unity of the Triune God," *JECS* 8, no. 1 (2000), 40–41, 54–55, 80.

134. Strawn, "And These Three Are One," 204.

135. Augustine, *Trin.* 1.17–18. English translations of *De Trinitate* are from Augustine of Hippo, *The Trinity*, ed. John E. Rotelle, trans. Edmund Hill, OP, *The Works of Saint Augustine* I/5, electronic ed.

> Christ *can* be found in the Old Testament because of its witness to God, whom Christians know to be triune . . . . But that is not the same thing as saying that Christ *is* or *must be* found in the Old Testament or that "the Old Testament is a witness to Jesus Christ" or that "the" subject matter of the Old Testament (!) or even of Scripture as a whole is Jesus Christ. In light of the doctrine of the Trinity, this is simply unnecessary. The subject matter of the Old Testament can simply be God.[136]

If one understands God as the subject of the Old Testament, then, from a Christian perspective, the Old Testament witnesses to Christ. But this does not mean that readings of the Old Testament need to be explicitly christological in order for them to be robustly Christian.

In light of the doctrine of inseparable relations and Strawn's claim that the subject matter of the Old Testament is "simply" God, it may be possible to extend Frei's claim that the main point of gospel stories is their ascriptive relationship to their subject, Jesus Christ, to say that the ascriptive subject of the Old Testament is God. One will need to allow for the distinctive reality of the Word incarnate; Jesus Christ is a coherent personality—a character—in gospel stories in a way that God is not (at least not to the same extent) in the Old Testament. Yet, one might say that the doctrine of inseparable operations means that the perception of Jesus Christ as the ascriptive subject of the New Testament is at the same time the perception of the Father and the Spirit as acting subjects of the New Testament—if in fact the incarnation demonstrates divine unity by inseparable action. Furthermore, surely Strawn's claim that "the subject matter of the Old Testament can simply be God" suits well Frei's emphasis on the literal sense as both the basic sense of the text and the text's self-referential character. The subject of the Old Testament is God, Father, Son and Holy Spirit. It *is* the gospel stories and their ascriptive subject, Jesus Christ, which bind the two testaments precisely because the unity of God—Father, Son, and Spirit—is revealed in Jesus Christ. Thus, these stories and their subject make clear that it is the identity and unity of God that binds the two-testament canon.

In summary, I have argued that an etymological approach to the divine name in Exod 3:13–15 does not aid interpretation of the received form of this text, and I have suggested that a canonical approach may provide better means of understanding how אֶהְיֶה אֲשֶׁר אֶהְיֶה (Exod 3:14) relates to יְהוָה (Exod

---

136. Strawn, "And These Three Are One," *PRS* 31, no. 2 (2004): 206.

3:15). In the latter portion of the chapter, I use the Christian concept of the literal sense, building on Frei's account of it, to bring together various contexts that inform my reading of Exod 3:13–15. Whereas Childs struggled to show how the various historical and literary contexts that he brought to bear on the biblical text are mutually informative, by viewing these contexts within the overarching framework of the literal sense, I seek to present a more unified reading of the text. This sense, for Frei, is primarily a Christian theological claim about Jesus Christ, the true reference of the gospel narratives about him. Building on Frei's understanding of the literal sense by drawing on the doctrine of Trinitarian inseparable operations, I have argued that 1. the character of this Hebrew narrative is realistic, and as such, the reader must be limited by "the way the words go," or the semantic potential of the text;[137] 2. the context in which I account for "the way the words go" is the Christian church broadly speaking; 3. within two-testament Christian Scripture, the subject matter of Old Testament texts is God, known to Christians as Father, Son, and Holy Spirit. These three elements comprise my use of the phrase "literal sense" in reading Exod 3:13–15.

---

137. "Semantic potential" is Watson's phrase. Cf. Francis Watson, *Paul and the Hermeneutics of Faith* (London; New York: T&T Clark, 2004), 4.

Chapter 2

Augustine's Literal-Sense Reading of Exodus 3:14–15

In the previous chapter, I have argued, contra von Rad, that etymology is not a helpful means of understanding the text of Exod 3:13-15. The negative portion of von Rad's argument is that the text of Exod 3:14 is not, "a definition of his nature in the sense of a philosophical statement about his being (LXX Ἐγώ εἰμι ὁ ὤν)—a suggestion, for example, of his absoluteness, aseity, etc."[1] To assess this part of von Rad's claim, I turn to St. Augustine, who—if von Rad is right—should be an example of a major figure within Christian tradition who read this biblical text as referring to God as abstract, static being. However, Augustine does not view God as abstract and static, but rather living, active, and faithful. Augustine provides resources for the theological interpretation of Exod 3 that I propose, one that addresses both God's identity and actions in the lives of God's people.

For Augustine, Exod 3:14 attests to God as God is in himself, which is beyond the grasp of human comprehension. Since God is immaterial and unchangeable, God cannot be perfectly thought or discussed according to the constraints of mortal existence. However, all is not lost for the one who seeks God in faith, for God continuously makes himself known to his creatures, through creation, Scripture, and the people of God. The Old Testament witnesses to the truth of God, just as the New Testament does in its own ways. This reality is known in Christ, who did not consider equality with God as something to be grasped, but became man and took up the cross (cf. Phil 2:6–8) in order that the world could know him. Augustine interprets Exod

---

1. Von Rad, *Old Testament Theology*, 180.

3:14–15 as demonstrating the dynamic that though who God is in himself is incomprehensible to us (v. 14), God makes himself known in a form that humans can grasp: the God of Abraham, the God of Isaac, and the God of Jacob (v. 15). This same dynamic is present in the incarnation, and Augustine explores the reality of God's self-revelation in this text with reference to Christ. I argue that Augustine's reading of Exod 3:14–15 can best be understood according to a literal sense of the Old Testament, which includes 1. close attention to the words of the text and their self-referential quality; 2. divine address to the individual reader, who is transformed in the context of the reading; 3. witness to the one true God, Father, Son and Holy Spirit.[2] I refer to the three aspects as the literal, existential, and Trinitarian dimensions, though these are interrelated and overlapping categories.

1. The Literal Sense in Augustine

Before I address Augustine's reading of Exod 3:13–15, it will be helpful to outline Augustine's approach to Scripture more generally. The modern reader should note that Augustine, like other ancient readers, did not view reading Scripture as a matter of texts analyzed for their meanings. As Cameron articulates clearly,

> Augustine did not view [Scripture] as a textual object that yields correct content to those operating upon it with the proper analytic method.... He did not work analytically *upon* Scripture ("What can we observe about this text?"), but hermeneutically from *within* Scripture ("How does this text disclose the mind of God?").... Augustine looks not so much for *meaning* as for *understanding*, and this appears on every page he wrote.[3]

---

2. The second point differs from how I articulate my own understanding of the threefold literal sense of Scripture. In the Conclusion, I reflect in more detail on the contemporary significance of spiritual journey in Augustine's mode of reading.

3. Michael Cameron, "Augustine and Scripture," in *A Companion to Augustine*, ed. Mark Vessey, Blackwell Companions to the Ancient World (Malden, MA; Oxford: Wiley-Blackwell, 2012), 201–2.

Informed by his study of Frei among others, Dawson makes a similar point about figural reading: "Whether we still think naively that texts 'have' their meanings, the way capitalists own their property, or—with more sophistication or readerly effort—that textual meaning is forever distanced and deferred—we still instinctively bring to

With Augustine's exegesis, one is not in the realm of meanings analytically extracted from texts. Rather, one receives a text and seeks to understand it and its place within the larger framework of salvation and history, God's creation and redemption of the world. Augustine views texts as texts, to be sure, but they are not texts that the reader ought to manipulate or wield control over. Rather, God uses these texts to guide the reader along the path of salvation. Thus the entire plot of Scripture—the story of history and salvation— matters for understanding the individual parts.

Augustine writes of reading Scripture as a journey, and a journey home.[4] This journey is the journey of salvation, toward true rest in God. Along the way, Christ accommodates himself to our humanity; Christ is both the way and the destination. The words of Scripture, their historical reference, and their authorial intention are integrated into the drama of Christ offering himself for the world and drawing the world into himself. Reading specific portions of Scripture informs one's reading of the whole, and reading the whole informs one's reading of the parts. To read the parts in light of the whole is to address not only the letter of the text but also the spirit, the intention of divine and human authorship.

Christian figural reading the assumption that, whatever else it may be about, it must concern texts and meanings. The question about the intelligibility of a divine performance is something we would rather not consider, for the idea that the prophet Isaiah had, in his own right and not only as a consequence of some later reader's strange interpretation, once referred in some oblique fashion to the person of Jesus who had not yet appeared in history and, in so doing, sought to render intelligible a certain divine performance, is, for most of us, historiographically absurd; it is, in fact, the height of unintelligibility. Yet any effort to understand Christian figural reading as fundamentally a matter of texts and the presence or absence of meaning, rather than a matter of rendering God's historical performances intelligible, is doomed to theological irrelevance, however much contemporary theoretical sense it might make." Dawson, *Christian Figural Reading*, 6.

4. This paragraph draws from Eden's chapter on Augustine, which includes substantial attention to Augustine's use and modification of rhetorical principles. Kathy Eden, *Hermeneutics and the Rhetorical Tradition: Chapters in the Ancient Legacy & Its Humanist Reception* (New Haven; London: Yale University, 1997), 53–63. On Augustine's use and modification of the Neoplatonic journey of ascent in *Doctr. chr.*, see John C. Cavadini, "The Sweetness of the Word: Salvation and Rhetoric in Augustine's *De doctrina christiana*," in *De doctrina christiana: A Classic of Western Culture*, ed. Duane W. H. Arnold and Pamela Bright, CJA 9 (Notre Dame: Notre Dame University, 1995), 164–81.

A basic rule for Augustinian exegesis is well-known: true exegesis fosters faith, hope and primarily love, of God and of neighbor.[5] If the proper sense does not encourage these virtues, then the text must be read figuratively: the text must be a *figura* of what is edifying. Augustine writes,

> *Et iste omnino modus est, ut quidquid in sermone divino neque ad morum honestatem neque ad fidei veritatem proprie referri potest, figuratum esse cognoscas. Morum honestas ad diligendum Deum et proximum, fidei veritas ad cognoscendum Deum et proximum pertinet;*

> Generally speaking, it is this: anything in the divine discourse that cannot be related either to good morals or to the true faith should be taken as figurative. Good morals have to do with our love of God and our neighbour, the true faith with our understanding of God and our neighbour.[6]

Within the guidelines of the Rule of Faith—love of God and neighbor—a range of interpretations are appropriate. Augustine disagrees with those who argue for right reading as governed by a strict understanding of authorial intention. While in principle it is best to follow the intention of the author, practically it is difficult to see how one can do so. Given "historical and linguistic barriers to understanding," how can one be certain what Moses intended, for example? How could Moses have known that he would be speaking to generations of people of faith? "In any case, writes Augustine, we know that the Holy Spirit has taken all possible meanings into account. If someone chooses an interpretation that misses the author's intention but still teaches love, then it is a case of 'no harm, no foul': a wrong road to the right place remains useful."[7] However, misunderstanding authorial intention, even in love, can cause difficulties for understanding the parts of Scripture within the whole. If a reader finds a passage that does not square with his reading of a first, misunderstood, passage, then the reader may cling to

---

5. Cf. *Doctr. chr.* 1.35, 39–40; 3.10,15.

6. Ibid., 3.10,14. English translations of *Christian Instruction* are from Augustine, *De doctrina christiana*, trans. R. P. H. Green (Oxford: Oxford University, 1996). Cf. James Samuel Preus, *From Shadow to Promise: Old Testament Interpretation From Augustine to the Young Luther* (Cambridge, MA: Harvard University, 1969), 9–23.

7. Cameron, "Augustine and Scripture," 208. Cf. *Doctr. chr.* 1.36.41.

his first interpretation and become frustrated and angry with Scripture. Within the author's intention, the whole of Scripture coheres.[8]

In some cases, the proper, or literal, sense is edifying, and in these instances the text ought not be read figuratively. Greater clarity must be reached in what Augustine means by "literal," "proper," and "figurative." Greene-McCreight observes that Augustine contrasts between "literal" and "figurative" or "allegorical," the "proper" and "symbolical," and the "historical" and "prophetic." Literal, proper, and historical senses are overlapping categories. Literal or proper sense may indicate events that occurred in past time; material persons, places or things; or words referring in their usual way. Figurative and allegorical senses refer to events in the future (thus, the prophetic sense); participation of material things in the being of God; or words referring in secondary, atypical, ways.[9]

An example of an allegorical understanding of the bush in Exod 3 may provide a contrast to Augustine's literal understanding of the self-revelation of God in this chapter. In both *Sermon 6* and *Sermon 7*, Augustine states that the bush, burning but unconsumed, refers to "the Jews," by which he seems to mean the Israelites as well as his Jewish contemporaries. The image of the bush burning but unconsumed arouses Moses' curiosity and the reader's as well: "So, to put it as briefly as possible: it is not in vain, not without point, not without some hidden meaning, that there was a flame in the bush and the bush was not being burned up."[10] The perplexity of the image cannot go

---

8. Eden, *Hermeneutics and the Rhetorical Tradition*, 54.

9. K. E. Greene-McCreight, *Ad Litteram: How Augustine, Calvin, and Barth Read the "Plain Sense" of Genesis 1-3*, Issues in Systematic Theology 5 (New York: Peter Lang, 1999), 40-43. Augustine recognizes a fourfold sense of Scripture: historical, aetiological, analogical, and allegorical. These do not correspond precisely to the traditional fourfold structure, and they refer both to different genres of Scripture as well as to distinct, superimposed modes of reading the same passage. However, the fourfold sense does not factor strongly in Augustine's practice of exegesis, for which the literal/allegorical distinction and refuting Manichaean objections to the Old Testament are more significant. Henri de Lubac, SJ, *Medieval Exegesis: The Fourfold Senses of Scripture*, vol. 1, trans. Mark Sebanc (Grand Rapids: Eerdmans, 1998), 123-32.

10. *Quod ergo breviter possumus dicere, non frustra, non inaniter, non sine alicuius significatione secreti. In rubo flamma erat, et rubus non cremabatur.* Serm. 7.2. English translations of *Sermons* are from Augustine of Hippo, *Sermons on the Old Testament*, ed. John E. Rotelle, OSA, trans. Edmund Hill, OP, *The Works of Saint Augustine* III/1, electronic ed.

unnoticed, and for Augustine that means that there must be more depth here to plumb. It is not clear whether or not we are to imagine that Moses himself understood the bush as a symbol for the Israelites, but at least Augustine has not entirely lost the importance of the strange image for the narrative flow: it catches the curiosity of Moses and causes him to draw closer to it, providing the context in which the Lord appears to him.

Having deemed that the bush must be a symbol, Augustine further explains that it must be a negative symbol, because of its thorns; סְנֶה, βάτος, and *rubus* all designate thorn bushes. Specifically, the thorns stand for the sins of the Israelites, which the law (fire) does not consume.[11] In *Sermon 7*, Augustine uses Gen 3:18—which he reads as "the earth will bring forth for you thorns and thistles"[12]—part of the curse pronounced to the man after eating fruit from the tree of the knowledge of good and evil, as evidence that thorns are associated with sin. In contrast, the fire is something good, associated with the Holy Spirit in the New Testament.[13] Augustine then admonishes believers saying, "then we ought to catch alight from this fire and not fail, because of our hardness, to be burnt up."[14]

I am not interested in defending Augustine's interpretation of the burning bush; it is not Augustine's finest exegetical moment.[15] However, this can provide a counterexample to Augustine's reading of Exod 3:14–15. Augustine observes the function of the bush in the story—that its peculiarity

---

11. *Serm.* 6.3; 7.2. Augustine's Bible is the *Vetus Latina*, whose Pentateuch includes Latin translations from Greek. These Latin translations are distinct from Jerome's translation from Hebrew. A critical edition of most books of the *Vetus Latina* is available in Kurt Aland et al., eds., *Vetus Latina. Die reste der altlateinischen Bibel* (Freiburg: Herder, 1949–2004). For discussion, see Pierre-Maurice Bogaert, "La Bible latine des origines au moyen âge" *RTL* 19 (1988): 137–59.

12. *Terra spinas et tribulos pariet tibi. Serm.* 7.2.

13. Augustine refers to Acts 2 in *Serm.* 7.2.

14. *Comprehendi debemus hoc igne, non autem propter duritiam non cremari. Serm.* 7.2.

15. A Jewish tradition likewise suggests that the bush represents Israelites, who endure amidst the oppression of the Egyptians. See Exodus Rabbah 2:1; Nahum M. Sarna, *Exodus = [Shemot]: The Traditional Hebrew Text with the New JPS Translation*, JPS Torah Commentary (Philadelphia: JPS, 1991), 14. Of course, it is not only the New Testament that represents the presence of God with fire (cf. Exod 19–20; Deut 4–5). But surely there would be a less negative way of saying that the thorn bush, aflame but not consumed, represents the presence of God coming in the midst of the Israelites, despite their transgression of the covenant (of which Christians also are convicted).

grabs Moses' attention, and so ours—but in the course of his symbolic reading of the bush, the bush, Moses, and the story at hand recede from view. The bush symbolizes a spiritual truth which is no longer moored in the narrative; Moses is not said to understand its symbolic nature, nor could he. Surely this is a nonliteral reading, and the difference between this exposition and how Augustine discusses Exod 3:14–15 will be evident: the association of the bush with the Jews pulls attention away from the text, while association of the dynamic of God's self-revelation with the incarnation further explains the nature of God's response to Moses, who could have recognized the character of this self-revelation. In contrast to Augustine's reading of the burning bush, Augustine's reading of Exod 3:14–15 explores the nature of divine self-revelation which is clearly the subject of this text.

However, one would not want to reduce the literal/proper versus allegorical/figurative distinction in Augustine to a simple dualism. That Augustine uses "literal" in two different ways is suggested by Eden, who notes that Augustine distinguishes between spiritual/corporeal-literal opposition and figurative/literal opposition. There are two kinds of literal rules: "the one is broadly legal and includes the equitable or spiritual interpretation; the other is broadly stylistic and covers all kinds of figurative statement."[16] So when Augustine critiques those who miss the intention of Scripture (the spiritual part or the goal) because they cling to the letter, he is not discussing a matter of style (figurative versus literal), but the failure of such readers to see the parts within the whole, and thus failure to reach the intention (*voluntas*) of Scripture (letter versus spirit).[17] When Augustine states that whatever cannot be understood literally/properly to encourage love of God and neighbor must be understood figuratively, this suggests a priority of the literal/proper sense over the figurative sense, within the spiritual rule of love. Eden writes, "In many cases, then, the spiritual (*spiritualis*) and the literal (*propria*) reading coincide. Whereas Augustine never advises the interpreter to read carnally (*carnaliter, corporaliter*), attending only to the words and not to the intention behind them, he finds ample occasion for reading literally (*proprie*)."[18] It is this coincidence of the literal/proper sense of the words of Scripture and their spiritual meaning within

---

16. Eden, *Hermeneutics*, 60–61.
17. Ibid., 58.
18. Ibid., 59–60.

the full narrative of salvation that I observe in Augustine's reading of Exod 3:14–15.

To see how this is the case and to gain further clarity regarding Augustine's distinction between the literal/proper and figurative sense, one can look to Augustine's discussion of signs in *De doctrina christiana*. Augustine identifies signs as "those things which are employed to signify something."[19] Doctrine consists of signs and things, and one learns of things through signs.[20] One would expect that Augustine would immediately discuss the nature of signs and how one learns about things through signs. However, Book 1 of *De doctrina* is not about signs, but things. According to Babcock, this "suggests that he is acutely aware, from the beginning, that signs can be construed wrongly; that they can be given the wrong *terminus*; that they can be arranged in patterns of signification that point away from, rather than toward, what he considers the true content, the true meaning, of Scripture."[21] Augustine reveals his expectation in reading Scripture, that its words will signify a particular thing (or set of things). Yet I argue that this does not foreclose the interpretive process.

Augustine categorizes things into what is to be enjoyed, what is to be used, and what (or who) does the enjoying and using. "To enjoy something is to hold fast to it in love for its own sake,"[22] whereas to use something is "to apply whatever it may be to the purpose of obtaining what you love."[23] While the only thing that ought to be loved for its own sake is God, it is possible for one to love a thing which ought only to be used, and to use a thing which ought only to be loved. Such disordered love needs to be re-ordered. Rightly ordered love follows "the objective order of things;"[24] it neither fails to love what should be loved nor loves what should not be loved nor loves in an unfitting degree.[25]

Moving to signs in the second book, Augustine identifies two broad types: *signa naturalia*, or "natural signs," and *signa data*, typically translated

---

19. *Res eas videlicet quae ad significandum aliquid adhibentur. Doctr. chr.* 1.2.2,5.
20. Ibid., 1.2.2,4.
21. William S. Babcock, "*Caritas* and Signification in *De doctrina christiana* 1–3," in *De doctrina christiana*, 146–47.
22. *Frui est enim amore inhaerere alicui rei propter se ipsam Doctr. chr.* 1.4.4,8.
23. *Venerit ad id quod amas obtinendum referre, si tamen amandum est.* Ibid.
24. Babcock, "*Caritas* and Signification," 148.
25. See *Doctr. chr.* 1.27.28,59.

"conventional signs." The latter are signs intended for communication. Written words, including in Scripture, are *signa data*, and these can be further categorized as either *signa propria* or *signa translata*. *Signa propria*, "proper signs," are verbal signs "employed to signify the things for which they were instituted in the first place (as when we use the word *ox* to signify an ox)," and they are *signa translata*, "figurative signs," "when the things they signify are themselves employed to signify some further thing (as when we use the word *ox* to signify an ox and the ox to signify an evangelist.)"[26] It is important to note that the signification of the *signa translata* builds on proper signification; in the second example, the word "ox" does not signify the evangelist, but rather the word "ox" signifies an ox which signifies the evangelist. In reading Scripture, it is possible to misunderstand *signa propria* as *signa translata* and vice versa. This is why it is important to first determine the goal of reading. Babcock summarizes,

> [I]t is precisely by knowing what Scripture signifies that we put ourselves in a position to discern how it signifies what it signifies, whether by proper or by figurative signs, and thus put ourselves in a position to resolve the ambiguity about whether to read scriptural locutions as *signa propria* or as *signa figurata* in any given case.[27]

One's understanding of the subject matter informs whether one takes the words of Scripture as literal/proper or figurative. However, being able to recognize what (or whom) the words signify is not to foreclose the interpretive process for two reasons. First, *signa propria* is the normative category of signs; the literal/proper sense of a text is the first avenue for interpretation. Only if this fails to direct the reader toward the subject matter of Scripture is it permissible to think in terms of *signa translata*. So the specific words of Scripture continue to have a limiting, guiding function. Second, love of God and neighbor is by definition not self-serving. God is the only one who ought to be enjoyed for his own sake. That the interpretive process is built on ordered, and ordering, love keeps it from self-service and ideology.[28]

When I speak of literal sense in this chapter, I mean *proprius*, the proper/literal sense which Augustine contrasts with the figurative/allegorical

---

26. Babcock, "*Caritas* and Signification," 149.
27. Ibid., 154.
28. Cf. Ibid., 154–55.

sense. The proper/literal sense includes accounting for how a particular text fits within the whole of Scripture, and thus how it coincides with the spiritual sense. It might be argued that because Augustine has the whole of Scripture in view (and not exclusively the Old Testament) in his reading of Exod 3:13–15, one ought to use the phrase "extended literal sense" rather than "literal sense" to describe it. From the standpoint of Childs, for example, one could imagine the phrase "extended literal sense" to be more appropriate. Childs argues that Old Testament texts have a literal sense within the context of this testament and the concepts available to original writers, readers, and hearers prior to the New Testament; Old Testament texts also have an "extended literal sense" within the context of the two-testament canon, whereby it is possible to allow what Christians know to be true about God as revealed in Christ to influence how one reads the Old Testament. By contrast, there is no "extended literal sense" in Frei. The notion of the literal sense was used first by Christians who identified the subject of the gospels with the one particular, historical person Jesus Christ. When the notion of literal sense is applied to the Old Testament, from a Christian standpoint, this necessarily includes seeing how the words of the Old Testament text fit within the context of the wider story of salvation. Thus, Frei's account of the literal sense is closer to Augustine's than is Childs's account of the literal and extended literal senses.

My argument, that Augustine's reading of Exod 3:14–15 be understood as a reading of the literal sense of the text, will proceed in three parts. These parts do not directly correspond to the three aspects of this literal sense, identified above as the literal, existential, and Trinitarian dimensions. To divide my argument in these terms would be inappropriate, given the interrelated nature of the dimensions. To separate them would be true neither to Augustine, who would not have said that the literal sense was other than that which attests to the Triune God, nor to my argument, in which I claim that both the existential and Trinitarian dimensions are encompassed in a literal sense. Instead, the argument will proceed as follows. In the first part, I argue that Augustine's account of his conversion in *Confessions* Book 7 demonstrates the conditions for reading the literal sense: Augustine's conviction that God is known through creation and Scripture, and that humble attention to the lowly forms of this revelation is necessary for an individual to contemplate God's divine nature (to the extent that such contemplation is possible). The next section is truly the heart of my argument. In it, I describe

Augustine's characteristic reading of Exod 3:14–15.[29] In the final section, I explore the nature of divine being, according to Augustine. I defend Augustine against the possible charges that his identification of God and being involves a Hellenistic imposition on the Hebrew text, and argue that, for Augustine, to talk about divine being is to talk about how Father, Son, and Spirit can be distinct from each other but still one God.

2. *Confessions* Book 7

I argue that *Confessions* Book 7 is exegetically centered on Rom 1:20, that God is "understood through the things that are made"; *Confessions* Book 7, together with Book 8, is christologically focussed.[30] Neither of these points is new. I depend on Cameron's account of exegesis for the insight that Rom 1:20 is central to Book 7 and on Dubarle for the insights that the spiritual ascent recounted in Book 7 is incomplete, according to Augustine's telling of it, without the "taking on Christ" recounted in Book 8, and that this further demonstrates the christological nature of Augustine's theological ontology.[31] However, my argument has a different focus than these, as I claim that this account of Augustine's conversion demonstrates the theological and exegetical underpinnings of Augustine's literal reading of Exod 3:14–15.

Augustine's *ascensio ad veritam* begins with his attempt to think of God in a non-material fashion,[32] but he is unable.[33] At the same time, questions about the nature and origin of evil plague Augustine.[34] Augustine then

---

29. Augustine refers to Exod 3:14 in forty-six places, in works ranging from *Tractates on the Gospel of John* and *Expositions of the Psalms* to *The Trinity*. For a complete list, see zum Brunn, *St. Augustine*, 119.

30. *Confessions* was written between 397 and 400. Henry Chadwick, "Introduction," in Augustine of Hippo, *Confessions*, trans. Henry Chadwick (Oxford: Oxford University, 1991), xiii.

31. Michael Cameron, *Christ Meets Me Everywhere: Augustine's Early Figurative Exegesis* (Oxford; New York: Oxford University, 2012), esp. 97–129; Dominique Dubarle, "Essai sur l'ontologie théologale de Saint Augustin," *RechAug* 16 (1981): 230–41. Relatedly, I have learned from zum Brunn's discussion of *magis esse* and *minus esse* in zum Brunn, *St. Augustine*, 69–90.

32. *Conf.* 7.1,1.

33. Ibid., 7.2,2.

34. Ibid., 7.2,3. Having heard (likely from Ambrose, according to Chadwick, 113, fn. 4) that evil is a result of the will that turns away from God (1.3,5), Augustine does

describes a transformation (in humility) through instruction in the "books of the Platonists." He has already come to accept Catholic teaching,[35] but he does not yet have the appreciation for, or the understanding of, Christian Scripture that he gains over the course of the book. In retrospect, Augustine recounts reading the "books of the Platonists" and finding nearly the whole of the Prologue to the Gospel of John there, that through the Word, who is God and with God since the beginning, all things were created, and that this Word is "born not of the flesh, nor of blood, nor of the will of man nor of the will of the flesh, but of God" (John 1:13).[36] However, that "the Word was made flesh and dwelt among us" (John 1:14) and that "he was in the world, and the world was made by him, and the world did not know him" (John 1:10), he does not find in the "books of the Platonists," and these are crucial. He begins to critique the Platonists and his former self as "those who, like actors, wear the high boots of a supposedly more sublime teaching [but] do not hear him who says, 'Learn of me, that I am meek and humble in heart, and you shall find rest for your souls'" (Matt 11:29).[37]

The Platonic books suggest turning within himself, and it is "with [God] as [his] guide" that Augustine enters.[38] Augustine spiritually perceives "the immutable light," which is difficult to describe precisely: it is not light as one would know it from everyday experience, but rather greater in a qualitative sense. This light transcends Augustine's mind, and he describes the difference according to creation: "It was superior because it made me, and I was

---

not yet understand how God, the supreme Good (*ipsum bonum*) could create humans with the capacity for evil.

35. . . . *ea fide, qua credebam et esse te et esse incommutabilem substantiam tuam et esse de hominibus curam et iudicium tuum et in Christo, filio tuo, Domino nostro, atque Scripturis sanctis, quas Ecclesiae tuae catholicae commendaret auctoritas, viam te posuisse salutis humanae ad eam vitam, quae post hanc mortem futura est.* ". . . the faith which I held, that you exist and are immutable substance and care for humanity and judge us; moreover, that in Christ your Son our Lord, and by your scriptures commended by the authority of your Catholic Church, you have provided a way of salvation whereby humanity can come to the future life after death." Ibid., 7.7,11. English translations of *Confessions* are from Augustine, *Confessions*, trans. Chadwick.

36. Ibid., 7.9,13–14.

37. *Qui autem cothurno tamquam doctrinae sublimioris elati non audiunt dicentem: Discite a me, quoniam mitis sum et humilis corde, et invenietis requiem animabus vestris.* Ibid., 7.9,14.

38. Ibid., 7.10,16.

inferior because I was made by it."³⁹ This light is truth, eternity, and love: "Eternal truth and true love and beloved eternity: you are my God."⁴⁰ Moreover, it is Being (*esse*), in contrast to Augustine who is "not yet being."⁴¹ From the "region of dissimilarity,"⁴² Augustine questions whether this light, truth, eternity, love which transcends him is nothing, since it is not spatial, and hears God cry from far away, "I am who am" (*ego sum qui sum*).⁴³ This satisfies Augustine's question and provides him assurance that the one who has met him is not nothing, and he knows this without any doubt: "I would have found it easier to doubt whether I was myself alive than that there is no truth 'understood from the things that are made' (Rom 1:20)."⁴⁴ Augustine uses this verse from Romans to communicate not only what he knew certainly, but also *how* it might known: "through the things that are made."⁴⁵ In other words, Augustine has finally been able to think of God as immaterial ("I woke up in you and saw you to be infinite in another sense, and this way of seeing you did not come from the flesh").⁴⁶ Simultaneously, led by the Platonists and Scripture, he has been able to understand creation as good. The latter idea is dependent on the former and is the catalyst for the repetition of Rom 1:20 throughout this book.

Augustine looks to the "things below" God and finds that they both are and are not. They are because they are from God, but are not because they are not God:⁴⁷ "to you they owe their existence, and that in you all things are finite, not in the sense that the space they occupy is bounded but in the sense that you hold all things in your hand by your truth."⁴⁸ Each thing is harmonious with a place and time, except God, who alone abides permanently. Furthermore, the books of the Platonists allow Augustine to move more fully out of his Manichaean way of conceiving creation. Whereas he once

---

39. *Sed superior, quia ipsa fecit me, et ego inferior, quia factus ab ea.* Ibid.
40. *O aeterna veritas et vera caritas et cara aeternitas! Tu es Deus meus.* Ibid.
41. *ut viderem esse, quod viderem, et nondum me esse, qui viderem.* Ibid.
42. *in regione dissimilitudinis.* Ibid.
43. Ibid.
44. *Dubitarem faciliusque dubitarem vivere me quam non esse veritatem, quae per ea, quae facta sunt, intellecta conspicitur.* Ibid.
45. *quae per ea, quae facta sunt, intellecta conspicitur.* Ibid., 7.14,20.
46. *Evigilavi in te et vidi te infinitum aliter, et visus iste non a carne trahebatur.* Ibid.
47. Ibid., 7.11,17.
48. *Tibi debere quia sunt et in te cuncta finita, sed aliter, non quasi in loco, sed quia tu es omnitenens manu veritate.* Ibid., 7.15,21.

thought of the things that God had made in creation by saying that there are two substances,[49] the Platonists enable him to view creation as good, which resonates with the biblical statement: all created things are corruptible because God made them good (Gen 1:31).[50]

That Augustine still has need of a further transformation in thought is suggested when he recounts the momentary experience of conceiving God immaterially: "in the flash of a trembling glance [the power of reasoning] attained to that which is. At that moment I saw your 'invisible nature understood through the things which are made' (Rom 1:20). But I did not possess the strength to keep my vision fixed."[51] To gain the "strength" to keep his attention focussed for more than a moment, healing will be necessary, and it may be unpleasant: "bread which is pleasant to a healthy palate is misery to an unhealthy one; and to sick eyes light which is desirable to the healthy is hateful."[52] In the following section, Augustine explains more specifically: he loved God but not in a stable manner on account of his "sexual habit."[53] With this, Augustine points to the transformation that occurs in Book 8.

Augustine identifies Christ as the mediator he must find to hold on to God. But Christ is only mediator to the humble, those who become Christ's subjects.[54] In part, Augustine's struggle to submit himself to Christ takes the form of uncertainty regarding the association of divinity and humanity in

---

49. Ibid., 7.14,20.

50. Ibid., 7.12,18.

51. *Pervenit ad id, quod est in ictu trepidantis aspectus. Tunc vero invisibilia tua per ea quae facta sunt intellecta conspexi, sed aciem figere non evalui.* Ibid., 7.17,23.

52. *Palato non sano poena est et panis, qui sano suavis est, et oculis aegris odiosa lux, quae puris amabilis.* Ibid., 7.16,22.

53. *consuetudo carnalis.* Ibid., 7.17,23.

54. *Verbum enim tuum, aeterna veritas, superioribus creaturae tuae partibus supereminens subditos erigit ad se ipsam, in inferioribus autem aedificavit sibi humilem domum de limo nostro, per quam subdendos deprimeret a se ipsis et ad se traiceret, sanans tumorem et nutriens amorem, ne fiducia sui progrederentur longius, sed potius infirmarentur;* "Your Word, eternal truth, higher than the superior parts of your creation, raises those submissive to him to himself. In the inferior parts he built for himself a humble house of our clay. By this he detaches from themselves those who are willing to be made his subjects and carries them across to himself, healing their swelling and nourishing their love. They are no longer to place confidence in themselves but rather to become weak." Ibid., 7.18,24.

Christ: "But the mystery of the Word made flesh I had not yet begun to guess.... I thought that he excelled others not as the personal embodiment of the Truth, but because of the great excellence of his human character and more perfect participation in wisdom."[55] He identifies this as the heresy of Photinus; the Catholic understanding is not that the Word *participates* in wisdom, but that it *is* wisdom, *is* truth, as a person.[56]

In the last section of the book, Augustine recounts how, with great zeal, he turned to the works of the apostle Paul. Augustine identifies his difficulty in maintaining his mind's vision of God with the tension Paul explains in Rom 7:22-33: though a person delights in God's Word inwardly, outwardly a person can remain enslaved to sin.[57] This solution to Augustine's difficulty is not found in the "books of the Platonists."[58] The Platonists do not learn from the meekness of Christ. Augustine contrasts two ways of attuning one's attention toward its goal:

> *Et aliud est de silvestri cacumine videre patriam pacis et iter ad eam non invenire et frustra conari per invia circum obsidentibus et insidiantibus fugitivis desertoribus cum principe suo leone et dracone, et aliud tenere viam illuc ducentem cura caelestis imperatoris munitam;*

> It is one thing from a wooded summit to catch a glimpse of the homeland of peace and not to find the way to it, but vainly to attempt the journey along an impracticable route surrounded by the ambushes and assaults of fugitive deserters with their chief, "the lion and the dragon" (Ps. 90:13). It is another thing to hold on to the way that leads there, defended by the protection of the heavenly emperor.[59]

---

55. *Quid autem sacramenti haberet Verbum caro factum, ne suspicari quidem poteram ... non persona veritatis, sed magna quadam naturae humanae excellentia et perfectiore participatione sapientiae praeferri ceteris arbitrabar.* Ibid., 7.19,25.

56. Ibid.

57. Ibid., 7.21,27.

58. *Hoc illae litterae non habent. Non habent illae paginae vultum pietatis huius, lacrimas confessionis, sacrificium tuum, spiritum contribulatum, cor contritum et humiliatum, populi salutem, sponsam civitatem, arram Spiritus Sancti, poculum pretii nostri.* "Those pages do not contain the face of this devotion, tears of confession, your sacrifice, a troubled spirit, a contrite and humble spirit (Ps. 50:19), the salvation of your people, the espoused city (Rev. 21:5), the guarantee of your Holy Spirit (2 Cor. 5:5), the cup of our redemption." Ibid., 7.21,27.

59. Ibid.

The Platonists know the goal, but not the way there, which requires submission to Christ as known through creation and Scripture.

At the end of Book 7, Augustine has attained contemplation of "that which is," but only for a fleeting moment, through guidance by the "books of the Platonists." Ironically, to gain the strength to fix his gaze permanently on the divine, Augustine must humble himself, to make his way to God through "the things that are created," and further, to the personal Truth through whom they were created. For Augustine, becoming weak is also a matter of perceiving Christ as equal to the Father, and it is this that certifies that the way of humility, through the things which are made, does in fact lead to God.

Contemplating God requires not only an attunement of the mind but a laying-aside of outward acts which would, if not for Christ, stand in judgment over Augustine. The latter act of laying aside his "sexual habit" to "take on Christ" is the subject of Book 8. Augustine has discovered, in Christ, not only the goal but also the way to it. Yet he has not fully submitted himself to the way, to Christ himself.[60] Because of this, Book 8 concerns the nature of the will and action, and the possibility (or reality) of a divided will:

Early in Book 8, Augustine describes this new desire,

> *Voluntas autem nova, quae mihi esse coeperat, ut te gratis colerem fruique te vellem, Deus, sola certa iucunditas, nondum erat idonea ad superandam priorem vetustate roboratam. Ita duae voluntates meae, una vetus, alia nova, illa carnalis, illa spiritalis, confligebant inter se atque discordando dissipabant animam meam.*
>
> The new will, which was beginning to be within me a will to serve you freely and to enjoy you, God, the only sure source of pleasure, was not yet strong enough to conquer my older will, which had the strength of old habit. So my two wills, one old, the other new, one carnal, the other spiritual, were in conflict with one another, and their discord robbed my soul of all concentration.[61]

Augustine does not yet possess the ability to *act* out of this new will. To fully enjoy God, he must wrest himself free from the habits of his old life.[62] This is

---

60. Ibid., 8.1,1.
61. Ibid., 8.5,10.
62. Ibid., 8.8,20.

achieved only once Augustine hears of the possibility of life completely devoted to God and detached from worldly desires.[63]

Famously, the crucial turning point for Augustine is hearing a voice chant, "Pick up and read, pick up and read,"[64] and he immediately opens Paul's writings to read, "Not in riots and drunken parties, not in eroticism and indecencies, not in strife and rivalry, but put on the Lord Jesus Christ and make no provision for the flesh in its lusts" (Rom 13:13–14).[65] At this point, his hesitation disappears, and he is determined henceforth to devote his entire life to God.

In the final section of Book 8, Augustine tells his mother of his conversion. In doing so, he recalls how his mother had seen, in a dream, that he would one day convert.[66] In this way, the book concludes more decisively than Book 7. Whereas the end of Book 7 finds Augustine unsettled and grasping for a way to maintain the vision of God he has had for the first time, the end of Book 8 brings greater closure; Augustine arrives at stability as a Christian, which has been the direction of the *Confessions* since at least Book 3.

Though little has been said about Exod 3:14–15 specifically, *Confessions* Books 7 and 8 describe, from the perspective of hindsight, the theological and exegetical discoveries of Augustine at the time of his conversion. These set the stage for his subsequent theology and exegesis. Most significantly, conversion required Augustine not only to appreciate the unchangeability, eternality, and incomprehensibility of God—characteristics of God's inherent immateriality—which he found both in Scripture and the the "books of the Platonists," but conversion formed Augustine in humility and acceptance that God graciously comes to humanity in the form of material things in creation and the tales of concrete events in Scripture. In these books, Augustine describes his learning that humanity can be healed and come to know the ungraspable, immutable God only through the mediation of the Son and through the things which are made. Understanding and accepting Catholic Christology was not simply a matter of abstract ideas for Augustine but a matter of humble attention and response to Scripture. Thus, existential

---

63. Ibid., 8.6,14ff.
64. *Tolle lege, tolle lege.* Ibid., 8.12,29.
65. *Non in comessationibus et ebrietatibus, non in cubilibus et impudicitiis, non in contentione et aemulatione, sed induite Dominum Iesum Christum et carnis providentiam ne feceritis in concupiscentiis.* Ibid.
66. Ibid., 3.11,19–20.

transformation is dependent upon "the way the words go," and literal reading involves divine address, calling the individual to transformation. Both of these are true in light of Christ, and so the Trinitarian dimension is also present (though not in as mature a form as we will see later in our argument). These central aspects of Augustine's conversion supply the basis for his reading of Exod 3:14–15.

3. Augustine's Characteristic Reading of Exodus 3:14–15

So far, I have argued that Augustine's conversion required a change in attitude toward creation and Scripture; rather than attempting to understand God's immateriality itself, Augustine had to learn, in humility, that God makes himself available in ways that mortals can understand. This is a step toward a literal sense hermeneutic. In this section, I describe Augustine's characteristic reading of Exod 3:14–15 and explain why it should be understood as a reading of the literal sense rather than of a figural sense. To do this, I first turn to *Expositions of the Psalms* 121[122], in which Augustine describes this dynamic of God as immutable and ungraspable *idipsum*—the Selfsame—who simultaneously offers himself in humility and in what God has created in order to draw creation to himself.[67]

3.1. Expositions of the Psalms 121

Augustine interprets Ps 121[122] as descriptive of the movement by faith toward the heavenly Jerusalem. Augustine reads, *Cuius participatio eius in idipsum*, "It shares in the Selfsame" (Ps 121[122]:3), which gives further evidence for the spiritual nature of the Jerusalem of which the psalmist speaks.[68]

---

67. Good overviews of Augustine's reading of Exod 3:14–15 are available in English in zum Brunn, *St. Augustine*, 97–118 and Allen, "Hellenization Thesis," 183–96.

68. *Enarrat. Ps.* 121.5. All English translations of *Enarrat. Ps.* 121 are from Augustine of Hippo, *Expositions of the Psalms 121–150*, ed. Boniface Ramsey, trans. Maria Boulding, OSB, *The Works of Saint Augustine* III/20, electronic ed.

Augustine argues at length that Ps 121[122]:1–4 is not about the earthly Jerusalem, but the heavenly one. He points out the present passive participle, "being built" in the Greek of verse 3, Ιερουσαλημ οἰκοδομουμένη ὡς πόλις ἧς ἡ μετοχὴ αὐτῆς ἐπὶ τὸ αὐτό (LXX), which Augustine reads as *Ierusalem quae aedificatur ut civitas*, "the Jerusalem that is being built as a city" (rather than the Hebrew *qal* passive participle, יְרוּשָׁלַ͏ִם הַבְּנוּיָה כְּעִיר, "Jerusalem—built as a city"). He suggests that since the building of

What is *idipsum*?[69] The first step in Augustine's discussion of *idipsum* is its undefinability:

> *Iam ergo, fratres, quisquis erigit aciem mentis, quisquis deponit caliginem carnis, quisquis mundat oculum cordis, elevet, et videat idipsum. Quid est idipsum? Quomodo dicam, nisi idipsum?*

> Now, brothers and sisters, if anyone can apply the keen edge of the mind, if anyone can lay aside the murk of the flesh, if anyone can cleanse the eye of the heart, let him or her look up and see. What is *idipsum*? It is simply *idipsum*, Being-Itself.[70] How can I say anything about it, except that it is Being-Itself?[71]

Idipsum is utterly undefinable, so that Augustine can say nothing about it save that it is *idipsum*. Marion glosses this text: "The *idipsum*, thus, remains radically and definitively apophatic."[72] Yet, Augustine does not urge his hearers and readers to ignore *idipsum*, but to continue the impossible task of contemplating it, understanding it:

> *Fratres, si potestis, intellegite idipsum. Nam et ego quidquid aliud dixero, non dico idipsum. Conemur tamen quibusdam vicinitatibus verborum et significationum perducere infirmitatem mentis ad cogitandum idipsum.*

> Grasp it if you can, brothers and sisters, for whatever else I may say, I shall not have defined Being-Itself. All the same, let us attempt to direct the gaze of our minds, to steer our feeble intelli-

---

the brick-and-mortar Jerusalem would have been completed by the time of the writing of the psalm (traditionally attributed to David), then the author must have been referring to the heavenly Jerusalem, which continues to be built by those who spiritually ascend into it. *Enarrat. Ps.* 121.4.

69. My summary of this text is indebted to that of Marion. Jean-Luc Marion, "*Idipsum*: The Name of God According to Augustine," in *Orthodox Readings of Augustine*, ed. Aristotle Papanikolaou and George E. Demacopoulos (Crestwood, NY: St. Vladimir's Seminary, 2008), 167–89.

70. Boulding makes some surprising translation choices: she does not include an object of "see" where the Latin has *videat idipsum*, but she includes both the Latin, *idipsum*, and her translation, "Being-Itself," where *idipsum* does not repeat.

71. *Enarrat. Ps.* 121.5. Boulding chooses to translate *idipsum* as "Being-Itself," though its sense may be closer to "the Selfsame," without invoking "being." Translation of this term is a major aspect of Marion's argument. Marion, "*Idipsum*," passim.

72. Ibid., 180.

gence, to thinking about Being-Itself, making use of certain words and meanings that have some affinity with it.[73]

Idipsum is what it is; any words used to describe it only "have some affinity with it," but cannot quite pinpoint its meaning. It would seem that even immutability, a negative description, is not truly a description of God in a direct sense but only has "some affinity with," or is in the vicinity of, *idipsum*.

These first two steps in Augustine's articulation of *idipsum* exemplify this dynamic: *idipsum* is undefinable, ungraspable; at the same time, the appropriate response to it is an attempt to understand it, to articulate something about it. Marion outlines two additional steps in Augustine's explanation of *idipsum*, which may be seen as a circling back and specification of the nature of the first two steps.

The third step that Marion outlines is rather important to him. In it, Exod 3:14 comes to the fore:

> *Et quid est quod est, nisi ille qui quando mittebat Moysen, dixit illi:* Ego sum qui sum? *Quid est hoc, nisi ille qui cum diceret famulus eius:* Ecce mittis me: si dixerit mihi populus: Quis te misit? quid dicam ei? *nomen suum noluit aliud dicere, quam:* Ego sum qui sum; *et adiecit et ait:* Dices itaque filiis Israel: Qui est, misit me ad vos. *Ecce* idipsum: Ego sum qui sum: Qui est, misit me ad vos. *Non potes capere; multum est intellegere, multum est apprehendere.*
>
> And what is That Which Is if not he who, when he wished to give Moses his mission, said to him, I AM WHO AM (Ex 3:14)? What is That Which Is if not he who, when his servant objected, "So you are sending me. But what shall I say to the sons of Israel if they challenge me, Who sent you to us?' (Ex 3:13), refused to give himself any other name than I AM WHO AM? He reiterated, "Thus shall you say to the children of Israel, HE WHO IS has sent me to you" (Ex 3:14). This is Being-Itself, the Selfsame: I AM WHO AM. HE WHO IS has sent me to you. You cannot take it in, for this is too much to understand, too much to grasp.[74]

---

73. *Enarrat. Ps.* 121.5.
74. *Enarrat. Ps.* 121.5.

The *Vetus Latina* and the Vulgate translations of the key phrases of both verse 14a and 14b are identical. It seems unlikely that Jerome would not have based his translation on Hebrew text, given his strong commitment to doing so, though he must have been aware of the *Vetus Latina* translation that was circulating. For discus-

Augustine identifies *ego sum qui sum* with *idipsum* and returns to the point with which he began the passage: that this *idipsum*, or *sum qui sum*, does not exist in such a way that the human mind can, finally, understand it. *Ego sum qui sum* exemplifies *idipsum* in a narrative framework: the sending of Moses to deliver the Israelites.

Marion argues that because Augustine only mentions Exod 3:14 *after* discussing *idipsum*, the latter, with its apophasis, governs *sum qui sum* and not the other way around. "God is therefore not being, but the immutable one" may be too strong a way of putting Augustine's prioritization of immutability over being, but the priority is there.[75]

Finally, in the fourth step, Augustine identifies *idipsum* with Christ:

> Quid enim debes tenere? Quod pro te factus est Christus, quia ipse est Christus; et ipse Christus recte intellegitur: Ego sum qui sum, quo modo est in forma Dei. Ubi non rapinam arbitratus est esse aequalis Deo, ibi est idipsum. Ut autem efficiaris tu particeps in idipsum, factus est ipse prior particeps tui; et Verbum caro factum est, ut caro participet Verbum.
>
> To what am I telling you to hold fast? Hold onto what Christ became for you, because Christ himself, even Christ, is rightly understood by this name, I AM WHO AM, inasmuch as he is in the form of God. In that nature wherein he deemed it no robbery to be God's equal (Ph 2:6), there he is Being-Itself. But that you might participate in Being-Itself, he first of all became a participant in what you are; the Word was made flesh (Jn 1:14) so that flesh might participate in the Word.[76]

This fourth step mirrors the second in that it identifies more specifically how the hearer/reader can continue to press on towards God, *idipsum, ego sum qui sum*, despite the latter's fundamental ungraspability. Christ, who is *idipsum* even as he is God, makes possible human knowledge of God by taking on our finite experience in the flesh.

---

sion and bibliography, see den Hertog, *Other Face*, 231, 256–62.

75. Marion, "*Idipsum*," 182. See zum Brunn, *St. Augustine*, 97, 105–6. Contra Anderson, who argues that Augustine correctly identifies Exod 3:14 as suggesting, in opposition to Neoplatonism, that immutability is a consequence of being in God; God is "is," first and foremost. James F. Anderson, *St. Augustine and Being: A Metaphysical Essay* (The Hague: Martinus Nijhoff, 1965), esp. 5, 12–18, 21, 30.

76. *Enarrat. Ps.* 121.5.

Augustine's use of Exod 3:14 in the context of discussing this psalm demonstrates his characteristic association of the verse with who God is in himself, ungraspable by human intellect. However, and also characteristically, this does not mean that humanity has no means by which to hear from and understand God. Rather, God comes to us in a form we can understand. This dynamic is further explained by the incarnation: Christ, who was in the form of God, took on the form of man; the Word was made flesh for our salvation. In *Sermon 6* and *Sermon 7*, Augustine again reads Exod 3:14 as referring to the ungraspability of God.

3.2. *Sermon 6 and Sermon 7*

These sermons contain Augustine's fullest account of Exod 3:14–15 within its narrative context. Similarities far outweigh differences between the sermons;[77] in both, Augustine addresses three key aspects of the narrative: the image of the burning bush, the theophany, and the revelation of the divine name. The most important of these subjects for our argument is, of course, the revelation of the divine name. Augustine interprets these verses according to the movement from God as he is in himself—incomprehensible to the human mind—to God as he is for us. This is the same movement that we saw, above, in *Expositions of the Psalms* 121, but in these sermons, the name given in verse 15—the "God of Abraham, the God of Isaac, and the God of Jacob"—is the graspable, comprehensible name.

Expounding on the divine name, Augustine suggests how this name would have affected Moses, and he perceives Moses as having a contemplative experience similar to his own:

> *Si intellexit, immo quia intellexit Moyses, cum ei diceretur: Ego sum qui sum; qui est misit me ad vos, multum hoc. credidit esse ad homines, multum hoc vidit distare ab hominibus. Qui enim hoc quod est et vere est digne intellexerit, et qualicumque lumine veracissimae essentiae, vel strictim sicut coruscatione afflatus fuerit, longe se infra videt, longe remotissimum, longe dissimillimum.*

> If Moses understood, indeed because he understood what he was told, I am who I am—he who is has sent me to you, he believed this meant a lot for men, he saw at the same time the vast difference

---

77. *Sermon* 6 and *Sermon* 7, though numbered sequentially, were not given in succession but rather a few years apart. The former may be dated after 400, and the second, Pentecost of 409. Hill, "Notes," in *Sermons on the Old Testament*.

between this and men. Having properly understood that which is and truly is, and having been struck however fleetingly, as by a flash of lightning, by even the slightest ray of light from the only true being, he sees how far, far below he is, how far, far removed, how ever so widely unlike it he is.[78]

Augustine describes Moses' experience much like his own contemplative experience.[79] He imagines that the words of God in Exod 3:14 are meant as a kind of lesson in ontology,[80] on the difference, how far in fact, the creature is from the Creator. That is, it is a "lesson in ontology" by way of referring to the contemplative life of the one who seeks after God. Augustine finds proof that pursuit of God, that contemplation, is characteristic of Moses in his request, *Ostende mihi temetipsum*, "Show me your yourself!" (Exod 33:18).[81]

In *Sermon* 6, Augustine questions how it is proper for God to have multiple names, if the first concerns God's immutability:

> *Quomodo illae hoc vocor quia sum, et ecce hac aliud nomen:* Ego sum Deus Abraham, Deus Isaac, et Deus Iacob. *Quia quomodo est Deus incommutabilis, fecit omnia per misericordiam et dignatus est ipse Filius Dei mutabilem carnem suscipiendo, manens id quod Verbum Dei est, venire et subvenire homini. Induit ergo se carne mortali ille qui est, ut dici posset:* Ego sum Deus Abraham Deus Isaac, et Deus Iacob.

---

78. *Serm.* 7.7.
79. Cf. *Conf.* 7.10,16; 7.13,19.
80. In this, Augustine follows a tradition that dates at least to Philo, who writes, "At first say unto them, I am that I am, that when they have learnt that there is a difference between him that is and him that is not, they may be further taught that there is no name whatever that can properly be assigned to me, who am the only being to whom existence belongs." *Mos.* 1 13.75; *The Works of Philo: Complete and Unabridged*, trans. Charles Duke Yonge (Edinburgh; Peabody, MA: Hendrickson, 1993). The major difference is that for Philo, the name is clearly a concession or negation since God cannot be named. For Augustine, the name "God of Abraham, the God of Isaac, and the God of Jacob," is not so much a concession as an act of mercy; as such, this name carries power to reveal God to humanity and to lead the contemplative person towards the fundamental ungraspability of God.
81. *Serm.* 7.7. The *Vetus Latina* of Exod 33:18 Augustine reads follows the Septuagint B variant: εμφανισον μοι σεαυτον, *Septuaginta*, eds. Alfred Rahlfs and Robert Hanhart (Stuttgart: Deutsche Bibelgesellschaft, 2006). The dominant Septuagint and Vulgate follow the Hebrew Masoretic Text: הַרְאֵנִי נָא אֶת־כְּבֹדֶךָ = Δεῖξόν μοι τὴν σεαυτοῦ δόξαν = *Ostende mihi gloriam tuam*.

> How is it that there I am called this name that shows *I am*, and lo and behold here is another name: *I am the God of Abraham, the God of Isaac and the God of Jacob*? It means that while God is indeed unchangeable, he has done everything out of mercy, and so the Son of God himself was prepared to take on changeable flesh and thereby to come to man's rescue while remaining what he is as the Word of God. Thus he who is, clothed himself with mortal flesh, so that it could truly be said, *I am the God of Abraham, the God of Isaac and the God of Jacob*."[82]

The incarnation more clearly demonstrates how God reveals himself to humanity, an act that was already being accomplished in the Old Testament. How does God reveal himself to humanity? By taking on human form. Here, God identifies himself as the "God of Abraham, the God of Isaac, and the God of Jacob," because, in some way—not in the fashion in incarnation, but, we might say, in the way of covenant—God takes on the vulnerability of created humanity without becoming changeable himself. Augustine's account might suggest that taking the doctrine of divine immutability seriously does not mean denying that God makes himself vulnerable to changeable humanity in God's covenant with Israel. Just as God, in Christ, is the unchangeable one who took on changeable flesh, so God, in Israel, is the unchangeable one who makes himself manifest in the changeability of this people. This is the nature of mercy, which accomplishes our salvation by descending among us.[83]

Furthermore Christ, the Word made flesh, fulfills Exod 3:15 and demonstrates how it can rightly be said that God is "the God of Abraham, the God of Isaac, and the God of Jacob." Augustine's reflection on the text moves from the condescension of Christ to the phrase "the God of Abraham, the God of Isaac, and the God of Jacob," so that Christ informs what the phrase means while affirming the truth that this name correctly identifies who God is. In other words, it is not suggested that this name is no longer valid. Rather than eclipsing the name "the God of Abraham, the God of Isaac, and the God of Jacob," Christ *validates* and affirms this name.

---

82. *Serm.* 6.5. Augustine often conflates the texts of Exod 3:15 and 3:6. The *Vetus Latina* version that he is reading likely reads the following for verse 15: *Haec eis dices: Dominus Deus patrum vestrorum, Deus Abraham et Deus Isaac et Deus Iacob misit me ad vos. Hoc mihi nomen est in aeternum.* Cf. *Serm.* 7.1.

83. Augustine does not dwell on the soteriological significance of the exodus in these two sermons.

In *Sermon 7*, Augustine explains verse 15 as pointing toward the church. Moses' request in Exod 33:18 is only partially granted (Exod 33:19–34:7). In light of the human inability to grasp *ego sum qui sum*,

> Quasi ergo ab illa excellentia essentiae longe dissimilis desperaret, erigit desperantem quoniam vidit timentem, tamquam diceret: Quoniam dixi: Ego sum qui sum; et: Qui est misit me, intellexisti quid sit esse, et desperasti te capere. Erige spem: Ego sum Deus Abraham Deus Isaac et Iacob. Sic sum quod sum, sic sum ipsum esse, ut nolim hominibus deesse.

> God encourages the desperate man whom he sees so fearful, and it's as if he said, "Because I said *I am who I am*, and *He who is has sent me* (Ex 3:14), you have understood what it means to be, and have despaired of being able to attain to it yourself. Courage, there's hope yet: *I am the God of Abraham, the God of Isaac and the God of Jacob* (Ex 3:15). I am what I am, I am what it is to be, in such a way that I do not wish to 'un-be' for men and women."[84]

Here Augustine suggests not only that God provides content of revelation that Moses can understand (i.e., "I am the God of Abraham, the God of Isaac, and the God of Jacob"), but also that in the course of revealing Godself to humanity, God will not cease to be "I am that I am." Revelation does not change the immutable and eternal nature of God. Similarly,

> Forte multum erat et ad ipsum Moysen, sicut multum est et ad nos, et multo magis ad nos, intellegere quid dictum sit: Ego sum qui sum; et: Qui est, misit me ad vos. Et si forte caperet Moyses, illi ad quos mittebatur quando caperent? Distulit ergo Dominus quod capere homo non posset, et addidit quod capere posset: adiunxit enim et ait: Ego sum Deus Abraham, et Deus Isaac, et Deus Iacob. Hoc potes capere: Nam Ego sum qui sum, quae mens potest capere?

> Perhaps it was too much even for Moses himself, as it is too much for us also, and much more so for us, to understand the meaning of such words, "I am who am;" and, "He who is has sent me to you." And supposing that Moses comprehended it, when would those to whom he was sent comprehend it? The Lord therefore put aside what man could not comprehend, and added what he could; for He said also besides, "I am the God of Abraham, and the

---

84. Serm. 7.7.

God of Isaac, and the God of Jacob." This you can comprehend; for "I am who am," what mind can comprehend?[85]

The ungraspable "I am who I am" is coupled with "I am the God of Abraham, Isaac, and Jacob." Even if Moses, a Hebrew man unsurpassed in spiritual intimacy with YHWH, understood the former statement, the latter, a name that people could comprehend, was given for the sake of the people.[86]

Furthermore, in *Expositions of the Psalms* 134, Augustine suggests that "Abraham, Isaac, and Jacob" means all of Israel, and that Israel includes the church, all of those who have been grafted in.[87] In the same way, in *Sermon 7*, Augustine emphasizes the existential dimension, that God is in relation to people, in relation to the reader. Indeed, God is "ensconced *not far from each one of us; for in him we live and move and have our being* (Acts 17:27-28)."[88]

In sum, in *Sermon 6* and *Sermon 7*, Augustine uses Exod 3:14 to explore who God is in himself, which is ungraspable to human intellect, but admonishes his readers (or hearers) to take heart in the mercy of God whereby he makes himself known to humans in created forms. As in *Expositions of the Psalms* 121, the created form whereby one can know God is identified as the humanity of Christ. But further, Augustine suggests in these sermons that this form is also "the God of Abraham, the God of Isaac, and the God of Jacob" (Exod 3:15). Exod 3:14-15 witnesses to the mercy of God in Christ, but this testimony is given in the Old Testament's own idiom: *I am who I am* is also *the* Lord *God of Abraham, the God of Isaac, and the God of Jacob*. Augustine's recognition of this incarnational dynamic present in Exod 3:14-15 allows him to more fully explore the text at hand; reference to Christ does not replace or supersede the Old Testament text.

---

85. *Tract. Ev. Jo.* 38.8. English translations of *Tractates on the Gospel of John* are from *Gospel According to St. John*, ed. Philip Schaff, trans. John Gibb and Rev. James Innes, NPNF 1, vol. 7 (Buffalo: Christian Literature, 1888).

86. Augustine does not address the fact that the name "the God of Abraham, the God of Isaac, and the God of Jacob" is already given in 3:6 and acknowledged by Moses in 3:13. He is more concerned with the dynamic of the answer to the question (vv. 14-15) than in trying to understand the particularities that may have motivated the question (v. 13).

87. *Enarrat. Ps.* 134.7.

88. *Non longe positum ab unoquoque nostrum: In illo enim vivimus et movemur et sumus. Serm.* 7.7.

3.3. Christ the mediator

This revelatory movement from who God is in himself to who God is for us, exemplified in the incarnation, is central both to Augustine's reading of Exod 3:14-15 and to his theology as a whole.[89] Augustine often uses the metaphor of Christ (as man) the way, and Christ (as God) the homeland or goal.[90] I have already discussed this analogy, which appears at the end of *Confessions* Book 7, where Augustine describes the Platonists as those who saw the goal but knew not how to get there, which is to say that they knew not the humble humanity of Christ which could lead them to the eternal and unchangeable God.[91] Another classic example of this is in *The City of God*:

> *Per hoc enim mediator, per quod homo, per hoc et via. Quoniam si inter eum qui tendit et illud quo tendit, via media est, spes est perveniendi; si autem desit, aut ignoretur qua eundum sit, quid prodest nosse quo eundum sit? Sola est autem adversus omnes errores via munitissima, ut idem ipse sit Deus et homo; quo itur Deus, qua itur homo.*

> For it is as man that He is the Mediator and the Way. If there is a way between one who strives and that towards which he strives, there is hope of his reaching his goal; but if there is no way, or if he is ignorant of it, how does it help him to know what the goal is? The only way that is wholly defended against all error is when one and the same person is at once God and man: God our goal, man our way.[92]

Here, Augustine seems more pessimistic than in *Confessions* about the situation of one who knows the goal but not the way to it. In his comments on John 1, Augustine uses this analogy of the way and the goal to describe how the humanity of Christ leads one to *ego sum qui sum*:

> In principio erat Verbum. *Idipsum est, eodem modo est; sicut est, semper sic est; mutari non potest: hoc est est. Quod nomen suum dixit famulo*

---

89. See the succinct summary of Studer in Basil Studer, OSB, *The Grace of Christ and the Grace of God in Augustine of Hippo: Christocentrism or Theocentrism?*, trans. Matthew J. O'Connell (Collegeville, MN: Liturgical, 1997), 150-51.

90. Cf. ibid., 44-47.

91. *Conf.* 7.21,27.

92. *Civ.* 11.2. English translations of *The City of God* are from Augustine of Hippo, *The City of God Against the Pagans*, trans. R. W. Dyson, CTHPT (Cambridge: Cambridge University, 1998).

suo Moysi: Ego sum qui sum; *et:* Misit me qui est. *Quis ergo hoc capiet, cum videatis omnia mortalia mutabilia; cum videatis non solum corpora variari per qualitates, nascendo, crescendo, deficiendo, moriendo, sed etiam ipsas animas per affectum diversarum voluntatum distendi atque discindi: cum videatis homines et percipere posse sapientiam, si se illius luci et calori admoverint; et amittere posse sapientiam, si inde malo affectu recesserint? Cum videatis ergo ista omnia esse mutabilia; quid est quod est, nisi quod transcendit omnia quae sic sunt ut non sint? Quis ergo hoc capiat? Aut quis, quomodocumque intenderit vires mentis suae, ut attingat quomodo potest id quod est, ad id quod utcumque mente attigerit, possit pervenire? Sic est enim tamquam videat quisque de longe patriam, et mare interiaceat; videt quo eat, sed non habet qua eat. Sic ad illam stabilitatem nostram ubi quod est est, quia hoc solum semper sic est ut est, volumus pervenire; interiacet mare huius saeculi qua imus, etsi iam videmus quo imus: nam multi nec quo eant vident. Ut ergo esset et qua iremus, venit inde ad quem ire volebamus. Et quid fecit? Instituit lignum quo mare transeamus. Nemo enim potest transire mare huius saeculi, nisi cruce Christi portatus. Hanc crucem aliquando amplectitur et infirmus oculis: et qui non videt longe quo eat, non ab illa recedat, et ipsa illum perducet.*

"In the beginning was the Word." He is the same, and is in the same manner; as He is, so He is always; He cannot be changed; that is, He is. This His name He spoke to His servant Moses: "I am that I am; and He that is has sent me." Who then shall comprehend this when you see that all mortal things are variable; when you see that not only do bodies vary as to their qualities, by being born, by increasing, by becoming less, by dying, but that even souls themselves through the effect of various volitions are distended and divided; when you see that men can obtain wisdom if they apply themselves to its light and heat, and also lose wisdom if they remove themselves from it through some evil influence? When, therefore, you see that all those things are variable, what is that which is, unless that which transcends all things which are so that they are not? Who then can receive this? Or who, in what manner soever he may have applied the strength of his mind to touch that which is, can reach to that which he may in any way have touched with his mind? It is as if one were to see his native land at a distance, and the sea intervening; he sees whither he would go, but he has not the means of going. So we desire to arrive at that our stability where that which is, is, because this alone always is as it is: the sea of this world interrupts our course, even although already we see whither we go; for many do not even see whither

> they go. That there might be a way by which we could go, He has come from Him to whom we wished to go. And what has He done? He has appointed a tree by which we may cross the sea. For no one is able to cross the sea of this world, unless borne by the cross of Christ. Even he who is of weak eyesight sometimes embraces this cross; and he who does not see from afar whither he goes, let him not depart from it, and it will carry him over.[93]

The Word is constant, always *is*, in contrast to mortal beings which by nature are born, live, and pass away. "In the beginning was the Word" means that the Word is *ego sum qui sum*. Surrounded by variable things, how can the human mind understand one who does not exist according to changeability? As in *Confessions* Book 7,[94] Augustine compares the spiritual journey to a physical one: here it is a sea which needs to be crossed, and Christ the mediator makes this possible. In *Confessions*, it was the Platonists who saw the goal but knew not how to arrive at it; here the land is well-known—one's native land—but the resources for making the journey are unavailable. Or, Augustine acknowledges that the resources for seeing the destination may not be available—for those who are "weak of eyesight"—but this matters not for the one who embraces the cross. For the *cross* here is what mediates, whereas in *Confessions*, Augustine speaks of Christ's humility and weakness.[95]

Augustine's *Tractates on the Gospel of John* may be another key text for understanding his reading of Exod 3:14-15. Zum Brunn argues that no Greek or Latin theologian before Augustine associated Exod 3:14 with the ἐγώ εἰμι sayings.[96] While this association may have been influenced by an anti-Arian concern to demonstrate the full divinity of the Son, it does more than act as a prooftext certifying Christ's divinity. It shows that Christ is not only the way, but also the goal; and that though the Son is God, the Son is not the Father (because the Son does what the Father instructs, John 8:28).[97] This association also gives Augustine occasion for a lengthy reflection on the un-

---

93. *Tract. Ev. Jo.* 2.2.
94. *Conf.* 7.21,27.
95. Cameron demonstrates that Augustine's acknowledgment of the cross increases as his Christology develops and as he repudiates elements of residual Manichaeism and learns from Paul. Christ's death on the cross becomes for Augustine the quintessential act of humility. Cameron, *Christ Meets Me Everywhere*, 97-164.
96. Zum Brunn, *St. Augustine*, 110. Cf. *Tract. Ev. Jo.* 38.8-11; 40.2-3; 43.17-18.
97. *Tract. Ev. Jo.* 38.8-11; 40.2-3.

graspability of the divine nature, and for a sermon that is primarily prayer, a plea to understand God as he is distinct from every created thing.[98] In other words, the association of Exod 3:14 with the "I am" statements of John serves Augustine's discussion of several of the main themes of his theology, and with attention to contemplation and prayer of the believer.

In the previous section of this chapter, I described the important role of the Scriptures in Augustine's conversion, as he describes it in *Confessions* Books 7 and 8, and the requirement of humble attention to the material forms in which God makes himself known for the salvation of humanity. I also began to discuss Augustine's reading of Exod 3:14–15, which is more fully explored in the current section of this chapter. In Augustine's mature reflection on these verses, verse 14 demonstrates the difference between Creator and creature: God is unchangeable, eternal, and ungraspable; God is unknown except that he mercifully willed to make himself known and comes to us in forms that we can understand, as the God of Abraham, the God of Isaac, and the God of Jacob (v. 15), and as man, in Christ. Augustine interprets these verses as witnessing to Christ as the self-revelation of God, but not in a way that eclipses the fact that 3:14–15 witnesses to the same character of God's self-revelation prior to Christ. So Augustine's interpretation of these verses attends to the literal sense of the text. Moreover, Augustine addresses the existential dimension, since reading these verses is always simultaneously for the reader to ask, with Moses, about the name and nature of God: how can I know God? However, the third aspect of Augustine's literal-sense reading—that exposition of Exod 3:14–15 is not only christological but fully Trinitarian—remains to be explored.

4. Divine Being

This fourth section concerns several of Augustine's texts on the nature of divine being, many of which refer to Exod 3:14. My goal is to show that Augustine's discussions of divine being involve a variety of terms, drawn from Scripture, used to identify an active, living, and constant God; and that these terms do not prioritize divine unity over trinity, but rather express the principle that to reflect on the nature of God is to reflect on how Father, Son, and Spirit are truly distinct and yet one God.

---

98. Ibid., 38.9–10.

4.1. Idipsum, Est, and the Nature of Divine Being

Augustine uses a variety of terms to discuss divine being. We have already seen Augustine's characteristic term *"idipsum"* used to identify the undefinable, ungraspable God in himself. Augustine's commentary on Ps 101[102] further explores the dynamic of God's self-revelation. Augustine reads in verse 27[26], "[Earth and heaven] will all wear out like old clothes, and you will discard them like a garment, and so they will be changed, but you are the selfsame (σὺ δὲ ὁ αὐτὸς εἶ), and your years will not fail."[99] Whereas in *Expositions of the Psalms* 121, the immutability and ungraspability of the divine nature is identified as *idipsum*, here the term is *"idem ipse es." "Idem ipse"* on its own would be basically equivalent to *"idipsum,"* but here the phrase does not occur without *"es,"* just as the psalm reads *"tu vero idem ipse es." "Tu vero idem ipse es"* distinguishes between Creator and creature, between the one who is constant and the one who comes into being. Earlier in his commentary on the psalm, Augustine glosses *"ipsum es"* with *"est"*:

> Ego sum qui sum: qui est, misit me ad vos. Magnum ecce Est, magnum Est! Ad hoc homo quid est? Ad illud tam magnum Est, homo quid est, quidquid est? Quis apprehendat illud esse? quis eius particeps fiat? quis anhelet? quis aspiret? quis ibi se esse posse praesumat?

> I AM WHO AM. HE WHO IS has sent me to you. What a mighty "is"! What an incomparably great "is"! What is any human being beside that? A human being "is" something, but what is he or she, alongside that great "is"? Who can grasp that being? Who could share in it? Who pant for it, who aspire to it? In its presence, who dare even think he "is"?[100]

Like *"idipsum," "est"* identifies a subject existing in a categorically different (and much greater) way than humanity, who can strive to apprehend *est* but will not finally succeed. But why *"est,"* a term of being, and not *"idipsum"*? It is possible that Augustine chose the term because of its fittingness to the exegetical context of Ps 101[102]. Augustine seems to use *"est"* here because of its semantic relation to the *"ego sum qui sum"* of Exod 3:14, a text that is not

---

99. *Et omnes sicut vestimentum veterascent, et sicut opertorium mutabis eos, et mutabuntur; tu autem idem ipse es, et anni tui non deficient.* Enarrat. Ps. 101.2.12. English translation from Augustine of Hippo, *Expositions of the Psalms, 99–120*, ed. Boniface Ramsey, trans. Maria Boulding, OSB, *The Works of Saint Augustine* III/19, electronic ed.

100. Enarrat. Ps. 101.2.10.

explicitly referenced in the psalm, but which Augustine finds appropriate to discuss. Further, "*est*" makes the point about eternity that Augustine is considering, following Ps 101[102]:25[24], which Augustine reads, "Do not recall me when only half my days are done. Your years abide in the generation of generations."[101] Augustine asks, "What are 'your years'?" He answers that human experience of time in which every year (month, day, minute) at first does not exist, then comes and is, and then ceases to be. But with God, there is no change, "Your eternal years are not like that; your years are unchanging and will abide with the generation of generations," that is, the community of believers from among Israel, Jew and Gentile.[102] In God, the present tense is appropriate because it is not as though God was something that God has since ceased to be, or will be something that God is not yet. In this generation, God will makes God's years present: "What is that generation? It truly exists, and if we understand properly we shall exist in it, and God's years will exist in us. How can they be in us? In the same way that God himself will be in us, so that, as Scripture says, 'God may be all things in all of us' (1 Cor 15:28)."[103] Believers have eternal life because they are found in God, and God in them, such that God transforms their time into God's.

In *Sermon 7*, Augustine refers to Ps 101[102]:27[26], just as in *Expositions of the Psalms* 101, he refers to Exod 3:14,

> *Esse nomen est incommutabilitatis. Omnia enim quae mutantur desinunt esse quod erant et incipiunt esse quod non erant. Esse est. Verum esse, sincerum esse, germanum esse non habet nisi qui non mutatur.*

> "Is" is a name for the unchanging. Everything that changes ceases to be what it was and begins to be what it was not. "Is" is. True "is," genuine "is," real "is," belongs only to one who does not change.[104]

---

101. *Ne revoces me in dimidium dierum meorum. In generatione generationum anni tui.* Ibid.

102. *Illi ergo anni tui aeterni, anni tui qui non mutantur, in generatione generationum erunt.* Augustine takes the final phrase literally as "generation of generations," rather than simply "forever." Ibid.

103. *Quae est ista? Est quaedam, et si bene agnoscamus, in illa erimus, et anni Dei in nobis erunt. Quomodo in nobis erunt? Quomodo ipse Deus in nobis erit: unde dictum est: Ut sit Deus omnia in omnibus.* Ibid.

104. Serm. 7.7.

"*Esse est.*" The phrase is not a final choice of terms for Augustine, but followed by the gloss, *verum esse, sincerum esse, germanum esse*. Augustine reaches for language to articulate something that is ultimately beyond description. This fluidity of terms may seem confusing or counter-productive. Was not Augustine giving us a unique account of *idipsum*, and does this account not lose its particularity when he also uses the terms "*est*" and "*ipsum esse*"? I have already suggested that such a fluidity of terms should be expected for exegetical reasons, but it should be expected for theological reasons as well. Augustine consistently argues that the nature of God is fundamentally ungraspable; it would be odd if he advocated a single term for identifying this ungraspability. As these terms communicate the ungraspability of an undefinable God, they simultaneously suggest some ambiguity as to whether "being" is *really* what Augustine is getting at or whether the central issue lies elsewhere. Again, it seems to me that Marion is right that Augustine is more concerned with immutability than "being," and further, eternity is of concern only as a corollary to immutability.[105] This does not mean that Augustine avoids use of terms for being; instead he uses a variety of terms that have an "affinity"[106] with the truth he is trying to articulate.

Marion writes of *Expositions of the Psalms* 101.2.10 that "eternity, which replaces immutability, is considered to be a *substantia*, despite Augustine's reluctance to do so in the *De Trinitate*," and finds this as running counter to his thesis.[107] Yet, I am not convinced that eternity "replaces" immutability here. Rather, eternity, which is discussed at all because the idea is present in the biblical text, is discussed in terms of "*est*" because of the priority of immutability. Only if God does not change can God be said to be the true and constant *est*. The claim that eternity is the substance of God is also exegetically driven, for it identifies how it is that God's years are found in believers (the "generation of generations"): as God himself dwells in those who have faith in him, so God's time does as well, because God and his eternity are not different things. *Expositions of the Psalms* 101.2 does not contradict the claim that being is subordinate to immutability. Rather, this text makes clear that

---

105. Marion, "*Idipsum*," passim.
106. Cf. *Enarrat. Ps.* 121.5.
107. Marion, "Idipsum," 186. Cf. *sed anni Dei, aeternitas Dei est: aeternitas, ipsa Dei substantia est, quae nihil habet mutable*; "God's years are God's eternity, and eternity is the very substance of God, in which there is no possibility of change." *Enarrat. Ps.* 101.2.10.

eternality and immutability are interrelated in Augustine's account: "What is 'I am who I am' if not 'I am eternal'? What is 'I am who I am' if not 'who cannot change'?"[108]

However, that eternality and immutability are interdependent notions in Augustine raises the question, is this eternal, immutable being static and therefore lifeless? I suggest that Augustine's understanding of God's eternity has the character of abiding, living constancy rather than static and abstract being. The familiar discussion of Exod 3:14 in *Sermon 6* suggests this:

> *Cum enim quaereret nomen Dei, hoc dictum est:* Ego sum qui sum. Et dices filiis Israel, Qui est misit me ad vos. Quid est hoc? O Deus, o Domine noster, quid vocaris? "Est vocor" dixit. Quid est, "Est vocor"? Quia maneo in aeternum, quia mutari non possum. Ea enim quae mutantur non sunt, quia non permanent. Quod enim est, manet. Quod autem mutatur, fuit aliquid et aliquid erit; non tamen est, quia mutabile est. Ergo incommutabilitas Dei isto vocabulo se dignata est intimare*: Ego sum qui sum.

> When he asked God's name, you see, this is what was said: I am who I am. And you shall say to the children of Israel, He who is sent me to you. What's this all about? O God, O Lord of ours, what are you called? "I am called He-is," he said. What does it mean, I am called He-is? "That I abide for ever, that I cannot change." Things which change are not, because they do not last. What is, abides. But whatever changes, was something and will be something; yet you cannot say it is, because it is changeable. So the unchangeableness of God was prepared to suggest itself by this phrase, I am who I am.[109]

Augustine explains *ego sum qui sum* first in terms of the unchangeability of God—the phrase "*ego sum qui sum*" suggests as much. To be sure, Augustine does not understand unchangeability in a static sense, but as living constancy: *Quod enim est, manet*. The unchangeability of God is further expressed in God's eternity:

---

108. *Quid est:* Ego sum qui sum, *nisi*, aeternus sum? *Quid est,* Ego sum qui sum, *nisi, qui mutari non possum? Sermon* 7.7. Furthermore, immutability and eternity are correlate with ungraspability; because God is without change and time, which characterize material life, God exceeds the grasp of human intellect.

109. *Serm.* 6.4.

> ...sed anni Dei, aeternitas Dei est: aeternitas, ipsa Dei substantia est, quae nihil habet mutabile; ibi nihil est praeteritum, quasi iam non sit; nihil est futurum, quasi nondum sit. Non est ibi nisi: Est; non est ibi: Fuit et erit; quia et quod fuit, iam non est; et quod erit, nondum est: sed quidquid ibi est, nonnisi est.
>
> God's years are God's eternity, and eternity is the very substance of God, in which there is no possibility of change. In him nothing is past, as though it no longer existed, and nothing is future, as though it had not yet come to be. There is nothing in God's eternity except "is." There is no "was," no "will be," because anything that "was" has ceased to be, and anything that "will be" does not yet exist. Whatever "is" in God simply is.[110]

Augustine is clear, here as elsewhere, that the eternity of God is not a matter of static immobility but a matter of consistent, constant presence: there is no "was" or "will be" in God, because it is not as though God will cease to be something that God is. Nor is it the case that God will begin to be something that God is not. This is what *"idipsum"* means: "And so you, Lord, are not one thing here, another thing there, but the selfsame, very being itself, 'holy, holy, holy Lord God almighty'" (Isa 6:3; Rev 4:8).[111] Divine simplicity supports this, as the passage from *Expositions of the Psalms* 101.10 quoted above begins: "God's years are not something different from God himself."[112] Moreover, the eternity of God is something in which those who are saved will share; we who were once only past and future will become, with God, only present. Augustine commends his readers, "Sift the mutations of things, you will find was and will be: think on God, you will find the is, where was and will be cannot exist. To be so then yourself, rise beyond the boundaries of time."[113] God's unchangeability and eternity are concepts that guard the difference between Creator and creation in the present, and they show the promise of God, the transformation that awaits those who are being saved.

So far in the fourth part of this chapter, I have suggested that Augustine uses a variety of terms to refer to divine being. These terms are exegetically

---

110. *Enarrat. Ps.* 101.2.10.

111. *Itaque tu, Domine, qui non es alias aliud et alias aliter, sed id ipsum et id ipsum et id ipsum, sanctus, sanctus, sanctus, Dominus Deus omnipotens. Conf.* 12.7.7.

112. *Non enim aliud anni Dei, et aliud ipse. Enarrat. Ps.* 101.2.10.

113. *Discute rerum mutationes, invenies Fuit et Erit: cogita Deum, invenies Est, ubi Fuit et Erit esse non possit. Ut ergo et tu sis, transcende tempus. Tract. Ev. Jo.* 38.10.

and theologically driven, since a plurality of terms is necessary to refer to something that is finally beyond human comprehension. However, in Augustine's thought, discussing the nature of divine being is necessarily coupled with the reality that Father, Son, and Holy Spirit are each God and together, one God. Thus, discussion of the being of God must take account of the mystery of divine unity and trinity.

4.2. Divine Being, Holy Trinity

In this subsection, I provisionally address the heart of Augustine's mature discussion of the Trinity. Recently, Lewis Ayres and Michel Barnes have challenged prominent, modern interpretations of Augustine's theology that he begins from the unity of God, and have suggested that greater attention be paid to Augustine's doctrinal concerns such as Scripture and its exposition by prior and contemporary theologians.[114] Since in this chapter I suggest that exegetical concerns are central to the development of several of the main points of Augustine's theology, my sympathy with Ayres and Barnes's arguments may already be suspected. In this subsection, I will present my own account of Augustine's discussion of the Triune unity of God, in which to consider divine being, such as it differs from created being, is simultaneously to consider how the Father, Son, and Spirit can be distinguished from one another while remaining one God. It is not so much that Augustine begins with the unity of God as that his discussions of the unity and trinity of God mutually inform each other, such that separating the two ideas would be impossible without doing injustice to one or the other.

Augustine suggests that recognition of the ontological difference between Creator and creature also enables one to express how the Father begets the Son and how the Spirit proceeds from the Father, while the three remain one God. The connection is suggested in an incipient form in *Expositions of the Psalms* 101. God has established the heavens and earth, which will die, but, Augustine writes, "Although all those things would not exist except as deriving from you, and coming to be through you, and existing in you, nonetheless they are not what you are, for *you are the selfsame, and your years*

---

114. Summaries of the issues can be found in Michel René Barnes, "Augustine in Contemporary Trinitarian Theology," *TS* 56 (1995): 237–50 and Ayres, "'Remember That You Are Catholic'," 39–82. For an extensive argument, see Lewis Ayres, *Augustine and the Trinity* (Cambridge: Cambridge University, 2010).

will not fail."¹¹⁵ For God to create is for God to make something that is not himself. On the other hand, it is possible to conceive of a mode of generation that might result in a distinction whereby the resulting party is none other than God himself. Similarly, in *Confessions* Book 12, Augustine writes,

> *in principio, quod est de te, in Sapientia tua, quae nata est de substantia tua, fecisti aliquid et de nihilo. Fecisti enim caelum et terram non de te; nam esset aequale Unigenito tuo ac per hoc et tibi, et nullo modo iustum esset, ut aequale tibi esset, quod de te non esset. Et aliud praeter te non erat, unde faceres ea, Deus, una Trinitas et trina Unitas.*
>
> In the beginning, that is from yourself, in your wisdom which is begotten of your substance, you made something and made it out of nothing. For you made heaven and earth not out of your own self, or it would be equal to your only-begotten Son and therefore to yourself. It cannot possibly be right for anything which is not of you to be equal to you. Moreover, there was nothing apart from you out of which you could make them, God one in three and three in one.¹¹⁶

On the one hand, there is wisdom, "which is begotten of your substance," and on the other hand is that which, through wisdom, is made from nothing. Augustine explains that, in the beginning, there could only have been God, so anything generated would either be from God—hence equal to God, the Son—or not equal to God, and thus not generated of God, or necessarily generated from nothing. Reflection on the ontic difference between Creator and creature illuminates the nature of Triune life because the difference between Creator and creature casts in stark relief the unity and equality of Father, Son and Spirit.

In the previous example, Augustine identifies the wisdom of God as "begotten from [God's] substance" (*nata est de substantia tua*). What exactly does Augustine mean by "*substantia*"? Augustine explores the meaning of this term in *Expositions of the Psalms* 68.1. In Ps 68:3, Augustine reads, "I am stuck fast in the mud of the deep, and there is no substance," and he asks, what does "there is no substance" mean? In the context of the psalm, it seems obvious that the psalmist refers to some foothold on which he might be able to

---

115. *Et quamvis etiam ipsa non essent nisi ex te, et per te, et in te, tamen non quod ipse es: Tu enim idem ipse es. Et anni tui non deficient. Enarrat. Ps.* 101.2.12.

116. *Conf.* 12.7.7.

stand so as to keep from sinking further. Augustine does not address this most plain meaning, but instead his attention is caught by the significance of the word "*substantia*." Does it suggest that the mud itself is not a substance? Or does the act of "sticking fast" cause the sticking person to become a non-substance?[117] If one will make progress toward understanding what this statement means, one needs to understand what exactly a substance is. Augustine first considers a material definition of substance as riches and of non-substance as poverty.[118] From this perspective and reading the psalm as from the mouth of Christ, either as head or body (that is, the church), Augustine suggests that the text points to Christ taking on poverty for our sake (cf. 2 Cor 8:9; Phil 2:6). "He reached the very pinnacle of poverty when he clothed himself in the form of a servant."[119] But there are other ways the text can be read.

Augustine then moves to a philosophical understanding of substance: "It means what we are—whatever we are."[120] Created things are substances, but God too is a substance, "for anything that is not a substance is not anything at all. A substance is something that is."[121] Augustine defines "*substantia*" in terms of "*esse*"; the former indicates the latter. Augustine continues, expounding the Catholic view that the Son is of the same substance as the Father, in two points:

1. "Whatever the Father is as God, that the Son is, and that the Holy Spirit is."[122] In other words, the Father is God, and the Son is God, and the Holy Spirit is God.

2. "But the Father's name as Father is not the name of a substance, but indicates his relationship to the Son; and therefore we do not say that the Son is the Father, in the manner in which we say that the Son is God."[123] Whatever is said about God as a substance is not to be predicated of the Fa-

---

117. *Enarrat. Ps.* 68.1.4.
118. Augustine recognizes that Ps 68 does not mention riches explicitly. Ibid.
119. *Ad summam enim paupertatem pervenit, quando formam servi induit.* Ibid.
120. *Illud quod sumus quidquid sumus.* Ibid., 68.1.5.
121. *Nam quod nulla substantia est, nihil omnino est. Substantia ergo aliquid esse est.* Ibid.
122. *Quidquid est Pater quod Deus est, hoc Filius, hoc Spiritus sanctus.* Ibid.
123. *At vero quod Pater est; quia non substantiae nomen est, sed refertur ad Filium, non sic dicimus Filium Patrem esse, quomodo dicimus Filium Deum esse.* Ibid.

ther specifically, for speaking in terms of substance is not the same thing as speaking in terms of intra-Triune relationship.

The second point requires further explanation. The principle that what is said of God, as God is in himself, is not predicated of the Father alone follows also for speaking of God as the one who is, as Augustine writes, "But as Father he is not that which is; for he is called Father not with reference to himself, but in relation to the Son, whereas he is called God with reference to himself."[124] Augustine goes on to say that, of course, if one were to ask what the Father is, the answer would be "God," so also with the Son and the Spirit. Thus the rules for predicating *substantia* of the Father, Son and Spirit are different from the rules of predicating "God" of the same.

This logic underscores the difference between speaking about human and divine "persons" (though Augustine does not use the term *persona* in this sense in *Expositions of the Psalms* 68.1). If one asks what Abraham is, one could answer "a man," and so for Isaac. Whereas Abraham and Isaac together are two men, the Father and Son together is one God. "The communion of substance in God is so great that it admits of equality, but not of plurality."[125]

In sum, Augustine's account of the nature of God in *Expositions of the Psalms* 68.1 does not offer the substantial unity of God as a point of departure for Trinitarian reflection. Rather, Augustine's exposition demonstrates his concern to remain true to two guiding principles of Trinitarian faith: that the Father is God, as is the Son and the Spirit, and that "Father," "Son," and "Spirit" are not titles of substance but of relationship. These principles are

---

124. *Cum autem Pater est, non illud est quod est. Pater enim non ad se, sed ad Filium dicitur: ad se autem Deus dicitur.* Ibid.

125. *Tanta enim ibi est substantiae societas, ut aequalitatem admittat, pluralitatem non admittat.* Ibid. The technical discussion of "*substantia*" seems to have little to do with Ps 68, but Augustine quickly returns to the exposition at hand, combining the christological reading of "no substance" as "poverty" with the more technical discussion of *substantia* and God. He concludes that "there is no substance" refers to the iniquity of people among whom Christ was sent, based on another principle: everything that God created has substance, and nothing has substance which was not created (and not God himself). Vice, which is the result of human will and action, does not have substance, because it was not created. (Augustine reaches a similar conclusion about evil in *Confessions* 7.13,19). Proof that sin does not have substance is given in the fact that, while all creation is said to praise God including even the lowliest of creatures (e.g., snakes), vice does not praise God.

possible because the grammar of divine being—that is, the rules for speaking about divine being—differs from the grammar of created being.

Moreover, Augustine's discussion of God and *substantia* in *Expositions of the Psalms* 68.1 anticipates his account of the same in *The Trinity* Book 5. Augustine's primary concern in Book 5 is to suggest, against the "Arians," that some things may be predicated of God by way of relationship. These "Arians agree" with Catholic faith that nothing is to be predicated of God by way of accident, which would suggest modification or change. However, Augustine disagrees with his opponents who argue that therefore, everything must be predicated of God by way of substance, and he suggests that some things may be predicated of God by way of relationship.

Augustine begins Book 5 with a qualification and a principle: 1. who God is in himself cannot be grasped by the mind, and even what can be thought of God cannot be expressed precisely; and 2. "whatever we say about that unchanging and invisible nature, that supreme and all-sufficient life, cannot be measured by the standard of things visible, changeable, mortal and deficient."[126] Keeping in mind the immutability and immateriality of God guards against thinking of God as a creature.

Then Augustine qualifies what he means by "substance" in God:

> *Est tamen sine dubitatione substantia, vel, si melius hoc appellatur, essentia, quam Graeci* οὐσία *vocant. Sicut enim ab eo quod est sapere dicta est sapientia, et ab eo quod est scire dicta est scientia, ita ab eo quod est esse dicta est essentia.*
>
> There is at least no doubt that God is substance, or perhaps a better word would be being; at any rate what the Greeks call *ousia*. Just as we get the word "wisdom" from "wise," and "knowledge" from "know," so we have the word "being" from "be."[127]

Augustine identifies "*substantia*" with "*esse*" and "*ousia*." In speaking of God, better than "*substantia*" is "*essentia*," deriving as it does from "*esse*," and further, as it is used in Exod 3:14.[128] In any case, either "*esse*" or "*substantia*,"

---

126. *Quae de natura incommutabili et invisibili summeque vivente ac sibi sufficiente dicuntur, non ex consuetudine visibilium atque mutabilium et mortalium vel egenarum rerum esse metienda.* Trin. 5.2,3.
127. Ibid.
128. Ibid.

when referring to God, must not be understood as though God has accidents or undergoes modification.

Because God cannot be changed, nothing can be predicated of him according to accidents or modification. Augustine will continue to assert that this does *not* mean that everything said of God is so substance-wise, though this would be the case with created things.[129] With created things, predicates of relationship are accidents; if one ceases to be a friend or spouse or parent, one does not cease to be as such. But with God, predications of relationship are not accidental, for one cannot say anything of God according to accidents. Nor are they substantial, or the Father would be the Son and vice versa; one would not be able to distinguish between Father, Son, and Spirit.

In chapter 1, Augustine argues that "Father," and "Son," as well as "begotten" (which is the same as "Son," because the latter is the consequence of the former) are all named according to relation, not substance. For one can only be father of a child, or son of a parent, and begotten likewise implies being begotten of another.[130] Further, Augustine specifies that what is said about the Son substance-wise establishes the Son's equality with the Father, not what is said relation-wise. While neighbors perhaps may be equal in neighborliness, the Son does not share sonship with the Father, who is unbegotten, nor the Father share fatherhood with the Son. Augustine writes, "It remains that what makes him equal must be what he is called with reference to himself," therefore, substance-wise.[131] Since what God is called with reference to himself (*ad se*) is the same as substantive predication, therefore, Father and Son are equal in substance.[132]

Augustine further explains what is said of God according to substance, following his central principle: "the Father is God and the Son is God and the Holy Spirit is God, and no one denies that this is said substance-wise; and yet we say that this supreme triad is not three Gods but one God."[133] Augustine applies this principle to other things that may be said of God *ad se*, i.e., that God is good, great, etc. Then, to explain how this is the case, Augustine gives

---

129. Ibid., 5.4,6.
130. Ibid., 5.6,5–7; 7,8.
131. *Restat ut secundum id aequalis sit quod ad se dicitur.* Ibid., 5.6,7.
132. Ibid.
133. *Quemadmodum enim Deus est Pater, et Filius Deus est, et Spiritus Sanctus Deus est, quod secundum substantiam dici nemo dubitat, non tamen tres deos sed unum Deum dicimus eam ipsam praestantissimam Trinitatem.* Ibid., 5.8,9.

examples of position, possession, time and place, how these are said of God metaphorically rather than properly, so that there are not three almightys, but one. As Ayres writes, "Lacking any accidents, God must be any qualities we predicate of God. But if so, Augustine implies, there cannot be three divine beings each of whom possesses the quality greatness, there can only be one greatness itself."[134] An immaterial understanding of God requires such simplicity, as does the substantial equality of the Father, Son and Spirit.

In Book 6 and the beginning of Book 7, Augustine further explores how one can express the relationship between Father, Son, and Spirit. Here, he takes up exegesis of the phrase "Christ the power of God and the wisdom of God" (1 Cor 1:24). This phrase was understood by some as meaning that the Son is the power and wisdom of the Father by which the Father is powerful and wise[135]—thus that the Father is not powerful or wise without the Son. While this exegesis does not suggest any inequality between divine persons, Augustine has two critiques of it, as Barnes succinctly explains.[136] First, it would follow from this exegesis that the Father would lack power and wisdom apart from begetting the Son, which makes it difficult to see how the language of "God from God, light from light" would be true.[137] In this Nicene phrase, Augustine understands all of the properties that are said of God in himself—power, wisdom, goodness, greatness, and so on—that is, all of what can be attributed to divine simplicity. To interpret 1 Cor 1:24 as meaning that the Son is the very wisdom and power of the Father in such a way that the Father has power and wisdom only by begetting the Son, then the Father is no longer wisdom and power but begetter of wisdom and power, which would make the phrase not "light from light" but "light from begetter-of-light," and "power from begetter-of-power." Moreover, even the Son could not truly be called any of these characteristics in itself, but only in relation to the Father, whose power, wisdom, greatness, and so on, it is.[138]

Augustine's second critique depends upon the logic of the first. If the Father is not wisdom or power, then the Father's being also depends on the

---

134. Ayres, *Augustine and the Trinity*, 216.
135. Barnes calls this the "Neo-Nicene" understanding of the power of God. Michel René Barnes, "Augustine and the Limits of Nicene Orthodoxy," *AugStud* 38, no. 1 (2007): 194.
136. Ibid., 200.
137. *Trin.*, 6,1,2.
138. Ibid., 6,2,3.

being of the Son, and vice versa. Thus "Son" and "Father" do not refer to relation but being—the Son is the being of the Father. The critique is clarified at the beginning of Book 7:

> At enim multo magis unius eiusdemque essentiae, quia una eademque essentia Pater et Filius, quandoquidem Patri non ad se ipsum est ipsum esse, sed ad Filium quam essentiam genuit et qua essentia est quidquid est. Neuter ergo ad se est, et uterque ad invicem relative dicitur. . . . Restat itaque ut etiam essentia Filius relative dicatur ad Patrem. Ex quo conficitur inopinatissimus sensus, ut ipsa essentia non sit essentia, vel certe cum dicitur essentia, non essentia, sed relativum indicetur.

> It means that Father and Son are one and the same being, seeing that the Father's very "is" has reference not to himself but to the Son, and that he has begotten this being, and by this being is whatever he is. So neither of them is with reference to himself, and each is said with reference to the other. . . . So we are left with the position that the Son is called being by way of relationship, with reference to the Father. And this leads us to the most unexpected conclusion that being is not being, or at least that when you say being you point not to being but to relationship.[139]

If sonship becomes a statement of substance, then being becomes a statement of relationship, which seems to go against standard usage.

In contrast with the neo-Nicene exegesis of 1 Cor 1:24, which considers the Son as the very wisdom, power (and thus, being) of the Father, Augustine concludes that—fitting for the discussion of predicates of substance and relationship beginning in Book 5—"Father," "Son," and "Spirit" are predicated only by way of relationship and not by substance. Using relational terms and distinctions such as these does not threaten the unity of the Father and Son (and, presumably, Spirit) as one being:

> Unde Pater et Filius simul una sapientia quia una essentia, et singillatim sapientia de sapientia sicut essentia de essentia. Quapropter non quia Pater non est Filius, et Filius non est Pater, aut ille ingenitus, ille autem genitus, ideo non una essentia quia his nominibus relativa eorum ostenduntur. Uterque autem simul una sapientia et una essentia, ubi hoc est esse quod sapere; non autem simul uterque Verbum aut Filius, quia non hoc est esse quod Verbum esse, aut Filium esse, sicut iam satis ostendimus, ista relative dici.

---

139. Ibid., 7.1,2.

> So Father and Son are together one wisdom because they are one being, and one by one they are wisdom from wisdom as they are being from being. And therefore it does not follow that because the Father is not the Son nor the Son the Father, or one is unbegotten, the other begotten, that therefore they are not one being; for these names only declare their relationships. But both together are one wisdom and one being, there where to be is the same as to be wise; they are not however both together Word or Son, because it is not the same here to be as to be Word or Son, since as we have quite sufficiently shown, these are terms of relationship.[140]

This conclusion, however, actually says very little. Augustine has not returned to give a full account of how one ought to read 1 Cor 1:24 or a comprehensive understanding of the nature of divine unity and distinction. Rather, the conclusion given is more of a guideline than an explanation: terms predicated by way of relationship do not infringe upon the unity of being between the divine persons.

In sum, *The Trinity* Books 5–7 present a mature reflection on how one can rightly speak about divine relations of Father, Son and Spirit without positing change within God. This reflection does not begin from the unity of God, though it does take as axiomatic divine immateriality and immutability, so that certain modes of speaking about the divine relations are rejected because of their inappropriateness to the subject matter. The principle of divine simplicity does not deny the relation of Father, Son and Spirit in God, but rather enables Augustine to designate a category of speech about God that is according to relation.

4.3. Trinity and Exodus 3:14–15

It might seem as though I have, in the previous section, lost sight of Exod 3:14–15. Though I did not explicitly trace Augustine's reading of this biblical text, these verses are never far from his Trinitarian thought, in which the negative principles of the immutability, immateriality, and incomprehensibility of God are paramount. Augustine references Exod 3:14 to express that God truly is and is unchanging, which is the basis of divine simplicity and qualifies Augustine's use of *substantia*.[141] The judgments that

---

140. Ibid., 7.2,3.
141. Ibid., 5.2,3; 7.5,10.

Augustine observes in these verses and related texts (the theophany of Exod 3, Ps 101[102]:25-28[24-27], Ps 121[122]:3, Rom 1:20, John 1, 8:28, and so on) guide his exposition of the divine Triune life.

Yeago argues that the Nicene language of "*homoousion*" correctly identifies the theological judgments that the early church observed in Scripture. Observing such judgments requires attention to the literal sense of biblical texts. Modern arguments which seek to place a wedge between the New Testament and later doctrinal formulations are ill-conceived if they fail to acknowledge the difference between concepts and judgments.[142] Concepts are tools of judgments, since,

> We cannot concretely perform an act of judgement without employing some particular, contingent verbal and conceptual resources; judgement-making *is* an operation performed with words and concepts. At the same time, however, the same judgement can be rendered in a variety of conceptual terms, all of which may be informative about a particular judgement's force and implications.[143]

This distinction dovetails with what I have argued about Augustine's description of divine being. Divine being is not a concept that he extracts from Exod 3:14 alone. Rather, Augustine looks to Exod 3:14 and other biblical texts for judgments about the nature of divine life. Augustine does not advocate a set concept of being, but uses a variety of terms to show the theological and exegetical appropriateness of some negative principles.

In this fourth section of the chapter, I have summarized Augustine's account of divine being in several aspects. The terms Augustine uses to discuss divine being are often exegetically driven, as he chooses terms that he finds in the biblical text. Moreover, divine being, for Augustine, is not a static concept but a way of marking the enduring character of the true God and distinguishing between Creator and creature. Relatedly, Augustine does not logically begin from a concept of the unity of God; rather, discussion of the nature of divine being is necessarily already a discussion of how the Father, Son, and Spirit are truly distinct and yet one God. Augustine's mature discussion of Trinitarian relations is possible because the grammar for discussing created being differs from the grammar for discussing divine being.

---

142. Yeago, "Nicene Dogma," 162.
143. Ibid., 159.

Thus, the Trinitarian aspect of the threefold literal reading comes to the fore in this section.

5. Summary

How best to summarize Augustine's reading of Exod 3:14-15? God is the one who most truly and unchangeably *is*: only God remains eternally constant, the Creator whose nature cannot be defined in creaturely terms. Yet this God has deemed it good to reveal himself to those who believe, including Moses and the people of Israel, and so gave them a second name by which to know him: "the God of Abraham, the God of Isaac, and the God of Jacob." God's appearance in the angel testifies to the coming mission of the Son, the Word made flesh, who provides sure healing for weak and sinful humanity to draw near to God in faith.

Throughout this chapter, I have suggested that Augustine's reading of Exod 3:14-15 can be understood within the context of a threefold interpretation of the literal sense of the text, which includes attention to the words of the text as self-referential, the reader's (or hearer's) contemplation of God and transformation, and the unity and equality of Father, Son, and Holy Spirit, the one God. All of these elements are inter-related, so it is difficult to know where to begin to speak of the dramatic movement, as a circle has no start or end. Scripture points to God the Creator, distinct from creation, in which God is revealed. Contemplation leads one to recognize that the immutable God cannot be thought precisely, much less expressed, and leads one back to Scripture and creation, which testify to the work of the Son, revealer of the Father, but not lesser in divinity. The Triune God makes himself known through the testimony of creation and Scripture.

To summarize Part I: in the first chapter, I argue that etymology and historical reconstruction of Yahwism do not significantly aid reading Exod 3:13-15, because these approaches ask questions that the text does not answer. Then, I suggest that a canonical approach is a more fruitful starting place and build on the work of Brevard Childs in holding in tension various historical, literary, and theological concerns that may be brought to bear on the text. Furthermore, I build on Frei's discussion of the literal sense to articulate my own threefold concept of "literal sense," including the following claims: 1. that Old Testament texts are realistic in character and that "the way the words go," or the semantic potential of the text, limits interpretative possibilities; 2. that the Christian church, broadly speaking, is the context in which this semantic potential is understood as the literal sense; 3. that in this context, the ascriptive subject of the Old Testament is understood as God, whom Christians know as Father, Son, and Holy Spirit. Furthermore, I argue in chapter 2 that Augustine's reading of Exod 3:13–15 does not posit a static, abstract God and that Augustine offers an example of a reading that takes seriously the place of this biblical text within the wider context of all of Christian Scripture. Because Augustine's reading attends to its literal sense and concerns God's dynamic relationship with humanity, Augustine's reading of this passage can provide resources for theological interpretation in a Christian context. Thus, in Part I, I critique both portions of von Rad's claim that Exod 3:14 is an etymology of the divine name and not a statement about God's being. Then, I begin to offer suggestions for a way forward. In Part II, I turn to the constructive, exegetical portion of my argument.

PART II

Rebuilding Theological Interpretation of Exodus 3:13–15

CHAPTER 3

The Divine Name in the Book of Exodus

Having argued that neither of von Rad's two claims about the text of Exod 3:14—that it is an etymology and that it is not a statement about God's being—are helpful in reading the literal sense of this text in a Christian context, in this chapter I begin to develop an account of how one might fruitfully read Exod 3:13-15 within its narrative, canonical context. Augustine's reading serves as a model for Christian reading that takes seriously the flow of the text itself as well as the context of the text within two-testament Christian Scripture. However, Augustine's interpretation should not simply be repeated in the present but must be brought into dialogue with approaches that draw attention to the literary context of the Old Testament within the canonical limits of this testament.

In this chapter I draw on resources from recent Old Testament scholarship and argue that Exod 3:13-15 within the context of the book of Exodus—and more specifically, references to the name "YHWH" in the book of Exodus—suggests something about the identity of God, who is known through (but not reduced to) God's action in delivering Israel from slavery in Egypt and establishing a covenant with them. This text suggests that God is free and faithful such that God cannot be limited to the categories of created being but rather exceeds these.

The argument undertaken in this chapter is grounded in current discussions of the exegetical task. As discussed in chapter 1, that the Old Testament can be read according to its literal sense is a statement about the realistic character of Old Testament narrative as well as a statement about the ascriptive character of the narrative's witness to the one God, known to Christians as Father, Son, and Holy Spirit. While my primary conversation partners in this chapter are modern exegetes, the discussion is compatible with the theological convictions that both inform and are informed by Augustine's reading of Scripture: that reading Scripture is a journey toward God through detailed attention to the literal sense of the text, that God is immaterial, and that knowledge of God is not exhaustively available to humans. Thus, Augustine's hermeneutic provides a broad framework from which to engage modern exegetical arguments about specific passages. Moreover, in the section on Exod 3–4, I will attend to Augustine's reading of this passage, as elements of that reading relate to issues raised in current discussions.

Texts in the book of Exodus that refer to the divine name—either through use of שֵׁם or the name "YHWH," or through a phrase that emphasizes the being or action of YHWH under this name—include some of the most significant moments in Exodus: 3:13–15; 5:2; 6:3; 7:5; 7:17; 8:6[8:10]; 18[22]; 9:14, 16, 29; 10:2; 12:12; 14:4, 18; 15:3, 11; 15:26; 16:12; 20:2, 5, 7; 23:21; 29:45–46; 33:19; 34:5–7. Since there is not space in this chapter to address all of these texts thoroughly, I will highlight the most significant texts in four groups: the call of Moses (Exod 3:1–4:17); the plagues and exodus (Exod 5–15); the Decalogue (Exod 20); and the story of the golden calf and its aftermath (Exod 32–34). The textual units are large because each reference to the divine name will be considered in its immediate literary context. While each section has a different nuance, they share themes of God's continuing faithfulness to be among and act on behalf of Israel, and of the paradox of God's self-revelation: while God makes Godself known to Moses and Israel in and by the name "YHWH," such knowledge is not exhaustive as God retains the freedom to make Godself known as God will.

1. Call of Moses (Exod 3–4)

1.1. Paronomasia and Translation (Exod 3:14)

In chapter 1, I concluded that etymological approaches do not assist the reader in understanding the received form of Exod 3:13–15. In this chapter, I present an alternative: reading these verses within the literary context of the book of Exodus. More specifically, my proposal for reading Exod 3:13–15 builds on the idea that verse 14 is not an etymology of the divine name, but rather wordplay or paronomasia. This is not a new argument; many commentators address both etymological and wordplay elements in these verses.[1] Already in 1950, Vriezen identified אֶהְיֶה אֲשֶׁר אֶהְיֶה as a *paronomastische*

---

1. E.g., Childs, *Book of Exodus*, 76; Dozeman, *Exodus*, 133; Moberly, *Old Testament*,

Relativsätze indicating indefiniteness, and he proceeded to investigate biblical parallels in order to identify more precisely the nature of the indefiniteness expressed there, without addressing the issue of etymology.[2] More recently, Beitzel has argued, in greater detail, that it is better to understand verse 14 as paronomasia rather than etymology, so it will be helpful to briefly address his argument.[3]

Beitzel argues on historical and philological grounds that Exod 3:13–15 includes paronomasia. Citing occurrences of the Tetragrammaton or shortened form outside of the biblical text (as an Ugaritic divine name, an Egyptian place name, a Byblian divine name, and as an element in Babylonian proper names and personal names at Ebla), Beitzel observes that place and personal names are often named after names of deities, but not typically vice versa. Further, he argues that the name "YHWH" is a "genuine tetragrammaton," which is to say that the *yod* is intrinsic to the name. The text of Exod 3:14 is better understood as paronomasia rather than etymology, because the divine name "YHWH" and הָיָה have no etymological relation.[4]

In 1893, Casanowicz suggested that even etiological Old Testament texts—texts that present themselves as etymologies of proper names—do not express more than popular understandings. For example, Gen 2:23b reads לְזֹאת יִקָּרֵא אִשָּׁה כִּי מֵאִישׁ לֻקֳחָה־זֹּאת, "this one shall be called Woman, for out of Man this one was taken." However, אִישׁ and אִשָּׁה come from different roots (אִשָּׁה being a contracted form of אֲנָשָׁה, the feminine form of אֱנוֹשׁ). Similarly, Casanowicz argues that מֹשֶׁה is more likely a Hebraized version of the Egyptian *mesu*, meaning "child," rather than the explanation given in Exod 2:10: וַתִּקְרָא שְׁמוֹ מֹשֶׁה וַתֹּאמֶר כִּי מִן־הַמַּיִם מְשִׁיתִהוּ, "She named him Moses, 'because,' she said, 'I drew him out of the water.'"[5] Seventy years later, Guillaume

---

22. There is a fine line between regarding God's responses in verse 14 as wordplay on the divine name, versus commentary on the same.

2. Th. C. Vriezen, "'EHJE 'AŠER 'EHJE," in *Festschrift Alfred Bertholet zum 80 Geburtstag*, ed. W. Baumgartner and L. Rost (Tübingen: Mohr Siebeck, 1950), 489–512. For the "paronomastic relative clause" in German scholarship, see overview in den Hertog, *Other Face*, 81–82.

3. B. J. Beitzel, "Exodus 3:14 and the Divine Name: A Case of Biblical Paronomasia," *TJ* 1 (1980): 5–20.

4. Ibid., 18–19.

5. Immanuel M. Casanowicz, "Paronomasia in the Old Testament," *JBL* 12, no. 2 (1893): 115–16. For a bibliography of research on paronomasia in the Old Testament until 1980, see Beitzel, "Exodus 3:14," 6.

assumed that Casanowicz's point held true, as he began his article with similar examples from the book of Genesis and declares, "Seldom had these explanations any philological basis. Everyone must have known that Reuben meant 'lion,' and was not an exclamation."[6]

Thus it seems wise to distinguish between what moderns, given philology and archeological evidence, are likely to think about the history of proper names and how ancient authors, editors, and readers of the Old Testament would have understood the history of these names. Casanowicz's argument regarding the etiology of proper names in the Old Testament highlights the fact that Exod 3:13–15 does not present itself as an etymology. There is no formula, for example, involving קרא; God is not named "YHWH" by Moses, according to the text, but rather YHWH names himself "YHWH." If the text were to follow the etiological form, then one would expect something like, "And God said, 'I am who I am.' Therefore God was called 'YHWH' for he said, 'I am who I am.'" If texts that present themselves as etiologies are possibly better understood as paronomasia, how much more, then, should Exod 3:14–15 be so understood, if it does not include the etiological formula.[7] Even if the text presents a folk etymology, the use of modern historical tools to uncover the etymological roots of the name "YHWH" will not aid one in understanding the popular etymology attested in this biblical text.

In fact, some studies of Exod 3 have used the term "etymology" in precisely this sense, as wordplay. Already in 1950, Vriezen identified the phrase in 3:14a as a *paronomastische Relativsätze* before embarking on a thorough discussion of the syntax and meaning of the statement in the biblical text.[8] Similarly, though his focus is understanding the syntax of Exod 3:13–15 within the literary context of the received form of the biblical text, den Hertog moves from literary analysis of the question in verse 13 and divine names in Genesis and Exodus to discussing verses 14–15 as etymology without comment; later in the book, he refers to the nature of these verses as "etymological wordplay."[9] However, use of the term "etymology" to refer to the wordplay in the text is confusing given the history of research addressed in chapter 1. Moreover, using the term in this way depends upon an assump-

---

6. A. Guillaume, "Paronomasia in the Old Testament," *JSS* 9, no. 2 (1964): 282.

7. However, Exod 3:14–15 does not appear in Casanowicz's list of occurrences of paronomasia in the Old Testament. Casanowicz, "Paronomasia," 123–63.

8. Vriezen, "'EHJE 'AŠER 'EHJE," 489–512.

9. Den Hertog, *Other Face*, 30–55, esp. 51–55, 182.

tion that the original authors, editors, and readers of Exod 3 understood this text in terms of the origins of the name "YHWH," but this is not self-evident; they may simply have understood these verses as commentary on the name. Therefore, because Exod 3:13–15 does not present an etymology in a modern sense and may not even present an ancient etymology, I argue that one should identify the content of these verses as wordplay or paronomasia and thereby seek to understand them within the received form of the text.

I address what the wordplay may communicate in what follows. However, first I address another issue that was raised in chapter 1: translation of Exod 3:14. Part of von Rad's claim is that the Septuagint translation of 3:14a—Ἐγώ εἰμι ὁ ὤν—produces a significantly different interpretation than the Masoretic Text's אֶהְיֶה אֲשֶׁר אֶהְיֶה. However, in this chapter I read the Hebrew text and argue that it is open to the type of reading that Augustine has supplied, though Augustine was reading the *Vetus Latina*. How can this be?

Lindblom and Schild have argued that the most natural translation of the Masoretic Text of Exod 3:14a is akin to the Septuagint: "I am the one who is." This is because, according to Hebrew syntax, if a principal clause is in the first or second person and is followed by a relative clause, the relative clause continues in the same person as the principal clause.[10] On account of this rule, the writer would have been restricted from writing אֶהְיֶה אֲשֶׁר יִהְיֶה. Schild and Lindblom give 1 Chr 21:17 as a parallel: וַאֲנִי־הוּא אֲשֶׁר־חָטָאתִי וְהָרֵעַ הֲרֵעוֹתִי, "I am the one who sinned and did wrong."[11]

However, Lindblom and Schild's translation is not the consensus. Albrektson argues that the parallels that Lindblom and Schild offer are not strictly parallels. In 1 Chr 21:17, the main clause (וַאֲנִי־הוּא) is a nominal clause, not a verbal one as in Exod 3:14 (אֶהְיֶה). Furthermore, this is true of *all* of Lindblom's parallels, as well as the examples Schild presents.[12]

Albrektson goes a step further, arguing not only that the translation of Lindblom and Schild is not proved, but that it is wrong. Albrektson advocates

---

10. Johannes Lindblom, "Noch einmal die Deutung des Jahwe-Namens in Ex 3, 14," *ASTI* 3 (1964): 4–15; E. Schild, "On Exodus III 14: 'I Am That I Am'," *VT* 4, no. 3 (1954): 296–302. This translation was suggested in the mid-nineteenth century by Knobel and then Ruess; cf. de Vaux, "Revelation," 69.

11. Schild, "On Exodus III 14," 300; Lindblom, "Die Deutung des Jahwe-Namens," 9. Cf. Bertil Albrektson, "On the Syntax of אהיה אשר אהיה in Exodus 3:14," in *Words and Meanings*, ed. Peter R. Ackroyd (Cambridge: Cambridge University, 1968), 18–19.

12. Albrektson, "Syntax," 23.

a syntactical rule which he finds voiced only in J. Pedersen's Hebrew grammar (written in Danish), that in the case of subordinate clauses where the principle clause is a nominal clause, then the subordinate clause may be its predicate. In other words, the crucial element for translation of the so-called "parallels" is precisely the point at which they are not parallel to the statement in Exod 3:14. In contrast, if the Hebrew writer wanted to write "I am the one who is," he could have used a participle to express this (for example, אֲנִי הַהֹיֶה).[13]

In my view, these arguments raise questions about the purpose and limits of translation. Albrektson writes, "For a rule of syntax is a statement of how words are in fact connected. 'Philology is an empirical science,' and to formulate a syntactical law is to say that such and such a pattern has been observed in several instances."[14] Is this an adequate account of translation and syntax? For the rules that moderns have generated for translating biblical Hebrew are modern rules; they are not rules that practitioners themselves agreed upon, and they are rules generated from a limited reservoir of examples. Moreover, the parallel that Albrektson gives for the traditional translation—וַאֲנִי הוֹלֵךְ עַל אֲשֶׁר אֲנִי הוֹלֵךְ, "I go where I go" (2 Sam 15:20)[15]—contains the independent personal pronoun and participle rather than the imperfect verbal form. It would seem that a precise parallel has not been given, and this imprecision calls into question Albrektson's account of the scientific nature of syntactical rules.

Moreover, Frei's account of the integration of words and meaning might suggest a different understanding of translation, in which translation would be viewed as a re-contextualization of a text, and as such, any translation would be an imprecise rendition of the original. It may be unwise to think in terms of the author wanting to write "I am the one who is" but being restricted by the rules of his language. The author wanted to say, and did say, אֶהְיֶה אֲשֶׁר אֶהְיֶה, which is a unique formulation in biblical Hebrew.

Therefore, it is a benefit to Lindblom and Schild's arguments that they have argued for the appropriateness of the translation "I am the one who is," but not for the *in*appropriateness of the more traditional translations, "I am who I am" and "I will be who I will be." Lindblom and Schild give imprecise

---

13. Ibid., 24–25. The masculine singular participle הֹיֶה is not attested in biblical Hebrew, but the feminine singular participle הֹיָה occurs in Exod 9:3.
14. Ibid., 24.
15. Ibid., 27. NRSV translates, "while I go wherever I can."

parallels, but these parallels may be what the Septuagint translator(s) had in mind. Moreover, that the Hebrew of Exod 3:14 has been translated as Ἐγώ εἰμι ὁ ὤν and the importance of the latter for Christian biblical interpretation and theology cannot be undone. One must assume that the translators were attempting to render the Hebrew in as accurate a way as they could, according to their understanding of the meaning of the verse. Most importantly, the Septuagint translation represents at least one early tradition of understanding the Hebrew text.

In sum, the traditional renderings of the phrase in English as either "I am who I am" or "I will be who I will be" is preferable when dealing exclusively with the Hebrew text. This does not mean that "I am the one who is" is an *inaccurate* translation, but only that, within a range of possible translations, the traditional rendering is a better one. Thus, in the account that follows, I prefer the translations "I am who I am" or "I will be who I will be." At the same time, "I am the one who is" and the Septuagint translation stand within the semantic potential of אֶהְיֶה אֲשֶׁר אֶהְיֶה.

The next question to consider is whether one can reasonably choose between "I am who I am" and "I will be who I will be"; is the present or future tense preferable in English translation? Beginning with the Septuagint and *Vetus Latina*, the phrase in Exod 3:14 has typically been translated in the present.[16] Augustine emphasizes the present tense in *Sermon 6*, writing,

> *Cum enim quaereret nomen Dei, hoc dictum est: Ego sum qui sum. Et dices filiis Israel, Qui est misit me ad vos. Quid est hoc? O Deus, o Domine noster, quid vocaris? "Est vocor" dixit. Quid est, "Est vocor"? Quia maneo in aeternum, quia mutari non possum. Ea enim quae mutantur non sunt, quia non permanent. Quod enim est, manet. Quod autem mutatur, fuit aliquid et aliquid erit; non tamen est, quia mutabile est. Ergo incommutabilitas Dei isto vocabulo se dignata est intimare: Ego sum qui sum.*

> When he asked God's name, you see, this is what was said: I am who I am. And you shall say to the children of Israel, He who is sent me to you. What's this all about? O God, O Lord of ours, what are you called? "I am called He-is," he said. What does it mean, I am called He-is? "That I abide for ever, that I cannot change." Things which change are not, because they do not last. What is,

---

16. For example, Childs translates it in the present without further discussion of tense. Childs, *Book of Exodus*, 48, 50.

> abides. But whatever changes, was something and will be something; yet you cannot say it is, because it is changeable. So the unchangeableness of God was prepared to suggest itself by this phrase, I am who I am.[17]

In the above quotation, Augustine employs an almost pedantic concern with the specific phrasing of the text. Surely Augustine's point is the continuing action of God, which one might argue could be communicated either through the present or the future tense. However, with recent interpretive emphasis on the presence of God with the Israelites and the dynamic nature of God's involvement in the exodus, one might expect the future tense to be more common.[18] Childs's commentary expresses this tension, as he translates the phrase with the present tense in the translation section, but then interprets it according to the future tense under "Old Testament Context."[19]

Statistically, אֶהְיֶה and other preformative forms of היה are usually rendered with future tense (e.g., Exod 3:12);[20] in support of a future rendering, one can also say that the existent form contrasts with a verbless form, which might more clearly indicate present tense.[21] However, to translate the אֶהְיֶה in verse 14b as a future tense ("I will be has sent me to you") results in an odd juxtaposition between future and past.[22] Perhaps most importantly, the enigmatic and indefinite character of the statement (which I describe at greater length in what follows) indicates that the context will be of little assistance in clarifying an appropriate tense in English. In light of the indefinite and enigmatic character of the statement, I suggest that one not choose between the future and present tense, where space allows.[23] This would mean observing the possibility of a future tense translation without denying the appropriateness of Augustine's reflections on the received text.

---

17. *Serm.* 6.4.

18. For example, Dozeman, *Exodus*, 116, 119; Schmid, *Genesis and the Moses Story*, 190.

19. Childs, *Book of Exodus*, 48, 50, 76.

20. Benno Jacob, *The Second Book of the Bible: Exodus*, trans. Walter Jacob and Yaakov Elman (Hoboken, NJ: Ktav, 1992), 73; den Hertog, *Other Face*, 95.

21. Den Hertog, *Other Face*, 95.

22. Den Hertog suggests a modal rendering, thus including "may," "can," "want," etc., which might supply philological support for Kearney's interpretation. Ibid., 97, 100–5; Kearney, *God Who May Be*, 77–85.

23. See, for example, Sarna, *Exodus*, 17; Seitz, "Call of Moses," 154.

1.2. Exodus 3:13-15 in Its Immediate Literary Context

Exodus 3:1–4:17 recounts the call of Moses. In chapter 4, I highlight Moses' vocation as covenant mediator in the Pentateuch as the direction toward which this passage points. Thus the prophetic aspects may be somewhat more muted in the reflection in this chapter. In this chapter, I address the character and disposition of Moses as seen in his various responses to the theophany throughout the passage. Though at first Moses demonstrates curiosity if not also reverence, as the narrative progresses, Moses is portrayed as one who, like the Israelites, has "weakness of will that is to be overcome by a demonstration of power."[24] Put differently, Moses' hesitation to follow the call of God is attached to his perception of his own weakness vis-à-vis the power of Pharaoh, and God seeks to transform Moses' perception by directing his attention toward God. Like Pharaoh and the Israelites (as I will argue), Moses is in need of more than information in order do what YHWH is calling him to do. Moses needs to understand who God is.

Moses is shepherding his father-in-law's flocks in Midian when וַיֵּרָא מַלְאַךְ יְהוָה אֵלָיו בְּלַבַּת־אֵשׁ מִתּוֹךְ הַסְּנֶה, "an angel of the Lord appeared to him in the flame of the fire in the midst of the bush" (Exod 3:2). The narrator informs the reader from the outset that this is a theophany, but, from Moses' perspective, initially only a burning bush is in view. At least, he does not mention a personal figure when he says (to himself or to the flocks), "I must turn aside and look at this great sight, why the bush is not burned up" (Exod 3:3). Moses' response is appropriate to what he has seen and to what the reader has been told about what he has seen. Seeing Moses turn toward the bush, YHWH calls his name twice (Exod 3:4),[25] and Moses responds, "Here I am." With this response, the reader understands that Moses is an obedient recipient of this revelation and expects that he will act in faith.[26] So the narrative begins by portraying Moses as one who has had a relatively normal day interrupted by a theophany, but who has responded to this surprising course of events with openness.

---

24. Moberly, *Old Testament*, 63.
25. Cf. Gen 22:11; 1 Sam 3:10, though in both of these texts, the double-name calling is not the first time YHWH has called the name of his servant, but rather at a climax in the narrative.
26. See Gen 22:1; cf. 1 Sam 3:4; Isa 6:8. Houtman translates הִנֵּנִי, "Yes, I am listening." Cornelis Houtman, *Exodus vol. 1*, trans. Johan Rebel and Sierd Woudstra, Historical Commentary on the Old Testament (Kampen: Kok, 1993), 345.

However, when YHWH commands Moses to remove his sandals, the reader is not told whether or not Moses does this. Moreover, the character of Moses' response changes once YHWH introduces himself: "I am the God of Abraham, Isaac, and Jacob" (v. 6a). Moses then hides his face, because he is afraid to look at God (v. 6b; וַיַּסְתֵּר מֹשֶׁה פָּנָיו כִּי יָרֵא מֵהַבִּיט אֶל־הָאֱלֹהִים). Later in Exodus, YHWH limits Moses' sight as YHWH passes by (Exod 33:18–34:9). In chapter 34, Moses bows in worship (34:8), but is Moses' response in 3:6b out of appropriate reverence? Probably but not necessarily. In the Old Testament, humans hide from danger or from something that would be disgraceful to see (e.g., Isa 53); neither is the word positive in reference to the hiddenness of YHWH (Ps 89:47[46]).

Once the call has been announced (Exod 3:7–10), Moses clearly hesitates and resists it, as he raises four concerns (3:11, 13; 4:1, 10). The first concern is in the form of a rhetorical question: "Who am I that I should go to Pharaoh, and bring the Israelites out of Egypt?" (v. 11) Through this rhetorical question, Moses expresses his humility, or at least his lack of confidence. Moses seems to presume that he will be alone in this venture,[27] and that the match for Israel will be waged between himself and Pharaoh. This question falls into the category of the "self-abasement or insult formula," as Coats explains.[28] However, in this context the question is strange. It presents a much different scenario than, for example, Gideon's resistance on account of being the youngest son, from a small clan (Judg 6:15; cf. 1 Sam 9:21). Though Moses' lowly social position may be communicated by the chapter's rural setting,[29] Moses does not make this, but rather the greatness of Pharaoh, the focus of his question. In fact, where this type of rhetorical question is used in the Old Testament, it is typically in reference to humility before God (e.g. 2 Chr 2:5; 2 Sam 7:8; Ps 8:5; Ps 144:3) or in comparison with an agent of God, such as the king of Israel (2 Sam 9:8; 1 Sam 18:18).[30] This form is also used in Exod 16:7b–8, where Moses states,

---

27. Moshe Greenberg, *Understanding Exodus*, Heritage of Biblical Israel (New York: Behrman House, 1969), 74.

28. George W. Coats, "Self-Abasement and Insult Formulas," *JBL* 89, no. 1 (1970): 14–26.

29. Childs, *Book of Exodus*, 74.

30. C. J. Labuschagne, *The Incomparability of Yahweh in the Old Testament*, POS 5 (Leiden: Brill, 1966), 23–24. Possible exceptions include 1 Kgs 18:9; the several occurrences in Job should be analyzed in their own right: 3:12; 6:11; 7:17; 15:14; 21:15.

"For what are we, that you complain against us?" And Moses said, "When the Lord gives you meat to eat in the evening and your fill of bread in the morning, because the Lord has heard the complaining that you utter against him—what are we? Your complaining is not against us but against the Lord."

I suggest that a good reader should be puzzled, and a bit troubled, by Moses' question. True humility would require him to say something like, "Who am I that you should send me to bring out the Israelites?"

In response to Moses' resistance, YHWH declares, "I will be with you." This is not reassurance of something Moses already knows; it contrasts sharply with the question he has posed. The writer may be hinting at the fact that the *true* confrontation in Egypt will not be between Moses and Pharaoh, but between YHWH and Pharaoh (Exod 7–15).

The second half of YHWH's answer is more difficult to explain. Moses did not ask for a sign; YHWH volunteers it.[31] But what is the sign, and how does it connect with YHWH's being with Moses? Greenberg suggests that the interpretive crux is whether the זֶה refers backwards in the sentence (meaning that the sign is YHWH's presence with Moses) or forwards (the sign is the future worship on the mountain), and he opts for the latter perspective.[32] On the basis of his form-critical analysis, Childs argues that "the point of the verse is as follows: this burning bush is a sign, that it is I who send you, and it is your guarantee that when you have rescued the people from Egypt, you will worship God on the same mountain."[33] Either way, here YHWH discloses more than is asked of him and points to, not the freedom of the Israelites, but worship of God on the mountain as the fulfillment of Moses' call.[34]

Since Moses' second resistance-question is the primary subject of discussion, I will discuss it last. The third question begins, "Suppose they do not believe me or listen to me, but say, 'The Lord did not appear to you'?" (4:1). Because the second question mentions the Israelites, they are the presumed subject of this verse. Moses is concerned that the Israelites will not trust him, and so he is given ominous signs that demonstrate the Lord's power

---

31. Greenberg, *Understanding Exodus*, 78; Childs, *Book of Exodus*, 74.
32. Greenberg, *Understanding Exodus*, 78.
33. Childs, *Book of Exodus*, 60. Cf. Sarna, *Exodus*, 17.
34. YHWH's deliverance of the Israelites for the purpose of serving YHWH is a clear theme throughout Exod 3–15.

over the creation and that suggest judgment.[35] Indeed, though Moses asks for reassurance vis-à-vis the trust of the Israelites, he is given signs of judgment against Pharaoh. Later in the story, Aaron performs "the signs" before the Israelites, and the people are immediately convinced (4:30–31). The reader is not told whether "the signs" in 4:30 are those of the snake and leprous hand, as in 4:3–8 (though presumably they are). However, the first sign, the staff becoming a snake, is performed before Pharaoh in 7:8–13 and serves as a prelude to the plagues. Moreover, the final sign that YHWH gives in 4:9 specifically foreshadows the first plague, in 7:14ff. While Moses believes that the Israelites will be difficult to persuade, as the story unfolds, the more significant conflict in Egypt is YHWH and Moses versus Pharaoh.

Moses' fourth expression of resistance is not a question but a statement: "O my Lord, I have never been eloquent, either in the past nor even now that you have spoken to your servant; but I am slow of speech and slow of tongue" (4:10). Because Moses begins his response with בִּי אֲדֹנָי, the reader might, for a brief moment, wonder if Moses' perception has finally changed away from his own weakness, but it has not.[36] Then YHWH responds with rhetorical questions: "Who gives speech to mortals? Who makes them mute or deaf, seeing or blind?" (4:11a). The correct answer to these rhetorical questions is, "None but YHWH alone" (cf. Isa 40:12–14, 26; Deut 3:24; Prov 30:4; Job 38–39),[37] and YHWH presents this answer in another rhetorical question, "Is it not I, the Lord?" (4:11b). As Creator, YHWH is the ultimate decider of who will speak and who will not. Whereas from Moses' perspective, the concern is a matter of whether he is qualified for the job, from YHWH's perspective, Moses' resistance is a result of failure to trust in YHWH, the Creator, to do what YHWH promises.

YHWH continues, commanding Moses again to go, get himself to Egypt, and in language resonant with that of 3:12, assures Moses that he will be with "[Moses'] mouth" and will teach him what to say (4:12). Yet even this does not convince Moses, who finally asks to be excused from the mission (4:13). This is the final straw for YHWH, who to this point has patiently tried to redirect Moses from fear of the Israelites and Pharaoh to trust in YHWH. YHWH becomes angry and appoints Aaron to speak for Moses (4:14–17). Then the conversation promptly ends. Moses does not make any declarations

---

35. Greenberg, *Understanding Exodus*, 88.
36. Here, Moses' response is not unlike that of Jeremiah in Jer 1:6.
37. Labuschagne, *Incomparability of Yahweh*, 27.

suggesting that YHWH has won him over to complete trust, but he does immediately make arrangements to go to Egypt (4:18).

To summarize, in this text, Moses is first awestruck by the sight of the burning bush and the appearance of the God of Abraham, Isaac, and Jacob. This fascination, however, does not immediately lead to obedience and trust in the power of God to accomplish what he is calling Moses to do. Moses fears the power of Pharaoh, in comparison to whom Moses is nothing (3:12). He also fears the Israelites, though YHWH's response foreshadows the fact that the Israelites will not be Moses' true rivals in Egypt. On the other hand, YHWH is patient and self-disclosing; YHWH consistently reiterates Moses' call, emphasizes his presence with Moses, and presents more signs and demonstrations of YHWH's power and the success of his mission than Moses asks for.

How then should the reader understand Moses' question in 3:13 and YHWH's response? The question cannot simply be a rewording of the question in 4:1. So far, each of Moses' responses has identified a different issue that causes him to hesitate. So it would be strange to claim that Moses, here, is concerned that the Israelites will not believe that the Lord has appeared to Moses unless he can supply a particular name. The issue of the Israelites believing Moses is addressed in chapter 4.

If the question is not best understood as the Israelites testing Moses, and one leaves to one side the question of whether or not the Israelites and/or Moses knew the name "YHWH" prior to Moses' sending, there remains another way of understanding the question pragmatically. In the book of Genesis, when God has something to say to the patriarchs, God appears to them directly. Exodus 3 marks the beginning of a new situation, in which God sends Moses and other prophets to communicate with the people of God and to accomplish certain tasks. Thus, the people may be asking under what name (either a new name or which among the names used in Genesis) can God be known as one who sends people.[38] The text supports this in that the phrase אֱלֹהֵי אֲבוֹתֵיכֶם occurs once in the question and twice in the answer.

Additionally, Moberly identifies the nature of the question in 3:13 as didactic, similar in form to "child's questions."[39] That is, it is a rhetorical

---

38. See den Hertog, *Other Face*, 49–50; 59–71; Moberly, *Old Testament*, 23.
39. Moberly adequately accounts for the differences between the question in 3:13 and the "child's question formula" while nevertheless drawing important parallels. Ibid., 20.

device; to imagine the question genuinely occurring once Moses has come to Egypt is to "misconstrue the significance of the text."[40] Instead,

> within the immediate context of Exodus, Israel's imagined reluctance to believe that YHWH has really spoken to Moses (Exod 4:1) is in no sense a theoretical problem of the identity of the deity but is rather a matter of weakness of will that is to be overcome by a demonstration of power.[41]

Indeed the verse seems to present the question of under what name—what understanding of the nature of God—the Israelites will be able to trust. Or, at least, this is the reader's view of the question once the answer has been supplied. For Moses inquires about the name of God, but he receives both a name and a statement of who God is. For both Moses and for the Israelites, the sending of Moses marks a new act of God, one that will require new and substantial trust in YHWH.

As in other cases, YHWH responds more than aptly. The response comes in two parts: first, a discussion of the name of God (vv. 14-15), and second, a restatement of Moses' mission (vv. 16-24). The first response can further be divided in three parts, each separated by a narrator's introduction:

> וַיֹּאמֶר אֱלֹהִים אֶל־מֹשֶׁה אֶהְיֶה אֲשֶׁר אֶהְיֶה וַיֹּאמֶר כֹּה תֹאמַר לִבְנֵי יִשְׂרָאֵל אֶהְיֶה שְׁלָחַנִי אֲלֵיכֶם: וַיֹּאמֶר עוֹד אֱלֹהִים אֶל־מֹשֶׁה כֹּה־תֹאמַר אֶל־בְּנֵי יִשְׂרָאֵל יְהוָה אֱלֹהֵי אֲבֹתֵיכֶם אֱלֹהֵי אַבְרָהָם אֱלֹהֵי יִצְחָק וֵאלֹהֵי יַעֲקֹב שְׁלָחַנִי אֲלֵיכֶם זֶה־שְּׁמִי לְעֹלָם וְזֶה זִכְרִי לְדֹר דֹּר:

> God said to Moses, "I Am Who I Am." He said further, "Thus you shall say to the Israelites, 'I Am has sent me to you.'" God also said to Moses, "Thus you shall say to the Israelites, 'the Lord, the God of your ancestors, the God of Abraham, the God of Isaac, and the God of Jacob, has sent me to you':
>
> This is my name forever,
> and this my title for all generations." (Exod 3:14-15)

Because the narrator introduces God's response three times, scholars have often viewed the text as an overloaded combination of sources and/or editing. Thus some have argued either that verse 15 is a later addition,[42] or

---

40. Ibid., 63.
41. Ibid.
42. For example, Schmid, *Genesis and the Moses Story*, 191-92.

(more likely), that verse 14 is.[43] However, the evaluation of these verses as overloaded "runs the risk of being highly subjective," and multiple speech introductions carry a rhetorical function in at least some cases.[44] In this case, it seems likely that the repeating introductions mark each statement as worthy of attention in its own right; the repetition focuses the reader's attention on each portion of the response.[45] Regardless of the text's possible prehistory, at some point an author or editor decided that the text should read as it does, and the three-part answer contains its own logic.

The forms in both verse 14a (אֶהְיֶה אֲשֶׁר אֶהְיֶה) and 14b (אֶהְיֶה) resonate with the language of 3:12 and 4:12. YHWH's presence with Moses is again contextually implied. However, 3:14 suggests much more than this.

God names himself and the description of this name can only be made through self-reference, in the first person. Thus, God's uniqueness is communicated in the answer. Moreover, as S. R. Driver argued, this is an example of the *idem per idem* construction, which is used "where either the means, or the desire, to be more explicit does not exist."[46] It remains an open question whether one can be more precise about the nature of the statement and what is communicated in this grammatical construction. Vriezen has argued that the function of the *idem per idem* statement in this case is to communicate intensification, as if to say "I am surely here."[47] However, as den Hertog has argued, the sense is more likely indefinite than intensive. The phrase in question is a posterior type *idem per idem* statement, because the main clause is followed by the relative clause. (This contrasts with the anterior type, in which the relative clause comes first.)[48] Thus, as in Exod 33:19; 1 Sam 23:13; 2 Sam 15:20; 2 Kgs 8:1; and Ezek 12:25,

---

43. See Childs, *Exodus*, 64–70; Martin Noth, *Exodus: A Commentary*, reprint ed., OTL (Philadelphia: Westminster, 1974), 43.

44. Den Hertog, *Other Face*, 31; E. J. Revell, "The Repetition of Introductions to Speech as a Feature of Biblical Hebrew," *VT* 47 (1997), 91–110.

45. Propp, *Exodus*, vol. 1, 367; cf. Revell, "Repetition of Introductions," 109.

46. Driver, *Book of Exodus*, 362–63; Driver, *Books of Samuel*, 185–86. Cf. Joüon and Muraoka, *A Grammar of Biblical Hebrew*, §158o, and Exod 16:23; 33:19.

47. Vriezen, "'EHJE 'AŠER 'EHJE," 506–8. Cf. Childs, *Book of Exodus*, 69.

48. Den Hertog acknowledges that anterior and posterior types of the construction cannot always be neatly distinguished; however, he then argues that Exod 3:14 fits clearly within the standard posterior type. Den Hertog, *Other Face*, 87–89.

the impact of the *idem per idem* construction can be described as follows: in the sentences concerned, the relative construction suggests that a complement (object, adjunct or nominal predicate) will be specified; however, because the relative clause essentially describes this complement in terms of what has already been said, its content remains in fact undefined.[49]

According to den Hertog, the indefiniteness of the construction is further supported by the fact that both instances of אֶהְיֶה are copulative in function, and by the preformative conjugation of this word.[50]

Still, contra den Hertog, it is difficult to see how there could not be an emphatic sense to אֶהְיֶה אֲשֶׁר אֶהְיֶה, given the similarity between the construction and the cognate accusative.[51] Thus, through wordplay and commentary rather than through definition or etymology, the repetition of אֶהְיֶה in verse 14 suggests that this term is not merely rhetorical but also substantially significant.[52] One can say at least that this repetition of the אֶהְיֶה suggests something about the nature of YHWH—who YHWH is—but that human knowledge of YHWH is always dependent upon the gracious act of God's self-revelation. God is, but God's ways and being are known fully only to God.

At the same time, to say that the phrase is indefinite is not to say that it is purely evasive. The response is a substantive revelation—it carries content—but at the same time who God is remains at least partially hidden.[53] This partially evasive answer suggests something about the nature of God, as Karl Barth explains:

> There is therefore no objective definition that we can discover for ourselves. We might say of this revelation of His name that it consists in the refusal of a name, but even in the form of this substantial refusal it is still really revelation, communication and illumination. For *Yahweh* means the Lord, the I who gives Himself to be known in that He exists as the I of the Lord and therefore acts only as a He and can be called upon only as a Thou in His action,

---

49. Ibid., 86–87.
50. Ibid., 89–92.
51. Moberly, *Old Testament*, 77.
52. Freedman, "God of Moses," 153; Moberly, *Old Testament*, 77.
53. See Magne Sæbø, "God's Name in Exodus 3.13–15: An Expression of Revelation or of Veiling?" in *On the Way to Canon: Creative Tradition History in the Old Testament*, JSOTSup (Sheffield: Continuum, 1998), 78–92.

without making Himself known in His I-ness as if He were a creature.⁵⁴

God cannot be known as an "item in the universe," but only as a subject who meets Moses in Midian and the reader in the text, pronouncing his own name. Thus, Moses' perspective must again shift from concern about a name to give the Israelites to attention toward the reality of the God who is sending him, who addresses Moses directly.⁵⁵

Against this interpretation of verse 14, it might be argued that the hiddenness of God could not possibly encourage Moses to accomplish the task that has been set before him. However, I suggest that, in response to Moses' concerns about his own weakness, YHWH reveals himself as the one who is able to carry out the task. YHWH's self-disclosure as subject in verse 14 is precisely in opposition to Moses' self-concern, because it draws Moses' attention away from himself and into God's "I." Knowledge of YHWH will require Moses' ongoing attention, because God does not describe himself according to a definition or by means of an object that can be mastered.

Augustine's characteristic reading of Exod 3:14-15, as described in chapter 2, recognizes the character of God's response to Moses in verse 14 as revelation that is indefinite or inexhaustible. The "I am who I am" and "I am" of this verse, to Augustine, point to the reality of God toward which Moses' and the reader's gaze is directed, but which is too much for the human mind to grasp. Though Augustine reads the *Vetus Latina*, his interpretation of these verses is affirmed by current scholarship on the syntax of the Hebrew *idem per idem* formula in its literary context.

Returning to the Hebrew text: the term אֶהְיֶה is repeated in verse 14b; this is what Moses is to tell the Israelites. On the one hand, this verse appears to function primarily as a transition between verses 14a and 15, and so perhaps it is not a very significant statement in itself. On the other hand, this second portion of God's response to Moses is marked by its own introduction, suggesting that it is important in its own right.

Is אֶהְיֶה a name?⁵⁶ The phrase in verse 14a would seem not to be a name, since it is not specifically stated that this is how Moses should answer the

---

54. Karl Barth, *Church Dogmatics*, trans. G. W. Bromiley, ed. G. W. Bromiley and T. F. Torrance vol. 2/1 (London: T&T Clark, 2009), §61.
55. Den Hertog identifies the statement as a "reorientating response"; *Other Face*, 121–22.
56. Den Hertog argues persuasively that it is a name. Ibid., 53–59.

Israelites' question, and the characteristic phrase שְׁלָחַנִי אֲלֵיכֶם does not follow it, as in 14b. In the context of Exod 3:14b, אֶהְיֶה could be a name. Yet it is not a name that is used elsewhere in the Old Testament (except perhaps Hosea 1:9).[57] There is a strong tendency among recent commentators to view אֶהְיֶה not as a name but as an explanation of the name "YHWH."[58] Childs appears to view the אֶהְיֶה of verse 14b as shorthand for the longer phrase in 14a, as he explains, "Moses' answer to the people can only reflect what God has revealed to him. He knows no more of God's intention than has been revealed in the formula."[59] To Childs, verse 14b concerns the question of significance of the name, whereas verse 15 provides the answer to the question about the name itself.[60] Yet, if Childs's interpretation is correct, one might rather think that the text of 14b would read, כֹּה תֹאמַר לִבְנֵי יִשְׂרָאֵל אֶהְיֶה אֲשֶׁר אֶהְיֶה, "Thus you shall say to the Israelites, 'I am who I am.'" Put differently, the phrase שְׁלָחַנִי אֲלֵיכֶם suggests that a name will precede it.

Seitz proposes that verse 14a contains God's name, אֶהְיֶה אֲשֶׁר אֶהְיֶה, but that this is "not a proper name in the strict sense (like Jim or Sally), but a name appropriate to God's character as God."[61] While I argue that, in the narrative, this phrase appears less like a name than the אֶהְיֶה of verse 14b, given Seitz's qualification, verse 14a could also function as a name. If אֶהְיֶה in 14b is functionally a name, this would not detract from the interpretations that suggest this term has to do with the meaning or significance of the name "YHWH" and that it points back to verse 14a. If אֶהְיֶה is a name, then it

---

57. Though on Hos 1:9 and Exod 3:14, see den Hertog. Ibid., 132-54.
58. So Houtman, *Exodus vol. 1*, 95–96, 368; Moberly, *Old Testament*, 22. Though the JPS transliterates the phrases in verse 14a and 14b, Sarna does not suggest that "'Ehyeh" is a name. Sarna, *Exodus*, 17–18.

Durham is unclear on this point, because he places "I am" in small caps (even in 3:12), perhaps indicating that it is a name, but summarizes the point of the repetitive phrase אֶהְיֶה by saying, "The redactor's point is just too important to be missed, and so he has labored to make it obvious: Yahweh Is." Thus Durham also suggests that 14b concerns the meaning of the name "YHWH." Durham, *Exodus*, 35, 39.

59. Childs, *Book of Exodus*, 76.
60. Childs distinguishes two phases in the tradition-history of verses 13-15: an earlier phase in which the identification of the God of the fathers with YHWH needed to be made, and a later one in which this connection was taken for granted and the meaning of the question (v. 13) understood in terms of the significance of the name. Ibid., 68–70, 76.
61. Seitz, "Call of Moses," 154.

carries the full weight of this meaning. Moreover, that this name is not used as a name for God elsewhere in the Old Testament (with one possible exception) is explained in verse 15: אֶהְיֶה is the name that YHWH gives himself, but "YHWH" is the name that God gives the people in order for them to call upon him. Obviously, it would be rather strange for the Israelites to refer to God in the first person (though Moses is permitted to do so, at least on one occasion), and though biblical Hebrew includes a few third-person verb forms used as proper names, no first-person forms are attested.[62]

I do not see any reason why אֶהְיֶה in verse 14b should not be understood as a name. This further supports the point made in conjunction with verse 14a that only God can reveal himself. God names himself, and the name with which God knows himself differs from the name by which the people of God know him. Moreover, identifying this word as a name does not necessarily support the naming of God as "Being," which is not a good translation of אֶהְיֶה. However, identifying this interpretation does call to mind Augustine's claim that verse 14 draws the reader's attention toward the incomprehensible nature of who God is.

The text of Exod 3:15 looks both backwards, to the patriarchs, and forwards, to the coming generations. The God who appears to Moses has been identified as the God of Abraham, Isaac, and Jacob (v. 6), and Moses acknowledges this name (v. 13). The name "YHWH," only alluded to in verse 14, is given and identified with the God of the patriarchs in verse 15; YHWH is none other than the God of Abraham's family. Whether the intended subject of verse 15b is simply "YHWH" or the longer "YHWH, the God of your fathers, the God of Abraham, the God of Isaac, and the God of Jacob" is of little consequence, for the longer form is understood in the singular name; YHWH *is* the God of the fathers. This name receives special emphasis as it will be the name by which people will call on God forever.[63]

---

62. Den Hertog, *Other Face*, 53–54.
63. At this point, it should be clear that the text of Exod 3:13–15 differs significantly from Gen 32:30. Prior to his question, Jacob has not been given the identity of this "man" (אִישׁ) with whom he wrestles; Moses has been told that it is the God of Abraham, the God of Isaac, and the God of Jacob who meets him (3:6). So Jacob's question would seem to be more a matter of identification, whereas Moses' has more to do with character. In response, Jacob receives no answer; Moses receives a very complex answer. Both answers suggest that naming God is not a simple or straightforward task. Only a general association can be made, that in both cases, the response shifts

Whereas אֱלֹהִים is a titular name, יְהוָה is a personal name.⁶⁴ Yet, one must clarify what is meant by "personal name" in light of the content of 3:14. The movement from this verse to verse 15 is one from divine freedom to manifestation, from hiddenness to accessibility. YHWH maintains the right to be whom YHWH will be, and this declaration is prelude to presenting the name by which Israel may call on this YHWH. Moreover, that divine freedom is the subject of the initial answer may suggest that this is not a qualification to YHWH's responsiveness to his people, but rather the reason for it. YHWH will choose whom YHWH will choose, and YHWH's will to deliver Israel is not contingent on anything. Moses should have confidence in this mission because YHWH, who is ultimately free, stands behind it.

A significant difference between the Hebrew text and its Greek and Latin translations is the use of a titular name in place of the Tetragrammaton in verse 15. In the Septuagint, this is Κύριος ὁ θεός; in the Vulgate, *Dominus Deus*. Likewise, the text of the *Vetus Latina* would not have included the personal name of God. Thus, for Greek and Latin interpreters, including Augustine, the line between names and titles are blurred; without a personal name for God, titular names are the only means of naming available.⁶⁵

Though one interpretive tendency in reading the Hebrew text is to see the Tetragrammaton as the only true name in this passage, I have argued that אֶהְיֶה also functions as a name, syntactically. While this does not resolve the differences between the Hebrew and its Greek and Latin translations, it does suggest that the Hebrew text of verse 14, not only verse 15, has to do with naming God. Therefore, reflections on naming God that omit the name "YHWH" are still relevant to interpretation of the Hebrew passage.

With verse 16, the narrative returns to its primary plot: the installation of Moses as prophet and the deliverance of the Israelites from Egypt. The Lord restates the call from the beginning: "Go and assemble the elders of Israel . . . ." At this point, YHWH adds information not previously given to

---

the attention of the one who inquires, as also in Judg 13. Ibid., 33–37.

64. See den Hertog for discussion and bibliography. Ibid., 43–45.

65. For Augustine, the situation is particularly complex, because the two phrases of God's self-introduction with which Augustine is primarily concerned are *Ego sum qui sum* and *Ego sum Deus Abraham Deus Isaac, et Deus Iacob*, the latter of which may be a conflation of verses 6 and 15.

The theological implications of the lack of personal divine name in Greek and Latin traditions are explored further in chapter 6.

Moses regarding the difficulties he will encounter in Egypt (3:16–24). The point of the restatement of Moses' call in these verses may be twofold. First, they function to try to motivate Moses again. YHWH has answered his most recent question of resistance; now it is time for him to go to Egypt! Second, this narrative is relevant to the question about the nature of God, whose power and character is demonstrated through his choosing of Moses and redemption of Israel. This power and character will be displayed all the more through the difficulties that Moses will encounter in Egypt.

In summary, Moses' resistance in Exod 3:1–4:17 suggests that Moses is hesitant to receive the call because he continually focuses on his own weakness and lack of preparation for the task rather than the identity and power of YHWH who is certainly capable of delivering the Israelites from Pharoah. YHWH goes out of his way to reveal himself to Moses, and finally, perhaps unwillingly, Moses heads toward Egypt. The text characterizes the revelation of YHWH in terms of YHWH's name, which is identified with the God of the patriarchs (3:6, 15), in a way that suggests that YHWH will be present with Moses (3:12, 14; 4:15). But this YHWH who is with Moses maintains his own freedom to reveal or withhold himself and to "be who [he] will be." Therefore, the name "YHWH" enables the Israelites to call upon their God, but it does not offer a means by which they might control God.

2. The Name in Exodus 5–40

2.1. Plagues and Exodus (Exod 5–15)

References to the name "YHWH" in the narratives of the plagues and exodus involve YHWH's self-disclosure in the form of the declaration, אֲנִי יְהוָה "I [am] YHWH," and in the recognition statement, לְמַעַן תֵּדַע כִּי אֲנִי יְהוָה "so that you will know that I [am] YHWH" (and variations on this phrase). My use of brackets around "am" in translation highlights the absence of the copulative in these characteristic statements. Ricoeur argues that this absence of היה in the characteristic phrase makes all the more surprising the use of this term in Exod 3:13–15, which is precisely the point at which our text and the self-disclosure and recognition statements in Exod 5–15 diverge.[66] However, some of the theological judgements suggested by the statements "I [am] YHWH," "so that you will know that I [am] YHWH," and similar phrases

---

66. Ricoeur, "From Interpretation to Translation," 333–34.

resonate with Exod 3:13-15. As in the narrative of Moses' call, in Exod 5-15 knowledge of YHWH involves more than factual acknowledgement of a name; knowledge of YHWH is typically construed as knowing YHWH rather than knowing *about* YHWH. Moreover, that one knows YHWH is demonstrated in actions that correspond to what YHWH is doing (namely, delivering the Israelites from Egypt and establishing a covenant with them). At the same time, knowing YHWH is not simply reducible to knowing what YHWH is doing among Israel. Knowing YHWH is a matter of receiving YHWH's self-revelation and responding appropriately.

2.1.1. "Who is YHWH?" (Exod 5:2) The text of Exod 4-5 portrays contrast between the Israelites' response of immediate faith and Pharaoh's response of rejection. Moses and Aaron appear before the Israelites (4:27ff.), who are easily persuaded. Though Moses was concerned that the Israelites would not believe him (4:1; וְהֵן לֹא־יַאֲמִינוּ), following the display of signs (4:30, though Aaron, not Moses, appears to be the one to perform the signs), the Israelites do believe (4:31). As Childs notes, the story seems to proceed with the telling of another event, Moses and Aaron's appearance before Pharaoh,[67] which is linked in the same sequence with וְאַחַר, which begins 5:1.[68]

At 5:1, the narrative slows, giving way to an extended dialogue of the interaction between Moses and Aaron, on the one hand, and Pharaoh on the other. Moses and Aaron speak boldly to Pharaoh, using the characteristic prophetic formula, "Thus says the Lord, the God of Israel," followed by YHWH's demand, "Let my people go, so that they may celebrate a festival to me in the wilderness" (5:1). Perhaps the two leaders of Israel betray their naïvety in this statement,[69] which introduces the form that YHWH's command to Pharaoh will take prior to several of the plagues. In response to this command, Pharaoh asks "Who is the Lord that I should heed him and let Israel go? I do not know the Lord, and [so?] I will not let Israel go" (5:2; מִי יְהוָה אֲשֶׁר אֶשְׁמַע בְּקֹלוֹ לְשַׁלַּח אֶת־יִשְׂרָאֵל לֹא יָדַעְתִּי אֶת־יְהוָה וְגַם אֶת־יִשְׂרָאֵל לֹא אֲשַׁלֵּחַ). Moses and Aaron try again, explaining their request in greater detail and leaving out the name "YHWH," but Pharaoh still refuses.

What exactly does Pharaoh mean by the question, "Who is YHWH?" It could be simply that Pharaoh has never heard of this divine name, and thus

---

67. The Lord tells Moses to go before Pharaoh with the elders of Israel in 3:18, but they do not appear before Pharaoh in Exod 5.
68. Childs, *Book of Exodus*, 104-5.
69. Durham, *Exodus*, 64.

he is not persuaded by a command in this name.[70] Moses and Aaron's choice of "God of the Hebrews" (v. 3) makes sense in light of this explanation. However, more could be going on here. Fretheim suggests that "ironically, Pharaoh gets the question right,"[71] which is only true if the words of the question can be separated from their rhetorical force. For surely Pharaoh is not asking for more information, that is, "Please tell me more about your God YHWH." Pharaoh's opposition toward this God and his people remains intact once YHWH is further identified as the God of the Hebrews.

Surely Exod 5:2 contains a rhetorical question which voices Pharaoh's contempt for (if also his ignorance of) YHWH. The question contrasts sharply with Moses' humble (if in the face of the wrong authority) "Who am I?" in 3:11.[72] In Prov 30:9, the teacher asks for no more than sufficient food, so that satisfaction of being full does not cause him to "deny" (כחשׁ), presumably the Lord, or, in other words, say, "Who is the LORD?" (מִי יְהוָה), the same phrase Pharaoh uses. In Job 21:15, Job similarly suggests that the wicked (רְשָׁעִים, vs. 7) say, "What is the Almighty (מַה־שַׁדַּי) that we should serve him? And what profit do we get if we pray to him?" (cf. Job 22:17). The force of the question is similar to that of the king of Assyria in 2 Kgs 18:35: "Who among all the gods of the countries have delivered their countries out of my hand, that the LORD should deliver Jerusalem out of my hand?" As in these examples, the speaker of the phrase in question shows disrespect toward God and suggests that God does not have the power to act in the way suggested. So also does Pharaoh express his contempt toward YHWH, the God of the Hebrews.[73]

In sum, in Exod 5, Pharaoh admits that he does not know YHWH and responds to YHWH's messengers, Moses and Aaron, with contempt. Instead of receiving the will of God openly, Pharoah tightens the chains on the people the Lord has set out to deliver.

2.1.2. "I [am] YHWH" (Exod 6:2)   At the end of chapter 5, the reader watches as the decree for the same amount of production with fewer resources works its way from Pharaoh through the "taskmasters and foremen"—that is, Hebrew collaborators with Egypt—to the people, and back again, and

---

70. Cassuto, *Book of Exodus*, 66.
71. Terence E. Fretheim, *Exodus* IBC (Louisville: Westminster John Knox, 1991), 86.
72. Sarna, *Exodus*, 27.
73. Pharaoh's lack of understanding of YHWH is a theme that runs throughout the plague narratives. Childs, *Book of Exodus*, 105.

finally to Moses and Aaron (5:6–21). Pressured by the collaborators, Moses doubts his call and blames YHWH for failing to secure his success (5:22–23).

Moses' plea leads YHWH to restate that he will use a great display of power to change the mind of Pharaoh (6:1). Then YHWH gives a response to Moses that further explores the nature of this name by which Moses speaks (6:2): "I [am] YHWH" (אֲנִי יְהוָה). Zimmerli's classic exposition of this phrase is still authoritative.[74] He writes, "The most important element here is the disclosure of Yahweh's personal name, a name containing the full richness and honor of the One naming himself."[75] The formula attests to the fact that only YHWH can make himself known in this way:

> The expression "I am Yahweh" asserts that this truth can only be revealed through Yahweh's own free revelation; it can never be usurped from outside. This distinguishes it in an essential fashion from every other predication of Yahweh. From his works one can recognize that Yahweh is king, that he is the holy judge, indeed, even that he is God. But the revelation that he is Yahweh can be heard from his mouth alone. The name encloses the unassailable mystery of his singularity and uniqueness just as, if we can risk this comparison *ad minus*, a name is a human being's own most personal mystery.[76]

In this lengthy quote, Zimmerli makes two significant points. First, the self-introduction formula indicates an event by which YHWH makes himself known. Further, Exod 6 links the theophanic event with the prophetic vocation. God presents himself first to the prophet, then to Israel and the world through the prophet. YHWH describes his intent to deliver the Israelites (vv. 2–5), then recommissions Moses (vv. 6ff.). The key phrase, אֲנִי יְהוָה occurs throughout the passage: as the introduction (v. 2); as the content of Moses' future speech before the Israelites (v. 6); as part of his speech, in the recognition formula ("You shall know that I am the Lord your God," וִידַעְתֶּם כִּי אֲנִי יְהוָה אֱלֹהֵיכֶם, v. 7); and finally, at the conclusion of YHWH's speech, verifying the promise of land (v. 8). Thus, "the messenger is advised to speak in the style of revelation under the auspices of the formula of self-introduction."[77]

---

74. Walther Zimmerli, *I Am Yahweh*, ed. Walter Brueggemann, trans. Douglas W. Stott (Atlanta: John Knox, 1982).
75. Ibid., 1–2.
76. Ibid., 83.
77. Ibid., 12.

Moses' task is to allow God to speak and reveal himself through Moses. Only YHWH can reveal this name, which expresses the mystery and uniqueness of who God is.

Exodus 6:3 has been a crucial verse for source criticism. Since the rise of source criticism, interpretation of this verse has surrounded whether or not Moses and/or Israel knew the name "YHWH" prior to the time of Moses. The Documentary Hypothesis, in its classic articulation, held that whereas the Yahwist source uses the name consistently prior to the time of Moses (e.g., Gen 4:26), the Elohist and Priestly sources attest to a particular moment in which this name is given to the Israelites, narrated in Exod 3 and 6 respectively. On the other hand, scholars who reject source criticism's division of the text on methodological grounds also reject readings of Exod 3 and 6 as substantially different in meaning from Gen 4:26.[78] Instead, they argue that the Pentateuch as a whole testifies to the fact that Israel knew and used the name "YHWH" since time immemorial. The difference between what was known before and after Exod 3 is not the name itself but the meaning or significance of this previously-used name.[79] Thus, much modern scholarship of a previous generation positioned itself with reference to the following question: did Moses and/or the Israelites already know the name "YHWH" prior to the exodus? The question can be asked in truly historical terms, or in literary terms: that is, does the text ask the reader to imagine that the Israelites did or did not know the name "YHWH" prior to the exodus? Because this question has governed so much recent discussion of Exod 3 and 6, and because two prominent voices in theological interpretation of the Old Testament disagree on how to read these texts in light of this question, I devote considerable space to consideration of their proposals.

---

78. E.g., Jacob, *Exodus*, 65–67; Cassuto, *Book of Exodus*, 77–79. Moberly also lists Christian scholars Keil and Delitzsch, Motyer, Martens, and Kaiser, as well as Jewish scholars Segal and Leibowitz. Moberly, *Old Testament*, 53.

79. Cf. Martin Buber, *Moses* (Oxford; London: East & West Library, 1944), 49ff. Greenberg takes a more moderate position. He notes that, among other names, the patriarchs used "YHWH" in Genesis, but that this name was not considered the proper name of God until the time of Moses. This proper name is "one expressing his essence (of which all the other names were only partial evocations), the one that would make him accessible in his fulness to the call of men." Greenberg, *Understanding Exodus*, 80.

Moberly and Seitz have voiced two different approaches to reading Exod 3 and 6 within the final form of the Pentateuch. Moberly argues that all of the writers of the Pentateuch, particularly those of Gen 4:26, Exod 3:13–15 and 6:2–8, agreed that the Israelites did not know the name prior to the exodus. He attributes occurrences of the name in Genesis to the work of a redactor who, theologically convinced that "the God of Abraham, the God of Isaac, and the God of Jacob" and "YHWH" were two names for the one God, inserted the name. On the other hand, Seitz argues that the Old Testament never explicitly addresses the question of when the Israelites came to know the name "YHWH," though Exod 3 and 6 attest that the meaning of this name was more fully understood in the course of the exodus events.

The textual evidence Moberly gives in support of his reading is twofold. When YHWH introduces himself to Moses (Exod 3:6), the self-introduction given is not by this name but "I am the God of Abraham, the God of Isaac, and the God of Jacob." That the name "YHWH" is not used "allows, and indeed suggests" that Moses would not have recognized it. Indeed, "I [am] YHWH," is the self-introduction in Exod 6:2, indicating that Moses now knows this name.[80] Also, and more importantly, Exod 3 introduces prophecy within the Old Testament. The phrase "has sent me to you" appears in each verse, suggesting that "the concern of the text is with the relationship between the name of God and the sending of Moses to Israel. All three elements (YHWH, Moses, and Israel) need to be held together if the text is to be understood."[81] That is, the name "YHWH" is an integral part of the whole complex of YHWH-Sinai-Moses-Israel, which marks the age of Mosaic Yahwism in contrast to the age of the patriarchs.

Moberly's distinction between Mosaic Yahwism and the religion of the patriarchs is not, on the whole, controversial. Seitz agrees that the understanding of the one God significantly changes between the time of the patriarchs and that of Moses.[82] Moreover, a cluster of characteristically Yahwistic concepts in a characteristically Yahwistic logical relationship does not require that can be maintained without arguing that the Israelites' knowledge, use, or recognition of this name originates within this theological context.

---

80. Moberly, *Old Testament*, 11–12.
81. Ibid., 23.
82. Seitz, "Call of Moses," 161, fn. 18.

However, according to Moberly, this is tantamount to "driving a sharp wedge between a name and its meaning,"[83] which has curious results:

> It means supposing that the patriarchs called God YHWH but that this was essentially meaningless to them, a mere sound without significance (since what they understood about God was represented by El Shaddai). That the writers of either Exodus 3 or Exodus 6 could have supposed, and intended to convey, that the divine name YHWH functioned as a meaningless sound prior to Moses seems to me simply incredible.[84]

Thus Moberly argues that it would be illogical to think that the pentateuchal writers had in mind that the patriarchs used the name "YHWH" without any understanding of its significance. Furthermore, "it is simply not the case that the name is used in Genesis with any difference of meaning from that which it customarily has elsewhere in the Old Testament." Moberly gives the example of Gen 15:7, "I am the LORD who brought you from Ur of the Chaldeans, to give you this land to possess," noting its similarity to Exod 20:2, for example.[85]

Contra Moberly, Seitz argues that "[both Exod 3 and Exod 6] presuppose a long-standing use of the proper name for God," because "the Old Testament never takes up the question of how the name as such first came to be uttered by humanity."[86] In the absence of raising and answering the question, "when did the Israelites come to know God as YHWH," the Old Testament writers simply use the name throughout the history of Israel, from prehistoric days through to Moses and beyond. Furthermore, to Seitz, Exod 6 reveals that the name "YHWH" will not be fully understood until the events of the exodus have taken place:

> The issue is not knowledge of the name *per se* but how God most fully makes himself known as YHWH. "I was not known in respect of my name YHWH" God tells Moses, because this knowledge turns on the events of the exodus, which are as yet unexperienced. The main burden of the unit is revealed in verse 7: "And I will take you for my people, and I will be your God; and you shall know that I am YHWH your God, who has brought you up from the burden of

---

83. Moberly, *Old Testament*, 65.
84. Ibid.
85. Ibid., 66–67.
86. Seitz, "The Call of Moses," 150.

the Egyptians." God has not been truly known as YHWH because this involves the mighty deliverance yet to be accomplished.[87]

After the exodus, the אֲשֶׁר אֶהְיֶה of 3:14a "found its proper content: 'I [am] YHWH your God who brought you out of the land of Egypt' (Exod 20:2)."[88]

In analyzing the disagreement between Seitz and Moberly, I find that neither precisely explains the argument of the other. Moberly's description of scholars who argue for a harmonizing reading does not plainly describe Seitz. Seitz is not arguing that the biblical writers held that the patriarchs used the name "YHWH" without any significance attached to it, so much as that these writers did not entertain a time when the name "YHWH" was not known, even though they do entertain a time when its *meaning* was not known, since its meaning is tied to the exodus. The exodus so changed the Israelites' understanding of the name "YHWH" that it came to be understood as it had never been understood before. To say that the patriarchs pronounced "YHWH" without understanding its meaning would be anachronistic and inaccurate. To the patriarchs, "YHWH" meant *something*, but this meaning was eclipsed by the exodus, which brought about an understanding of the name which came to dominate in the Old Testament. Moberly's insistence on keeping the name and its meaning together seems to ignore the fact that the meaning of a name could develop over time.

On the other hand, Seitz does not seem to have clearly understood Moberly's argument. His challenge, which he claims "might prove very problematic for Moberly's reading," that the text of Exodus does not describe Moses declaring the name to the Israelites for the first time—an event which should be accompanied by "fanfare"[89]—is a moot point since Moberly argued that the question (Exod 3:13) is not to be taken as a description of what will happen when Moses arrives in Egypt, but rather rhetorically. Exodus 3:15 itself, while not "fanfare," is certainly an emphatic declaration. Further, Seitz could clarify his argument against Moberly by addressing whether or not the occurrences of the name "YHWH" in Genesis differ substantially from those of Exodus, and if there are substantial differences, why these are present. Seitz could also address the use of אֵל in proper names, such as בֵּית־אֵל, in

---

87. Ibid., 158.
88. Ibid., 160.
89. Ibid., 155–56.

Genesis. Without addressing the possibility that a redactor included the name in Genesis, Seitz has failed to attend fully to Moberly's argument.

As both scholars observe, part of what is at stake between them is the legacy of source criticism: does the question with which source criticism was so concerned—when did the Israelites come to know the name "YHWH"?— help us understand the passage at hand? It seems that the most important point in understanding both Exod 6:3 and 3:13-15 is that YHWH is doing something new in delivering the Israelites from Egypt and in establishing a covenant with them, and that these unforeseen acts involve a new revelation of the identity of God which is associated with the name "YHWH." This is one of the many ways that Mosaic Yahwism differs from patriarchal religion:[90] the book of Genesis is not concerned with the meaning of the name "YHWH," though this name is used there. On the other hand, Mosaic Yahwism is rather so concerned; the book of Exodus makes clear that the name "YHWH" and its meaning can be known through the events narrated in it.

In summary, throughout Exod 5-6, the name "YHWH" is clearly linked with God's actions towards God's people and with God's faithfulness to the intent he has already declared, including both the promises to Abraham and his descendants, and to Moses.[91] Moses should take heart and have patience; God's will and resolve to act have not changed. Thus, in chapters 5 and 6, Pharaoh takes his stand against YHWH, who reassures Moses of his commission. Moreover, the name "YHWH" is used in reference to God's authority and power, which Pharaoh renounces. The important phrase, "I [am] YHWH," is introduced, as self-introduction and in the recognition formula.

Drawing on this discussion, I raise two questions, which will guide my subsequent discussion. First, if the name "YHWH" suggests the power of God, what kind of power is this? Second, why does YHWH respond to Pharaoh's "I do not know YHWH" by revealing himself to Moses and Israel (6:3-8)? Put differently, to whom does YHWH make himself known in the story, and to what extent is this knowledge received by various characters?[92] Keeping

---

90. Cf. Samuel L. Terrien, *The Elusive Presence: Toward a New Biblical Theology* (Eugene: Wipf & Stock, 2000), 108.

91. Davies, "Divine Name in Exodus," 147.

92. Much research on these chapters in recent decades has attended to the seeming theological problem of YHWH hardening Pharaoh's heart. Is God fabricating a conflict by motivating Pharaoh's opposition? Our discussion will address this question somewhat indirectly, since related concerns of the nature of the power of God

these questions in mind, I turn to the many occurrences of the phrase, "so you will know that I [am] YHWH," and similar phrases in Exod 7–14.

2.1.3. "So you will know that I [am] YHWH" (Exod 7–14)   Rather than "so that they will know me," the phrase is, "so that you will know that I [am] YHWH" (and the like).[93] The narrative emphasizes YHWH's action, not only in the deeds by which YHWH is known to the people, but in the act of their recognition. Indeed, YHWH is the protagonist of the story, the main subject, from calling Moses (ch. 3) straight through to the miracle at the sea (chs. 14–15).

The occurrences of the recognition formula and seemingly parallel statements in Exod 7–14 are as follows:

וְיָדְעוּ מִצְרַיִם כִּי־אֲנִי יְהוָה

The Egyptians shall know that I [am] the Lord... (7:5a).

כֹּה אָמַר יְהוָה בְּזֹאת תֵּדַע כִּי אֲנִי יְהוָה

Thus says the Lord, "By this you shall know that I [am] the Lord" (7:17a).

לְמַעַן תֵּדַע כִּי־אֵין כַּיהוָה אֱלֹהֵינוּ

... so that you may know that there is no one like the Lord our God... (8:6b [8:10b translations]).

לְמַעַן תֵּדַע כִּי אֲנִי יְהוָה בְּקֶרֶב הָאָרֶץ

... that you may know that I the Lord [am] in this land (8:18b [8:22b translations]).

בַּעֲבוּר תֵּדַע כִּי אֵין כָּמֹנִי בְּכָל־הָאָרֶץ

... so that you may know that there is no one like me in all the earth (9:14b).

---

and knowledge of God are more immediately relevant to understanding the name "YHWH" in Exodus. On the theme of the hardening of Pharaoh's heart, see William A. Ford, *God, Pharaoh and Moses: Explaining the Lord's Actions in the Exodus Plagues Narrative* (Milton Keynes; Waynesboro, GA: Paternoster, 2006); Fretheim, *Exodus*, 96–103; David M. Gunn, "The Hardening of Pharaoh's Heart: Plot, Character and Theology in Exodus 1–14," in *Art and Meaning: Rhetoric in Biblical Literature*, ed. David J. A. Clines and Alan J. Hauser, *JSOT* 19 (Sheffield: JSOT, 1982), 72–96; Robert R. Wilson, "The Hardening of Pharaoh's Heart," *CBQ* 41 (1979): 18–36; Childs, *Book of Exodus*, 170–74.

93. Zimmerli, *I Am Yahweh*, 84–85.

וְאוּלָם בַּעֲבוּר זֹאת הֶעֱמַדְתִּיךָ בַּעֲבוּר הַרְאֹתְךָ אֶת־כֹּחִי וּלְמַעַן סַפֵּר שְׁמִי בְּכָל־הָאָרֶץ

But this is why I have let you live: to show you my power, and to make my name resound through all the earth (9:16).

לְמַעַן תֵּדַע כִּי לַיהוָה הָאָרֶץ

... so that you may know that the earth is the Lord's (9:29b).

וִידַעְתֶּם כִּי־אֲנִי יְהוָה

—so that you may know that I [am] the Lord (10:2b).

וּבְכָל־אֱלֹהֵי מִצְרַיִם אֶעֱשֶׂה שְׁפָטִים אֲנִי יְהוָה

... on all the gods of Egypt I will execute judgments: I [am] the Lord (12:12).

וְאִכָּבְדָה בְּפַרְעֹה וּבְכָל־חֵילוֹ וְיָדְעוּ מִצְרַיִם כִּי־אֲנִי יְהוָה

... so that I will gain glory for myself over Pharaoh and all his army; and the Egyptians shall know that I [am] the Lord (14:4).

וְיָדְעוּ מִצְרַיִם כִּי־אֲנִי יְהוָה בְּהִכָּבְדִי בְּפַרְעֹה בְּרִכְבּוֹ וּבְפָרָשָׁיו

And the Egyptians shall know that I [am] the Lord, when I have gained glory for myself over Pharaoh, his chariots, and his chariot drivers (14:18).

Regarding this list, several observations can be made:

In every instance, YHWH speaks to Moses directly, even when the statement of recognition is intended for Pharaoh and/or the Egyptians. Though Pharaoh has challenged the authority of YHWH (5:2), YHWH only speaks to Moses. This perhaps emphasizes both Moses' role as prophet—primarily speaking to kings—as well as Pharaoh's true position, which is significantly removed from God. Pharaoh does not recognize the power of the one whom Moses represents.

The occurrence in 7:17 unusually follows the prophetic formula, כֹּה אָמַר יְהוָה. In this verse, YHWH declares to Moses the purpose of the first plague (blood). The message to be relayed to Pharaoh is, "Thus says the Lord, 'By this you shall know that I am the Lord.'" In these chapters, the prophetic phrase, "Thus says the Lord," is not typically followed by the self-introduction formula, but rather "let my people go so that they may worship me" (as begins the second, fourth, fifth, seventh and eighth plagues, or every plague that is preceded by a warning, with the exception of the final plague; 7:25,

8:16[20], 9:1, 9:13, 10:3).[94] For Pharaoh to set free the Israelites requires that Pharaoh know YHWH, and vice versa.

The recognition formula appears as part of the warning that Moses is to give Pharaoh prior to several of the plagues (7:5; 8:18[22]; 9:14, 16). However, in two cases (8:6[10]; 9:29), the formula is associated with the taking away of the plague. Similarly, the formula appears in the context of YHWH describing his restraint in 9:14–16. In his careful reading of the latter passage, Ford emphasizes YHWH's restraint as indicative of the kind of patient power that he exemplifies. This power differs significantly from the power of domination that Pharaoh wields, and likewise, Pharaoh does not understand it, but rather abuses YHWH's forbearance by ignoring him.[95] Ford's point can be overstated. For the text seems to suggest nothing less balanced than that the Lord both brings about the plagues and causes their ceasing. Pharaoh and the Egyptians shall know that he is YHWH when the plagues are brought forth (7:5; 9:14, 16), and Pharaoh will also be shown this when the frogs and hail cease (8:6[10]; 9:29).[96]

In two cases the recognition formula is associated with YHWH attaining "glory" (14:4, 18). The Hebrew root, כבד, is important in Exodus, where it appears (with חזק and קשה) as one of three words denoting the hardness of Pharaoh's heart. Differently, in Exod 33:18, Moses asks YHWH to

---

94. The ten plagues can be grouped in three series of three plagues each, followed by the final, culminating plague of the firstborn. Each group of three plagues begins with a forewarning, to be given before Pharaoh "in the morning" (בַּבֹּקֶר) at which time Moses or Aaron is to stand (נצב) before Pharaoh. The second plague in each group begins with YHWH telling the agent to "come/go to Pharaoh" (בֹּא אֶל־פַּרְעֹה; that is, into the palace) and present him with a warning. The third plague in each group of three is given without warning and without instruction to the agent. The final plague is set apart in both content and form. Jože Krašovec, "Unifying Themes in Ex 7,8–11,10," in *Pentateuchal and Deuteronomistic Studies*, ed. C. Brekelmans and J. Lust (Leuven: Leuven University, 1990), 47–66; Sarna, *Exodus*, 38; Nahum M. Sarna, *Exploring Exodus: The Origins of Biblical Israel* (New York: Schocken Books, 1986), 76; contra Dennis J. McCarthy, "Moses' Dealings with Pharaoh: Exod 7:8–10:27," *CBQ* 27, no. 4 (1965): 336–47; Dennis J. McCarthy, "Plagues and Sea of Reeds: Exodus 5–14," *JBL* 85, no. 2 (1966): 137–58.

95. Ford, God, *Pharaoh and Moses*, 73.

96. That the recognition formula does not occur in the same place in the recounting of each plague is not particularly surprising, given that the plague narratives follow a loose literary structure.

see "your glory" (כְּבֹדֶךָ). The book ends with a beautiful and dramatic description of the glory of YHWH filling the tabernacle (40:34–35). In this case, "gaining glory" or "being glorified" (*nipʿal*) appears to refer to the elevation of stature of YHWH in the eyes of those who see that YHWH is mightier than Pharaoh and the Egyptian warriors. YHWH's acts at the sea involve YHWH's reputation. These constructions are quite similar to that of 9:16, where "my name" (שְׁמִי) suggests YHWH's reputation before the nations.

At several points, the reader expects to see "so that you will know that I [am] YHWH," but instead finds something else. In 8:18b[22b] and 9:29b what YHWH intends for the people to recognize is, respectively, "that I the Lord am in this land" and "that the earth is the Lord's." Both statements challenge Pharaoh's sovereignty in his own territory. In the first case, YHWH's presence in the land is associated with YHWH's distinction between his own people and Pharaoh's people; God's people, in Goshen, will be spared from the insects (8:18–19[22–23]). In the second case, Pharaoh (momentarily) humbles himself, confessing his own guilt (9:27; וַיֹּאמֶר אֲלֵהֶם חָטָאתִי הַפָּעַם) and YHWH's righteousness (יְהוָה הַצַּדִּיק). Pharaoh then pleads to Moses to end the hail, and Moses foresees that it will cease, so that "you will know that the earth is the Lord's" (9:28–29). Clearly Pharaoh has lost control, and his temporary recognition of YHWH's power is affirmed when the hail ceases. YHWH's presence in and possession of the land benefits those YHWH chooses and demonstrates that YHWH's power exceeds any earthly power, even Pharaoh's.

Comparative constructions occur in Exod 8:6b[10b] and 9:14b: there is no one like YHWH, either on earth or in heaven. How much distinction should be made between the more frequent recognition formula and this one? Is knowing YHWH tantamount to knowing YHWH's incomparability? Perhaps. The incomparability statement is here specifically coupled with Moses' intercession for Pharaoh. There is none like YHWH because only YHWH grants mercy to all who ask, even those who have heretofore rejected him.[97] Further, comparison-language appears again in the seventh plague, though here not in reference to YHWH but to the destruction of the plague:

> There was hail with fire flashing continually in the midst of it, such heavy hail *as had never fallen in all the land of Egypt since it*

---

97. On incomparabilty constructions, see Labuschagne, *Incomparability of Yahweh*, passim.

> *became a nation.* The hail struck down everything that was in the open field throughout all the land of Egypt, both human and animal; the hail also struck down all the plants of the field, and shattered every tree in the field (Exod 9:24-25).

Similarly, the locusts are "something that neither your parents nor your grandparents have seen, from the day they came on earth to this day" (Exod 10:6). The incomparability of the plagues manifests the incomparability of the one who sends them.

Points 5a and 5b (above) supply background for the declaration in 12:12, in which the Lord says, "For I will pass through the land of Egypt that night, and I will strike down every firstborn in the land of Egypt, both human beings and animals; on all the gods of Egypt I will execute judgments: I [am] the Lord." In the final plague, YHWH demonstrates jurisdiction over Egypt, and thus sovereignty over Egypt's gods.[98] The narrative does not elsewhere explicitly refer to Egyptian deities, so the meaning of this reference is uncertain. Perhaps, as Sarna has argued, some of the plagues were specifically directed against Egypt's gods (e.g., the Nile river god Hapi, the frog-headed goddess Heqt).[99] Rendtorff suggests that Pharaoh, in his audacious rejection of YHWH, makes himself "an Anti-God," so that "in him at the same time the 'gods of Egypt' stand against the one God."[100] Either way, here the narrative makes explicit what is only implicit elsewhere: the plagues are demonstrations of YHWH's power that prove him superior to other so-called gods, and moreover, the final plague is an act of judgment against these gods.

Throughout the narrative, creation is the instrument of YHWH's power. Sarna compares the literary structures of Exod 7-14 with Gen 1 and Job 1-2 in the received form of the text.[101] In these examples and in Exod 7-14, "The

---

98. Cf. Num 33:4 and Jer 46:25.

99. Sarna, *Exodus*, 39-40.

100. Rolf Rendtorff, *The Canonical Hebrew Bible: A Theology of the Old Testament*, trans. David E. Orton (Leiderdorp: Deo, 2005), 45.

101. Cf. Z. Zevit, "The Priestly Redaction and Interpretation of the Plague Narrative in Exodus," *JQR* 66, no. 4 (1976): 193-211. Zevit views the text diachronically and shows how the Priestly redactor edited and arranged literary material from J, E, and P with this theological conviction in mind.

In Gen 1, YHWH creates in eight pronouncements on six days, with two pronouncements occurring on the third and sixth days. The seventh day pertains only to God. Within each set of three days, creation occurs first in heaven, then in earthly

meaning and function of the structural symmetry is always to emphasize that what has occurred is the vindication of God's active presence in the life of the world."[102] YHWH is Lord of creation, and literary formulas punctuate the design of the text. Differently, Fretheim views the plagues as active "signs" or "portents" (4:17, 21; 7:3, 9; 8:17[8:23]; 10:1-2; and 11:9-10),[103] participating in the destructive consequences of Pharoah's breach of the moral order inherent in creation. God is active in these events "in the interplay of Pharoah's sin and its consequences," giving "Pharaoh up to reap the 'natural' consequences of his anti-creation behaviors."[104] The plagues cannot be described as natural phenomena, because they are not part of the normal ebbs and flows of creation. Rather, "the plagues are hypernatural at various levels—timing, scope, and intensity."[105] Creation has gone berserk.

The contrast between Fretheim's interpretation and Sarna's is acute. For Sarna, the plagues could be described in natural terms, but God uses these natural occurrences to achieve his historical will. For Fretheim, the plagues are hypernatural signs of disaster brought about by trespassing the moral order that God instilled in creation. Though Fretheim has observed some important links in the text between the language of creation and that of plagues, as well as the language of the plagues and what happens at the Sea of Reeds (chs. 14-15), his interpretation is hard-pressed to deal with some of the most basic aspects of the narrative. Pharaoh's sin is drawn to the foreground, while knowledge of YHWH and the redemption of Israel are placed in the background. This does not seem true to the text, in which YHWH's first statement of intent begins with the declaration that he has heard the cries of the Israelites (3:7), and in which Moses' (YHWH's) command before Pharaoh is continually not only "Let my people go," but "Let

---

water, and then on dry land. "Further, the creations of the first three days become the resource to be utilized by the corresponding creature in the second group." Job's catastrophes occur in three groups of two difficulties. In all three groups, the first difficulty deals with livestock and the second, with humans. "The cause of each series is alternately human and divine, and the whole culminates in a climactic, divinely wrought, seventh calamity." Sarna, *Exploring Exodus*, 77-78.

102. Ibid., 78.

103. Terence Fretheim, "The Plagues as Ecological Signs of Historical Disaster," *JBL* (1991): 385-96.

104. Fretheim, *Exodus*, 395.

105. Ibid., 393.

my people go *that they may serve me.*" Pharaoh's "moral order" is indeed "bankrupt,"[106] leading to disastrous consequences, but in the narrative, this is consistently tied to Pharaoh's rejection of YHWH's authority, faithfulness to the promises made to the ancestors, and deliverance of Israel. Thus deed-consequence is not the best conceptual lens for viewing this narrative.[107]

Which is not to say that YHWH does not desire a response from Pharaoh. Most certainly the prophetic language, "Thus says the Lord: 'Let my people go, so that they may worship me,'" suggests that Pharaoh needs to act in response to this demand of YHWH. Yet that response will not be *simply* a policy change regarding state slavery,[108] but true recognition of YHWH as Lord and all of the implications of that recognition. Moreover, the narrative increasingly portrays Pharaoh's resistance as illogical, even in comparison to that of the other Egyptians. Pharaoh's first indication of lessening his stubbornness comes in 8:4[8], after the second plague. Pharaoh suggests that he will let the Israelites go if Moses and Aaron successfully implore God on his behalf to end the plague. YHWH's servants do as Pharaoh requests, but upon the disappearance of the frogs, Pharaoh changes his mind and becomes stubborn once more (8:11[15]). In 9:27, he seems to relent again, saying, "This time I have sinned; the Lord is in the right, and I and my people are in the wrong." Yet, once the hail ceases, the Egyptian king is as obdurate as ever. Some commentators explain these reversals as indicative, not of repentance, but of fear of punishment.[109] Moses suggests "that Pharaoh's confession of guilt is just empty words;"[110] Pharaoh does not yet "fear YHWH" (9:30), though some of his officials do (and so save their property, 9:20). Gunn argues that Moses understands that Pharaoh's confession is less than complete because Moses has privileged information: YHWH has hardened Pharaoh's heart,

> so there is no need to doubt the sincerity of Pharaoh's confession. What is being demonstrated is that he is now so totally under Yah-

---

106. Ibid., 394.

107. Cf. Donald E. Gowan, *Theology in Exodus: Biblical Theology in the Form of a Commentary* (Louisville: Westminster John Knox, 1994), 140.

108. Levenson well describes Torah as against state slavery, in light of the Exodus, rather than all slavery. Jon D. Levenson, "Exodus and Liberation" *HBT* 13, no. 1 (1991): 134–74.

109. Cf. Krašovec, "Unifying Themes in Ex 7,8–11,10," 59; Cassuto, *Book of Exodus*, 121.

110. Sarna, *Exodus*, 47.

weh's control that he is unable to sustain any consistency in his responses. His initial responses show him, like those around about, growing in awareness of the true state of affairs. His subsequent turn-abouts are irrational by comparison. He is like a schizophrenic.[111]

After the next plague, members of Pharaoh's court lose patience with him; the Hebrew slaves are not worth the ruin of Egypt (10:7). In this light, Pharaoh's attempt at negotiation does not seem to be an improvement, but only a further display of ridiculous stubbornness (10:24ff.).[112] Gunn argues that, because Egyptian king has elevated himself over YHWH, so YHWH manipulates him to make a point about God's sovereignty:[113]

> [Yahweh] can turn the wisdom of the king to folly, to a ruinous recalcitrance which, moreover, leaves the king starkly isolated in his folly. It is Yahweh who decides <u>when</u> Pharaoh shall know that he, Yahweh, is truly God. It is Yahweh who prompts refusal so that the signs are heaped up as "punishment." In the theme of mastery, the two functions of hardening noted by Childs—to prevent the signs from revealing knowledge of God, and to multiply the signs as judgment—are subsumed. Yahweh can and does manipulate Pharaoh. Yahweh is truly master.[114]

As Gunn aptly recognizes, Exod 3–15 concerns the sovereignty of God, whose power is not in a zero-sum relationship with human power. God's power does not end where human freedom begins, but rather, human freedom begins in service to YHWH. Pharaoh's rejection of YHWH's authority makes him a puppet; Moses' following the call of God, perhaps even against his will (4:13ff.), makes him a true leader. When the Israelites lose heart again at the edge of the Reed Sea, Moses (not Aaron, who has receded into the background), declares, "Do not be afraid, stand firm, and see the deliverance that the Lord will accomplish for you today; for the Egyptians whom you see today you shall never see again. The Lord will fight for you, and you have only to keep still" (14:13-14). Though verse 15 may suggest that an inquiry from Moses to YHWH is missing in the final form of the text, the narrative as it stands indicates that Moses acts without consulting YHWH. Certainly this fits

---

111. Gunn, "*Hardening of Pharaoh's Heart*," 77–78.
112. Ibid., 78.
113. Ibid., 83.
114. Ibid., 80.

the later chapters' portrayal of Moses as an audacious disputer with YHWH. By obeying his call as a servant of YHWH, Moses has become truly free, truly independent. In this way, he remains a model of faith for Israel, leading them into the wilderness, as they receive the law and consider their lives in relation to keeping the covenant.

Does God ever truly make known to Pharaoh "that I [am] YHWH"? YHWH reveals himself, through Pharaoh, as sovereign Lord of creation and God of Israel. The Egyptian magicians recognize YHWH's handiwork (8:15[19]); some of Pharaoh's officials fear YHWH (9:20); and the Egyptian army recognizes who their opponent is, and they flee (14:25), though it is too late to save themselves (14:27). Like Pharaoh, the Egyptians see that YHWH is the powerful God of Israel, ruler of creation, and yet they continue to be the object of YHWH's magnificent display of power. They perceive the power of God but they do nothing to participate in YHWH's deliverance of Israel, and so they are overcome. On the other hand, Israel sees the power of God triumphing over the Egyptians, and Israel knows and fears YHWH (14:31). Only Israel's knowledge of YHWH leads to deliverance and obedience. Knowledge of YHWH is finally dependent upon God's freedom to reveal as God chooses.

2.1.4. "YHWH is a warrior" (Exod 15:3) Given the increasing authority of Moses and Israel's knowledge and fear of YHWH, it is unwise to follow Eslinger in distrusting the voice of Moses and the people in chapter 15.[115] Rather, this text provides a hymn that summarizes lyrically what has occurred in the previous chapter.[116] Though the poem is more truly a hymn than a victory song,[117] here the writer expresses that it is the triumph of YHWH over Israel's (and thus the YHWH's) enemies that presents the occasion for his praise.

---

115. Lyle Eslinger, "Freedom or Knowledge? Perspective and Purpose in the Exodus Narrative (Exodus 1–15)," *JSOT* 16, no. 52 (1991): 43–60.

116. This hymn of praise to YHWH is similar to those of the Psalter both in form and content. Childs writes, "Yahweh is praised for his greatness and strength (v. 6) which is then joined to his attribute of holiness (v. 13; cf. Ps 89:14, 15). His specific deeds of redemption are without comparison (v. 11; cf. Pss 77:14; 95:3). Above all, the display of divine power is to create for himself a people (v. 13; Ps 77:16) before the astonished eyes of the nations (v. 14; Ps 98:2) whose gods are proven to be worthless before the might of Yahweh (Ps 96:5). Finally, he rules the world as king from his holy abode (v. 18; Pss 93:1ff.; 96:7ff.)" Childs, *Book of Exodus*, 250.

117. Ibid.

As the Egyptian army noted YHWH's fighting for Israel and fled, so here (15:3) Israel identifies this God who has fought for them: "The Lord is a warrior; the Lord is his name" (יְהוָה אִישׁ מִלְחָמָה יְהוָה שְׁמוֹ). The difference between this statement and that of 14:31 is one of perspective. Whereas in 14:31, the narrator recounts Israel's turn to faith, here the reader is invited to praise through Israel's own perspective. YHWH is lauded as the one who acted in history on behalf of Israel, right before their eyes, in a display of terrific power, using creation as his instrument. The song gives voice to the Israelites' faith in YHWH, their deliverer, once they have experienced deliverance. The particle אָז (v. 1a) indicates that the Israelites' singing immediately follows the events in Exod 14.[118]

"The Lord is a warrior." On the one hand, the violence of this ancient metaphor should not be overemphasized, for the song does not dwell on the gory details of YHWH's triumph, but rather Israel's concrete and immediate experience of deliverance. On the other hand, the divine warrior motif cannot simply be ignored, for it grounds the Old Testament understanding of war and significant theological concepts such as divine kingship (cf. Exod 15:18) and the imperative to trust YHWH rather than fear one's enemies.[119] One must acknowledge that central to YHWH's identity is the fact that the one God fights for Israel. At the same time, as we will see, YHWH's anger is not only aroused against Israel's enemies but, at times, against Israel. Thus Israel avoids ideology with its confession of God as its divine warrior, for this fact is subject to YHWH's freedom to act according to divine justice and holiness.[120]

Still, the reader ought not to focus too much on the militaristic imagery in this verse, for several reasons. First, this is not a case of Israel's "holy war," since they do not fight, at all, and neither do they have weapons. One could imagine Israel running *away* from the Egyptian army, rather than towards them; they are not trying to engage battle, but merely escape. Second, we have seen throughout the plague narratives that YHWH's power cannot be reduced to the ways we typically understand cause-and-effect or human

---

118. See Dozeman, *Exodus*, 327.
119. Patrick D. Miller, Jr., "God the Warrior: A Problem in Biblical Interpretation and Apologetics," *Int* 19 (1965): 44–46; Millard Lind, *Yahweh is a Warrior* (Scottdale, PA: Herald, 1980), passim.
120. See Patrick D. Miller, Jr., *The Divine Warrior in Early Israel* (Cambridge, MA: Harvard University, 1973), 173–74.

power. If YHWH is a "man of war," then this phrase is meant as a metaphor to describe what has already occurred in Exod 14. The strong anthropomorphism seems to be simply restating in more vivid, poetic language what has already been described. What it means for YHWH to be a "man of war" (Exod 15:3) is necessarily related to the narrative context surrounding the verse.[121] What can be observed in 15:3 is that the central act of the exodus—the crossing of the sea—manifests the identity of YHWH.

Commentators typically claim that the Septuagint translation of Exod 15:3, κύριος συντρίβων πολέμους, κύριος ὄνομα αὐτῷ, "The Lord, when he shatters wars, the Lord is his name" (NETS) reveals embarrassment at the warrior imagery and seeks to replace it with an image of YHWH as the one who brings wars to an end.[122] However, if this was the translator's intention, he was unsuccessful, given that the context of the verse clearly shows YHWH as victor in battle. As Perkins argues, this fits the meaning of the same terminology in Jdt 9:7 and 16:2.[123] The action of YHWH is more specifically described: "for he has triumphed gloriously; horse and rider he has thrown into the sea," כִּי־גָאֹה גָּאָה סוּס וְרֹכְבוֹ רָמָה בַיָּם; (ἐνδόξως γὰρ δεδόξασται, ἵππον καὶ ἀναβάτην ἔρριψεν εἰς θάλασσαν, LXX; v. 1) and "Pharoah's chariots and his army he cast into the sea" מַרְכְּבֹת פַּרְעֹה וְחֵילוֹ יָרָה בַיָּם (ἅρματα Φαραω καὶ τὴν δύναμιν αὐτοῦ ἔρριψεν εἰς θάλασσαν, LXX; v. 4). Throwing the Egyptian army into the sea is perhaps an act of war, and certainly a final one. Regardless the reasoning behind the Septuagint translation, YHWH is the one who ends the battle with the Egyptians.

In this section, I have argued that Pharaoh's rejection of YHWH's authority leads into the plague cycle, in which the divine self-introduction and recognition formulas, together with their parallels, demonstrate that YHWH

---

121. Hamori argues that אִישׁ is meant metaphorically in Exod 15:3, and therefore, that this text differs significantly from Gen 18 and 32, theophany texts in which God appears in the form of a man. Esther J. Hamori, *"When Gods were Men": The Embodied God in Biblical and Near Eastern Literature* BZAW 384 (Berlin; New York: de Gruyter, 2008), 3.

122. See Dozeman, *Exodus*, 322; Durham, *Exodus*, 206. Cf. den Hertog's claim that the translator's goal was to avoid association between YHWH and other known warrior gods; *Other Face*, 190. Houtman more cautiously writes that "LXX has blunted the bold expression through its rendering." Houtman, *Exodus vol. 2*, 280.

123. Larry Perkins, "'The Lord is a Warrior'—'The Lord Who Shatters Wars': Exod 15:3 and Jdt 9:7; 16:2," *BIOSCS* 40 (2007): 121–38.

uses the plagues for the purpose of self-revelation. The more disastrous the plagues become, the more YHWH's power, and Pharaoh's weakness and folly, become apparent. YHWH sends the plagues and causes them to cease; YHWH hardens Pharaoh's heart and protects his chosen people, who have no reason to be afraid. In this way, Israel's story of deliverance prepares the reader for the covenant, for Israel's true freedom is found in service to YHWH.

Throughout Exod 5–15, the name "YHWH" is associated with God's self-revelation in the declaration, אֲנִי יְהוָה "I [am] YHWH," and in the recognition statement, לְמַעַן תֵּדַע כִּי אֲנִי יְהוָה "so that you will know that I [am] YHWH," and similar phrases. Through speech and action, God reveals himself as YHWH. Knowing that God is YHWH involves receiving this revelation of God's identity and responding in accordance with his will and action. Through YHWH's deeds, people are given opportunity to know him, yet God is not reducible to these deeds. YHWH remains free and powerful. The forces of nature and the political leaders of the world are—willingly or unwillingly—subject to YHWH, who alone is able to make himself known.

2.2. Decalogue (Exod 20)

The first three commandments of the Decalogue are interrelated and concern right human living in light of the identity and nature of God as YHWH. The self-introduction formula occurs again in Exod 20:2, in the introduction to the Decalogue: "I am the Lord your God who brought you out. . ." This statement acts as a prologue for all of what follows.[124] The phrase has occurred earlier in Exodus in narrative context, but what difference does this genre—law—make for understanding the phrase? God reveals himself in covenant with Israel, and "in the act of creating a people for himself history and law are not antagonistic, but different sides of the one act of divine self-manifestation."[125] The revelatory act of YHWH's self-declaration not only generates YHWH's relationship with Israel, which includes the story of Israel's life as well as the community guidelines which make this life possible (and, one might add, the resources of its liturgy, hymns and poetry). Thus, the Decalogue can be viewed as articulating the implications of the revelation of the divine name. The first section (20:3–12) describes the

---

124. The phrase is an independent clause, not dependent on verse 3. Zimmerli, *I Am Yahweh*, 1–2; cf. Childs, *Book of Exodus*, 386; Dozeman, *Exodus*, 465.

125. Childs, *Book of Exodus*, 402.

implications of the name for divine-human relationship, and the second (20:13–17), the implications for the community of God's people.¹²⁶

The first commandment (v. 3) declares that YHWH refuses to be worshipped alongside other gods. Viewing the Decalogue in the context of the Old Testament as a whole, Childs presents the example of Elijah at Mount Carmel in 1 Kgs 18. The issue was not that the Israelites wanted to stop worshipping YHWH and worship Baal instead, but that they believed they could worship both. Elijah forces the people to choose between the two (v. 21).¹²⁷

The second commandment prohibits the worship of images, "for I the LORD your God am a jealous God" (כִּי אָנֹכִי יְהוָה אֱלֹהֶיךָ אֵל קַנָּא; vv. 4–5).¹²⁸ Zimmerli states that the content of this statement is interchangeable with that of the Decalogue's prologue, and that verse 5 reflects back on the first commandment.¹²⁹ Yet, this verse has a slightly different nuance than 20:2. The "(possibly imagined) infringement of someone's rights or injury to the subject's honor" causes קנא, which is typically translated "jealousy."¹³⁰ Though it is common for commentators to offer the relationship between one and one's spouse as the primary metaphor for understanding this term (human jealousy, Prov 6:34; Num 5; divine, Ezek 16:38, 42; 23:25),¹³¹ to what degree divine "jealousy" can be likened to human jealousy is debatable. The issue is not simply one of attributing human characteristics, or even human passions or emotions, to God, but the nature and direction of the passion, as it were.¹³² YHWH's jealousy is not directed against other rival gods, but against Israel.¹³³ As Brongers writes, "es sind nicht die fremden Götter, die Israel abtrünnig gemacht haben, Israel hat selbst die Initiative ergriffen. *Sie* ist ihren Buhlen nachgelaufen, nicht die Abgötter Israel!"¹³⁴ Further, YHWH's "jeal-

---

126. Dozeman, *Commentary on Exodus*, 479.

127. Brevard S. Childs, *Old Testament Theology in a Canonical Context* (London: SCM, 1985), 65.

128. An extension of the first commandment according to an alternative way of numbering the commandments (in Roman Catholic teaching, for example).

129. Zimmerli, *I Am Yahweh*, 25–26. Cf. Childs, *Old Testament Theology*, 65–66.

130. *NIDOTTE*, "קנא."

131. George A. F. Knight, *Theology as Narration: A Commentary on the Book of Exodus* (Edinburgh: Handsel, 1976), 136; Gowan, *Theology in Exodus*, 181–82; Dozeman, *Commentary on Exodus*, 485–86.

132. *TDOT*, "קנא."

133. *NIDOTTE*, "קנא."

134. H. A. Brongers, "Der Eifer des Herrn Zebaoth," *VT* 13, no. 3 (1963): 283–84.

ousy" is not petty or unrighteous, because "God has every right to make an absolute claim upon those he has created."[135] Renaud emphasizes the covenantal context of YHWH's jealousy and writes, "loin de rabaisser la divinité, la jalousie divine qui exprime cette volonté de communion de Dieu avec l'homme, de Yahvé avec son peuple, fait prendre conscience, dans cette expérience même, des exigences sélectives et purificatrices de sa Sainteté."[136] Within the covenant, YHWH brings Israel into an exclusive relationship appropriate to YHWH's holiness.

In verses 5a–6, in contrast to the similar formula in Exod 34:14, God's judgment is described prior to God's mercy, which may emphasize the former. However, God's faithfulness, which extends to the thousandth generation, lasts longer than God's judgment, which extends only to the third or fourth generation.[137] The formula presents a contrast between "those who reject me," whose children will be punished, and "those who love me and keep my commandments," to whose family God will extend faithfulness for a thousand generations.

Childs argues that nowhere in Exodus is an explicit reason for the prohibition of images given, and that von Rad and Zimmerli's attempts at articulating reasons are both "somewhat speculative" and unconvincing.[138] Yet, I would suggest that YHWH's fundamental immateriality and freedom are continually communicated in Exodus. "I am who I am" remains hidden even as God is revealed, and thus the name only functions in a qualified sense. In Exod 32–34, the Israelites' act of making a golden calf is strongly condemned, not because this involves the worshipping of a god other than YHWH, but because the Israelites believe they can produce their own means of relating to YHWH (apart from Moses). Furthermore, YHWH remains at least partially hidden even from Moses (Exod 33:18-23). Childs acknowledges the canonical importance of Exod 32, and recognizes other passages that raise similar issues (Jdg 17; 1 Kgs 12; Dan 3). Childs continues, claiming,

---

135. Gowan, *Theology in Exodus*, 181.
136. Bernard Renaud, *Je suis un Dieu jaloux: évolution sémantique et signification théologique de* qine'ah (Paris: Éditions du Cerf, 1963), 152.
137. Gowan suggests that the length of judgment is based on how many generations could be living at one time. Sin causes consequences for one's entire community, especially one's family, so it would make sense that one's living relatives would bear the consequences of one's sin. Gowan, *Theology in Exodus*, 237-38.
138. Childs, *Old Testament Theology*, 66-67.

> In spite of different theological emphases, the issue at stake turns on guarding the purity of God's self-revelation lest Israel confuse its own image with that of God's. In the case of this commandment, the narrative material within the Old Testament did not move in the direction of expounding the negative commandment in such a way as to bring out the positive dimensions of the imperative, but rather continued to probe the full implications of this threat to the divine nature.[139]

The line between "explicit reason" and "positive dimension of the imperative," on the one hand, and "the full implications of this threat to the divine nature," on the other, seems rather thin. Surely the more important point is that the prohibition of images fits squarely with the characteristics of divine nature as suggested in both narrative and law in Exodus.

The third commandment (v. 7) contains a prohibition directly involving the divine name: "You shall not make wrongful use of the name of the Lord your God" (לֹא תִשָּׂא אֶת־שֵׁם־יְהוָה אֱלֹהֶיךָ לַשָּׁוְא), "for the Lord will not acquit anyone who misuses his name." While swearing falsely by the name of God is prohibited elsewhere (Lev 19:12 and Deut 6:13), Exod 20 suggests broader application than a legal context.[140] YHWH's name is to be honored and used in praise and prayer. The prohibition could be against any number of misuses of the divine name. Dozeman suggests that "the magical use of power for evil purposes" could be in view;[141] and Cassuto indicates a warning against "any worthless practice, in connection with which the gentiles mention the names of their gods, such as incantation, sorcery, divination, and like."[142] Knight identifies the wrong in question as using the power of the name "for selfish ends."[143] Childs reflects, "As a source of truth [God] cannot be linked to falsehood or deception. Nor can God's freedom be infringed by human manipulation. The third commandment is radically theocentric in focus, and thus differs from the concerns of the eighth commandment, which prohibits the injuring of another human being by means of false witness."[144] The third commandment demands that the name "YHWH" be treated in accordance

---

139. Ibid., 65–66.
140. Ibid., 68.
141. Dozeman, *Commentary on Exodus*, 487.
142. Cassuto, *Book of Exodus*, 243–44.
143. Knight, *Theology as Narration*, 137.
144. Childs, *Old Testament Theology*, 68.

with YHWH's character, as the one who is most true and free, thwarting human attempts at control, manipulation, and deception.

Thus in Exod 20:5-7, the name "YHWH" is associated with the rights that YHWH exercises: to be the only, imageless God that Israel worships; to have his name (and thus himself) treated with due reverence. Likewise, elsewhere in this section (Exod 20-23), the divine name is specifically associated with God's judgment; YHWH is Israel's God but remains free to judge this nation. The text of 20:7 prohibits worthless or false use of the name "YHWH" and states that those who do this will not go without punishment (נקה, *pi'el*). YHWH is the imageless God whose claim on Israel is exclusive, whose name must be treated with due reverence, and whose justice will have devastating consequences. YHWH has delivered Israel (chs. 14-15) will provide for and protect her (chs. 15-16), but the people must follow certain guidelines in order to maintain this privileged life with YHWH.

2.3. Threatening the Presence of God (Exod 32-34)

Exodus 33:19 and 34:6-7 bear strong similarity to 3:13-15 in different ways, and these texts will be the primary focus of the discussion in this section. However, beginning with a brief discussion of the prescriptions for the tabernacle in Exod 25-31, I address some of the interpretive issues in the larger narrative in order to explain what is at stake in these verses in chapters 33 and 34.

2.3.1. Setting the scene: the tent of meeting (Exod 25-31) In chapters 25-31, YHWH gives Moses the prescriptions for building the tabernacle and for worship surrounding it. The purpose of the tent of meeting (אֹהֶל־מוֹעֵד) is clear from its title: this is where God will meet with the Israelites (29:42a-43). Note that YHWH is not here said to dwell in the tabernacle; the dynamic term "meet" (יעד, *nip'al*) is used. Subject to divine will and freedom, God will descend to meet with the Israelites at particular times. Further (v. 45), YHWH declares that he will abide, not in the tabernacle specifically, but "among the Israelites" (וְשָׁכַנְתִּי בְּתוֹךְ בְּנֵי יִשְׂרָאֵל). The verbal root שכן, from which "tabernacle" (מִשְׁכָּן) derives, does not have the same locational significance as, e.g., ישׁב; it may suggest a more nomadic way of dwelling.[145] Thus the narrative resists the suggestion that YHWH's presence can be presumed to be locally present as though not present elsewhere. YHWH abides in the tabernacle for the purpose of Israel's worship, maintains the freedom of dynamic presence,

---

145. Sarna, *Exodus*, 158; HALOT, "שכן."

and resists objectification.

The tent of meeting will be sanctified by "my glory," the כְּבוֹד יְהוָה. This phrase is a technical term for the presence of YHWH, found especially in texts generally referred to as P and in Ezekiel.¹⁴⁶ In Exod 29:43, the phrase refers to the means by which YHWH will sanctify the tent of meeting, and in 40:34, the glory fills the tent at the same time as a cloud descends to cover it. In 16:7, Moses tells the Israelites that they will see the כְּבוֹד יְהוָה; later, they do see it, in a cloud (v. 10). In 24:17, Moses and the Israelites see it in the form of a "consuming fire" (כְּאֵשׁ אֹכֶלֶת). These images evoke the tension that is at the heart of the theological mystery of YHWH's care and provision (cloud) as well as his consuming holiness (fire).

YHWH communicates that though Moses is to prepare the rituals for the sanctification of the tent, altar, and priests, God will sanctify them (Exod 29:44).¹⁴⁷ Further, YHWH's abiding with the Israelites is identified with being their God (cf. 6:7). All of this serves the purpose that the Israelites will know YHWH. The section ends with the recognition formula and self-declaration:

וְיָדְעוּ כִּי אֲנִי יְהוָה אֱלֹהֵיהֶם אֲשֶׁר הוֹצֵאתִי אֹתָם מֵאֶרֶץ מִצְרַיִם לְשָׁכְנִי בְתוֹכָם אֲנִי יְהוָה אֱלֹהֵיהֶם

> And they shall know that I am the Lord their God, who brought them out of the land of Egypt that I might dwell among them; I am the Lord their God (Exod 29:46).

The force of the divine self-revelation in the recognition formula is supported by self-identification in verse 46b. Cassuto suggests that this is suggestive of a king, "who signs his name at the end of the declaration that he has issued, in order to validate it and accept full responsibility for its implementation."¹⁴⁸ If one emphasizes the revelatory significance of the phrase "I am the Lord their God," this statement may mark what precedes it as integral to what it means for YHWH to be YHWH. The strong language of YHWH's will and action throughout the passage and reference to the כְּבוֹד יְהוָה suggest as much. Yet, as I will argue, this act of dwelling, or promising to dwell, is not constitutive of YHWH such that it cannot be taken away. All of this—the tent of meeting, the abiding of YHWH among the Israelites, and thus YHWH being their God—are threatened by what the Israelites do in chapter 32.

---

146. *TDOT*, "כבד."
147. Cassuto, *Book of Exodus*, 388.
148. Ibid., 389.

2.3.2. Golden calf (Exod 32–34) My primary concern in this section will be with Exod 33:19 and 34:5-7. However, as chapters 32–34 are a (complex) unit,[149] I need to address some of the interpretive cruxes of the narrative whole. First, what is the nature of the wrongdoing in chapter 32? There are various ways of asking about this sin, but the main focus of the text is the sin of the people, rather than on Aaron's role, which is debatable.[150]

In 32:1, the people are concerned with who will lead them in the absence of Moses, who has been away on Sinai for some time. In Moses' absence, the narrative suggests that the calf will replace him. However, once they create the calf, the people's intent changes. They exclaim that this calf is their God (33:4), which seems incredible to the reader. As Brichto writes, "Are we really asked to believe that mature adults would hail as their liberator from Egypt a man-made image that had not come into existence until that very moment?"[151] The initial intent of the calf is not to represent another god, as opposed to YHWH, but a mediate presence—alternative to Moses—between the people and YHWH.[152] As Durham writes,

> The composite of Exod 32:1-6 is not an account of the abandonment of Yahweh for other gods; it is an account of the transfer of the center of authority of faith in Yahweh from Moses and the laws and symbols he had announced to a golden calf without laws and without any symbols beyond itself. Moses is the representative of a God invisible in mystery. The calf is to be the

---

149. Three important attempts to reading Exod 32–34 as a coherent literary unit are Dale Ralph Davis, "Rebellion, Presence, and Covenant: A Study in Exodus 32–34," *WTJ* 44 (1982): 71–87; R. W. L. Moberly, *At the Mountain of God: Story and Theology in Exodus 32–34*, JSOTSup 22 (Sheffield: JSOT, 1983); and Herbert Chanan Brichto, *Toward a Grammar of Biblical Poetics: Tales of the Prophets* (New York; Oxford: Oxford University, 1992), 88–121.

150. Jewish, more than Christian, commentators tend to defend Aaron. Cf. Cassuto, *Book of Exodus*, 408, 413; Childs, *Book of Exodus*, 570; Moberly, *Mountain of God*, 54. Brichto argues that Aaron's statement in 33:22-24 should be taken as true, given that Moses accepts it, and that God produced the calf against Aaron's expectation; Brichto, *Grammar of Biblical Poetics*, 95–97. There may be continuity between Brichto's understanding of how God treats the people of Israel in chapter 32 and Gunn's understanding of God's treatment of Pharaoh in chapters 5–14.

151. Brichto, *Grammar of Biblical Poetics*, 92.

152. Moberly, *Mountain of God*, 46–47.

representative of that same God, whose invisibility and mystery is compromised by an image he has forbidden.[153]

The act of manufacturing an alternative medium through which to experience YHWH cannot hold. In fabricating a new mediator for themselves, the people reject God, who is characteristically known in self-revelation.[154] In this sense, the psalmist declares,

> They exchanged the glory of God
>   for the image of an ox that eats grass.
> They forgot God, their Saviour,
>   who had done great things in Egypt (Ps 106:20-21).[155]

The people who so boldly proclaimed that they would adhere to the covenant (19:8) have broken the first two elements of the Decalogue while still at the base of Sinai.[156]

The consequences of their disobedience are manifold. Early in the dialogue cycle, Moses succeeds in easing the Lord's anger and saving the people from complete destruction (32:9-14). However, Moses himself commands the death of those implicated in the act (32:25-29). Having secured survival for a remnant of the people, in 32:30, Moses begins to work toward forgiveness on their behalf. But YHWH is not easily persuaded. Sin has consequences, and YHWH makes clear that there will be further punishment of Israel (32:34b). Further, though the Lord agrees to continue to guide the people to the promised land, YHWH will not go "in the midst" of the people. Given their manifest tendency to idolatry, YHWH's presence with the people would threaten their safety; YHWH's anger could be provoked, and the people, destroyed (33:3).[157] What is at stake is not the messenger promised for guidance in 23:20ff., but YHWH's presence in the tabernacle, the provisions for

---

153. Durham, *Exodus*, 421-22.

154. Childs, *Book of Exodus*, 564.

155. The NRSV of verse 20a is based on Greek manuscripts; MT reads וַיָּמִ֥ירוּ אֶת־כְּבוֹדָ֖ם, "They exchanged their glory"; cf. Childs, *Book of Exodus*, 564.

156. Moberly, *Mountain of God*, 49.

157. The sense of 33:2-3, that the leading angel will not cause Israel harm, sits awkwardly with 23:21-22, in which the promise of the leading angel is followed by the stipulation that the angel must be obeyed, because it will have the power to execute justice against Israel.

which are made beginning in chapter 25.[158] Yet it is not *merely* the tabernacle, as if this were of minor importance. The people mourn (33:4), for though the tabernacle has not yet been built, YHWH's reversal of this promise would suggest that Israel's identity as the people of God—set apart from other peoples because of YHWH's presence among them—is at stake.[159]

So the stage has been set for this narrative to develop an understanding of the nature of God's presence (or absence) among the Israelites. This issue was first raised in chapters introducing the tabernacle, where the language used for the presence of YHWH suggests temporary dwelling subject to YHWH's freedom. However, in chapters 32-34 the problem focuses acutely on the situation of Israel's breaking of the covenant. How can God, who is holy and jealous, be present among a people prone to idolatry? As Gowan writes, "The choices throughout these chapters seem at first to be only two: dying in their sins, if God visits them, or, if God distances himself, existing in their sins, without hope for anything good to come."[160]

Time passes, during which Moses continually meets with God in his customary tent, which is (as it must be) located outside of the camp of Israel.[161] Then Moses is emboldened to intercede for Israel once more (33:12ff.). The logic of Moses' petition is difficult to discern. Whereas Moses' plea begins with reference to the angel (v. 12), it becomes clear that the real concession that he presses for is that YHWH will go in the midst of the people and commit himself to them once more.[162] Moberly resolves this tension by arguing that the shrine is the subject already in verse 12, on the basis that אֲשֶׁר could be impersonal, thus, ". . . what you will send with me" rather than ". . . who you will send with me," and that "with me" recalls 3:12, in which YHWH promises to be with Moses.[163] YHWH first concedes that "[his] face"

---

158. Ibid., 63.
159. Durham may exaggerate the consequences of this, though he is certainly correct in seeing that the center of Israel's life as the people of God is at stake. Durham, *Exodus*, 437.
160. Gowan, *Theology in Exodus*, 218.
161. Moberly, *Mountain of God*, 63ff.
162. Childs, *Book of Exodus*, 594.
163. Moberly, *Mountain of God*, 69. Differently, Durham resolves the tension by suggesting that what Moses requests in verse 12 is a deeper understanding of YHWH, in similar fashion to his questions in 3:11, 13. Thus 33:12, 13 are parallel requests for understanding YHWH's intention with Israel. Durham, *Exodus*, 446-47. According to Brichto, Moses raises the issue of the angel (v. 12) only to demonstrate that the angel

(פָּנַי) will go with Moses, to lighten his burden (v. 14). It is possible to read YHWH's response in this verse not as a statement, but a question, that is, "Shall my face go with you?"[164] Regardless, the point that Moses presses is that God must choose again *this people* and commit himself again to them, so that Israel will be restored as the people of YHWH (vv. 15–16).[165]

On the basis of Moses' righteousness, God grants his request in verse 17. YHWH's response suggests that he will go in the midst of the Israelites, but the problem of their potential destruction is not explicitly resolved.[166] This is the issue that Moses presses in verse 18, in which he exclaims, "Show me your glory!" (הַרְאֵנִי נָא אֶת־כְּבֹדֶךָ). Moses requests some demonstration of God's character so that he can understand how YHWH will deal with Israel.[167] Brichto and Durham read the petition differently, suggesting that Moses desires the means by which to recognize YHWH in the midst of Israel; the request to see YHWH's presence is for assurance that God really will accompany them.[168] It seems likely that Moses is asking not only about the character of God, but about the nature of God's presence, which, in some form, he desires to see. That this is to "prove" YHWH's presence within Israel seems to suggest, without rationale, that Moses distrusts God. Certainly (as Moberly suggests) YHWH will respond to the issue of whether his presence in the midst of Israel will threaten the life of the people.

In verse 19, YHWH indicates that he will grant Moses' request, saying, "I will make all my goodness pass before you, and will proclaim before you the name, 'The Lord'; and I will be gracious to whom I will be gracious, and will show mercy on whom I will show mercy." The subject here is emphatic, אֲנִי אַעֲבִיר. On account of the qualification that follows (v. 20ff.), some have argued that "my goodness" should be read as the blessings that YHWH pro-

---

is altogether unnecessary (v. 13). If YHWH will reveal his intention to Moses, they can dispense with the angel completely. God's response suggests that he knows what Moses truly wants—YHWH to accompany them. Brichto, *Grammar of Biblical Poetics*, 105. Brichto's reading, in which the issue at hand is whether YHWH himself or an angel accompany Israel, contrasts with my reading of the issue as whether YHWH will go "in front of" or "in the midst of" Israel. See Moberly, *Mountain of God*, 63; Davis, "Rebellion, Presence, and Covenant," 76.

164. Ibid., 77; Brichto, *Grammar of Biblical Poetics*, 104–105.
165. Moberly, *Mountain of God*, 69–75.
166. Davis, "Rebellion, Presence, and Covenant," 77.
167. Moberly, *Mountain of God*, 68.
168. Brichto, *Grammar of Biblical Poetics*, 106–107; Durham, *Exodus*, 437.

vides for his people, or the "whole story of God's saving love for his people."[169] Another option is to understand טוב as the beauty of YHWH.[170] Yet what Moses experiences is neither a vision nor a description of God's acts in history, but rather a recital of God's attributes (34:6-7).[171] Further, the passing over of God's goodness is here in parallel with the declaration of the divine name (v. 19a), suggesting that goodness is central to God's identity.[172] Brichto's identification of the goodness of YHWH as the part that Moses sees, and the judgment of YHWH as what is kept from Moses, is an overzealous attempt to divide the character of YHWH into comprehensible parts.[173] The goodness of YHWH is not here described as a part of YHWH's character, but as the whole of it, as the proclamation of the divine name. God's goodness is manifest in God's acts of redemption, but these acts do not exhaust his goodness. In the Psalms, YHWH's goodness is said to extend to eternity, so that God can be called upon to work future good in the lives of those who pray to him.[174] Though elsewhere in the Pentateuch, YHWH reveals his glory though judgment (for example, Num 14:10-12; 16:19ff.), at this crucial point in Israel's history, YHWH reveals his glory as goodness.[175]

The *idem per idem* formula links Exod 33:19 with 3:14a. Moberly suggests that these two descriptions of the name "YHWH" constitute two stages of revelation. Before the covenant, the revelation of the name is cast in nonmoral terms, but the covenant has changed Israel's relationship with YHWH. In 33:19, YHWH is described in terms appropriate to the context of sin and Israel's need for forgiveness.[176] God's essential mercy and compassion are revealed within the context of the covenant, not outside of it. Again, the *idem per idem* formula suggests that YHWH retains freedom to be merciful and

---

169. Knight, *Theology as Narration*, 196-197. Cf. Moberly, *Mountain of God*, 76.
170. Durham, *Exodus*, 437.
171. Sarna, *Exodus*, 214; Gowan, *Theology in Exodus*, 234.
172. Sarna, *Exodus*, 214.
173. Brichto, *Grammar of Biblical Poetics*, 107.
174. Ps 86:5-7; 100:5; 106:1-2; 107:1ff.; 118:1, 29; 145:9. See *NIDOTTE*, "טוב."
175. Moberly, *Mountain of God*, 77.
176. Further, Moberly suggests that, as a result of this, one ought not to consider 3:14 to the exclusion of other texts in exploring the meaning of the divine name. Ibid., 78-79.

compassionate at his discretion. God's mercy cannot be presumed upon, as though humans could sin intentionally, counting on YHWH's forgiveness.[177]

YHWH is receptive to Moses' request to see YHWH's glory, but in verses 20-23, he qualifies this receptivity. Moses will not be able to see God's face, because no one who does so lives (v. 20). Instead, God will set Moses on a safe place on a nearby rock, and when his glory passes by, God will shield Moses with his hand (v. 22). Here the כְּבוֹד יְהוָה refers to YHWH's very self.[178] When YHWH takes his hand away, Moses will be able to see YHWH's "back" (vs. 23). If what Moses was asking to see was the כְּבוֹד יְהוָה in the form of cloud and/or fire,[179] this response suggests YHWH going beyond Moses' request and endeavoring to give him as immediate an experience of YHWH's presence as is humanly possible. The term "back" is used as a counterpart to "face."[180] The reader needs to seek a balance between attending to the anthropomorphic language of the text and seeing that this language does not portray God in a concrete human form. So, on the one hand, Moberly advises the reader to take the anthropomorphic language seriously in order to fully imagine the dynamics of the story,[181] and on the other, Hamori acknowledges that in this text, "God is described in anthropomorphic terms and seems to be immanent, but is not explicitly depicted as physically embodied."[182] Some have argued that the "back" of YHWH be understood temporally, either as God's deeds in history,[183] or as the future, perhaps the leadership of Joshua,[184] but it may be more helpful to look to what happens in the narrative in chapter 34 in order to understand what is meant by "back." Cassuto's reading takes the context—the recital of YHWH's attributes—more fully into consideration:

---

177. Cassuto, *Book of Exodus*, 436.
178. Moberly, *Mountain of God*, 76; *NIDOTTE*, "כבד."
179. Gowan, *Theology in Exodus*, 232-33.
180. Moberly, *Mountain of God*, 82.
181. R. W. L. Moberly, "How May We Speak of God? A Reconsideration of the Nature of Biblical Theology" *TynBul* 53, no. 2 (2002): 197.
182. Hamori, *"When Gods were Men,"* 30.
183. Knight, *Theology as Narration*, 198.
184. Diana Lipton, "God's Back! What Did Moses See on Sinai?," in *The Significance of Sinai: Traditions About Sinai and Divine Revelation in Judaism and Christianity*, ed. George J. Brooke, Hindy Najman and Loren T. Stuckenbruck (Leiden: Brill, 2008), 287-311.

> *I will make all My goodness*—all My virtues (it is already implied here that fundamentally the Divine qualities are compassionate)—*pass before you*, that is, I shall not cause them to stand before you, so that you may contemplate them, but I shall make them pass before you in a momentary flash, whilst you stand at the side. . . . Here [in v. 23] it is obvious that figurative expressions are being used: you will be able to perceive only My works and to discern from them some of My attributes, but you will be unable to comprehend My essential nature.[185]

The form in which YHWH's glory (goodness, attributes, name) comes to Moses is not a visual representation of himself but a declaration which passes by him. He cannot grasp these attributes fully or hold onto them. Their passing by in the form of proclamation intimates the mystery of God's mercy and judgment that they articulate.

The text of 34:1–4 describes Moses' preparation for the coming theophany. In verse 5, the revelatory moment begins with the descending of a cloud, frequently associated with the glory of YHWH. The remainder of the verse is a heading for what follows in more detail in verses 6–7, indicating that the declaration that follows can be understood as constitutive of proclaiming the name "YHWH."[186]

The Lord then proclaims the name "YHWH" twice, for emphasis, perhaps, and as a confessional statement.[187] Cassuto glosses the double naming, "The Lord, He is the Lord,' and it is impossible to define His nature in any other words (compare iii 14: 'I am who I am')."[188] YHWH's double calling of a person's name occurs at crucial points in the lives of those whose names are called (e.g., Exod 3:4, Gen 22:11, and 1 Sam 3:10). From a form-critical perspective, Dentan observes that, as a third-person declaration, the formula is liturgical, and could have originally been from the perspective of an individual worshipper toward God.[189] Yet, in its current literary context, YHWH

---

185. Cassuto, *Book of Exodus*, 435, 437.
186. I follow Moberly's suggestion that YHWH is the subject of וַיִּקְרָא in verses 5 and 6. Moberly, *Mountain of God*, 86. Cf. Cassuto, *Book of Exodus*, 439. Though Childs suggests an earlier version of the narrative had Moses as the subject of both verbs in verse 5, he concedes that the flow of the current narrative suggests that YHWH is the subject of verse 5b. Childs, *Book of Exodus*, 603.
187. Durham, *Exodus*, 453.
188. Cassuto, *Book of Exodus*, 439.
189. Robert C. Dentan, "The Literary Affinities of Exodus 34:6f," VT 13, no. 1

declares the formula. As elsewhere in the book of Exodus, God is only revealed through God's own speech and actions.

The end of verse 6 repeats the terms of 33:19b, "a God merciful and gracious." Further, YHWH is "slow to anger, and abounding in steadfast love and faithfulness" (34:6b). In contrast to the form the confession takes in Exod 20:5-6, here the merciful elements are placed first, in extended form, as they are the more prominent features of the declaration in this context.[190] Further, in the Decalogue, the primary contrast is between those who keep the commandments and those who do not. However, in chapter 34, there is a dual contrast which emphasizes YHWH's character rather than human obedience. God is "keeping steadfast love for the thousandth generation" and "forgiving iniquity and transgression and sin," on the one hand, and "yet by no means clearing the guilty, but visiting the iniquity of the parents upon the children and the children's children, to the third and the fourth generation" (v. 7), on the other. Rightfully, the Decalogue emphasizes the importance of obeying the commandments; however, once these commandments have been broken (ch. 32), the issue turns to God's character.

The contrast between the judgment of God, which seems more prominent in Exod 20:5-6, and the mercy of God, the focus in chapter 34, can be overstated. Divine jealousy, and thus divine judgment, is not removed. Much in the spirit of the Decalogue, the text of verse 14 prohibits the worship of other gods, "because the Lord, whose name is Jealous, is a jealous God" (כִּי יְהוָה קַנָּא שְׁמוֹ אֵל קַנָּא הוּא). This statement of YHWH's jealousy is more emphatic than that of 20:5. "Jealous" is not the proper name of God, which has been identified in 3:15. Rather, the sense is similar to that of 15:3, where YHWH's name indicates his essential character. Jealousy is at the heart of God's identity. YHWH is, essentially, Israel's God, and as their God, he demands exclusive worship.

Finally, 34:6-7 brings the reader to a fuller understanding of YHWH's holiness in the midst of sin. Dozeman is right that "grace builds on jealousy, it does not replace it."[191] In the renewal of the covenant, the demands on Israel are not lessened by the mercy of God. YHWH's jealousy is not antithetical to YHWH's mercy, but rather, they seem to be correlated. Moberly writes, "Faithfulness to Yahweh must be all or nothing. . . . On the one hand Yah-

---

(1963): 37.
190. Sarna, *Exodus*, 216.
191. Dozeman, *Commentary on Exodus*, 737.

weh's mercy is revealed more fully than hitherto, but on the other hand his demand upon Israel is likewise intensified."[192] How these seemingly incompatible traits find compatibility in YHWH is not explained. These texts "do not tell us how Yahweh's grace and holiness kiss each other, but they do preach grace in such a way that we both fear Yahweh's wrath yet rejoice—with trembling—under his unexplainable grace."[193]

Yet, at the same time, the dominant voice in Exod 34 is one of mercy: through his own compassionate nature, YHWH overcomes the impossibility of his presence among a sinful people. The presence of God in the midst of Israel can never be taken for granted, but it is always a miracle, a mystery at the heart of the nature and identity of YHWH.

2.4. Summary

Throughout the book of Exodus, references to the name "YHWH" suggest God's faithfulness to Israel and freedom to be who God will be; YHWH's action among and presence with Israel is intertwined with revelation of YHWH's identity, nature, and character. YHWH delivers Israel and establishes a covenant with Israel; throughout these narratives, human knowledge of YHWH is both the purpose and the result of deliverance and covenant-making. The Decalogue specifies how the Israelites can worship an immaterial, incomparable God. When Israel jeopardizes the continuation of that covenant and God's faithful presence among Israel, YHWH overcomes the impossibility of dwelling among a sinful nation through revealing himself as essentially merciful, a revelation which involves reflection on how it is that the invisible, holy God can show himself to a human, Moses. Therefore, YHWH's continuing presence among Israel is to be received as a gift dependent on the identity of YHWH.

Though this argument has proceeded in dialogue with modern exegetes and without direct attention to Augustine's reading of these passages, the reading proposed supports, and is supported by, Augustine's hermeneutic and its theological underpinnings as described in chapter 2. Significant attention has been given to the details of the Hebrew text in its literal sense, the means through which one can know and journey toward God. Even within a modern approach to Exodus in its narrative and canonical form has

---

192. Moberly, *Mountain of God*, 97.
193. Davis, "Rebellion, Presence, and Covenant," 87.

revealed ways in which the text suggests the immateriality of God and human limitations in fully comprehending the one God.

3. Conclusion

As use of the divine name in Exod 5–40 suggests that God's action is not separated from revelation of God's identity, nature, and character, so Exod 3:14–15 suggests that something about the nature and identity of God as well as God's action and presence among the Israelites. YHWH gives the Israelites a name by which they can truly call on him, a name YHWH will recognize as his own, but this name does not give the Israelites power over YHWH, who remains hidden even in his revelation. Therefore, Exod 3:13–15 is open to ontological interpretation for at least two reasons. First, the repetition of the word אֶהְיֶה and the wordplay between the root היה and the divine name יְהוָה cannot be passed over as an inaccurate etymology. Nor is the best way to read this text to suggest that it presents an *accurate* etymology. Rather, the phrases אֶהְיֶה אֲשֶׁר אֶהְיֶה and אֶהְיֶה express that the nature of God is to be revealing in self-reference, calling the hearer into the reality of God and God's will for the world. Receiving this revelation requires a transformation of perception, whereby the world is absorbed into God's identity and action. Second, Exod 3:14–15 fits within the larger witness of the book of Exodus to God known by the name "YHWH," because this book as a whole suggests that the nature of God is revealed in God's actions for his people. However, knowing God cannot simply be reduced to knowing God's deeds but rather it must include human attention, and appropriate response, to God's "I."

It is surely correct to say, as recent commentators often do, that Exod 3:14–15 indicates that YHWH is present with his people and is known through sending Moses and through delivering the Israelites from Egypt. However, through these actions and this presence, the Israelites come to know the nature and reality of this God. Therefore, it is reasonable, within a reading of Exod 3:13–15 as a realistic narrative in the literary context of the book of Exodus, to say that in verse 14, God reveals himself to be one who cannot be known directly to humanity; אֶהְיֶה אֲשֶׁר אֶהְיֶה is an indefinite statement that one can reflect on but never fully grasp. Yet this God is known in the life of Israel, as the Lord God of Israel's ancestors, Abraham, Isaac, and Jacob, and known to the reader as the God who is the subject of Israel's Scriptures, the Old Testament.

CHAPTER 4

Moses as Covenant Mediator

On Exod 3:13-15, Moberly writes, "The text's concern with the disclosure of the name of God is in no sense an abstract concern raised for its own sake but is integrally related to Moses' role as the classic example of that phenomenon of prophecy by which historic Israel in practice encountered their God."[1] In this chapter I explore the nature of Moses' vocation as prophet and covenant mediator in the terms of his legacy expressed in Deut 34:10-12, before returning to Exod 3:1-4:17 to discuss how Moses' vocation sheds light on this text. Thus taking a synthetic approach to the exegesis of Exod 3:13-15 within the received form of the Pentateuch, I suggest that Moses' vocation as covenant mediator is best understood in terms of proximity to YHWH. Such proximity is manifest in Moses' unique perception of God—in terms of seeing and hearing—and in Moses' action as supremely obedient to God's will. Bringing attention to Moses' proximity to YHWH into reading Exod 3:1-4:17, I suggest that this text fits its context rather well, because Moses' proximity to and knowledge of YHWH has to do with him accomplishing certain tasks on YHWH's behalf. Furthermore, the narrative emphasizes Moses' perception, which can inform how one understands verses 13-15.[2]

---

1. Moberly, *Old Testament*, 24.
2. That the narrative of Exod 3:1-4:17 has rather much to do with Moses' vocation is not a new or surprising claim. According to form criticism, the call narratives in Exod 3, Judg 6, Isa 6, Jer 1, and Ezek 1 developed out of the same form. Habel identifies six components of this form—"1. divine confrontation, 2. introductory word, 3. commission, 4. objection, 5. reassurance, 6. sign" (N. Habel, "The Form and Significance of the Call Narratives," *ZAW* 77 (1965): 298)—though subsequent scholars (e.g., Zimmerli and Simon) have modified Habel's proposal, adjusting specific criteria. As skepticism increases on the subject of our ability to know the historical

Deuteronomy 34:10–12 presents a reflection on the role and significance of Moses from the end of his life:

וְלֹא־קָם נָבִיא עוֹד בְּיִשְׂרָאֵל כְּמֹשֶׁה אֲשֶׁר יְדָעוֹ יְהוָה פָּנִים אֶל־פָּנִים: לְכָל־הָאֹתוֹת וְהַמּוֹפְתִים אֲשֶׁר שְׁלָחוֹ יְהוָה לַעֲשׂוֹת בְּאֶרֶץ מִצְרָיִם לְפַרְעֹה וּלְכָל־עֲבָדָיו וּלְכָל־אַרְצוֹ: וּלְכֹל הַיָּד הַחֲזָקָה וּלְכֹל הַמּוֹרָא הַגָּדוֹל אֲשֶׁר עָשָׂה מֹשֶׁה לְעֵינֵי כָּל־יִשְׂרָאֵל:

> Never since has there arisen a prophet in Israel like Moses, whom the LORD knew face to face. He was unequalled for all the signs and wonders that the LORD sent him to perform in the land of Egypt, against Pharaoh and all his servants and his entire land, and for all the mighty deeds and all the terrifying displays of power that Moses performed in the sight of all Israel.

Though scholarship in the twentieth century tended to ignore this passage,[3] this situation is beginning to change. In 1994, Olson published his insightful, creative work on the death of Moses as a crucial and pervasive theme in the book of Deuteronomy.[4] A smaller step forward is Tigay's argument for reading these verses as countering polytheistic and syncretistic Yahwistic voices in the community; all subsequent teaching and leadership must be in conti-

---

development of texts, the genre designation "type-scene," classically described by Alter, may be usefully applied here. Savran has argued for such a transition in approach to call narratives. George W. Savran, *Encountering the Divine: Theophany in Biblical Narrative* (London; New York: Continuum, 2005), 5–30; Walther Zimmerli, *Ezekiel I*, trans. R. E. Clements, Hermeneia (Philadelphia: Fortress, 1979), 97–100; U. Simon, *Reading Prophetic Narratives* (Bloomington: Indiana University, 1997), 51–58; Robert Alter, *The Art of Biblical Narrative* (New York: Basic, 1981), 47–62.

Rather than reviewing the literature on Exod 3 as a call narrative, I build on the well-founded observation that this is the beginning of Moses' mission.

3. Chapman suggests that the lacuna stems from Noth's and subsequent scholars' identification of the text as a late Deuteronomistic addition. Tigay suggests a literary rationale: not much attention is paid to epitaphs generally. However, this text should not be ignored with other epitaphs, because this is not an ordinary epitaph but an account of Moses' enduring significance, an account which comes at the end of an "ideological" book. Stephen B. Chapman, *The Law and the Prophets: A Study in Old Testament Canon Formation* FAT 27 (Tübingen: Mohr Siebeck, 2000), 114; Jeffrey H. Tigay, "The Significance of the End of Deuteronomy (Deuteronomy 34:10–12)," in *Texts, Temples and Traditions: A Tribute to Menahem Haran*, ed. Michael V. Fox et al. (Winona Lake, IN: Eisenbrauns, 1996), 137–38.

4. Dennis T. Olson, *Deuteronomy and the Death of Moses: A Theological Reading*, OBT (Minneapolis: Fortress, 1994).

nuity with Moses' torah, which holds highest authority.⁵ Chapman builds on Blenkinsopp's argument that Deut 34:10-12 should be read as a guide for interpretation of Torah as a whole, judging from the text's inherent concern with determining the nature of the relationship between Moses and other Israelite prophets.⁶ These studies have persuasively demonstrated the significance of this passage for communicating the central themes of Deuteronomy and for understanding the relationship between the Pentateuch and the prophets. Given the subject matter of these verses and their canonical significance, Deut 34:10-12 is a fine place to begin to explore the nature of Moses' vocation in the received canonical portrayal.

As in chapter 3, my primary conversation partners in this chapter are modern exegetes. However, exploration of the vocation of Moses in the Pentateuch further supports reading of Exod 3:13-15 as to do with both the identity and action of the YHWH, the God of Israel. How the discussion of Moses' vocation relates to Augustine's reading of Exod 3:13-15 will be addressed at the conclusion of the chapter.

1. "Never Since Has There Arisen a Prophet in Israel Like Moses"

The text of verse 10 ascribes particular honor to Moses. But is the honor given to Moses by this text simultaneously a critique of later prophets? The relationship between Moses and subsequent prophets has been construed in a variety of ways. For example, on one end of the spectrum sits Tigay, who suggests that the Pentateuch does not identify Moses as a prophet precisely. The term "prophet" is at once too limiting and too magical for Moses. The Pentateuch prefers to call him the Lord's "servant" (עַבְדִּי; Num 12:7-8) and "man of God" (אִישׁ הָאֱלֹהִים; Deut 33:1). Moses is much more than a prophet, though prophecy is a role that he performs at various points.⁷ Moreover, the

---

5. Tigay, "Significance," passim.

6. Joseph Blenkinsopp, *Prophecy and Canon: A Contribution to the Study of Jewish Origins* SJCA 3 (Notre Dame: Notre Dame University, 1977); Chapman, *Law and the Prophets*, 112-31, especially 117-18. However, Chapman and Blenkinsopp disagree substantially in how they understand the relationship between Moses and subsequent prophets.

7. Jeffrey H. Tigay, *Deuteronomy*, JPS Torah Commentary (Philadelphia: JPS, 1996), 175.

term נָבִיא here is not for the purposes of designating Moses as a prophet, but for "declaring that he is superior to all other prophets."[8] On the other end of the spectrum stands Blenkinsopp, who argues that "Never since" or "never again" or "no longer" is the correct sense of עוֹד . . . לֹא. "Not yet," which would suggest hope for a future prophet that *would* be like Moses, is never the sense of this phrase with the past tense in the Old Testament.[9]

Both Tigay and Blenkinsopp's perspectives seem overstated. In response to Tigay, it may be observed that the Pentateuch (especially Deuteronomy) *does* refer to Moses as a prophet. If, as Exod 7:1 suggests, a prophet is one who speaks for God, then Moses spends quite a bit of his life acting as a prophet, speaking the word of God to Pharaoh and to Israel. Furthermore, the text of Deut 5:22-31 (cf. Exod 20:18-21) narrates Moses entering into this role at the people's request, which YHWH approves. Also, like subsequent prophets Isaiah, Jeremiah, and Ezekiel, Moses is "sent" (שלח; Deut 34:11; cf. Exod 3:1-4:17).[10] In response to Blenkinsopp, Chapman has persuasively argued that this text presents Moses as a preeminent example of the prophets. To accomplish this, Chapman builds on Knoppers's discussion of the incomparability formulae in 1-2 Kings (וְכָמֹהוּ לֹא־הָיָה לְפָנָיו מֶלֶךְ), "Before him there was no king like him," 2 Kgs 23:25; וְאַחֲרָיו לֹא־הָיָה כָמֹהוּ בְּכֹל מַלְכֵי יְהוּדָה וַאֲשֶׁר הָיוּ לְפָנָיו, "so that there was no one like him among all the kings of Judah after him, or among those who were before him," 2 Kgs 18:5; אֲשֶׁר כָּמוֹךָ לֹא־הָיָה לְפָנֶיךָ וְאַחֲרֶיךָ לֹא־יָקוּם כָּמוֹךָ, "no one like you has been before you and no one like you shall arise after you" 1 Kgs 3:12). These formulae refer to the unsurpassing nature of certain qualities of kings, rather than their utter singularity.[11] Therefore, future prophets are in continuity with Moses, though they have

---

8. Ibid., 339.

9. Blenkinsopp gives the example, "Jeroboam never again recovered his power during the lifetime of Abijah" (2 Chr 13:20) and cites several additional examples (Exod 2:3; Josh 2:11; 5:1, 12; Judg 2:14; 1 Sam 1:18; 2 Sam 3:11; 14:10; 1 Kgs 10:5, 10; 2 Kgs 2:12; 1 Chr 19:19; 2 Chr 9:4; Jer 44:22; and Ezek 33:22). Blenkinsopp, *Prophecy and Canon*, 86, 176, fn. 14.

Further, Blenkinsopp argues that this text is an expression of Second Temple conflict between theocratic and eschatological elements of the tradition and that it seeks to subordinate "free prophecy" to Mosaic law. Ibid., 89, 93-95.

10. R. W. L. Moberly, *Prophecy and Discernment*, CSCD (Cambridge: Cambridge University, 2006), 3-4.

11. Gary N. Knoppers, "'There Was None Like Him': Incomparability in the Book of Kings," *CBQ* 54 (1992): 411-31.

never reached the heights of his honor. Chapman goes so far as to suggest that subsequent prophets are elevated by being subordinated to Moses; judges, kings, and priests are never described by such a comparison.[12]

A look at the text of Deut 18:15-18 may help to clarify the relationship between Moses and subsequent prophets. In this text, Moses declares that "the LORD your God will raise up for you a prophet like me from among your own people; you shall heed such a prophet" (Deut 18:15). This verse contains a promise that, after Moses dies, the Lord will send (a) prophet(s) to mediate the word of God.[13] Scholars have debated whether what is meant is a single, future prophet or several prophets, perhaps even an ongoing office of covenant mediator within the cult.[14] However, the concern in the text seems to be who will mediate the word of the Lord to Israel after the death of Moses. In light of this, the text's immediate reference must either be to Joshua or to an ongoing set of future prophets.

After declaring that there will be a future prophet or prophets, Moses then references the story of Deut 5:22-31, perhaps to suggest that because

---

12. Chapman, *Law and the Prophets*, 123.

13. Walther Zimmerli, *Old Testament Theology in Outline*, trans. David E. Green (Edinburgh: T&T Clark, 1978), 104-5.

14. Moberly and Pope Benedict XVI follow a widespread scholarly understanding that the text envisages an ongoing prophetic office in Israel. R. W. L. Moberly, "The Use of the Old Testament in Pope Benedict XVI's Jesus of Nazareth," in *The Pope and Jesus of Nazareth*, ed. Angus Paddison and Adrian Pabst (London: SCM, 2009), 99, 103. Mayes may be correct in his argument for a distributive sense of the verb, meaning "I will raise up from time to time." A. D. H. Mayes, *Deuteronomy*, NCB (Edinburgh: Oliphants, 1979), 282. Von Rad is wary of the suggestion that by such a prophet, "Israel may be assured at all times of the most intimate association with this God," and so prefers a singular fulfillment, though he does not entertain the idea of occasional, non-permanent, fulfillment. Gerhard von Rad, *Deuteronomy: A Commentary*, trans. Dorothea Barton, OTL (London: SCM, 1966), 123-24.

A collaborative Jewish-and-Christian understanding of this text is possible. As Jesus Christ ultimately fulfills the role of the great prophet who speaks the word of God, he does so in historical continuity with prophets who spoke for God after Moses and before the incarnation. Moreover, Christ does not neatly fit the description of this text, for he not only speaks for God, but is the Word of God. However, a Christian reading that looks to Christ for the fulfillment of Moses and Old Testament prophecy cannot assume that these texts on their own terms anticipate a fulfillment greater than Moses and the prophets. Moberly, "Use of the Old Testament," 106.

the Israelites requested a mediator, they are bound to such mediation and to obedience to the words of future prophets.[15] This is Tigay's understanding of Deut 18:15-18, though it would seem to subvert the case that Moses is not a prophet.[16] Furthermore, the place of prophets in Israel clearly distinguishes this nation from its neighbors. The literary context of Deut 18:15-18 suggests this, for these verses immediately follow the prohibition of magic and divination in 18:9-14. Von Rad writes, "It is now possible to sweep aside, as with a wave of the hand, the motley arsenal of mantic and occult practices, all the attempts to obtain a share of the divine powers or of divine knowledge. A quite different possibility has been disclosed to Israel, namely the Word of its prophet."[17]

In summary, one can say that subsequent prophets in Israel fulfilled the same role as Moses to the extent that both spoke for God or, put differently, mediated the word of God to the people of God. In this, both the law and the prophets agree that the community of the people of God rests upon the authority of someone mediating God's word to the people. Thus later prophecy and Moses' speaking for God can mutually inform one another. Prophecy is essentially a matter of relaying the word of God, not a matter of abnormal psychological state or disposition, which Moberly calls "optional extras."[18] True prophetic words are known by their content, which enables God's peo-

---

15. Tigay, *Deuteronomy*, 176.

16. Furthermore, Tigay argues that the prophets' role of speaking for God included, "all matters of national life, including religion and domestic and foreign affairs. He is, in essence, the envoy through whom God, the divine king, governs Israel. . . . The prophets served, in sum, as the monitors of Israel's fulfillment of its covenant obligations to God and as the primary bearers of Israel's religious and moral ideals." Ibid., 176. The wider the frame of influence identified for the prophets, the more their role resembles that of Moses.

Olson's argument that the future prophet will be like Moses in that he will die is intriguing but does not withstand scrutiny. If Moses was considered a great prophet, as Deut 34:10-12 suggests, then it is unlikely that the Israelites would be expecting an even greater prophet, that is, one that would not die. More likely, the people are afraid that after Moses, the word of God will no longer be made available to them. Perhaps they are even afraid that they will have to hear the voice of YHWH directly, and therefore die themselves (Deut 18:16; cf. Deut 5:23-27). Olson, *Death of Moses*, 85.

17. Von Rad, *Deuteronomy*, 123; Cf. Peter C. Craigie, *The Book of Deuteronomy*, NICOT (Grand Rapids: Eerdmans, 1976), 262.

18. Moberly, *Prophecy and Discernment*, 10.

ple to live in accordance with the central aspects of the covenant: the Decalogue, *Shema*, and so on.

Yet, subsequent prophets were not equal to Moses. Craigie articulates the distinction in terms of their historical place: "However distinguished a subsequent prophet in Israel might be, his ministry would be within the community of God's people; the work of Moses, however, was instrumental, under God, in the formation of that community."[19] That Moses carries greater authority out of historical precedent is a fair claim. However, more in continuity with the terms of Deut 34:10–12 is Chapman and Knoppers's claim that the incomparability of Moses, like the incomparability of kings in similar statements, is according to certain qualities that Moses demonstrates.[20] Miller aptly writes,

> As chapter 34 indicates, no other prophet like Moses has arisen, or been raised up by the Lord, if one uses the criterion of mighty deeds and signs and wonders as a basis for comparison. But one *can* expect that the Lord will raise up a prophet (or prophets) who, like Moses, will faithfully convey God's word to the people and in so doing represent God's rule in the new order that God is creating in and out of this people.[21]

I would add that the phrase "whom the Lord knew face to face" is as significant a criterion as performing "signs and wonders." But the force of Miller's point holds: specific qualifications given in Deut 34:10–12 mark Moses as the greatest of the prophets, yet fundamentally, Moses' role is to relate the word of YHWH, and to the extent that future prophets perform the same function, they are in continuity with Moses.

It is to these unequalled qualities, for being the one "whom the Lord knew him face to face" and for the "signs and wonders that the Lord sent him to perform," I now turn.

---

19. Craigie, *Book of Deuteronomy*, 406.
20. Cf. Knoppers, "'There Was None Like Him';" Chapman, *Law and the Prophets*, 123; Moberly, "Use of the Old Testament," 104.
21. Patrick D. Miller, "Moses My Servant: The Deuteronomic Portrait of Moses," *Int* 41, no. 3 (1987): 248, emphasis original.

2. "Whom the Lord Knew Face to Face"

The first aspect of Moses' preeminence is that YHWH knew him "face to face," פָּנִים אֶל־פָּנִים (Deut 34:10b). This phrase occurs also in Gen 32:30; Exod 33:11; Judg 6:22; and Ezek 20:35. Similar phrases are attested in Num 12:8 (פֶּה אֶל־פֶּה) and Deut 5:4 (פָּנִים בְּפָנִים). In Gen 32:30 and Judg 6:22, Jacob and Gideon respectively expect to die as a result of this immediate encounter with God. (A variation on this theme emerges in conjunction with Moses' mediation in Exod 33:18ff. and Deut 5:22–27.) Exodus 33:11 and Num 12:8 concern the unique relationship between YHWH and Moses. Deuteronomy 5:4 addresses YHWH's speaking the Decalogue directly to Israel. Ezekiel 20:35 is an unusual occurrence, suggesting that the Lord will appear "face to face" with the Israelites in the wilderness, in order to judge them. No pentateuchal narrative seems to account precisely for this reference, though the general sense of judgment following an unmediated experience of YHWH's presence may be the fear voiced in Gen 32:30 and Judg 6:22.

There are several ways of understanding the phrase "face to face" as it is used in these texts. At the start, we can easily dispense with one. Blenkinsopp writes of the phrase "face to face," that "such a way of speaking would seem to indicate simply the easy and unstinted familiarity existing between friends."[22] This approach to understanding the phrase "face to face" is based on Exod 33:11, which adds "as one speaks to a friend" (וְדִבֶּר יְהוָה אֶל־מֹשֶׁה פָּנִים אֶל־פָּנִים כַּאֲשֶׁר יְדַבֵּר אִישׁ אֶל־רֵעֵהוּ) to the phrase in question. Despite its textual support, such an account is inadequate, for as Chapman argues, this description is based on a non-Hebraic, romanticized notion of "friend," רֵעַ.[23] That the relationship between YHWH and Moses should not be characterized in terms of the intimacy of friendship is demonstrated by the qualifications to their interaction in Exod 33:20–23. If Moses has unprecedented, immediate interaction with YHWH, it is not without limits. Moreover, the nature of the limits (cf. Exod 33:20) suggests that their interaction is not one of equals but

---

22. Blenkinsopp, *Prophecy and Canon*, 89.
23. Chapman, *Law and the Prophets*, 120, fn. 42. Blenkinsopp himself is dissatisfied with such a brief account, because he views the text of Exod 33:11 as attesting to an ancient tent-oracle tradition in which one could see the face of God and still live. Blenkinsopp, *Prophecy and Canon*, 90. However, my reading suggests that nowhere in Exod 33 is it claimed that Moses sees God's face in a physical, anthropomorphic sense.

one of grace; the Lord creates the possibility and determines the parameters of their interaction.

2.1. Moses as Covenant Mediator

I argue that "face to face" *does* indicate a type of immediacy of relationship between YHWH and Moses, but that this relationship is best understood within the context of Moses' role as covenant mediator. The text of Deut 5:22-31 provides an account of this role and its origin.

At the beginning of his speech in this chapter,[24] Moses interprets the Horeb covenant not as made with the people's fathers, but as being made with this very generation (5:3). The people need to take responsibility for the covenant as their own. Moreover, Moses describes the process by which the people received the covenant and stresses the immediacy of the people's experience of YHWH: "The LORD spoke with you face to face at the mountain, out of the fire" (פָּנִים בְּפָנִים דִּבֶּר יְהוָה עִמָּכֶם בָּהָר מִתּוֹךְ הָאֵשׁ) (v. 4). The phrase translated "face to face" in this verse differs, perhaps marginally, from that of Deut 34:10b (פָּנִים אֶל־פָּנִים). Still, the phrase and its narrative context suggest that, in giving the Decalogue, YHWH is present to the Israelites as a whole in the same way that he is present to Moses subsequently.[25]

---

24. The text of Deut 5 is central to Deuteronomy. Olson sees in the structure of Deut 5 a condensed version of the entire book. Verses 1-5 serve as an introduction. 5:6 covers Israel's past history, summarizing Deut 1-4. Like Deut 5-28, 5:7-21 gives the present law, the Decalogue. Verses 22-31 concern the future provision of Moses as covenant mediator for the rest of the law, just as Deut 29-31 concerns what happens after Israel's future disloyalty to YHWH. Finally, like Deut 33-34, 5:32-33 concerns the blessing of Israel. However, Olson's schema seems too neat; for example, if 5:6 is a summary of chapters 1-4, would it not need to include a bit more detail? However, Olson has at least demonstrated that the themes prevalent throughout the book are also integral to this chapter. Olson, *Death of Moses*, 40-41.

25. Cf. Chapman, *Law and the Prophets*, 120.

Childs has observed the tension between Deut 5:4 and 5:5. In 5:4, the people hear the words of YHWH directly; in 5:5, Moses stands between them and YHWH, in order to declare the Lord's words to the people. Elsewhere in Deuteronomy and also in Exod 19-20, the biblical writers are clear that the Decalogue is spoken directly to the people, whereas Moses mediates the divine words following this encounter. Childs concludes that, while verse 5 is residual from an earlier tradition, "Verse 4 is a reading of the tradition after the redaction of J and E placed the Decalogue in its present position within the narrative." Childs, *The Book of Exodus*, 351-60. Olson rightly observes

The context of the people's request is the theophanic proclamation of the Decalogue (Deut 5:1–21). This immediate experience of YHWH is associated with cloud, fire, and darkness (5:4, 23–26) and demonstrated in that the people hear the voice of YHWH directly (vv. 24–26). The point of these phenomena is that they "convey something of the awesomeness of the divine presence and speech."[26] The phenomena and the presence and speech they indicate cause the Israelites to fear for their lives, so they declare, "For this great fire will consume us; if we hear the voice of the Lord any longer, we shall die. For who is there of all flesh that has heard the voice of the living God speaking out of fire, as we have, and remained alive?" (vv. 25–26).

Craigie tries to identify exactly what caused the Israelites to fear: do they react to the speech of God or to the visual phenomena associated with the speech? Craigie suggests that it was the phenomena: "Though he could not literally be seen, God could be known, but to *see* the phenomena surrounding his presence was exceptional rather than normal. It was the exceptional occurrence that terrified the people and reminded them of their *mortality*."[27] This differentiation goes beyond the text, which seems intentionally ambiguous: the phrase "speaking out of fire" has to do with both seeing and hearing. While elsewhere in the Old Testament fear for one's life does accompany seeing God "face to face" (Gen 32:30; Judg 6:22), the overall account of the Sinai theophany in Deuteronomy is more concerned with hearing than seeing. For example, in Deut 4, the prohibition of images is founded on a formless theophany: וְנִשְׁמַרְתֶּם מְאֹד לְנַפְשֹׁתֵיכֶם כִּי לֹא רְאִיתֶם כָּל־תְּמוּנָה בְּיוֹם דִּבֶּר יְהוָה אֲלֵיכֶם בְּחֹרֵב מִתּוֹךְ הָאֵשׁ, "Since you saw no form when the Lord spoke to you at Horeb out of the fire, take care and watch yourselves closely, so that you do not act corruptly by making an idol for yourselves, in the form of

---

that at the level of final form, these verses "wrestle with the paradox of the intimate and mediated presence of God." Olson, *Death of Moses*, 41. The text of 5:22–28 clearly assumes that the people have heard the words of YHWH directly, and that therefore they have reason to petition Moses to mediate for them in the future. The purpose of 5:5 in the received text may be to explain the different wording of the Decalogue in Deuteronomy and Exodus, by inserting a reference to the situation after the giving of the Decalogue (Exod 20:18ff.).

26. Moberly, *Prophecy and Discernment*, 6.

27. Craigie, *Book of Deuteronomy*, 165, emphasis original. Craigie may be conflating Exod 20:18–21 with Deut 5, though in the latter text the people do see fire on the mountain and are concerned about mortality.

any figure." (Deut 4:15-16a). Moreover, Deut 18:16 restates the concern in 5:25-26 as "if I hear the voice of the Lord my God any more or ever again see this great fire, I will die." In light of this, it seems wise to retain the ambiguity of Deut 5:26: it is the immediate experience of YHWH and all that includes—hearing the voice of the Lord and seeing phenomena associated with his presence—which causes the Israelites to respond as they do. Specifically, it is the proximity of the "living God" (אֱלֹהִים חַיִּים) which reminds the people of their mortality.[28] So the text suggests a distinction between the nature of divine and human life, a distinction which is known in the context of hearing the voice of YHWH "speaking out of fire."

The people summon Moses to "Go near, you yourself, and hear all that the Lord our God will say. Then tell us everything that the Lord our God tells you, and we will listen and do it" (Deut 5:27). By committing themselves to heeding Moses' word, the people demonstrate that they are not avoiding responsibility in their request for mediation.[29] YHWH approves of the people's request, saying: שָׁמַעְתִּי אֶת־קוֹל דִּבְרֵי הָעָם הַזֶּה אֲשֶׁר דִּבְּרוּ אֵלֶיךָ הֵיטִיבוּ כָּל־אֲשֶׁר דִּבֵּרוּ, "I have heard the words of this people, which they have spoken to you; they are right in all that they have spoken" (v. 28). Even as this text describes the people sending Moses to act as their mediator, it includes YHWH's approval. In light of this approval and the people's commitment to obeying whatever instruction Moses relays to them, the people's fear should be understood not as weakness, but as strength. The reverence that the people exhibit in taking caution with the immediate presence of YHWH is commendable; God hopes that this type of reverence will continue to characterize the Israelites, so that they will keep the commandments (Deut 5:29).[30] Similarly, the text of verses 32-33 articulates the purpose of the narrative: further rationale for why the Israelites must heed YHWH's commandments, given through Moses. Articulating the authority of Moses, given to him by the Israelites as well as YHWH, is in service of the larger point of obedience.

Therefore, this passage serves as a rationale for prophecy, or more specifically, mediation of the covenant. Moses as covenant mediator is distinguished by his proximity to YHWH, the living God, a proximity which is demonstrated by both hearing and seeing. I hope it is clear that I am

---

28. Ibid.
29. Ibid., 166.
30. Tigay, *Deuteronomy*, 73. Cf. Moberly's critique of von Balthasar's "Protestant" reading of this text. Moberly, *Prophecy and Discernment*, 39-40.

suggesting that Moses has proximity to YHWH in neither a geographical sense (with reference to Mount Horeb)[31] nor an ontological one,[32] if by "ontological" one means that Moses is a different kind of being than human. Moberly argues that Moses' proximity to YHWH is "moral" or "spiritual," while acknowledging the problematic nature of these terms.[33] Similarly, Briggs argues that Moses' uniqueness lies in his "dependence" on YHWH, for the divine word and the virtue to handle it well.[34] Therefore, Moses' proximity to YHWH, understood as moral or spiritual closeness, is grounded in an act of God rather than a specific quality or characteristic that Moses attains for himself (though this proximity, by virtue of being moral and spiritual, will be demonstrated in action). Thus I agree with both Moberly and Briggs and add that this proximity is associated with Moses' *perception* of YHWH, which leads to action appropriate to this perception. (Why the emphasis on perception is appropriate is examined in greater detail later in this chapter.) Again, Moses' perception of YHWH is grounded in YHWH's revelation of himself to Moses in a characteristically different way than God appeared to other Israelites or to the prophets after Moses.

2.2. Risk and Intercession

The explanation of Moses' vocation in Deut 5 highlights the riskiness of his position. The people want him to stand between them and YHWH so that they will not die, but will *Moses* die? Olson argues that "the office of mediator carries with it the price of premature death, a death Moses will experience while still strong and vigorous in Deuteronomy 34."[35] At no point does the Old Testament state explicitly that Moses dies on account of his vocation. While the precise reason for his death before entering the land is a matter of interpretive dispute,[36] biblical references (Deut 1:37; 32:51; Num 20:12) sug-

---

31. See Moberly, *Prophecy and Discernment*, 9.
32. See Richard S. Briggs, *The Virtuous Reader: Old Testament Narrative and Interpretive Virtue*, Studies in Theological Interpretation (Grand Rapids: Baker, 2010), 60–61.
33. Moberly, *Prophecy and Discernment*, 9.
34. Briggs, *Virtuous Reader*, 60–64.
35. Olson, *Death of Moses*, 47.
36. Milgrom identifies eleven different explanations for Moses' death outside the land; Tigay, on the basis of Deut 1:37, suggests a twelfth. Jacob Milgrom, "Magic, Monotheism and the Sin of Moses," in *The Quest for the Kingdom of God: Studies in Honor of George E. Mendenhall*, ed. H. H. B. Huffmon, F. A. Spina and A. R. W. Ravinell (Winona

gest a wrongdoing committed either by the Israelites or Moses. In contrast, Moses' vocation is risky, but it has divine approval (cf. Deut 5:28–31).

The text of Exod 32 describes Moses' first attempt to convince the Lord to forgive the people for the golden calf incident;[37] in doing so, Moses declares, "But now, if you will only forgive their sin—but if not, blot me out of the book that you have written" (Exod 32:32). Presumably, being "blotted out of the book" is the penalty for breaking the covenant. If the Lord will not forgive without exacting penalty, Moses suggests that YHWH will direct punishment toward Moses instead. But his request is refused: though God will not yet forgive the people, only those who have sinned will be "blotted out" (Exod 32:33); the Lord would not judge anyone who was not guilty. Moses put his life on the line for the sake of the Israelites. Augustine beautifully compares the compassion of Moses for the people with that of a mother:

> Mark that, as it were, mother's fondness, of which I have often spoken. When God threatened the sacrilegious people, Moses' tender heart trembled, and on their behalf he opposed himself to the wrath of God. "Lord," he says, "if Thou wilt forgive their sin, forgive; but if not, blot me out of Thy book which Thou hast written." With what a father's and mother's fondness, yet with what assurance said he this, as he considered at once the justice and the mercy of God; that in that He is just, He would not destroy the righteous man; and that in that He is merciful, He would pardon the sinners.[38]

So, for Augustine, Moses becomes the model of one who does not turn his back on the wicked, but while inwardly choosing a different course from their wrongdoing, outwardly has compassion upon them.[39] Moses' intercession for the Israelites is deeply self-involving, even risky.

The text of Deut 9 heightens the drama of Moses' intercession for the people in response to the calf episode and the self-denial he exhibits in such intercession. When Moses retells the story, he adds, "Then I lay prostrate before the LORD as before, for forty days and forty nights; I neither ate bread nor drank water, because of all the sin you had committed, provoking the

---

Lake, IN: Eisenbrauns, 1983), 251–65; Tigay, *Deuteronomy*, 425.

37. The intercession of Exod 32:11–14 does not concern forgiveness but whether the people can be allowed to live after breaking the covenant.

38. *Serm.* 38.24.

39. Ibid., 38.25.

Lord by doing what was evil in his sight" (Deut 9:18). Having completed forty days and nights of fasting while receiving the stone tablets (Deut 9:9), Moses descends the mountain only to fast again. Also, according to Moses' retelling, the self-denial works; the Lord listens to his intercession (v. 19).

Childs writes, "Increasingly Moses became a type of the innocent suffering servant, bearing the sins of the nation, who stood in Israel's place but could not himself enter the promised land."[40] Indeed, this theme is more prevalent (and more successful) in Deuteronomy than in Exodus;[41] Moses' self-denial is also much more of a theme in this book, leading as it does to Moses' death. This self-denial is not only associated with Moses' intercession, but also with him receiving the covenant (Deut 9:9). If this leader "bear[s] the sins of the nation," then he also stands in the dangerous position of immediately receiving the word of God.

2.3. "Face to Face"

Regarding the repetition of פָּנִים in Exod 33, commentators have observed a seeming contradiction in its use. In 33:11, the reader learns that YHWH would speak with Moses "face to face" פָּנִים אֶל־פָּנִים, whereas in 33:20, the Lord declares that neither Moses nor anyone else will be able to see the God's face and live (33:20). Though the Septuagint translates verse 11 with ἐνώπιος ἐνωπίῳ ("presence to presence"), *Targum Onqelos* reads ממלל עם ממלל, "speech with speech," and *Targum Neofiti*, ממלל לקבל ממלל, "speech towards/opposite/against/in the presence of speech."[42] By interpreting this phrase in this way, the Targumic traditions suggest two things: first, that the matter at hand is speech rather than sight, and second, that one ought to imagine a dialogue rather than a monologue. Both of these elements of the Targumic versions resonate with the sense of the wider narrative. The text of Exod 33:7–11 is clearly preparatory for the story of Moses' intercession in verses 12ff., in which Moses audaciously negotiates with YHWH. Further, YHWH fulfills the request and qualification of 33:18–22 with a primarily auditory proclamation of his presence in Exod 34:5–7. Though the cloud is seen, the more significant elements of YHWH's presence are the repetition of the divine name and the explanation of the name in terms of characteristics of God. Seeing God's face is impossible, but Moses hears God in both passages.

---

40. Childs, *Old Testament Theology*, 111.
41. See von Rad, *Old Testament Theology*, 294–95.
42. Cf. *Tg. Ps.-J.*

So, with the Targums, there is some basis for claiming that the primary sense of Exod 33:11 might be *hearing* rather than *seeing*, for it is YHWH's speaking that is in view. However, as in Deut 5:25-26, Moses' role as covenant mediator cannot be exclusively defined in terms of sight, for the Israelites feared the close presence of YHWH, including the sight of the fire and the sound of YHWH's voice. What then is the sense of the phrase "face to face" in Deut 34:10? Like Deut 34:10-12, Exod 33 suggests that Moses is unlike other prophets in that he has a heightened perception of God. Both visual and auditory language is used to describe this perception, which is perhaps neither visual nor auditory in a straightforward sense.

2.4. Numbers 12:6-8

Though my primary concern in this section is Num 12:6-8, it will be helpful to set these verses in context. The narrative as a whole tells of the rebellion of Miriam and Aaron, who have two seemingly unrelated complaints: first, that Moses has taken a Cushite wife, and second, that the Lord has spoken also to them, intimating that Moses' authority is not unique in the community (Num 12:1-2). The second complaint relates to the narrative in Num 11, in which the spirit rests on seventy elders so that they prophesy. Eldad and Medad continue to do so (Num 11:16-20). Moses defends these prophets, saying, "Would that all the Lord's people were prophets, and that the Lord would put his spirit on them!" (Num 11:29b).[43] Aaron's question in 12:2 suggests a situation in conflict with that of chapter 11: it is supposed that Moses is the only one to whom the Lord has spoken. If verse 2 requires some reading between the lines to determine what Miriam and Aaron mean by their statement, verse 1 presents an interpretive puzzle. At the level of the text's received form, "the precise identity of Moses' Cushite wife and the nature of Miriam and Aaron's objection against her remain unclear."[44]

---

43. Aaron is never identified as a prophet of God, yet the text of Exod 15:20 describes Miriam as a prophetess. Thus, it is unclear why Aaron is included in verse 2, except to voice Miriam's concern, particularly since, in verse 1, וַתְּדַבֵּר is feminine. Martin Noth, *Numbers: A Commentary*, trans. James D. Martin, OTL 7 (Philadelphia: Westminster, 1968), 95; cf. Bernard P. Robinson, "The Jealousy of Miriam: A Note on Num 12," *ZAW* 101, no. 3 (1989): 430-31.

44. Dennis T. Olson, *Numbers*, IBC (Louisville: Westminster John Knox, 1996), 71. If by "Cush," Ethiopia is intended (see LXX), then the wife in question is not Zipporah. However, if Moses divorced Zipporah or took an additional wife to Zipporah, this is

The narrator then gives us some information about Moses: וְהָאִישׁ מֹשֶׁה עָנָו מְאֹד מִכֹּל הָאָדָם אֲשֶׁר עַל־פְּנֵי הָאֲדָמָה, "Now the man Moses was very humble, more so than anyone else on the face of the earth" (Num 12:3). If we had hoped that this character portrayal of Moses would aid in understanding why Miriam and Aaron are speaking against Moses, we may be sorely disappointed. This text presents an incomparability statement, and one that is farther-reaching than that of Deut 34:10, as it compares Moses not only with prophets but with all of humanity.

To deal with the seeming discontinuities in the passage, Noth argues the the first three verses indicate three stages of textual development. The feminine singular verb וַתְּדַבֵּר in verse 1 suggests that Miriam was the original subject and instigator of the episode; this also explains why only Miriam is punished. The second stage of the text's development adds Aaron and the concern about leadership (v. 2). Additions of the third stage concern Moses' character and status before God and the people (v. 3).[45] However, even as Noth's explanation is a helpful way of accounting for some of the difficulties

---

never explicitly stated in the Pentateuch. Furthermore, Hab 3:7 puts "Midian" in parallel with the place name "Cushan." If "Cush" in Num 12:1 refers to Cushan, then this is Zipporah. If it is Zipporah, one might ask why Miriam has waited so long to voice her concern. Cf. Timothy R. Ashley, *The Book of Numbers*, NICOT (Grand Rapids, Eerdmans, 1993), 223–24.

Milgrom resolves this by observing that Zipporah would not have gone to Egypt, but joined the group at Sinai. Still, the Israelites are a distance from Sinai in Num 12! Jacob Milgrom, *Numbers*, JPS Torah Comentary (Philadelphia: JPS, 1990), 93.

Even once the identity of the wife has been determined, the complaint of Miriam might still be opaque for the modern reader. Perhaps she is jealous of the authority of Moses' wife among the women in Moses' house, or of her influence on Moses. Robinson, "Jealousy of Miriam," 431; David L. Stubbs, *Numbers*, BTCB (Grand Rapids: Brazos, 2009), 122; Olson, *Numbers*, 71.

Alternatively, the issue could be racial or ethnic, or perhaps the objection about the wife is only a "surface issue that concealed the deeper problem" discussed in verse 2. Hepner's suggestion that Moses' wife had a questionable sexual history seems far-fetched, but the ambiguity of the passage does open possibilities for imaginative construals. Ashley, *Book of Numbers*, 224; Gershon Hepner, "Moses' Cushite Wife Echoes Hosea's Woman of Harlotries: Exposure of Unfaithfulness in the Wilderness," *SJOT* 23, no. 2 (2009): 233–42.

45. That verse 3 is a later addition is seen from the close connection between verses 2b and 4. Noth, *Numbers*, 92–95.

in the narrative, the passage can fruitfully be read as a coherent literary unit, governed largely by the third stage in the text's development. In this way, Coats and Robinson have argued that the final form of the text concerns Moses' virtue or position, respectively.[46] Milgrom holds these two themes together under the overarching rubric of Moses' uniqueness, saying, "The uniqueness of Moses is the sole theme of this chapter. It is reflected in the challenge to his authority (v. 2); his humility (v. 3); God's affirmation of his uniqueness (vv. 6-8); the punishment of Miriam (vv. 9-10); and Moses' successful intercession on her behalf (vv. 11-15)."[47] I will argue that Moses' virtue and position, both before God and before Israel, are intrinsically related. Therefore, the meaning of the passage can be described as the preeminence of Moses according to the intersection of his virtue and his vocation.

One option for piecing Miriam and Aaron's concerns together with the narrator's statement is that the Lord has spoken to Moses, indicating that it is permissible for him to divorce Zipporah and take a foreign wife. If that is the case, then the narrator's comment would guard against the reader thinking that Moses has simply taken an exception to the law for himself without true divine direction.[48] Alternatively, according to the flow of the narrative, Moses' humility might explain why Moses does not respond directly to Miriam and Aaron; the reader is to understand that Moses' lack of response is not a sign of weakness, but of humility.[49] Moreover, this statement attunes the reader to the fact that the main point of the narrative will be its portrayal of Moses' character.

But precisely what does verse 3 indicate about Moses' character? The word ענו is difficult to translate, as this is the only occurrence of the word in the singular. The plural form is attested twenty times in the Old Testament (e.g., Isa 32:7; Amos 8:4; Ps 9:13, 19; 10:2; Prov 3:14; 14:21; 16:19; Job 24:4); in these texts, the word means bowed or crouched down, either willfully or

---

46. George W. Coats, "Humility and Honor: A Moses Legend in Numbers 12," in *The Moses Tradition* (Sheffield: JSOT, 1993), 88-98; Robinson, "Jealousy of Miriam," passim.
47. Milgrom, *Numbers*, 93.
48. See Fischer's argument as described in Briggs, *Virtuous Reader*, 58.
49. See Ashley, *Book of Numbers*, 224; Milgrom, *Numbers*, 94. This point only holds if the reader assumes that Moses heard Miriam and Aaron's complaints, whereas the narrator only tells us that YHWH heard.

forcefully, and by extension, humble or pious.[50] Moses being physically brought low does not seem to fit the narrative at hand. A psychological description—that by the challenging words of Miriam and Aaron, Moses is brought to a mental state of utter despondency—is possible, but "more so than anyone else on earth" would seem a rather exaggerated designation.[51] Thus, English translators tend to translate עָנָו as "humble."

However, if we should understand עָנָו in this text as "humble," this presents a further problem. As Briggs observes, humility is not something that can be sought after and achieved in comparative terms. One can only say, "I am the most humble person on earth" with a deep sense of irony, meaning that one is *not* humble. So Briggs asks, "Is Moses to be understood as the one who excels most noticeably in the area of self-effacement?"[52] This problem is not altogether alleviated by modern criticism which denies Mosaic authorship of the Pentateuch,[53] because the designation "more so than anyone else on earth" would seem odd for a description of humility even if one imagines it penned by a hand other than Moses'.

What was perhaps once an appropriate translation, "meek," now connotes too much passivity to describe Moses in this narrative.[54] While Moses does not rebuke Aaron and Miriam, he boldly intercedes on Miriam's behalf (Num 12:13). Coats helpfully suggests a comparison between עָנָו and כָּבוֹד, "honor," following the phrase וְלִפְנֵי כָבוֹד עֲנָוָה ("and/but humility comes before honor"), which occurs in both Prov 15:33 and 18:12. כָּבוֹד may refer to public honor, and עֲנָוָה "is therefore personal honor, the integrity of character that makes public honor well bestowed."[55] Further, in Prov 15:33 עֲנָוָה appears in parallel with יִרְאַת יְהוָה, "the fear of the Lord," and Ps 22:27 reads, יֹאכְלוּ עֲנָוִים וְיִשְׂבָּעוּ יְהַלְלוּ יְהוָה דֹּרְשָׁיו, "the עֲנָוִים will eat and be satisfied; those who seek him shall praise the Lord." In these contexts, עָנָו suggests obedience and pursuit of God. Might this sense also be present in Num 12? To answer this question, one must continue reading.

---

50. *HALOT*, "עָנָו"; cf. *TDOT*, "עָנָה II."
51. Contra Cleon Rogers, "Moses: Meek or Miserable?" *JETS* 29, no. 3 (1986): 257-63.
52. Briggs, *Virtuous Reader*, 49.
53. Contra George Buchanan Gray, *A Critical and Exegetical Commentary on Numbers* (Edinburgh: T&T Clark, 1903), 123.
54. Briggs, *Virtuous Reader*, 50; cf. Milgrom, *Numbers*, 94.
55. Coats, "Humility and Honor," 94.

The Lord calls the three to the tent of meeting (v. 4), and then, descending in a pillar of cloud, summons Miriam and Aaron apart from Moses in order to speak to them (v. 5). Whether or not Moses can hear what YHWH says in verses 6–8 is not stated, but one may gather that the Lord directs his speech toward Miriam and Aaron.

וַיֹּאמֶר שִׁמְעוּ־נָא דְבָרָי אִם־יִהְיֶה נְבִיאֲכֶם יְהוָה בַּמַּרְאָה אֵלָיו אֶתְוַדָּע בַּחֲלוֹם אֲדַבֶּר־בּוֹ: לֹא־כֵן עַבְדִּי מֹשֶׁה בְּכָל־בֵּיתִי נֶאֱמָן הוּא: פֶּה אֶל־פֶּה אֲדַבֶּר־בּוֹ וּמַרְאֶה וְלֹא בְחִידֹת וּתְמֻנַת יְהוָה יַבִּיט וּמַדּוּעַ לֹא יְרֵאתֶם לְדַבֵּר בְּעַבְדִּי בְמֹשֶׁה:

And he said, "Hear my words:
When there are prophets among you,
I the LORD make myself known to them in visions;
I speak to them in dreams.
Not so with my servant Moses;
he is entrusted with all my house.
With him I speak face to face—clearly, not in riddles;
and he beholds the form of the LORD.
Why then were you not afraid to speak against my servant Moses?"

This text differentiates Moses from other prophets in several ways.[56] First, the Lord declares, בְּכָל־בֵּיתִי נֶאֱמָן הוּא, "he is entrusted with all of my house" (NRSV) or "he is [the most] trusted of all of my household."[57] Interpreting this statement is complicated by at least two factors: First, this is the only place in the Old Testament that the *nipʿal* of אמן is attested with a בְּ preposition. This verb regularly occurs in the *hipʿil* with בְּ, meaning "to believe/trust in" something or someone.[58] Second, what is meant by YHWH's "house": Israel, or "God's celestial 'house'?"[59] So, following the two translation options given above, the text could mean that, among even the celestial beings, "Moses is the most trusted; he alone has direct access to the Deity

---

56. As in the text of Deut 34:10–12, here Moses is compared with other prophets. In this case, the prophets in view are contemporaneous with Moses rather than subsequent to him; possibly, these prophets refer to those on whom the spirit of the Lord rests in Num 11.

57. Milgrom, *Numbers*, 96.

58. In 1 Sam 3:20, the verb occurs in the *nipʿal* with an object carrying a preformative לְ. *HALOT*, "אמן."

59. Milgrom, *Numbers*, 96.

and obtains an audience with Him at will."⁶⁰ Or, it could mean that Moses is the head-servant of YHWH, charged with leading Israel. With regard to the second meaning, in Gen 24:2, Eliezer is given similar jurisdiction over Abraham's house, and Joseph is, with Potiphar's, in Gen 39:4–5.

However one understands this phrase, the text suggests that the authority or trustworthiness that Moses exemplifies is unlike that of other prophets, about whom the Lord would not say, בְּכָל־בֵּיתִי נֶאֱמָן הוּא. A series of phrases further specifies the contrast: to other prophets, YHWH makes himself known בַּמַּרְאָה, "in visions," and YHWH speaks to them בַּחֲלוֹם "in dreams."⁶¹ But YHWH's communication with Moses is to be distinguished from these media. God speaks with Moses פֶּה אֶל־פֶּה, וּמַרְאֶה וְלֹא בְחִידֹת and וּתְמֻנַת יְהוָה יַבִּיט. The first of these phrases, literally "mouth to mouth," or "face to face," bears strong similarity to the פָּנִים אֶל־פָּנִים of Exod 33:11 and Deut 34:10. Building on the sense of Moses as a head-servant (v. 7b), Milgrom writes, "The image is that of a royal house in which only the most trusted servant has regular access to the monarch. Such ones are called literally 'those who see the face of the king' (2 Kings 25:19)."⁶² The phrase suggests dialogue, which is further demonstrated by Moses' pleading prayer (v. 13).

The second phrase, וּמַרְאֶה וְלֹא בְחִידֹת, which the NRSV translates, "clearly, not in riddles," oddly repeats the term that, in verse 6, characterizes how YHWH speaks to other prophets, "in visions." Yet, in verse 8, the meaning seems to be different, as it is in contrast with בְחִידֹת. The sense of the statement might be that when Moses hears the word of YHWH, it does not require interpretation. Between verses 6 and 8, the term's vowels differ, first reading בַּמַּרְאָה and then, וּמַרְאֶה, suggesting that the Masoretes attempted a distinction; the latter could perhaps mean "visible appearance" rather than "vision."⁶³ Freedman applies the medial negative לֹא to both בְחִידֹת and וּמַרְאֶה, translating the phrase, "Not in a vision or in riddles, And the form of Yahweh he beholds."⁶⁴ Further, he suggests that "visions," through which

---

60. Ibid.
61. God speaking and making himself known appear synonymous.
62. Ibid.
63. David Noel Freedman, "The Aaronic Blessing (Numbers 6:24–26)," in *Pottery, Poetry and Prophecy: Studies in Early Hebrew Poetry* (Winona Lake, IN: Eisenbrauns, 1980), 237.
64. Ibid., 236; cf. Ashley, *The Book of Numbers*, 221. Both Freedman and Ashley acknowledge the significant textual evidence for changing בַּמַּרְאָה to וּמַרְאֶה (Sam. Pent.,

YHWH speaks to other prophets, are less immediate manifestations of the Lord's presence than "the form."[65]

In a more speculative move, Kselman has argued that the original text of verse 6 read לֹא where the received text has אֵלָיו, and thus the original text would have read, "in vision (theophany) I do not make myself known, (but) in a dream I speak with him."[66] However, I am not convinced that textual emendation is necessary to make sense of this passage, for a similar phenomenon occurs in Exod 3:2-3. The burning bush is first described, according to Moses' perception, וַיַּרְא וְהִנֵּה הַסְּנֶה בֹּעֵר בָּאֵשׁ וְהַסְּנֶה אֵינֶנּוּ אֻכָּל, which the NRSV translates, "he looked, and the bush was blazing, yet it was not consumed" (Exod 3:2). However, in the next verse, Moses speaks about his need to see מַדּוּעַ לֹא־יִבְעַר הַסְּנֶה (Exod 3:3). Whereas in verse 2, the bush is burning (בער, *qal* part.) but is not consumed (אכל), the bush does not burn (בער, *qal* imperf.) in verse 3. The NRSV smooths over this apparent contradiction by translating the latter בער as "burn up." In both Exod 3:2-3 and Num 12:6-8, the biblical writers struggle to communicate difficult and complex visual phenomena. How can a bush burn but not be consumed? What language can one use to describe this? Similarly, how can one precisely articulate how it is that YHWH appears to Moses? Words fail.[67]

Finally, unlike other prophets who have "visions" and "dreams," Moses וּתְמֻנַת יְהוָה יַבִּיט, "beholds the form of the Lord." Translating תְּמוּנָה with "form" is appropriate since all ten instances of the noun in the Old Testament suggest a visible form.[68] With this phrase, this biblical text refuses to classify Moses' reception of knowledge of God exclusively by means of hearing. Rather, it is possible to talk about Moses seeing. Waschke considers this text in conflict with passages suggesting that no one can see God and live (e.g., Exod 19:21; 33:18-23). He claims that Num 12:8 "underlines Moses' unique position in converse with Yahweh: he is granted a vision of God that would result in death for anyone else."[69] However, Waschke acknowledges

---

LXX, Syr., and Vulg.).

65. Cf. Gray, *Numbers*, 126.

66. J. S. Kselman, "A Note on Numbers XII 6-8," *VT* 26, no. 4 (1976): 501-2.

67. As Olson writes, "God's words strain to describe the intense intimacy of God and Moses." Olson, *Numbers*, 71.

68. See Exod 20:4=Deut 5:8; Deut 4:12, 15-16, 23, 25; Num 12:8; Job 4:16; Ps 17:15. *TDOT*, "תְּמוּנָה."

69. Ibid.

that the same term is used metaphorically in Ps 17:15, where it expresses the psalmist's desire for vindication in the morning, upon beholding (חזה) the תְּמוּנָה of YHWH.⁷⁰ In Num 12:8 there may be more ambiguity with respect to whether the term is meant metaphorically or literally. As in Deut 5, Moses is asked to experience regularly the type of communication that the Israelites as a whole had in receiving the Decalogue. The Septuagint translators made an intriguing choice in verse 8, translating וּתְמֻנַת יְהוָה יַבִּיט, "and he beholds the form of the Lord," as καὶ τὴν δόξαν κυρίου εἶδεν, "and he saw the glory of the Lord," perhaps referring to a particular experience of Moses. Thus the language of this verse, in Greek, reminds the reader of Exod 33:18ff., suggesting that one can read these two texts together. Moses sees "the glory of the Lord," and the Israelites have as well (cf. Exod 16:6-7, 10; 40:34-38). According to the Greek version, the sense is not that Moses saw God in a way that was unavailable to others, but that the most immediate manifestation of YHWH that the Israelites experienced was much more frequent for Moses: Moses regularly experienced what the Israelites only very occasionally experienced (cf. Deut 5:22-31). Though the Septuagint uses a different concept, in this verse, to communicate the nature of Moses' communication with God, it is not out of keeping with the sense of the Masoretic Text.

Richard Briggs has argued that the sense of "humility" in verse 3 should be understood within the context of the entire narrative. In this context, humility "is dependence upon God, and in particular, it is dependence upon God for any speaking of a divinely authorized word."⁷¹ Humility is a requirement for handling the divine word well.⁷² Thus, the statement about Moses' humility expresses how Moses deals with what he sees and hears, and his uniqueness is a matter of both the unmediated nature of Moses' interaction with God and how he conducts himself in light of this access. His intercession for Miriam later in the chapter (12:13) is another example of Moses employing his access to YHWH out of compassion for the Israelites, to convince YHWH to relent from punishment. It would seem, then, that perception (seeing and hearing) and action are interrelated.⁷³ Moses, who handled the di-

---

70. Ibid.
71. Briggs, *Virtuous Reader*, 60.
72. Ibid., 63.
73. Cf. Ellen Davis argues that contemplation requires *metanoia*—seeing truly requires change in action. Ellen F. Davis, *Scripture, Culture, and Agriculture: An Agrarian Reading of the Bible* (Cambridge: Cambridge University, 2009), 46-47.

vine word better than any other person on earth (Num 12:3), also regularly spoke with YHWH "face to face" (v. 8a) and saw "the form of YHWH" (v. 8b).

Thus in this section, I have argued that Num 12:6-8 portrays Moses as a prophet *par excellence*, in accordance with the particular directness with which YHWH presents himself to Moses' senses of hearing and sight. Moses perceives God more immediately than the other prophets, and this gives him unique authority. So far in this chapter, I have claimed that Deut 34:10 describes Moses as preeminent among the prophets in accordance with his unmediated, "face to face" interaction with YHWH, in which Moses regularly sees and hears YHWH with profound immediacy, constituting tremendous risk for Moses and requiring self-denial. This relationship enables Moses to declare the covenant to the Israelites, and to intercede on their behalf so that God will relent from punishing those who transgress the covenant. The goal of this chapter is to see how statements about Moses' vocation can shed light on Exod 3:1-4:17, but first I must address the final aspect of Moses' uniqueness articulated in Deut 34:10-12.

3. "Signs and Wonders," "Mighty Deeds," "Awesome Displays of Power"

The text of Deut 34 describes the next aspect of Moses' uniqueness:

לְכָל־הָאֹתוֹת וְהַמּוֹפְתִים אֲשֶׁר שְׁלָחוֹ יְהוָה לַעֲשׂוֹת בְּאֶרֶץ מִצְרָיִם לְפַרְעֹה וּלְכָל־עֲבָדָיו וּלְכָל־אַרְצוֹ: וּלְכֹל הַיָּד הַחֲזָקָה וּלְכֹל הַמּוֹרָא הַגָּדוֹל אֲשֶׁר עָשָׂה מֹשֶׁה לְעֵינֵי כָּל־יִשְׂרָאֵל:

> He was unequalled for all the signs and wonders that the Lord sent him to perform in the land of Egypt, against Pharaoh and all his servants and his entire land, and for all the mighty deeds and all the terrifying displays of power that Moses performed in the sight of all Israel (Deut 34:11-12).

Immediately one recognizes the awkward syntax of these verses, which presuppose verse 10. The לְ of specification ("with respect to"), which begins the verse (לְכָל־), unusually follows the אֲשֶׁר in verse 10b.[74] For this reason, the NRSV repeats the main clause of verse 10, "he was unequalled for," though this phrase does not appear in the Hebrew of verse 11. The construction is

---

74. Chapman, *Law and the Prophets*, 123.

awkward, but the force of the verses is clear: the "signs and wonders" that Moses performs in Egypt and the "mighty deeds" he does before Israel demonstrate his preeminence among the prophets. Further, the text appears to be repetitive, in contrast to "whom the Lord knew face to face," which speaks briefly but with significant meaning. The deeds of Moses are divided between those that happen in Egypt ("signs and wonders") and those that occur before Israel ("mighty deeds" and "terrifying displays of power.")[75]

3.1. Prophets and "Signs and Wonders"

The terms "sign" (אוֹת) and "wonder" (מוֹפֵת), both in the singular, appear in Deut 13:2-3[1-2], a passage that warns the people against heeding the words of false prophets. However, neither sign nor wonder constitute the falsity of the prophecy (v. 3a[2a]). On the contrary, these terms typically refer to the means by which a person can judge whether a prophet is true or false: if the foretold "signs and wonders" occur, then the prophet is true (cf. Jer 28:9). So, of Deut 34:11-12, Tigay writes, "No prophet so thoroughly proved his authenticity as Moses did."[76] In Exod 4:1-9, YHWH gives Moses two signs by which the Israelites will be able to discern that he has been sent by YHWH. The situation that Deut 13:2-3[1-2] asks us to imagine is one in which the signs are followed by teaching that leads people to serve other gods (v. 3b[2b]). It is this teaching that makes the prophets false, not the "signs and wonders."[77] Thus, in verse 2a[1a], prophets are neutrally described as those who "divine by dreams and promise you omens or portents" (חֲלֹם חֲלוֹם וְנָתַן אֵלֶיךָ אוֹת אוֹ מוֹפֵת). Moses meets the second criterion but exceeds the first, since he speaks with YHWH "face to face" rather than in a dream (Num 12:6-8). This does not make Moses a false prophet, but certainly it makes him a prophet, and more than one.

---

75. Chapman suggests that the text of verses 11-12 is a later addition, because the final statement "that Moses performed in the sight of all Israel" (אֲשֶׁר עָשָׂה מֹשֶׁה לְעֵינֵי כָּל־יִשְׂרָאֵל) repeats information found already in verse 10. Ibid. However, the phrase, "that Moses performed in the sight of all Israel," in verse 12 may be meant as a contrast with the location in Egypt (v. 11), and thus does not precisely repeat the sense of verse 10, which indicates that Moses is an Israelite prophet. This phrase in itself is not necessarily indicative of a later addition.

76. Tigay, *Deuteronomy*, 340.

77. See ibid., 129-30; Chapman, *Law and the Prophets*, 125.

Though "sign" and "wonder" in Deut 13:2-3[1-2] refer to the work of prophets,[78] more frequently throughout the book of Deuteronomy, these terms refer to the work of YHWH, especially (but not exclusively) in the Israelites' deliverance from Egypt through plagues. This is particularly true when אוֹת and מוֹפֵת are coupled with other important terms in Deut 34:11-12: הַיָּד הַחֲזָקָה and הַמּוֹרָא הַגָּדוֹל (e.g., Deut 4:34; 6:22; 7:19; 26:8; 29:2-4).[79] A look at Deut 4:32-40 may suggest a reason why these terms have been used to speak of Moses' incomparability.

3.2. The Incomparability of YHWH, Israel, and Moses (Deut 4:32-40)

The flow of 4:33-35 repeats in verses 36-40. In Moses' eloquent speech, he describes the deeds of YHWH for Israel: first, God spoke to Israel directly, out of fire (v. 33, 36; cf. Exod 19:16–20:21; Deut 5). Second, in a tremendous display of power, the Lord has brought the Israelites out of Egypt, making them God's own people (v. 34). In verse 37, this work is placed in broader historical context, between God's promises to the patriarchs and defense of Israel in conquest. These deeds are considered unprecedented, both in this generation and in previous times, both on earth and in heaven. It may not be far-fetched to argue that this text suggests YHWH's historical deeds for the Israelites are of eternal significance. What God has accomplished has fundamentally changed the possibilities for human life in Israel, for Israel is now a people taken as God's possession, and also among all the nations, since never before has such a thing occurred. The purpose of these acts is to cause Israel to know YHWH, which is described in terms of knowing "that the Lord is God" (v. 35), that there is no other God beside YHWH (vv. 35b, 39), that the Lord dwells both in heaven and on earth (v. 39), and in terms of keeping the commandments, which will bring blessing in the land (v. 40).[80] Through

---

78. Elsewhere in the Old Testament, prophets perform "signs and wonders" or are called "signs and wonders" themselves. See 1 Kgs 13; 2 Kgs 4–5; Isa 8; 20; Jer 13; Ezek 4; 12; 24; Joel 3:3[2:30]; Zech 3:8. Similarly, the prophets describe their experience as the "mighty hand" of God being upon them. Cf. Isa 8:11; Jer 1:9; 15:17; Ezek 1:3; 3:14; 37:1; 40:1; etc. Chapman, *Law and the Prophets*, 126.

79. Cf. Deut 11:3. In Deut 28:46, אוֹת and מוֹפֵת are attested without הַמּוֹרָא הַגָּדוֹל and הַיָּד הַחֲזָקָה, and they have a different reference: the future curses that the Lord will bring upon the people and their descendants for failing to obey the commandments.

80. Olson divides the text of chapter 4 such that verses 32-39 mirror verses 5-8. Thus, "the intimate nearness of God (4:7) is balanced by the terrifying majesty and

unique acts in the history of earth and heaven, YHWH shows himself to be unique, unsurpassed by other potential gods.

Rofé argues that it is specifically the acts of extracting the Israelites from within another nations (v. 34) that demonstrate that YHWH is the one and only true God. If every nation has its own god—as was commonly believed in the ANE—and,

> if the Lord "invaded" Egypt and took for himself from there the Israelite people thus revealing his supreme and sovereign power, he has proved by such both his dominion, which is beyond the borders of the traditional concept of "the Lord of the land"— "the inheritance of the Lord," and the impotence of Amon, the God of Egypt, that is, the futility of Egyptian faith in "a god who cannot save." The Lord is the God of the universe, and the other territorial gods cannot save, that is, cannot acts as gods. The Lord is thus found to be the only God in the universe.[81]

According to Rofé, if it is the exodus alone which identifies YHWH as Lord of the universe, then election is discussed in this text for the purpose of answering why only one people recognizes this God as their own: because YHWH chose them out of love for their ancestors (cf. 4:37-38). Furthermore, the point about YHWH speaking "out of a fire" (4:33; cf. v. 36), Rofé sees as a reference to the greatness of Israel, penned by a later hand (who is also responsible for Deut 5:21b, 23, the latter verse being similar to 4:33).[82] Yet, it is worth reconsidering whether Deut 4:32-40 can be read as a coherent unit, and whether the people's experience of YHWH speaking to them directly might be cause to consider YHWH's, and Israel's, uniqueness.

Thus I would argue that a more fruitful way of reading the text would be to see that the uniqueness of Israel and the uniqueness of YHWH are intrinsically linked. Israel could only withstand the direct voice of God because of his graciousness. When he sees an angel of YHWH, Gideon calls on him to

---

power of God (4:34-35). God's ongoing and quiet guidance through the wisdom of statutes and ordinances (4:8) is matched by the bold and dramatic saving events in the rescue from Egypt and the conquests at the edge of the promised land (4:37-38)." In this schema, 4:40 is less closely connected to verses 32-39 than I have argued; instead, it mirrors the introduction in verses 1-4. Olson, *Death of Moses*, 33.

81. Alexander Rofé, "The Monotheistic Argumentation in Deuteronomy IV 32-40: Contents, Composition, and Text," *VT* 35, no. 4 (1985): 439.

82. Ibid., 434-36.

protect him (Judg 6:22-24). In the book of Exodus, God regularly protects Moses and Israel from the dangers of direct contact with him, through commanding them to keep distance (Exod 3:5; 19:12-13) and by covering Moses with his hand (Exod 33:20-23). That the Israelites survive meeting YHWH is no cause for their own exaltation, but rather for the exaltation of God. Israel is unique because it has YHWH, the one true God, as its Lord. Furthermore, parallels between this text and Deut 34:11-12 give further support to the idea that the divine speaking and the exodus are linked. The two-pronged deeds of YHWH in Deut 4:32-40 mirror the terms of 34:10-12. Not only does the former text include the key terms of YHWH's deeds that are attributed to Moses in 34:11-12, but it also concerns Israel's seeing and hearing of YHWH (v. 33, 36), which bear similarity to YHWH knowing Moses "face to face" in 34:10 (cf. Exod 33:11; Num 12:8). Thus, contra Rofé, it must be acknowledged that the logic of the received form of the text stands without arguing that the portions about the greatness of Israel were written later; the "exceptional status" of Israel is itself an act of YHWH.[83]

Further, the text opens the possibility that in this act of speaking to Israel, YHWH reveals himself as the one true Lord. But what exactly is the logic of such a claim? There are strong parallels between Deut 4:32-40 and Exod 3:1-4:17. The two-pronged deeds of YHWH are fully present here: YHWH speaks to Moses "out of a fire," telling him to go to Pharaoh. Whether the phrase "out of a fire" was meant to refer to the Exodus text, the logic of the argument would fit if Exod 3:13-15, spoken "out of a fire," refers to YHWH's uniqueness. YHWH will be who YHWH will be, which is the one who exists differently than humanity and its gods.

In sum, Deut 34:10-12 and 4:32-40, taken together, describe a pattern whereby YHWH has a unique relationship with his people, through an auditory and visual encounter ("out of a fire"/"face to face") and the particular saving acts of the exodus, both of which are mediated by Moses. This gives a sense of why the terms, "signs and wonders," and so on, were used to describe Moses' unequalled status: because they were terms that referred to the uniqueness of YHWH and YHWH's relationship with Israel.

---

83. Ibid., 436.

3.3. Dual Agency

These "technical terms,"[84]—"signs and wonders," "mighty deeds," and "awesome displays of power"—are typically reserved for acts of YHWH. So, when they are used to describe works of Moses, this leads to questions about agency: who performed this acts? Was it YHWH? Was it Moses? Was it, in some sense, both, and if so, in what sense? In response to these questions, there is another interpretive spectrum. On one end of the spectrum stands Olson, who stresses the radicalism of the statement that Moses performs YHWH's actions: Moses is an agent of divine activity.[85] On the other end, Blenkinsopp states that the phrases in Deut 34:11-12 and its parallels (cf. Ps 105:26-27; 135:9) "belong invariably and routinely only to Yahweh."[86] Because the reference in 34:11-12 is to Moses rather than to YHWH, the closer parallel is Deut 13:2-3[1-2], in which these "signs and wonders" may or may not come true; "Hence, the emphasis is moved from the central issue of how God reveals himself to his people (v. 10) to the peripheral working of miracles and prediction of the future."[87] So, for Blenkinsopp, these verses do not add to Moses' authority or claim anything about his uniqueness, but rather are an incongruent anti-climax following the profundity of verse 10. Blenkinsopp's reading seems poor in light of the apparent sense of the text, which clearly assumes and expands upon verse 10.

Between these two poles, Chapman again takes a path through the center, stating that

> expressions usually reserved for God are applied in Deut 34 to Moses, but in a syntactically ambiguous way. Might this not indicate purposeful reflection on the ambiguous notion of agency which lies at the heart of the biblical portrayal of prophecy? The very form of messenger speech that the prophets employ creates or reflects this same ambiguity. In prophecy, who speaks—God or the prophet? . . . In my view, it is therefore entirely possible that here in the conclusion to the Torah the tradition has meaningfully preserved a theological conviction by means of an ambiguous grammatical construction, especially if the critical alternative consists of supposing that an unthinking and unskilled redactor

---

84. Olson, *Death of Moses*, 169.
85. Ibid., 169-70.
86. Blenkinsopp, *Prophecy and Canon*, 88.
87. Ibid., 88-89.

has simply heaped on barely grammatical phrases of fulsome praise. I would argue that to pull apart the biblical construal in either direction—toward the agency of Moses or the agency of God—ignores the fulcrum of the biblical balancing act that is in fact at the heart of the passage.[88]

According to Chapman, Deut 34:11–12 reflects a conscious ambiguity of agency that mirrors the ambiguity inherent in prophetic speech. Reflecting on his own position, Chapman describes it as "not narrowly theocentric" and "a both/and solution" rather than "the usual either/or."[89]

I have discussed how, in Exodus, agency blurs between YHWH and Pharaoh: does Pharaoh harden his own heart, or does YHWH accomplish this?[90] I have argued that, in the Exodus narratives, divine power does not function in a zero-sum relationship with human power, but rather, people have freedom when they act in service to YHWH. The same would apply here: Moses is preeminent among the prophets because he alone has served YHWH so persistently that YHWH's salvific actions can be described as his own. In other words, the two aspects of the dual agency function on different levels, with Moses' agency subservient to YHWH's. Describing the two aspects of agency as addressing different types of agency does not make this perspective "narrowly theocentric," though it does suggest that the two sides of the "both/and" are not equal in terms of the quality of their agency.

In other words, I agree with Chapman that the passage seems to include intentional ambiguity in describing the acts of Moses as sent by YHWH. However, I would add that the book of Exodus also contains what seems to be conscious ambiguity of agency that might inform how one reads Deut 34:11–12, since these verses call to mind the very narratives of Exodus. This type of agency, that of the most obedient to the divine will, is appropriate for Moses given his role as covenant mediator. Briggs has argued that Moses differs from all other humans in his deep humility (Num 12:3), defined as dependence on YHWH.[91] A kind of subordinate agency, whereby Moses' freedom and greatness is found within his service to YHWH, befits such dependence.

---

88. Chapman, *Law and the Prophets*, 127.
89. Ibid.
90. According to Exod 7:3, the hardening of Pharaoh's heart is directly related to the "signs and wonders"—that is, the plagues—that YHWH accomplishes in Egypt.
91. Briggs, *Virtuous Reader*, 59–63.

4. Moses Sees and Hears His Prophetic Call (Exod 3:1–4:17)

Thus far, in exegesis of Deut 34:10-12 and related passages, I have argued that Moses, as a prophet or more specifically, as mediator of the covenant, was unsurpassed in his proximity to YHWH, which was demonstrated in his unique perception of, and action on behalf of, God. These themes are also present in Exod 3:1–4:17.[92] The scene is the first dialogue between YHWH and Moses. This text anticipates much of the rest of Moses' career, as YHWH calls him to go to Pharaoh (3:10), to speak specific words to the Israelites and their elders (3:14-17), and to perform signs (אוֹת) to encourage the Israelites' trust (4:1-9). Further, Exod 4:10-17 presents its own explanation of Moses' prophetic role.

The narrative conveys the importance of seeing and hearing through repetition. Forms of ראה appear six times in 3:2-4 alone, and in these verses, הִנֵּה also appears twice. Whereas verse 1 presents the setting of the story, verse 2 begins the primary action with the מַלְאַךְ יְהוָה ("angel of the Lord") appearing (ראה, nip'al imperfect with waw consecutive). In verse 2b, the perspective turns to Moses, who sees (ראה, qal imperfect with waw consecutive) the burning bush. However, rather than simply telling the reader what Moses has seen, the biblical writer allows the reader to visualize the scene from Moses' perspective:[93] "and [what he saw was][94] the bush was blazing, yet it was not consumed." Alter translates, "and he saw, and look, the bush was burning with fire and the bush was not consumed."[95] Moses then thinks

---

92. What most people seem to remember about the story in Exod 3 is not the commentary on the divine name (vv. 13-15), but the burning bush, the portion of the story in which the reader is asked to picture something he/she will have never seen: a bush burning but unconsumed. It is possible that it is this act of visualization that imprints itself on readers' memories. Further, it is not only the modern reader to remembers the story this way; of all the places in the Old Testament that include the phrase "the God of Abraham, the God of Isaac, and the God of Jacob," Jesus, in Mark and Luke, refers to the one in Exod 3:15, identifying this story as ἐπὶ τοῦ βάτου, "about the bush" (Mark 12:26; Luke 20:37; cf. Matt 22:32).

93. On the use of הִנֵּה to mark movement from the narrator's perspective to a character's, particularly in a situation where the character sees something unexpected, see Robert Alter, *The Pleasures of Reading in an Ideological Age* (New York; London: Simon and Schuster, 1989), 176-77.

94. The NRSV leaves וְהִנֵּה untranslated.

95. Robert Alter, *The Five Books of Moses: A Translation with Commentary* (New York:

through his response, as though speaking to the reader about what they have seen together: "I must turn aside and look [ראה, *qal* imperfect] at this great sight" (הַמַּרְאֶה; the Hebrew word order places the cognate accusative next to the verb).[96] The phrase הַמַּרְאֶה הַגָּדֹל הַזֶּה suggests that Moses has begun to recognize the significance of what he sees.[97] All of this is prolegomena to YHWH's speech, which is in response to Moses' *sight* and *action*: "When the LORD saw [ראה *qal* imperfect with waw consecutive] that he had turned aside to see [ראה, *qal* infinitive construct], God called to him out of the bush, 'Moses, Moses!' And he said, 'Here I am' [הִנֵּנִי; v. 4]." YHWH acknowledges what Moses sees and how he responds to this sight; only then does YHWH speak. It would seem that if Moses had not turned aside to look, YHWH would not have spoken.[98] Furthermore, this speech is specified as coming "from the bush." Though the bush is not directly mentioned in the rest of the narrative, the reader may imagine that the voice of YHWH continues to come from the flaming bush, the phenomenon that accompanies God's immediate presence.[99] Savran cogently argues that the bush is the form in which מַלְאַךְ יְהוָה appears in verse 2. The active and passive forms of ראה in these verses suggest that what appears and what Moses sees are identical.[100] The angel or messenger does not have an active role in the story (contra, e.g., Judg 6:12 and 13:3); rather here, "the manifestation [of YHWH] is not anthropomorphic, but fiery."[101]

W. W. Norton, 2004), 318.

96. Moses' thoughts anticipate his conversation with YHWH, as Savran writes, "interior monologue is often used to offer an explanation for behaviour, but here the effect goes beyond clarifying an element of the plot (what will Moses do next?) to present a snapshot of the character's mind at that moment. Usually such interior monologue is limited to the protagonist (and the reader), but here, where YHWH is aware of the thoughts of the characters, it effectively begins a dialogue about which Moses himself is as yet unaware. In contrast to the minimalistic representation of thoughts common in biblical narrative, we are given a clear verbal (or mental) indication of Moses' decision making process." Savran, *Encountering the Divine*, 97.

97. Ibid., 97-98.
98. Ibid., 99.
99. See Moberly, *Prophecy and Discernment*, 6.
100. Savran, *Encountering the Divine*, 64.
101. Greenberg, *Understanding Exodus*, 70; quoted in in Savran, *Encountering the Divine*, 65. This differentiates Exod 3 from Deut 5, in which there is no appearance of an angel and no "form" (תְּמוּנָה) (Deut 4:12, 15).

The repetition of סְנֶה (vv. 2–3) offers three different descriptions of the bush: that it was burning with fire, that it was not consumed, and that it was not "burning up." The participles in verse 2 emphasize Moses' ongoing observation; the repetition of the sight in verse 3, in terms that do not align with those of verse 2, reveals that Moses does not comprehend the sight.[102] Savran argues that Moses' sight is set not on the source or essence of the flame, but rather on its quality, as demonstrated by the use of הִנֵּה in verse 2.[103] Yet, clearly what concerns Moses—why he considers the phenomenon a "great sight," and why he turns aside to see it—is the perplexing nature of a fire that requires no fuel. The flame is self-subsistent. Though elsewhere in the Pentateuch, fire is associated with the presence of YHWH, particularly on the mountain (Exod 19:18; 24:17; 40:38; Deut 4:12, 15, 33, 36, 5:4–5, 22–26; 9:10; 10:4; 18:16), never again is it given this description.

After Moses announces his own presence (v. 4b), YHWH commands him to remain at a distance and remove his sandals (v. 5). YHWH introduces himself as "the God of your father, the God of Abraham, the God of Isaac, and the God of Jacob" (v. 6a). In response, Moses "hid his face, for he was afraid [ירא *qal* perfect] to look at God [נבט, *hipʿil* infinitive construct; v. 6b]."[104] As Polak

---

102. Ibid., 68.
103. Ibid.
104. This is the only time in the passage that נבט occurs (cf. Moses' "seeing the form of the Lord" in Num 12:8).

Savran observes two types of midrash on this text. In the first, Moses demonstrates his humility before God in Exodus 3:6b, and so God rewards him by enabling him to see God "face to face" (Exod 33:11; Num 12:8). This goes against my reading, which suggests that Moses does not actually see God's face in Exod 33:11 and Num 12:8. The second type interprets Moses' response as "failure of nerve at a crucial moment." The limitation in Exod 33:20 is interpreted in response to this rejection; because Moses feared seeing the Lord's face in the earlier narrative, he is refused such an experience in the later narrative. The relationship between Moses' response to God's self-introduction and his future vocation can be more appropriately described. Savran writes, "The text records Moses' fear of seeing YHWH's face, but without the attendant fear of death found in other theophany narratives. . . . It is striking that nowhere in Moses' career does he give expression to such a sense of anxiety in the face of the divine." As the one who will respond to the Israelites' fear and regularly enter the liminal space of YHWH's presence, Moses expresses the fear that accompanies unmediated experience of YHWH without demonstrating the kind of anxiety that would hinder him from fulfilling the role of covenant mediator. Savran, *Encoun-*

observes, once Moses realizes what he sees—a manifestation of God—he must look away. The writers describe the scene carefully: "the more the narrator reduces the gap between the human and the divine, the more he has to emphasize the distance."[105]

In the next verse, YHWH prefaces his declaration of intent to deliver the Israelites with three statements: "I have observed [ראה *qal* infinitive absolute and *qal* perfect] the misery of my people who are in Egypt; I have heard [שמע *qal* perfect] their cry on account of their taskmasters. Indeed I know [ידע *qal* perfect] their sufferings" (v. 7). For these three reasons, YHWH has "come down to deliver them" (v. 8). The emphases on God's seeing and hearing return in verse 9: "The cry of the Israelites has now come to me; I have also seen" (ראה *qal* perf.) how the Egyptians oppress them." Polak observes the verbal phrase רָאֹה רָאִיתִי (v. 7), arguing that at the beginning of the narrative, with the burning bush, and in YHWH's subsequent declaration, "perception serves to establish the connection between deity and man."[106] So, in verses 6–10, the narrative links divine perception with divine and human action.

The connection between perception and action in this narrative is artfully demonstrated through Savran's examination of the text within a broader type-scene "theophany," consisting of several parts: "the setting of the scene, the appearance and speech of YHWH, human response to the presence of the divine, the expression of doubt or anxiety, and externalization of the experience."[107] By identifying a wider category than "call narrative" in which to place Exod 3:1–4:17, Savran highlights several aspects of the story that recede from view under the form-critical criteria (e.g., Habel's[108]), namely the visualization element of the divine confrontation and the "externalization of the experience," by which Savran means movement from the solitary theophanic experience to the corporate situation of public (or community) life, a movement which often extends beyond the limits of an individual narrative.[109] Put differently, Savran highlights the movement

---

tering the Divine, 103.

105. Frank Polak, "Theophany and Mediator: The Unfolding of a Theme in the Book of Exodus," in *Studies in the Book of Exodus: Redaction, Reception, Interpretation* BETL 126 (Leuven: Leuven University, 1996), 120–21.

106. Ibid., 121.

107. Savran, *Encountering the Divine*, 13; cf. 14–25.

108. Habel, "Form and Significance," 298.

109. Savran, *Encountering the Divine*, 22–25.

from an individual seeing and hearing to the public action that the divine encounter requires in response.

In Exod 3:1–4:17, externalization is highlighted in the third objection (Exod 4:1ff.). With this rebuttal, Moses admits explicit concern about the Hebrew people believing that YHWH has appeared to him. With YHWH's response to this objection, the visual sense of the narrative shifts from the bush to the staff, the symbol of Moses' authority, and to the other signs. These signs demonstrate Moses' authority, which can only come from an encounter with YHWH. For this must be the narrative logic: the signs are meant to demonstrate to the Israelites that YHWH has appeared to Moses (4:1). Signs typically serve to verify the authenticity of a prophet (cf. Deut 13:2–3[1–2]; Jer 28:9). However, Moses' question reveals heightened expectation for his words: the Israelites must not only verify that he speaks truthfully with respect to Pharaoh, but that YHWH actually appeared to him. The signs are linked to the appearance.

With the fourth objection (4:10ff.), externalization of the experience continues as YHWH appoints Aaron. Again, prophecy comes to the fore. Moses questions his own ability to speak (v. 10), after which YHWH assures him that his personal speaking abilities are irrelevant; the point is that YHWH will make possible Moses' speech: "Now go, and I will be with your mouth and teach you what you are to speak" (Exod 4:12). It is possible and appropriate for YHWH to teach Moses how to speak, as YHWH explains by asking: "Who gives speech to mortals? Who makes them mute or deaf, seeing or blind? Is it not I, the Lord?" As YHWH gives abilities of perception to, or withholds them from, all creatures, so YHWH also will be responsible for Moses' speech. When Moses refuses to go (4:13), YHWH makes a suggestion: could not Aaron go along with Moses, to act as Moses' prophet? "You shall speak to him and put the words in his mouth; and I will be with your mouth and with his mouth, and will teach you what you shall do. He indeed shall speak for you to the people; he shall serve as a mouth for you, and you shall serve as God for him" (4:15–16; see Exod 7:1, where the term "prophet," נָבִיא, describes Aaron's role).

According to Savran, externalization does not end in Exod 4:17 with YHWH's reminder to Moses to take the staff. Rather, it continues when, in Exod 19:19, the people hear YHWH speaking to Moses, validating his authority, and in Exod 20:15–18, when the people's anxiety demonstrates the dependence of the people on Moses as mediator of the word of God. The externalization is further developed in Deut 5:25-31 and chapter 18.[110]

5. Implications for Reading Exodus 3:13-15

Now for the most significant question at hand: how does this discussion of Moses' vocation, and the narrative context of Exod 3:1-4:17 as described in light of the importance of Moses' visual perception and response, shed light on verses 13-15? I begin reflecting on this question through raising a reading of this text that is interesting but open to questions. Polak provides a reading of these verses that, while acknowledging the strong relationship between this text and Moses' wider vocation, nevertheless unduly reduces the sense of 3:14.

YHWH responds to Moses' question about his suitability for confronting Pharaoh (3:11) with reference to the sign (3:12), "implicitly alluding to the burning bush and thus indicating divine authority," and foreshadowing the giving of the law at Sinai.[111] The suggestion of future relationship between YHWH and Israel makes the logical connection to Moses' question in verse 13, which has to do with this relationship. While the "practical answer" to this question is given in verse 15, "what counts is not the practical recognition of the name as such, but the theoretical insight into the nature of the power behind it."[112] Based on the repetition of phrases in verses 12, 14, and 15, Polak argues that "the four divine responses to Moses' question form one integrated system, which opens with the promise of divine succour to Moses (v. 12) and closes with the proclamation of God's name (v. 15)."[113] Polak then addresses each response in turn.

The response in 3:12 contains two parts: the promise כִּי־אֶהְיֶה עִמָּךְ and a statement about Moses' commission, וְזֶה־לְּךָ הָאוֹת כִּי אָנֹכִי שְׁלַחְתִּיךָ. Polak suggests that this introduces both of the key terms of the system: אֶהְיֶה and √שׁלח. The first of these terms occurs twice in the second response (v. 14a), once as אֶהְיֶה and a second time as אֶהְיֶה אֲשֶׁר. On its own, אֶהְיֶה means the same thing as "I will be with you" (v. 12a), a promise of divine assistance. Together with אֲשֶׁר אֶהְיֶה, it means that "divine succour is both indefinite and

---

110. Ibid., 163-64.
111. Polak, "Theophany and Mediator," 122.
112. Ibid.
113. Ibid., 122-23.

unlimited."[114] The *idem per idem* formula does not "convey specific information," because it occurs with an existential verb.

In the third response (v. 14b), as in the first (v. 12), we have both key terms. This response begins like the second, with אֶהְיֶה, but substitutes שְׁלָחַנִי אֲלֵיכֶם for אֲשֶׁר אֶהְיֶה. The substitution, according to Polak, suggests that אֶהְיֶה "signifies" שְׁלָחַנִי אֲלֵיכֶם. Finally, in the response in verse 15, the subject is יְהוָה, instead of אֶהְיֶה, and שְׁלָחַנִי אֲלֵיכֶם recurs. Thus the divine name and אֶהְיֶה are part of the same symbolic category. Polak concludes: "The YHWH name, then, means אֶהְיֶה עִמָּךְ and שְׁלָחַנִי אֲלֵיכֶם. It symbolizes divine action for the sake of his people. The structure of the response אֶהְיֶה אֲשֶׁר אֶהְיֶה turns this idea into a general and absolute principle without any limitations whatsoever. The certainty of divine succour is implied in God's very name."[115]

Polak has carefully observed repetition in the passage and articulated an interpretation of the text that highlights the significance of Moses' sending.[116] However, Polak's symbolic system does little more than define the difficult terms and phrases of the text (אֶהְיֶה שְׁלָחַנִי אֲלֵיכֶם and אֶהְיֶה אֲשֶׁר אֶהְיֶה and יְהוָה) in terms of more understandable phrases, namely אֶהְיֶה עִמָּךְ and שְׁלָחַנִי אֲלֵיכֶם. Thus Polak's reading surely flattens the text.

In what follows, I offer several reflections on the interconnection of Exod 3:13–15 and my reading of Deut 34:10–12 and related passages.

5.1. The Nature of the Question

In considering the meaning of the question in verse 13, Polak appropriately observes that it has to do with the future relationship between YHWH and Israel. Readings that understand the question as to do with the meaning or significance of the name, on the one hand, or the name as new itself, on the other, may not fully attend to the fact that verse 12 points to the covenant at Sinai, and thus to an entirely new mode of relationship between God and God's people. Further, my discussion of Moses' vocation may provide conceptual tools to elaborate on the nature of this question and on Moses' role in voicing it.

Augustine's characteristic reading of Exod 3:14-15, as described in chapter 2, suggests that God's response to Moses' question is not directed to that leader alone but also to every reader of the passage. Thus the reader is not

---

114. Ibid., 123.
115. Ibid., 123–24.
116. Cf. Moberly, *Old Testament*, 23–24.

existentially removed from, but rather self-involved with, God's response. One effect of this is that the question in verse 13 cannot be understood as simply requesting factual information, as it must also voice the reader's question regarding the identity of this God. At the same time, what modern, narrative exegesis can offer an Augustinian reading is appreciation for the new relationship between YHWH and the Israelites that comes about through the exodus and covenant.

Moses is the first prophet. Whereas in Genesis, God appears and speaks directly to the patriarchs, in Exodus a new situation arises: YHWH sends Moses to speak to the people of God. Thus the question may be about what name (either which among known names of God, or what new name) can be used in relation to the new situation of God sending someone.[117]

Furthermore, one can consider how Moses would act as covenant mediator in communicating the name and its meaning. The content of the speech may be indirectly identified with the covenant, in the sense that the Decalogue could be understood as an exploration of the significance of "I am the LORD your God, who brought you out of the land of Egypt, out of the house of slavery" (Exod 20:2). Though YHWH speaks the Decalogue, the center of the covenant, to the Israelites directly rather than through Moses, the giving of the name may prefigure the giving of the covenant, particularly in the context of Horeb, with YHWH speaking to Moses out of fire.

Further progress can be made on the role of Moses in relaying the name through comparison with the text of Gen 32:22-32. Jacob wrestles with a divine figure, and his struggle concludes with the endeavor to discover the name of the figure, whom he (later?) realizes is God, when he names the place Peniel, declaring, "For I have seen [ראה, qal perf.] God face to face, and yet my life is preserved" (Gen 32:30). Jacob seems to be "wrestling" with a great many things: his brother, who may or may not forgive him; himself, whom he may or may not forgive; a potential blessing; and the name of God. As a result of this experience, Jacob is renamed Israel. Though the etiology of the name explains that Israel is the one who has "striven with God and with humans" (Gen 32:28), the name itself stresses Israel's wrestling with God.

Thus, I suggest that Israel—through synecdoche understood as the twelve tribes or the entire people of God—is the people who struggle with God, for a blessing and to know God's name.[118] Likewise, in Exod 3:13, Moses'

---

117. See den Hertog, *Other Face*, 49–50; 59–71.
118. See Levering, *Scripture and Metaphysics*, 49.

question is explicitly expressed as the *people's* question rather than his own; Moses asks on behalf of the Israelites, in a kind of intercession. YHWH answers, giving Moses both something to ponder himself ("I am who I am," v. 14a) as well as some words for the Israelites, namely "'I will be' has sent me to you" (v. 14b) and "The LORD, the God of your ancestors, the God of Abraham, the God of Isaac, and the God of Jacob has sent me to you" (v. 15).

5.2. Divine Self-Reference in Exodus 3:14a

While Polak argues that the sense of verse 14a is that the divine assistance offered to Moses is unlimited, there is (understandably) much that he does not say. In part, this is because of Polak's assessment of the *idem per idem* formula. While it may be true that the import of the phrase with an existential verb differs from that of an active or stative verb, the repetition of אֶהְיֶה in these verses clearly impresses upon the reader something having to do with "being." The verse does not attempt a definition of God or of being, but it is an exaggeration to claim that the phrase, with היה, is meaningless. For example, the phrase suggests that God can only be described with reference to God; the first אֶהְיֶה is followed by yet another אֶהְיֶה. Allen illustrates this point with a comparison: individual persons can be compared with other individual persons, who may be taller, shorter, etc. than another within a given group. Further, Allen astutely observes the effect of this response on the reader: "Yet Exodus 3:14 jolts us by saying that God is not grouped with others. God can only be known by comparison to himself. The name seems tautologous at first glance. It humbles the reader."[119] This "humbling" response may resemble the model of dependence on God that Moses exhibits. If God is only defined by comparison to himself, the relationship this elicits from humanity is one of dependence on, and trust in, God.

Augustine's interpretation of Exod 3:14-15, the literary context of Exod 3:1-4:17, and this chapter's reflection on the role of Moses in the Pentateuch all contribute to recognition of divine self-reference in Exod 14. Divine self-reference is central to Augustine's interpretation of *Ego sum qui sum* and *Ego sum Deus Abraham, et Deus Isaac, et Deus Iacob*. God reveals Godself first, under a name toward which Moses and the reader can direct their attention but not fully grasp, and then by a name which is comprehensible. Both ways of naming God come from God and draw the hearer back to him.

---

119. Allen, "Exodus 3," 32.

Literary support for divine self-referentiality may be found in the narrative's focus on the burning bush. Moses turns aside to see the bush and, particularly, why it does not "burn up" (Exod 3:3). The flame—the appearance of the מַלְאַךְ יְהוָה and the location from which YHWH speaks—blazes without any external fuel, and this sight he cannot comprehend. Augustine's reading of Exod 3:14 suggests that "the one who is" reveals God to be self-subsistent, and it is a concept that no one is able to grasp.[120] Though Augustine does not explicitly connect the unconsumed bush to YHWH's self-subsistence,[121] the narrative impresses the image of the bush upon the reader, so that the reader mentally carries this strange sight through the rest of the story.

Furthermore, I have suggested that the people's fear for their lives after YHWH speaks to them "out of fire" (Deut 5:26; cf. 4:33) calls to mind Exod 3, even though in Exodus is it Moses, not the people, who hears the Lord speaking to him from fire. The experience of the immediate presence of God (in Deut 5) causes the Israelites to consider their mortality. Likely, their fear is not a conscious reflection on Exod 3:13–15. Yet, if in Deut 5 God speaking to one "from fire" solicits reflection on the difference between the living God and mortal humanity, the same type of dynamic may be at work in Exod 3.

5.3. Sight and Action

While it may be argued that Exod 3:13–15 constitutes a more abstract theological discussion than the rest of the chapter, my reading of Exod 3:1–4:17 in terms of Moses' perception of God and God's will reveals that these verses fit well in their context. Upon seeing the bush and hearing the voice of YHWH, he asks how the people might be able to call upon YHWH, so Moses must "see" and "hear" YHWH in some sense. If verse 14 suggests a limitation of such seeing and hearing on the basis of God's self-referentiality, then this limited knowledge is certainly appropriate for Moses, the one who is known for immediate experience of YHWH; even for Moses, there are limits to how "close" he can come to YHWH (Exod 3:5; 33:20–23). This leads to and qualifies the content of the giving the name (v. 15).

The relationship between sight and action is demonstrated both in the narrative of Exod 3:1–4:17 as well as in the legacy of Moses as described in Deut 34:10–12. The Israelites need a glimpse of this God in whom they must

---

120. See chapter 2.
121. Augustine understands the bush figuratively, as signifying the Jews. *Serm.* 7.2.

trust to lead them out of Egypt if indeed they are going to follow Moses. The text of verse 14 suggests that this glimpse (the name, v. 15) is but a glimpse; wholly dedicated to his people, God nevertheless is not determined by their history nor fully comprehended by those who seek him. The response in verse 14 is not a rejection of the question, but rather itself a burning bush which beckons the reader to draw nearer into the liminal space of reflection upon the only one who reveals himself while remaining hidden.

5.4. Perception and Knowledge of God

Moses perceives YHWH as no one else in Israel did before or after him. In this context, it is only fitting to understand the question in verse 13 as more than a matter of factual information. Moses perceives God "face to face," and so mediates YHWH's revelation to Israel. Moreover, this perception—seeing and hearing the reality of God—resonates with contemplative aspects of Christian tradition, so long as contemplation is viewed holistically within a life lived in right response to God.[122] Again, my reading intersects with Augustine's, since Augustine describes Moses' experience in Exod 3 as similar to Augustine's own contemplative experience in his conversion.[123]

5.5. "Face to Face" in the New Testament

In the New Testament, the phrase "face to face" returns in 1 Cor 13:12a: βλέπομεν γὰρ ἄρτι δι' ἐσόπτρου ἐν αἰνίγματι, τότε δὲ πρόσωπον πρὸς πρόσωπον, "For now we see in a mirror, dimly, but then we will see face to face." In this chapter, Paul encourages the Corinthians not to think too highly of ecstatic prophetic gifts, which are available only to a few and will come to an end, but rather to see the eternal significance of love, a gift available to all. This claim fits with the portrayal of Moses I have presented: his gifts of prophecy were for the sake of Israel, demonstrated in Moses' self-denying intercession on their behalf, and involved keeping covenant (that is, love of God and neighbor) rather than in his experience of an unusual psychological state.

In New Testament scholarship, the general consensus is that ἐν αἰνίγματι, literally "in a riddle," refers to Num 12:8. Hollander builds on this consensus and suggests that this phrase, together with πρόσωπον πρὸς πρόσωπον, sug-

---

122. Levering defends Aquinas's claim that Moses is a "contemplative of God's essence" in *Scripture and Metaphysics*, 65–66.
123. *Serm.* 7.7. Cf. *Conf.* 7.10,16; 7.13,19.

gests a conflated reference to both Num 12:8 and Deut 34:10.[124] Paul uses Moses' proximity to God as an analogy for how Christians will perceive God in the eschaton. Likewise, the image that Paul uses to explain the difference between Christian perception of God now versus in the eschaton resonates with the type of distinction between Moses' perception and the Israelites' or other prophets':

> Most modern interpreters of 1 Cor. 13 correctly assume that the mirror imagery does not allude to the quality of seeing, in the sense that in Paul's view the image of God that we have is obscure or distorted. It rather refers to the indirect nature of looking into a mirror, in the sense that the apostle wanted to underline that man's vision and knowledge of God and the divine world is indirect: we see no more than the image of God.[125]

It is not that others misunderstand God so much as that Moses' perception is more direct. Furthermore, surely the limitations on the Israelites' experience of God, demonstrated by Moses' more immediate experience (which was itself limited), suggests something about the nature of human limitation in knowledge of God; one cannot now perceive God as God truly is, in the fullness of God's self-referentiality (cf. Exod 3:14). For now, one sees God in God's actions, through Moses and the patriarchs (cf. Deut 34:11-12; Exod 3:15), creating and redeeming a people for Godself. However, in the end,

> What we shall contemplate as we live for ever is what he told his servant Moses: I am who I am. And so you shall say to the children of Israel, He who is sent me to you (Ex 3:14). . . . This will happen when the Lord comes and lights up the things hidden in darkness (1 Cor 4:5), when the darkness of this mortality and corruption passes away.[126]

---

124. Harm W. Hollander, "Seeing God 'In a Riddle' or 'Face to Face': An Analysis of 1 Corinthians 13.12," *JSNT* 32, no. 4 (2010): 398-400.
125. Ibid., 397.
126. *Trin.* I.3.17.

CHAPTER 5

Exodus 3:13–15 and Trinitarian Doctrine

In the preceding two chapters, I have developed a reading of Exod 3:13–15 within the context of the book of Exodus and its witness to the divine name, and within the context of Moses' role as covenant mediator, a prominent storyline in the Pentateuch. In chapter 3, I argue that within the book of Exodus, through the name "YHWH," God reveals himself to be both faithful to Israel and free to be "who [he] will be." God gives Israel a name by which God can be called upon, a name that God recognizes as his own. At the same time, the biblical witness continually suggests that Israel does not manage God under this name; YHWH is utterly free, his own reality, into which Israel is invited in relationship. Moreover, the phrases "I am who I am," "I am has sent me to you" and "the Lord God of Abraham, the God of Isaac, and the God of Jacob" are all implicitly ontological statements; they communicate something about what is real. Therefore, the literal sense of the text is patient of a kind of ontological interpretation,[1] which is not a philosophical imposition on the text but another way of saying that it makes true claims about the God to whom it bears witness, the one who encounters the reader through the text. In chapter 4, I argue that the context of Moses' vocation as covenant mediator suggests that Moses' uniqueness stems from his ability to "see" and "hear" YHWH and YHWH's voice. The obedience of Israel rests upon Moses' seeing and hearing; it is the paradigm for relation to YHWH

---

1. As stated in the Introduction (p. 9, fn. 23), I use the term "ontological" in a rather broad sense: referring to that which is real. I am not arguing whether God is a being, a different sort of being, or beyond being.

even though the Israelites generally do not perform this task. Moreover, I have argued for the verbal importance of "seeing" and "hearing" in Exod 3:1–4:17. These are tantamount to Moses' reception of the call. Therefore ancient interpreters are not mistaken in claiming that God's answer to Moses' question in Exod 3:13-15 involves something to which one must give concentrated attention; more than factual information, this is the mystery of God's identity disclosed to humanity.

In this chapter, I clarify the nature of this ontological reading of Exod 3:13-15 in conversation with two substantial recent proposals on the relationship between Christian Trinitarian doctrine and the Old Testament. In the first section, I argue that the ontological reading I am pursuing is not in conflict with Nathan MacDonald's argument that "monotheism" is a modern concept that cannot adequately describe the teaching of Deuteronomy (and perhaps the rest of the Pentateuch). In the second section, I argue, contra Soulen, that doctrinal theology's respect for and attention to the Old Testament should not include use of the divine name "YHWH" as the most proper name of God, that is, as a more direct name than "Father, Son, and Holy Spirit." The commentary on the divine name in Exod 3:14 serves as a qualification to the name "YHWH," and though this name was given to Israel as a true means of calling on God, the name does not constitute a more direct means of calling upon God than other personal names given in Scripture (notably, for Christians, "Father, Son and Holy Spirit"). In the third section, I offer some suggestions for continued reflection on Exod 3:13-15 and for the use of Old Testament exegesis in doctrinal theology.

1. Old Testament "Monotheism" and Divine Unity: Nathan MacDonald

One recent and rather convincing work on theological interpretation of the Pentateuch is Nathan MacDonald's reading of Deuteronomy, in which he argues that the term "monotheism" as it is typically understood does not apply to Deuteronomy.[2] In the process, MacDonald helpfully reorients the discussion in order to reassert the primacy of the relational context of Israel's sole loyalty to YHWH. In this section, I suggest that the reflection on God's

---

2. Nathan MacDonald, *Deuteronomy and the Meaning of "Monotheism,"* 2nd ed., FAT II 1 (Tübingen: Mohr Siebeck, 2003).

nature and identity that I advocate in interpretation of Exod 3:13–15 functions within the same relational context that MacDonald advocates for interpreting Deuteronomy. Ontology and relationship are not antithetical concepts. Through revealing his identity and nature as YHWH, God calls Israel into covenant relationship.

In his work drawing on his dissertation, MacDonald has persuasively argued that the term "monotheism" is inappropriate for application to Deuteronomy. The idea of monotheism, as it is typically understood, is an Enlightenment and post-Enlightenment construction used to describe belief that only one God exists. Old Testament scholarship has typically used the term to describe a coherent climax (for better or for worse) of religio-historical development in Israel, with scholars proposing different dates for Israel's "monotheistic" turn. MacDonald follows von Rad in suggesting that what one finds, for example in Deuteronomy, is not the affirmation that one God exists and no others, but the importance of loyal human response to YHWH. MacDonald summarizes von Rad's position: "Israel's monotheism, however, is not the fruit of abstract, rational discussion: a piece of knowledge that one obtains. Instead, it is the confession of trust and dependence on YHWH, the Lord of history. It is not, therefore, an intellectual stage that is reached, but something that constantly needs addressing."[3] Von Rad's definition of "monotheism" opposes how this term is usually meant: an intellectual decision that only one God exists, a cultural development that, once made, is not rescinded. In contrast, the Old Testament portrays confession of God's "oneness" as something that Israel must constantly remember, a claim that can be made only in the context of Israel's loving relationship with YHWH and YHWH's election of Israel. This confession and the relationship in which the confession is made are always in jeopardy because of Israel's temptation toward idolatry.

While I wholeheartedly support MacDonald's project and am in full agreement with his conclusion, I raise some questions about where the argument might turn once the thoroughly *relational* context of Israel's confession has been firmly established. Namely, is it possible for an ontological interpretation to build on, rather than negate, this relational context?

A key chapter in MacDonald's work is the second chapter, in which he begins to explain his understanding of God's oneness in Deuteronomy. Central to this chapter is his interpretation of Deut 6:4–9, the *Shema*. MacDonald

---

3. Ibid., 42.

provides a substantial discussion of the issues involved in translating verse 4b before suggesting that it contains a single predication, with the seemingly redundant second יְהוָה understood as a *casus pendens*.⁴ Thus he translates, "YHWH, our God, YHWH is one."⁵ MacDonald then moves into his interpretation of the verse, citing Janzen to say that interpretations tend to fall under two categories: those that argue that the word "one" makes a claim about God's nature, who God is *in se,* and those that argue that "one" refers to YHWH's claim on Israel.⁶ Though the latter interpretation usually follows from translations other than MacDonald's (that is, "YHWH is our God; YHWH is one" or "YHWH is our God, YHWH alone"), MacDonald asserts that the context of Deuteronomy overwhelmingly supports the second interpretation, as the book emphasizes loyalty to YHWH and the practical rejection of other gods. Perhaps because his entire book gives evidence to validate this claim, MacDonald immediately moves to a negative argument, against the idea that Deut 6:4 has to do with the nature of God, in one of the many ways this has been understood: "mono-Yahwism, there is only one god ('monotheism'), the integrity of YHWH's will, YHWH has no family, YHWH is unchangeable."⁷ After critiquing these interpretive options, MacDonald suggests that a strong parallel can be found in Song 6:8-9,⁸ which reads,

> There are sixty queens and eighty concubines,
> and maidens without number.
> My dove, my perfect one, is the only one,
> the darling of her mother,
> flawless to her that bore her.
> The maidens saw her and called her happy;
> the queens and concubines also, and they praised her.

---

4. Ibid., 62-70.

5. Cf. R. W. L. Moberly, "'Yahweh Is One': The Translation of the Shema," in *Studies in the Pentateuch*, ed. John Adney Emerton, VT.S 41 (Leiden: Brill, 1990), 209-15.

6. MacDonald, *Deuteronomy*, 71; cf. J. Gerald Janzen, "The Most Important Word in the Shema (Deuteronomy VI 4-5)," *VT* 37, no. 3 (1987): 280.

7. MacDonald, *Deuteronomy*, 71.

8. MacDonald is not the first to suggest this comparison, as he admits in calling Song 6:8-9 "a text which has often been held up as the most illuminating parallel to Deut. 6.4." Ibid., 74. However, the only work he cites in this section is R. W. L. Moberly, "Toward An Interpretation of the Shema," in *Theological Exegesis*, 124-44.

In the song, the lover declares his love to be "one," by which he does not mean that she is the only woman, nor is she necessarily the only child of her mother. Instead, as MacDonald summarizes, "she has a place in the affections of her mother and her lover that is unrivaled. In a similar way what Deuteronomy calls the people of Israel to affirm about YHWH is not that other gods do not exist, but that YHWH is unique for Israel, and to receive Israel's wholehearted love."[9]

Furthermore, MacDonald suggests that such an understanding of "oneness" is not purely subjective because, in 6:9b, the text states that others praise the beloved as they observe how blessed she is in light of this relationship. Therefore, "the uniqueness of YHWH is also open to recognition by others, but not detachable from their relationship (however this operates) to him," and "it is possible to undo the distinction between understanding Deut. 6.4 as a statement about YHWH *in se* or YHWH *ad extra*."[10] I am most interested in this final implication. If "*in se*" and "*ad extra*" are equivalent to "objectivity" and "subjectivity," then one has certainly encountered a problem: there is no "view from nowhere"[11] from which someone (or no one?) can identify God. But then, Augustine never supposed that there was such a "view from nowhere." That God is *idipsum* and says *ego sum qui sum*, is told in Scripture and made known to the person who encounters this God through contemplation. The rational is not divorced from the relational. Is MacDonald saying that the relational language is already ontological, so that there is no longer any distinction? Or is he saying that we must do away with ontological language and use only relational language because God can only be identified in relationship?

Throughout the book, MacDonald often contrasts ontological interpretation with the relational one he advocates, whether the relational dimension is considered in terms of experience,[12] confession,[13] or election.[14] In his conclusion, MacDonald contrasts ontological language with soteriological:

---

9. MacDonald, *Deuteronomy*, 74.
10. Ibid., 74–75.
11. This phrase is Roger Scruton's, but I take the claim to be a widely-held contemporary view. Roger Scruton, *The Face of God* (London; New York: Continuum, 2012), 1–21.
12. MacDonald, *Deuteronomy*, 85, fn. 152, quotation of Elnes.
13. Ibid., 92.
14. Ibid., 163, 180.

We might say, to use the language of theological discourse, that YHWH's claim to be God is not primarily an ontological claim, but more a soteriological one (though such a claim carries with it ontological implications). It is then, perhaps, not entirely inappropriate to compare this claim to the New Testament one that Jesus is Lord. This title derives from the exaltation of the one who has humbled himself even to death on a cross so that he might save his people.[15]

MacDonald's hint, that soteriology and ontology are not opposites, is certainly true to my reading of Augustine and to the reading of Exod 3:13-15 that I am advocating. Where MacDonald most strongly claims that he might not be opposed to *every possible* ontological interpretation is at the conclusion of chapter 6. The context is his discussion of the *Bilderverbot* in Deut 4, which he suggests is like oneness claims in Deuteronomy because both have to do with YHWH's uniqueness, which is situated in the context of YHWH's relationship with Israel and demonstrated in YHWH's actions on Israel's behalf. Therefore, "in both cases something is said about the nature of YHWH, an ontological statement, so to speak, but a statement that cannot be divorced from the personal claim on Israel. Thus, Deuteronomy's aniconism and its 'monotheism' are to be located in the relationship formed between YHWH and Israel."[16] Even this, MacDonald's strongest claim about the possibility of an ontological interpretation that does not sacrifice any portion of the relational dimension, is fairly weak. However, if one can make the most of these more positive hints, it might be said that MacDonald calls "ontological" those readings of Deuteronomy from which he dissents, and that though these interpretations do not do justice to the truly relational nature of of the book or Israel's unceasing challenge to claim that YHWH is God, Deuteronomy is not ontologically vacuous. MacDonald admits of the possibility of an ontological interpretation that would fall within his relational framework, but he seems a bit unsure about what this might look like, which is understandable since to specify this is beyond the scope of his illuminating and important work.

Keeping in mind MacDonald's intimation that a relational interpretation of Deuteronomy's message could include ontological statements, I return to MacDonald's list of ways the "oneness" of YHWH has been understood as a

---

15. Ibid., 215.
16. Ibid., 207.

statement about the divine nature and see whether there might be a way forward from within this list: "mono-Yahwism, there is only one god ('monotheism'), the integrity of YHWH's will, YHWH has no family, YHWH is unchangeable."[17] Though the final claim, that "YHWH is unchangeable," MacDonald does not address directly, my concern is with the second, "the integrity of YHWH's will." MacDonald cites Janzen as exemplifying this position, which MacDonald then critiques. However, I argue that MacDonald's critique of Janzen is ill-conceived at two key points.

First, MacDonald misunderstands what Janzen means by "integrity." The first of Janzen's claims that MacDonald critiques is that, in Job 23:13, אֶחָד refers to the integrity of YHWH; MacDonald argues that in this verse, within the context of Job, the man is not calling on YHWH's integrity but protesting against YHWH's sovereignty.[18] MacDonald is right, but only if by "integrity" one means *moral* integrity; obviously Job claims that what YHWH is doing is unjust. But if by "integrity" one means assurance or certainty, then Janzen's claim would hold.[19] This seems to be what Janzen intends, as he writes, "God's 'oneness' is the unity between desire and action, between intention and execution. Such is this 'oneness', that God's action cannot be turned or deflected from its goal. The divine 'integrity' consists in the unswerving dedication with which God pursues the divine purpose for Job."[20]

---

17. Ibid., 71.
18. Ibid., 72–73.
19. *Oxford Dictionaries Online* gives two definitions for "integrity": "1. the quality of being honest and having strong moral principles," which is MacDonald's definition, and "2. the state of being whole and undivided," what Janzen seems to mean. *Oxford Dictionaries Online*, s.v. "integrity," (Oxford: Oxford University, 2013), http:///oxforddictionaries.com/definition/english/integrity.
20. The second claim of Janzen that MacDonald critiques is that אֶחָד also refers to the integrity of YHWH in Job 31:15: "Did not he who made me in the womb make them? And did not one fashion us in the womb?" Janzen reads Job 31 as Job affirming his loyalty to YHWH, and verse 15 as Job claiming "from God an integrity which will answer to the integrity which he asserts in and through his oath of loyalty." MacDonald argues that Job is defending his own integrity, not YHWH's; God made both Job and his slaves. However, even if Job is not affirming his loyalty to God, the text seems to suggest that Job is speaking about the justice of his own and God's actions. Job imagines that if he treated his own slaves poorly, God might call him to account for this treatment, and therefore he makes a claim about his own just actions. At the same time, he observes the irony that God might question Job's morality when Job

Second, MacDonald and Janzen disagree on what evidence is relevant to interpreting Deut 6:4. Janzen explicitly states that the bulk of his argument is "indirect" as he discusses other texts in the Pentateuch, and then the Old Testament, which have to do with the divine identity. Meanwhile, MacDonald critiques Janzen, stating,

> The final criterion for assessing any interpretation of אֶחָד must be the wider context of Deuteronomy. Here, the evidence for Janzen's interpretation is thin. References in Deuteronomy to the promises given to the Patriarchs hardly necessitate understanding Deut. 6.4 as a statement of divine integrity. More significantly whilst divine integrity plays a central role in Exodus 32-34, the episode about the Golden Calf, other themes come to the fore in the Deuteronomic retelling of that story (Deuteronomy 9–10). It seems difficult to argue, then, that divine integrity is a major theme in Deuteronomy.[21]

MacDonald's final sentence is telling, for what he is trying to accomplish is an understanding of the theology of *Deuteronomy* while Janzen's concern is broader. For MacDonald, only evidence from Deuteronomy is relevant to his task, but the same cannot be said of Janzen. This distinction is important. One can observe that, for MacDonald, a key argument is that "oneness" in Deut 6:4 fails because obedience, not divine unity, is the subject of the rest of the book. This runs counter to, for example, Augustine's interpretation of Exod 3:14, in which he admits that while the Old Testament generally speaks of God in ways that we can understand (as God "for us"), in a few particular texts, such as Exod 3:14, the veil momentarily lifts and the reader is offered something different. One might ask MacDonald *why* the lack of discussion of ontology in the rest of Deuteronomy requires that Deut 6:4 be read similarly, particularly if Deut 6:4 is central to the book but its wording is unique. It seems entirely possible that here, for a moment, an ontological reference

---

treats his own slaves better than God has treated him, since both he and the slave have been made by the same Creator. Job does claim that his own ways are just, while at the same time arguing that God ought to be consistent in his dealings with humans. Thus אֶחָד is used somewhat differently in Job 23:13 than in 31:15, but it is the former use that Janzen explicitly connects to the *Shema*. Janzen, "Most Important Word," 286–87.

21. MacDonald, *Deuteronomy*, 73.

seeks to ground Israel's loyalty to YHWH, which is the more consistent point of the book given the difficulty Israel had with such loyalty.

Because I am chiefly interested in Exod 3:14-15 and whether Deut 6:4 might serve as a parallel, I am open to a larger spectrum of evidence than is relevant to MacDonald's argument. Janzen takes up Exod 3 explicitly in his article and suggests that the Israelites' deliverance from Egypt is connected to the identity of YHWH (Exod 3:13-15), which is revealed in the divine name "YHWH" and God's faithfulness to promises made to the ancestors (3:6, 15; cf. 2:23-25).[22] While MacDonald is right that "fidelity to prior promises" does not necessarily indicate "oneness" or the kind of unity that Janzen proposes, there may be other evidence in support of this type of unity, evidence not only in Exodus but also in Deuteronomy.

In the same chapter in which MacDonald addresses interpretation of the *Shema*, he also discusses other verses in Deuteronomy that are typically considered "monotheistic," including 4:35, 39. While I agree with MacDonald that the recurring phrase (מִלְבַדּוֹ) אֵין עוֹד is more suggestive of the uniqueness of YHWH than of the nonexistence of other gods, more can be said about יְהוָה הוּא הָאֱלֹהִים. MacDonald rightly notes that the word הָאֱלֹהִים might be used similarly to 1 Kgs 18: "if YHWH is הָאֱלֹהִים follow him, but if Baal follow him" (v. 21). MacDonald writes,

> YHWH's answer by fire shows that he is הָאֱלֹהִים (vv. 37, 39). In this conflict the underlying presupposition is that only one deity can be הָאֱלֹהִים. . . . It should be noted that in Deuteronomy, as also in 1 Kings 18, to call YHWH הָאֱלֹהִים is to make a claim about YHWH's uniqueness, but it is not, however, a denial of the existence of other deities. Thus, our use of "God" must be understood to be making no prejudgement on the existence or otherwise of other gods.[23]

MacDonald's main point is surely correct, but more can be said about what type of "uniqueness" the term הָאֱלֹהִים implies. Janzen's and Miller's approaches to the *Shema* show us that this uniqueness can be understood as unity: God's undivided will is powerful to accomplish what God intends. This may be how it is used in 1 Kgs 18, since what demonstrates that God is הָאֱלֹהִים is that God sends fire on the (wet!) altar. God has accomplished some-

---

22. Janzen, "Most Important Word," 282-83.
23. MacDonald, *Deuteronomy*, 80.

thing that Baal has not. So also in Deut 4:35, where YHWH is acclaimed as unique on account of God's marvelous deeds such as have never before been seen: only God has chosen a people for himself and delivered them from so mighty an enemy, with such a splendid display of power. The text of 4:37-39 also has the exodus in view, but with particular attention to this deliverance as the out-working of God's love for Israel's ancestors; because of this great act, resulting from God's faithfulness to Abraham, Isaac, and Jacob, Israel is to "acknowledge today and take to heart that the Lord is God" (v. 39).

The kind of divine unity that Janzen and Miller propose is not finally opposed to MacDonald's main argument against Deuteronomy (or even, the Old Testament more broadly speaking) being said to convey "monotheism" as that term is typically understood. Rather, it is fully possible that divine unity, understood as unconflicted, consistent will in relationship with Israel and her ancestors and the power to accomplish that will in the present, is a key element in at least Deut 4 and 6. If this is the case, then the loyalty to which Israel is called throughout Deuteronomy is built on YHWH's undivided, effective will.[24] Moreover, the bulk of MacDonald's argument, that Deuteronomy is about keeping the covenant with YHWH alone, still holds and is only strengthened by this ontological claim.

In his final example in the chapter, MacDonald argues against an ontological reading of Deut 32:29. He states that the antecedent of הוא in the phrase אֲנִי אֲנִי הוּא should be understood as צוּר; YHWH is here emphasizing that, in contrast to other gods, YHWH is the true rock and refuge. However, while the point that YHWH is a rock is clearly made throughout the song (vv. 4, 15, 18, 30, 31) in contrast to other gods (vv. 31, 37), there is no reason for the author to have chosen הוא over צוּר in verse 39. The last occurrence of the latter term is several lines away (v. 37), and whereas MacDonald suggests that הוא might have been chosen for emphasis, the more general term would seem to have the opposite effect. Moreover, if anything is emphasized in the phrase אֲנִי אֲנִי הוּא it is the divine self-referential "I." In this repetition, there may be a parallel with Exod 3:14—in the repetition of אֲנִי, not in אֲנִי הוּא.[25]

---

24. Surely this is the case at least in the first commandment. Cf. Patrick D. Miller, *Deuteronomy*, IBC (Louisville: Westminster John Knox, 1990), 97-98; Janzen, "Most Important Word," esp. 281-82, 294-96.

25. Contra Norman Walker, "Concerning *hû'* and *'anî hû'*," ZAW 74 (1962): 205-6; Catrin H. Williams, *I Am He: The Interpretation of 'anî hû' in Jewish and Early Christian Literature*, WUNT II 113 (Tübingen: Mohr Siebeck, 2000), 51; cf. MacDonald, *Deuteronomy*,

The parallel is at the level of judgment rather than concept,[26] since the Hebrew terms obviously differ.[27] This self-referentiality may not *quite* articulate self-existence, but it may suggest that God's will and being are identical; only God can determine or reveal who God is. Furthermore, what is questionable about MacDonald's reading of this verse is his claim that it can only mean that YHWH is a rock *or* be interpreted in some ontological sense. But surely if YHWH is a rock then he is a certain, unchanging place of refuge for the people; that is simply what the metaphor means. Other gods exist, but they are no rock as is the self-referencing "he" who alone has the power to save his people. In other words, even if the antecedent of הוא is צור, the verse may still have ontological implications.

In light of the potential for an ontological basis of personal loyalty in Deuteronomy, MacDonald's anti-rational argument may be overstated in much the same way that, at points, he overstates his case against ontology. In chapter 3, MacDonald continues to support his claim that the primary context in which to understand Deut 6:4 is that of love, which is at odds with typical understandings of "monotheism":

> Although the Deuteronomic portrayal of YHWH's oneness, love, a wholehearted commitment to YHWH, has no place in modern intellectualization of "monotheism." "Monotheism" is a truth to be comprehended, not a relationship in which to be committed.[28]

While MacDonald's characterization of modernity's "monotheism" is likely correct, this is not true to Augustine's reading of Exod 3:14, a text that convinced Augustine that truth exists, and a text that he reads while declaring that truth is a person.[29] Moreover, I have argued that Moses' role as covenant mediator is cast in terms of "seeing" and "hearing," which are both relational terms that invite cognitive reflection. Moses leads Israel because he is closest to YHWH in proximity, but this closeness is consistently described in terms of Moses seeing and hearing something that Israel, farther off, does not see and hear, and which Moses must relay to them. Thus Moses

---

87.

26. Cf. Yeago, "Nicene Dogma," 152–64.
27. The Masoretic Text of Exod 3:14 does not include the first person singular pronoun at all, though the Septuagint does.
28. MacDonald, *Deuteronomy*, 97.
29. *Conf.* 7.10,16; 7.19,25.

is an example of one whose relational nearness to God involves an element of contemplation, a direction of attention toward YHWH's self-disclosure.

Moreover, reading MacDonald with Augustine in mind, one can observe that the argument against using the term "monotheism" shares with Enlightenment accounts of monotheism a black-and-white description of being: either gods exist, or they do not. This assumption makes it possible to say that what Israel denies other gods is not existence but loyalty and significance, since, obviously, for other gods to create a temptation for Israel, they must exist. But Augustine's account of being is not so dualistic, since he can pray, "And I considered the other things below you, and I saw that neither can they be said absolutely to be or absolutely not to be. They are because they come from you. But they are not because they are not what you are."[30] What Augustine learns while reading Exod 3:14 is not that only Israel's God exists and the others are non-existent, but that all things—including other gods—are partial in comparison to the absolute consistency of God.[31] Their existence is incomplete: they cannot act and did not deliver Israel from Egypt, and so love of them is foolish and inappropriate. If we desire to avoid imposing Enlightenment conceptions of monotheism on the biblical text, then Augustine's more fluid account of ontology might be appropriate. However, contra MacDonald, rather than pushing aside *all* ontological interpretations, one would need to attend in some way to the ontological implications of the passage.

Augustine's ontological language fits squarely with the Pentateuch's tendency toward comparative statements about God's identity. Take, for example, Deut 4:32–40, which I have already addressed in conversation with MacDonald. MacDonald is surely correct in arguing that the statements about God's identity in verses 35, 39 have to do with divine uniqueness in the context of Israel's election: only this God, YHWH, has delivered Israel from Egypt and nothing so terrific has ever before occurred. Adding the possibility that these verses also contain ontological implications in no way detracts from MacDonald's argument. "The Lord is God; there is no other besides him" (Deut 4:35) is obviously a comparative statement; even as this statement does not deny that other gods exist, the statement may still be ontological. "No other god exists as YHWH does" is a statement about YHWH's character and

---

30. *Et inspexi cetera infra te et vidi nec omnino esse nec omnino non esse: esse quidem, quoniam abs te sunt, non esse autem, quoniam id quod es non sunt. Conf.* 7.11,17.

31. Cf. *Conf.* 7.10, 16.

existence, which are not finally separable. No other god has so grandiosely demonstrated such a single, consistent will on behalf of one people. In these acts, YHWH proves a new mode of being unwitnessed heretofore.

Before concluding this section, it may be helpful for me to clarify further what I mean by "ontological." In the foregoing discussion, I have argued that Augustine's understanding of existence is patient of degrees and that this type of ontology could help us move beyond Enlightenment notions of monotheism to a better understanding of Deuteronomy and Exodus. Yet at other points in the thesis, I have argued for a different understanding of the term "ontological": that the name "YHWH," as a sign given by God himself, opens into the reality of God who exceeds traditional theological claims. The logic is incarnational: God surely comes to humans in a form that we can grasp, but condescension in no way threatens God's power and fundamental distinction from all things as their Creator. God's name enables humanity to have access to him, but this access is entirely subject to the freedom and mercy of God rather than an achievement of human intellect or ingenuity. Hermeneutically, I am not saying that the Old Testament contains an ontology or a metaphysic, or that there is a "metaphysic of the Old Testament,"[32] if by that one means a clear structure of being that is readily apprehended and universally applicable, on the one hand, or on the other, a universal reality that makes unnecessary the sign of that reality. Rather what I mean is that the text of the Old Testament at times suggests that its stories do not exhaust the reality of God even as they guide the reader toward God. Exod 3:14 is one such witness to excess.

My second type of use of the term "ontological" is the same as the first, only seen from a different perspective. Theological ontology as degrees of being begins with God and compares all material, created reality to God; theological ontology as excess begins with created, material reality and compares this back to God. Both statements are Augustinian, and together they say something about how to speak of one who cannot be numbered as an item in the universe, a God who is Lover and Love: immaterial, personal unity. Deuteronomy's "other gods" *are* items in the universe; they are mortal, conflicted, and untrustworthy.[33]

To summarize, I have suggested that MacDonald's approach may be open to an ontological interpretation of the *Shema* as long as this interpreta-

---

32. Cf. Gilson's "metaphysics of Exodus." Gilson, *Spirit of Mediæval Philosophy*, 51.
33. Cf. Herbert McCabe, *God Still Matters* (Sheffield: Continuum, 2005), 56.

tion is thoroughly situated within the dynamic of YHWH's relation to Israel, God's relation with his people. MacDonald has difficulty articulating this openness clearly perhaps because he assumes, with the Enlightenment logic of monotheism, that there is no room for degrees in ontological speech. Such dualistic ontology is not what we find in Augustine and Augustine's understanding of Exod 3:14, and it not necessarily true of Deuteronomy.

Therefore, this study has significant implications for Old Testament theology. If MacDonald's argument is indicative of a prominent direction within Old Testament studies and theology, then I suggest that the field needs to be more careful about its use of the term "ontology." While the narrative, law, and poetry of the Old Testament do not contain a philosophical treatise that systematically outlines a philosophy of being, nevertheless, accounts of God's self-revelation to Moses and the Israelites in the Pentateuch do suggest that God's existence is unsuitable for images, unseen fully even by the most godly of people and unnameable without qualification, even as YHWH names himself for the Israelites, enables himself to be called upon, appears to Moses and the patriarchs, and offers Moses as covenant mediator and the covenant itself as the means by which Israel can be in relation with this God.

2. Naming God in Three Patterns: R. Kendall Soulen

If this study has implications for Old Testament theology, it also has significant implications for doctrinal theology that seeks to build on biblical theology. In *The Divine Name(s) and the Holy Trinity: Distinguishing the Voices* R. Kendall Soulen offers a carefully constructed argument for the renaissance of the Tetragrammaton in Trinitarian doctrine, and includes a lengthy exegetical discussion of Exod 3:13-15. I argue that Soulen's proposal is misguided, both theologically and exegetically. Though he argues for a renaissance of the divine name "YHWH" in doctrinal theology on the grounds that it indicates a unique theological pattern of naming God, Exod 3:14-15 does not suggest that God is named "YHWH" without qualification. Therefore, Soulen's three patterns of naming are not as distinct as he claims.

Soulen begins by asserting that there are three key "patterns of naming" the holy Trinity:

- A *theological* pattern of naming the persons of the Trinity that identifies the three persons in terms of the giving, receiving, and glorification of the divine Name, the unspoken Tetragrammaton.

This pattern is characterized by its tight orbit around a single personal proper name, which is alluded to obliquely by means of a number of different surrogates and pious circumlocutions, in keeping with the precedent of Jewish custom and the New Testament.

- A *christological* pattern of naming that identifies the three persons as the Father, the Son, and the Holy Spirit. This pattern is relatively fixed, not in the sense that it always appears in a single linguistic form, but rather in that it revolves chiefly around a limited set of male kinship terms, which occurs with relatively minor variations: "Our Father," "Abba," "Son of God," "spirit of adoption," and so forth.

- A *pneumatological* pattern of naming that identifies the three persons by using an open-ended variety of ternaries, such as "Love, Lover, Beloved," relations of persons in a variety of context-sensitive ways that multiply and coexist while always leaving room for more.[34]

These patterns are "distinct," "equally important," and "interrelated," as the Trinitarian persons are. Moreover, Soulen argues that wherever these three are not held in balance, there Christian identification of the Trinity is threatened.[35] Soulen then demonstrates how the New Testament witnesses to the Triune God using these three patterns, as does the Nicene-Constantinopolitan Creed. However, the Dionysian and Reformation traditions that come to dominate Christian tradition each obfuscate the first pattern in their own way, and it is against these weighty traditions that Soulen fights for the integrity of the name "YHWH."[36]

Soulen's proposal for Trinitarian naming seems creative and balanced. However, there are difficulties at several points. First, there is the minor concern of his choice of titles for the three patterns, e.g., why are the kinship terms "christological" rather than "theological"? Soulen draws these three patterns from three biblical scenes: the burning bush (Exod 3), the words of the risen Christ (Matt 28:19), and the morning of Pentecost (Acts 2). The three scenes illustrate biblical resources for dealing with three contemporary issues in theology: Christian-Jewish relations, the equality of women

---

34. Soulen, *Divine Name(s)*, 22.
35. Ibid.
36. See R. Kendall Soulen, "YHWH the Triune God," *MT* 15, no. 1 (1999): 25–54.

and men, and the growth of the church in the global east and south.[37] From the standpoint of these biblical narratives, one can see why the three names are loosely appropriate.[38]

A more significant problem is the relationship between the naming patterns and whether the personal titles are befitting of the relationships between these patterns. Soulen wants to indicate that the relations between Trinitarian persons serve as models for those between the patterns of naming. Yet, it is not clear that the grammar of how the Father, the Son, and the Holy Spirit relate ought to apply to these three patterns of divine naming (or any three elements of theological grammar). The three patterns are not Trinitarian persons; they are impersonal concepts, which do not substantially relate to the persons for which they are named.[39] Can a Trinitarian model of personal relationship supply an appropriate analogy for the relations of these conceptual patterns? That Soulen's proposal is a creative reflection on the Trinity goes without saying, but one must be theologically and exegetically convinced that these three patterns are actually "distinct," "equally important," and "interrelated." For example, Seitz argues that "Father, Son and Holy Spirit" is the normative name of the Trinity for Christians (with Jewish Christians excepted) because "Our Father" is how Jesus taught his disciples to pray. Seitz is not claiming priority for the New Testament over the Old in matters of Christian practice, but rather he argues that Christians only have access to the God of Israel through Christ. Seitz asserts,

> To call God "our heavenly Father" is to address God as Jesus did, and only from that christological point of standing does the name refer to The God, Israel's named Lord, YHWH. If "we Gentiles" do

---

37. In Part 2 of the book (beginning at p. 107), Soulen does relate these patterns of naming to the voices of Father, Son, and Spirit in the New Testament. However, Part 1 is my primary concern.

38. For the sake of simplicity, I refer to them as the first, second, and third patterns.

39. Yet, Soulen breaks from strict adherence to the equality of the patterns when he writes that the name "YHWH," "occupies a special place in the economy of trinitarian names because it alone orbits a personal proper name, indeed, the personal proper name. Precisely for this reason, the pattern of naming that orbits this name stands in relationship to the other patterns as a king of *fons divinitatis*, fountain of divinity, as the first person of the Trinity stands in relationship to the second and third persons." Soulen, *Divine Name(s)*, 23.

> not regard this language as a gift, privileging us to speak to God, in the first-person plural ("*our* Father") with Jesus, who is our only point of access to YHWH, then no amount of debate or "revision" will expose why this language is proper and good. Rather, it will only expose our forgetfulness about a gift of incorporation upon which our very lives depend. . . .
>
> To call God "Father" proceeds from Jesus' own language and perspective, and without this we have no access to Israel's life with the named God, YHWH. To call God "Son" is to recognize the nonnegotiable fact of access through Jesus, in the most elevated sense. To call God "Holy Spirit" is to confess that even how we address God is itself a gift from God, not to be debated or probed but received in humility and thanksgiving, with the same sense of reverence that God's people Israel had for the name YHWH, vocalized now for Christians, "Father, Son, and Holy Spirit."[40]

According to Seitz, Christians receive God's names as a gift and have no choice but to use the names which God has intended and offered: for Christians, this means first "Father, Son, and Holy Spirit" and only indirectly, through that name, the name "YHWH."

It is important for my argument in contrast with Soulen that Seitz's proposal comes neither from the Old Testament developing into the New nor from the New superseding the Old. Rather, for Seitz, the two testaments witness to the one God each in their own idiom and stand alongside each other in the canon. The specificity of the name "YHWH" is matched in the specificity of the New Testament name "Jesus."[41] In contrast, Soulen seems to assume that anything other than complete equity between the three naming patterns would indicate that the New Testament has superseded the Old. In an earlier article upon which his later book seems to be based, Soulen reasons that "classical trinitarianism affirms that God appears in the economy as YHWH, the God of Israel, but nevertheless treats God's identity as YHWH as finally dispensable for understanding God's *eternal* identity and *ultimate* purposes for creation."[42] But this description does not at all fit Seitz's argument, and yet Seitz can affirm that Christians only come to YHWH through

---

40. Christopher R. Seitz, *Word Without End: The Old Testament as Abiding Theological Witness* (Grand Rapids: Eerdmans, 1998), 259-61.
41. Ibid., 260.
42. Soulen, "YHWH the Triune God," 26.

Christ, who first teaches his followers to call God "*our* Father." Thus, one can begin to see that it is not self-evident that the three naming patterns should be treated equally.

Moreover, Soulen cites Scripture and the Nicene-Constantinopolitan Creed as positive examples of the three naming patterns, yet it is unclear whether Soulen's description does justice to the creed.[43] Having sufficiently introduced his argument, Soulen begins chapter 2 with a summary of recent research on oblique references to the divine name "YHWH" in the New Testament and early Christian practices of the *nomina sacra*, drawing particularly on the works of Larry Hurtado, Colin Roberts, and Schuyler Brown.[44] That the second and third patterns of Trinitarian naming are integral to the New Testament is not debatable. That the name "YHWH" is also integral might be debatable, and Soulen persuasively defends this claim. However, the latter portion of this chapter, in which Soulen argues that all three patterns of Trinitarian naming are presented in a beautiful and enduring way in the Nicene-Constantinopolitan Creed, is problematic because of what Soulen avoids, namely the phrase for which the Creed is best known: "of one being" and in the 325 version, "from the being." Soulen argues that these phrases have to do with "what is *common* to the three persons of the Trinity: the divine essence," and not specifically to do with naming any of the persons of the Trinity. Thus, Soulen believes that he is justified in giving very short space to the phrases, summarizing that they "are fully compatible with all three patterns of naming the persons of the Trinity, without themselves belonging directly to any one of them. This follows from the fact that the phrases do not actually name the persons of the Trinity, but instead express what is common to the three persons."[45] Stating that the divine essence is

---

43. It also seems at least odd, if not problematic, that Soulen finds no positive examples for his proposal in Christian tradition except for Scripture and the Nicene-Constantinopolitan Creed. Soulen argues that the contemporary issues of women's liberation, the growing global church and Christian repentance from supercessionism fuel his renewed look at tradition, but the proposal itself appears rather traditional. Patriarchy, the narrow geographical limits of the church in other historical periods, and supercessionism may have influenced tradition away from the equity of the three naming patterns, but it is at least theoretically possible that one could have advocated all three naming patterns even under these conditions. That the proposal cannot easily be found in tradition may indicate that its absence is not a mistake.

44. See references in Soulen, *Divine Name(s)*, 259, fn. 2.

45. Ibid., 45.

something that can be named apart from naming the persons of the Trinity sounds dangerously close to positing a fourth "thing" in God. Both Nicene phrases are prepositional; they name neither the persons of the Trinity nor the divine essence but rather indicate something about the generative relationship between Father and Son: "from the being of the Father" or "of one being with the Father." "*Ousia*" belongs to the kinship pattern, and for this reason, Soulen refers to it under the heading "A Christological Pattern Characterized by the Vocabulary of Father and Son," only to sideline the issue.[46]

In sum, Soulen's proposal for threefold naming of the Trinity is problematic with regard to the relationship it suggests between the three proposed patterns of naming and in its separation of these patterns from ontological discourse. The placement of being-language outside Soulen's framework becomes a problem when he addresses Exod 3:14–15. He claims that "Since 'He Who Is' and the Tetragrammaton *are two different kinds of names*, no amount of attention to the former—no matter how exemplary in itself—can take the place of comparable attention to the latter (YHWH), which is the more widely attested biblical name by several orders of magnitude."[47] Soulen wants to say that Exod 3:14 names God; but to what pattern of naming does it belong? Certainly not to any of the patterns he has proposed. Moreover, though Soulen's account of Exod 3:14–15 has many merits, it fails to portray adequately the relationship between the two verses, between the name "YHWH" and its explanation or, as I argue, qualification.

In several respects, Soulen's account of Exod 3:14–15 resonates with mine: the content of verse 14 is to be understood not etymologically, but as "*wordplays* that anticipate a reply yet to come: the Tetragrammaton."[48] In particular, the wordplay in verse 14a is a tautology, as Soulen proposes,

---

46. Ibid., 41.

47. Ibid., 267, fn. 24. In this footnote, Soulen clarifies his argument in the earlier article and defends it against Levering, stating, "In the essay to which Levering refers, I defend the justifiability of interpreting Exod. 3:14 in ontological terms. My criticism of the tradition's handling of 3:14 is not directed against its ontological interpretation per se, but against the assumption that such interpretation provides *an equivalent substitute* for a comparable analysis of the Tetragrammaton and its place in the Old and New Testaments," emphasis original. Cf. Soulen, "YHWH the Triune God," passim; Levering, *Scripture and Metaphysics*, 47–73.

48. Soulen, *Divine Name(s)*, 141, emphasis original.

"With these words, God declares who he is by referring God to—God!"[49] Treating the two verses together, Soulen writes,

> God's replies to Moses' question express God's uniqueness, each in a different way. "I am who I am" and "I am" express God's uniqueness by virtue of what they *mean*, albeit with subtle differences of color. The Tetragrammaton, in contrast to both, expresses God's uniqueness merely by what it *is*. These two main ways of expressing God's uniqueness illuminate and protect each other. . . . "I am who I am" illuminates and protects our understanding of the Tetragrammaton by driving home the insight that God's uniqueness is beyond every finite category, even (or perhaps especially) the category of named gods of the ancient Middle East. *Deus non est in genere!* Yet the Tetragrammaton also illuminates and protects our understanding of "I am who I am" by referring even this august description to the living God who bears the divine name.[50]

Soulen's primary concern, in his discussion of these two verses together, is to demonstrate their distinction, as different ways of naming God, and the priority of the divine name "YHWH." True, the two names and the two verses are related: the first "illuminates and protects" the second, and vice versa. Soulen also claims that both parts of verse 14 are "commentaries" on the divine name.[51] Even more, Soulen begins to recognize that the Tetragrammaton cannot be understood as a proper name in the sense that humans—and indeed other gods—have proper names—*Deus non est in genere!* So far, Soulen's interpretation has much in common with my own.

Soulen argues that "I am who I am" is its own name for God, distinct from, and dependent on, the name "YHWH." He continues:

> Nevertheless if there is no relationship of superiority and inferiority between these two kinds of names, there is a relationship of priority and logical sequence. The Tetragrammaton precedes "I am who I am," not in a literary or temporal sense, but in a logical sense, by virtue of its status as a personal proper name that fixes the referent of biblical discourse and of every other discourse that aspires to move in the orbit of the God attested by Scripture. The Tetragrammaton, we might say, leans on "I am who I am" for its

---

49. Ibid., 140.
50. Ibid., 141–42.
51. Ibid., 141.

elucidation in the language of "Being." But language about Being becomes discourse about the one true God only insofar as it willingly yields to the priority of the Tetragrammaton. Whenever Christian theology overlooks or withholds or denies this priority, it threatens its own integrity from within. For if the names of Exodus 3:14 were to disappear, the rest of the canon's witness to the living God would remain, however much our understanding of it might be impoverished. But if the divine name of Exodus 3:15 were to disappear, the canon itself would cease to exist as sacred Scripture.[52]

Soulen's thought experiment suggests that the the name "YHWH" carries greater weight, across the Old Testament, than does the context of verse 14. Surely this is correct. However, Soulen does not answer the question, *why* does "I am who I am" precede "YHWH"? In fact, the thought experiment may distract the reader from the flow of the received text.

I have suggested that verse 14 offers a qualification for how to understand the divine name: "I am who I am," or "only I can name myself." The uniqueness of God demands that the name "YHWH" not be understood as other proper names are understood. People do not name themselves, but are given names by their parents, or receive the names of their parents, while only God can name God. There is a distance, the space of "I am who I am" that keeps the name "YHWH" from acting as a proper name in a straightforward sense. Thus, that God is both nameable and nameless finds its roots in the literal sense of Exod 3:14-15. Soulen attributes the concept of God's namelessness to Neoplatonism. While perhaps philosophical winds of the first centuries after Christ enabled this element of the text to be brought out, Soulen must attend to the fact of the presence of Exod 3:14 and its counterintuitive placement prior to the divine name "YHWH."

As I have argued, there are resources in Augustine's work for seeing the relationship between Exod 3:14, an attempt to articulate who God is in himself, and the name in verse 15, the name given by God to humanity in time, God with us and for us. Soulen focuses on a few portions of *The Trinity*, and so misses the fullness of Augustine's reading of Exod 3:14-15 in texts such as *Expositions of the Psalms* 121, *Sermon* 6, and *Sermon* 7. In the "distinction between absolute and relative names of God,"[53] relative names include not only "Fa-

---

52. Ibid., 142.
53. Ibid., 67.

ther, Son and Holy Spirit," and "Lover, Beloved, Love" (which Soulen admits) but, I would suggest, also the "God of Abraham, the God of Isaac, and the God of Jacob" (e.g., Exod 3:15). All three are found in Scripture (as "Lover, Beloved, Love" is based on "God is love," 1 John 4:8, 16). As for the absolute name of God, or that which refers to who God is *in se*, Augustine uses a variety of terms for this as well, and as I have argued, the variety stems from Scripture and the challenge of naming the unnameable (*"idipsum," "ego sum qui sum," "est,"* etc.). In every case, God overcomes the essential impasse between divinity and humanity, offering himself to be known.

Of course, since Augustine himself does not acknowledge the divine name "YHWH," one can only speculate whether he would consider it an absolute or a relative name, had he acknowledged it. However, either way, Soulen's claim that recognition of the Tetragrammaton would necessarily subvert Augustine's logic of the essential namelessness of God seems untrue. Had Augustine recognized the divine name "YHWH," he could have argued that the name "YHWH" would be equivalent to *"idipsum," "ego sum qui sum," "est,"* etc., and thus one of the absolute names for God. If this were the case, then the name is absolute by virtue of association with Being, which Soulen wants to jettison. On the other hand, Augustine could have seen "YHWH" as a relative name, equivalent to "the God of Abraham, the God of Isaac, and the God of Jacob," as I have suggested. In this case, the logic of the Tetragrammaton would not be fundamentally different from the logic of the other two naming patterns: while "YHWH" constitutes a name that God recognizes as his own, God nevertheless exceeds this designation; the one who calls upon this name still does not have power over God. Therefore, while we should not ignore the Tetragrammaton, as Augustine has, Augustine's logic of the movement between the verses may be retained, whether the name "YHWH" is acknowledged or not.

The Tetragrammaton may be both a relative name and an absolute name. Insofar as the name "YHWH" can be described as "I am who I am" or "I am," to the extent it refers, through self-reference and indeed by way of negation, to who God is in himself, it is an absolute name. Insofar as the name identifies the one who acts among and on behalf of Israel, the name is relative. The logic of Exod 3:14–15 may demonstrate that a clean differentiation between these two types of names is ill-made. Exodus 3:14–15 refers to the movement of divine self-revelation from who God is in himself to who God is for us. The incarnational logic, that "God gives himself fully in finite words and deeds," but "God cannot be exhaustively expressed in finite words and deeds,"[54] is near at hand. In this way, the Old Testament text refers to who God is "in himself" (*in se*) and who God is "for us," without the former making the latter unnecessary, and without the latter constituting the former. Put differently, God reveals himself to humanity in such a way that we are assured that God, though *not* an "item in the universe," truly stands behind this revelation. God's self-disclosure reveals reality.

In summary, the divine name "YHWH" need not follow a substantially different logic than other ways of naming the Trinity. The text of Exod 3:14 provides a qualification to the divine name "YHWH" and a reminder, wherever this name is used, that though it truly refers to God, God nevertheless exceeds this reference. In the next section, I will offer brief and modest suggestions for a better way for exegesis of this passage and Trinitarian theology to proceed.

3. The Triune God and the Literal Sense of Exodus 3:13-15

In this chapter, I have attempted to clarify my ontological reading of Exod 3:13-15 by addressing some of the implications of this reading for biblical theology. First, using MacDonald's monograph as an example, I have argued that the tendency in Old Testament theology to dispense with ontological language in the name of focusing on relational language is both unnecessary and ungrounded. The text of Deut 6:4 may well be open to ontological interpretation on its own terms and within a reading of Deuteronomy as a realistic narrative.

Second, in dialogue with Soulen, I have argued that the divine name "YHWH" does not function in Exodus in a straightforward manner such that this name could be considered a direct, unqualified name of God. Rather, verse 14 functions as a qualification of the name. So while the name "YHWH" is used in particular textual contexts and so has its own storied meaning, this name does not function in relation to God in a categorically different way from other names found in Scripture, including the name "Father, Son and Holy Spirit."

My reading of Exod 3:13-15 can be briefly summarized as follows. In asking after the name of God, Moses foreshadows his vocation as covenant me-

---

54. D. Stephen Long, *Speaking of God: Theology, Language, and Truth*, The Eerdmans Ekklesia Series (Grand Rapids: Eerdmans, 2009), 4.

diator, in which God appears and speaks to him more directly than to anyone else in Israel. Thus Moses hears from God both God's name as well as commentary on that name, in the form of paronomasia or wordplay. That the wordplay involves the root היה suggests something about the nature of God, yet the nature of God is simultaneously withheld; אֶהְיֶה אֲשֶׁר אֶהְיֶה, in its indeterminacy and first-person form, is ascribed to God who can only be identified through self-reference and who cannot be fully described in words. Yet God makes himself available to Israel in the name "YHWH," which they can use to call upon him, and in YHWH's ongoing covenant relationship with them, fulfilling the promises made to the patriarchs. In Exod 3:13–15, God makes himself known through self-reference and identification with Israel. God acts faithfully among and on behalf of Israel while at the same time retaining God's own freedom to be and act according to his will.

This reading of Exod 3:13–15 has significant implications for Trinitarian doctrinal theology, and the direction that I propose for exploring these implications is through attention to the theological judgments evident in the biblical text when read according to its literal sense. While idioms through which the Hebrew text presents the Lord's self-identification to Moses are peculiar to this passage in its language, the theological judgments evident in the passage may be identified with theological judgments rendered through different idioms. Attention to the specific idioms in the Hebrew text enables this reading of the literal sense to be firmly grounded in "the way the words go,"[55] while exploration of the unity between Old Testament theological judgments and later Christian doctrinal developments enables the reader to perceive the ascriptive subject of the Old Testament as the one God, known to Christians as Father, Son, and Holy Spirit. Thus, the Hebrew Bible is a resource for Trinitarian theology, and modern readers of the Hebrew text of Exod 3:13–15 can dialogue with, and potentially learn from, traditions of Christian interpretation that stem from Greek and Latin translations.

In particular, the literal sense of Exod 3:13–15 suggests three sets of theological judgments that are relevant for Trinitarian theology:

1. *God's identity and action are intertwined in God's self-revelation.* God's self-revelation to Moses in Exod 3 involves both what God will do among the Israelites as well as who God is. The literary contexts of use of the divine name in the book of Exodus and passages describing Moses' vocation in the Pentateuch further support this point. This may suggest that theological

---

55. Marshall, "Absorbing the Word," 93–94

reflections on God's identity should also be reflections on God's acts in the world, and vice versa.

2. *Naming God is self-involving.* I have suggested that reading the question and answer in Exod 3:13–15 as to do with factual information of a name, previously known or unknown to the Israelites, amounts to a reduction of the literal sense of the passage. Rather, the question and response have to do with human experience of knowing God. Though within the narrative and its literary context, Moses and the Israelites are those seeking to know God, through reading the biblical text, the reader is invited to perceive God's self-disclosure. As God's self-revelation involves God's action and identity, so receiving it involves human cognitive and active response.

3. *God's self-revelation is both concrete and indeterminate.* The Lord speaks to Moses a name by which the Lord makes himself available to his people: YHWH, the God of Abraham, the God of Isaac, and the God of Jacob. Yet, this name is not given without qualification; the indeterminate phrase "I am who I am" suggests that one cannot presume to have exhaustively known or named God. This is true despite the fact that the Hebrew text gives the personal name of God; even this name must be qualified in light of human limitation to grasp fully the holy, invisible and immaterial God.

Read in this way and in Christian context, the reader can perceive strong resonance with the incarnation: God comes to humanity in an understandable form and, in revealing himself, accomplishes salvation for those who receive him. While Exod 3:13–15 is a realistic narrative about the self-revelation of God to Moses, within the context of Christian Scripture and Christian grammar it functions as a figure of the fullness of God's self-revelation in Jesus Christ. Moreover, that God is the only one who can reveal God, and that God can identify himself only through self-reference, provides a basis for confessing the Christian mystery that the one God is Father, Son, and Spirit. For the principles of divine life are known only to God and received in the community of faith and through Scripture.

Thus I have argued that Old Testament studies would do well to take greater care in addressing the ontological implications of Old Testament texts. Also, I have argued that intersection between exegesis of Exod 3:13–15 and doctrinal theology could fruitfully reflect on how the self-revelation of God in the Old Testament enables one to make theological judgments that are foundational for naming the Trinity. These are only two aspects of the many potential implications of reading Exod 3:13–15 in dialogue with premodern Christian interpretations.

Conclusion

I have offered a reading of Exod 3:13–15 that draws on a variety of sources. Mid-twentieth-century religio-historical approaches that sought to reconstruct the origins of the divine name and how it came to be known in Israel have not significantly aided the task of understanding the received form of the passage. Therefore, I have turned to the literary context of the received text, addressing the divine name in the book of Exodus and the role of Moses in the wider Pentateuch. In this context, the text of Exod 3:13–15 suggests Moses' question is more than a request for factual information; it is a question about the character and nature of God. אֶהְיֶה אֲשֶׁר אֶהְיֶה expresses indefiniteness; while God reveals himself, he also remains hidden, beyond human comprehension. The Lord instructs Moses to tell the Israelites that אֶהְיֶה has sent him to them, though the Israelites are given a different name to call upon God. The name "YHWH" is a name that God provides as part of the promise that he will deliver them from Egypt so that they can be a distinct people in covenant with him. Though the text suggests that he will be with Moses (v. 12), and by extension with the Israelites, God is not exhaustively known to the Israelites, since God identifies himself through self-reference and retains the freedom to be who he will be. Moreover, my study of Augustine's reading of Exod 3:13–15 has argued that Christian interpretive tradition building on Greek translations of the text does not necessarily declare God to be static or abstract, even if early Christian commentators may say more about the nature and being of God than modern Old Testament scholars have deemed appropriate. Nor, I have argued, can Augustine be indicted for flagrant eisegesis, concerned as he is with the reader submitting to the revelation in Scripture and in creation.

In light of this study, Old Testament scholarship of Exod 3:13–15 should not continue to promote reading Exod 3:13–15 as etymology or viewing the Masoretic text and Christian traditional readings in dichotomous relationship. Neither of the options that von Rad proposes—etymology or reference to abstract, static being—attend well to the features of this Hebrew text, which includes paronomasia that suggests indefiniteness and functions as a qualification of the divine name "YHWH." Scholarship on Exod 3:13–15 can, and should, turn toward the fields of history of interpretation and Septuagint studies to develop a more nuanced narrative of the ways that this text has been interpreted and the role of Greek and Latin translations in forming reading traditions.

Moreover, theological interpretation may consider how premodern readings might help us to read and perceive the biblical text. I have suggested that dialogue with Augustine's reading of Exod 3:13–15 can help current theological interpretation of this text. Precisely what reading this text in conversation with Augustine offers readings of this text in Christian, twenty-first century contexts merits further comment by way of conclusion.

First, reading with Augustine, as mediated by Strawn, helped me to articulate the possibility and legitimacy of christological readings within a Trinitarian approach without seeing christological reading as required in a Christian context. The doctrine of inseparable operations helps one to see the ascriptive subject of the Old Testament as simply God without anxiety that this will involve anachronism, on the one hand, or be removed from the self-revelation of God in the Word incarnate, Jesus Christ, on the other.

Second, Augustine suggests language to help one conceive of the intersection between careful attention to the specific words of the text and the goal of spiritual reading. In Augustine's terms, the literal/proper sense contrasts with the figurative sense, and spiritual reading contrasts with carnal (literal) reading. The literal sense is thus not divorced from the task of spiritual reading. What one, drawing from Frei, might call the self-referential character of the text may be aligned with Augustine's *proprie*, or literal sense reading, while attending to the subject matter of the Old Testament—namely God, whom Christians know as Father, Son, and Holy Spirit—may align with Augustine's *spiritualis*, or spiritual reading, which is in contrast with carnal reading. That the spiritual and literal reading coincide is precisely the point that that diverse texts in the canon hang together in the Old Testament's ascriptive subject, God.

Third, reading the Old Testament in light of God as its ascriptive subject may be a contemporary way of making Augustine's point that reading is a journey and a journey home. The direction of reading is from text to subject matter, *res* (as fits Childs's first and second stage of his multilevel reading). This *res* is none other than the one God. The point and purpose of reading is not only to understand how this God was known in the past but to see God's self-revelation through the text and so to be brought into the *res*. To say that the Old Testament draws the reader into understanding God, who is known to Christians as Father, Son, and Holy Spirit, is not to present an anachronism, but rather to be aware of the ontological *telos* of the act of reading. That this God is known particularly through the text of Scripture means that the reading process is never complete. Though Augustine uses the language of journey to describe the reader's movement toward God, the goal (the homeland) and the way (the words of the text; the name, "the Lord God of Abraham, the God of Isaac, and the God of Jacob;" and the humanity, or cross, of Christ) one does not arrive home, this side of the eschaton. Rather, the reader constantly returns to the task, asking how this text reveals the mind of God, and is drawn further on the journey toward God.

Fourth, considering the act of reading as a journey, and a journey home to God, involves not only the full two-testament canon, but even the entire story of salvation, from creation to eschaton, in which Christians find themselves. As Augustine claims that the parts of Scripture should be read in light of the whole, in conversation with Augustine a current reader might view Old Testament texts as having discrete integrity even while acknowledging that, in a Christian context, the God to whom they witness reliably is none other than Father, Son, and Holy Spirit. It is not necessary (if it is even possible) to leave at the doorstep all knowledge of God learned through texts and experiences on this side of the Old Testament; while historical inquiry may form and critique our understandings of the ancient world, it is only through the reader's current lens that one can view the Old Testament at all. An exegete can explicitly attend to particular statements, stories, or terms that are used in parts of the canon while simultaneously acknowledging that such a canonical selection exhausts neither what the reader will bring to the interpretive process nor the semantic potential of the text. One can read part of the story as coherent in itself, but since it is not an isolated story but rather part of a larger story, those for whom the larger story is their story will be able to observe vestiges of that larger story within the discrete passage. In sum, Old Testament texts have a particular place in the larger story from creation to eschaton, and thus while individual passages can be seen as partial and anticipating other events in the larger story, they also offer an entry point for the reader into the story of salvation.

Fifth, reading with Augustine helps one to articulate the limits of using anthropological language of "discrete voice" to make an interpretive argument. Regarding Exod 3:13–15, this type of language may be used to distinguish between reading the text within the context of Exodus or the wider Old Testament and reading it in light of its history of interpretation. Yet, in chapters 3 and 4, I interpret Exod 3:13-15 within the context of the book of Exodus and within the Pentateuch and find that the semantic potential of these verses, within these contexts, already points in directions that resonate with Augustine's reading. Similarly, in critiquing Childs's use of the phrase "the discrete voice of the Old Testament," Fowl argues that, "I can advance no argument by claiming that my interpretation conforms to the 'voice' of scripture and my opponent's does not allow the 'voice' of scripture to be heard."[1] It might be argued that Fowl's point is overstated. The phrase "discrete voice" does have limited use in interpretive disputes, because it can identify explicit reference appropriate to historical context; for example, one can use "discrete voice" to describe the fact that covenant is an important concept in the Old Testament, but that, since the text concerns times prior to the earthly life of Jesus Christ, the name "Father, Son, and Holy Spirit" is nowhere used in the Old Testament. However, "discrete voice" cannot address ambiguity in the text or the range of nuances which can be discerned once that text is read in a new historical context. Moreover, since Hebrew narrative is characteristically sparse and ambiguous,[2] the discrete voice will, at times, be significantly limited in its usefulness. Precisely because one can read the so-called "voice" of Scripture in multiple ways, this term is not always helpful in interpretive disputes.

Sixth, Augustine's articulation of the doctrine of the Trinity offers a starting point for understanding Father, Son, and Spirit as the reality into which Christians are drawn in faith as they read Scripture, Old and New Testaments. This reality may be articulated through ontological language; indeed, one may be forced to use language of being in order to articulate the reality-in-mystery of God who says, "I am who I am," and who is Father, Son, and Spirit. Yet, to articulate it thus should not be intended or misunderstood as identification of being as a fourth thing in God. Father, Son, and Spirit are one God even as the Father is not the Son, the Son is not the Spirit, and so on. Further, to consider how the Father, Son, and Spirit can be distinguished from one another while remaining one God is simultaneously to consider di-

---

1. Stephen E. Fowl, *Engaging Scripture* (Oxford; Malden, MA: Wiley-Blackwell, 1998), 26. Fowl refers to Brevard S. Childs, "Toward Recovering Theological Exegesis," *ProEccl* 6, no. 1 (1997): 16-26.

2. See the classic description of Old Testament narrative in contrast with Homer's Odyssey in Erich Auerbach, *Mimesis: The Representation of Reality in Western Literature*, reprint ed. (Princeton: Princeton University, 1953), 9-17.

vine being, such as it differs from created being. In Christian grammar, language of being is never removed from the Trinitarian reality of God, so to open Exod 3:13–15 to ontological interpretation is by no means to move away from the personal God with whom Christians are in relation. Quite the opposite: to consider Exod 3:13–15 as a witness to the reality of God (whom Christians know as Father, Son, and Spirit) is to be drawn into that reality, to be with God.

Therefore, I suggest that theological interpretation of the Old Testament broadly, and of Exod 3:13–15 in particular, should consider how exegesis can engage a plurality of literal sense interpretations across history and within the church, and that attention to the particularities of the textual witness not be considered divorced from the text's witness to the one living God, toward whom the reader is drawn through the task of reading. The usual arrangement of the argument, opposing the inherent meaning of the Old Testament against how the church fathers and others have read it, will not do for an approach to the Old Testament that claims to take traditional Christian readings seriously. Such an endeavor will be indebted to Childs, Frei, and others who have come before, but in order to make significant progress in interpretation of Exod 3:13–15, new steps will need to be taken to clarify the fact that the literal sense of Old Testament texts can be understood in different ways depending upon the context of the reading, and that one cannot necessarily compartmentalize the different contexts of Old Testament interpretation into different stages of interpretation. Perhaps then the future of Old Testament studies will be able to more fully acknowledge, understand, and engage the varieties of interpretation of Exod 3:13–15 that have resulted from serious consideration of the text in its received form.

Bibliography

Aland, Kurt, Jean-Marie Auwers, Pierre-Maurice Bogaert, Hugo S. Eymann, Bonifatius Fischer, Hermann Josef Frede, Uwe Fröhlich, Gesche Gesche, Roger Gryson, Jean-Claude Haelewyck, Adolf Jülicher, Walter Matzkow, Eva Schulz-Flügel and Walter Thiele, eds. *Vetus Latina. Die Reste der altlateinischen Bibel*. Freiburg: Herder, 1949–2004.

Albrektson, Bertil. "On the Syntax of אהיה אשר אהיה in Exodus 3:14." In *Words and Meanings*, edited by Peter R. Ackroyd, 15–28. Cambridge: Cambridge University, 1968.

Albright, W. F. "Contributions to Biblical Archaeology and Philology." *JBL* 43, no. 3/4 (1924): 363–93.

———. *From the Stone Age to Christianity: Monotheism and the Historical Process*. Garden City, NY: Anchor Books, 1957.

———. *Yahweh and the Gods of Canaan: A Historical Analysis of Two Contrasting Faiths*. Jordan lectures in comparative religion, 1965. Reprint ed. Winona Lake, IN: Eisenbrauns, 1968.

Allen, Michael. "Exodus 3." In *Theological Commentary: Evangelical Perspectives*, edited by R. Michael Allen, 25–40. London: T&T Clark, 2011.

———. "Exodus 3 after the Hellenization Thesis." *JTI* 3, no. 2 (2009): 179–96.

Alt, Albrecht. "The God of the Fathers." In *Essays on Old Testament History and Religion*, translated by R. A. Wilson, 1–77. Oxford: Basil Blackwell, 1966.

———. "Ein ägyptisches Gegenstück zu Ex 3 14." *ZAW* 58 (1958): 159–60.

Alter, Robert. *The Art of Biblical Narrative*. Reprint ed. New York: Basic Books, 1981.

———. *The Five Books of Moses: A Translation with Commentary*. New York: W. W. Norton, 2004.

———. *The Pleasures of Reading in an Ideological Age*. New York; London: Simon and Schuster, 1989.

Alm, Richard von der. *Theologische Briefe an die Gebildeten der deutschen Nation*. Leipzig: Otto Wigand, 1862.

Amzallag, Nissim. "Yahweh, the Canaanite God of Metallurgy?" *JSOT* 33, no. 4 (2009): 387–404.

Anderson, James F. *St. Augustine and Being: A Metaphysical Essay*. The Hague: Martinus Nijhoff, 1965.

Arnold, Duane W. H. and Pamela Bright, eds. *De doctrina christiana: A Classic of Western Culture*. CJA 9. Notre Dame; London: Notre Dame University, 1995.

Arnold, William R. "The Divine Name in Exodus iii: 14." *JBL* 24, no. 2 (1905): 107–65.
Ashley, Timothy R. *The Book of Numbers*. NICOT. Grand Rapids: Eerdmans, 1993.
Auerbach, Elias. *Moses*. Translated by Robert A. Barclay and Israel O. Lehman. Detroit: Wayne State University, 1975.
Auerbach, Erich. *Mimesis: The Representation of Reality in Western Literature*. Reprint ed. Princeton: Princeton University, 1953.
Augustine of Hippo. *The City of God Against the Pagans*. Translated by R. W. Dyson. CTHPT. Cambridge: Cambridge University, 1998.
———. *Confessions*. Translated by Henry Chadwick. Oxford: Oxford University, 1991.
———. *De doctrina christiana*. Translated by R. P. H. Green. Oxford: Oxford University, 1996.
———. *Expositions of the Psalms*. Edited by John E. Rotelle. Translated by Maria Boulding, OSB. Electronic ed. In *The Works of Saint Augustine*.
———. *Gospel According to St. John*. Edited by Philip Schaff. Translated by John Gibb and Rev. James Innes. NPNF 1. Buffalo: Christian Literature, 1888.
———. *Sermons on the Old Testament*. Edited by John E. Rotelle, OSA. Translated by Edmund Hill, OP. Electronic ed. In *The Works of Saint Augustine*.
———. *The Trinity*. Edited by John E. Rotelle. Translated by Edmund Hill, OP. Electronic ed. In *The Works of Saint Augustine*.
———. *The Works of Saint Augustine*. Edited by Boniface Ramsey. 2nd release, electronic ed. Charlottesville: InteLex Corporation, 2001. Originally published by New City Press in 50 vols., 1990–.
Axelsson, Lars Eric. *The Lord Rose Up From Seir: Studies in the History and Traditions of the Negev and Southern Judah*. Illustrated ed. Stockholm: Almquist & Wiksell International, 1987.
Ayres, Lewis. *Augustine and the Trinity*. Cambridge: Cambridge University, 2010.
———. "The Fundamental Grammar of Augustine's Trinitarian Theology." In *Augustine and His Critics: Essays in Honour of Gerald Bonner*, edited by George Lawless and Robert Dodaro, 51–76. London; New York: Routledge, 2000.
———. "'Remember That You Are Catholic' (serm. 52.2): Augustine on the Unity of the Triune God." *JECS* 8, no. 1 (2000): 39–82.
Babcock, William S. "*Caritas* and Signification in *De doctrina christiana* 1–3." In Arnold and Bright, eds., *De doctrina christiana*, 145–63.
Barnes, Michel René. "Augustine and the Limits of Nicene Orthodoxy." *AugStud* 38, no. 1 (2007): 189–202.
———. "Augustine in Contemporary Trinitarian Theology." *TS* 56 (1995): 237–50.
———. "Rereading Augustine's Theology of the Trinity." In *The Trinity: An Interdisciplinary Symposium on the Trinity*, edited by Stephen T. Davis, Daniel Kendall, and Gerald O'Collins, 145–76. Oxford: Oxford University, 1999.
———. "The Visible Christ and the Invisible Trinity: Mt. 5:8 in Augustine's Trinitarian Theology of 400." *MT* 19, no. 3 (2003): 329–55.
Barr, James. "The Literal, the Allegorical, and Modern Biblical Scholarship." *JSOT* 44 (1987): 3–17.
———. *The Semantics of Biblical Language*. Reprint ed. Oxford: Oxford University, 1961.

Barstad, Hans M. "The Understanding of the Prophets in Deuteronomy." *SJOT* 8, no. 2: 236-51.
Barth, Karl, and Rudolf Bultmann. *Letters, 1922-66.* Edited by Bernd Jaspert and Geoffrey W. Bromiley. London: T&T Clark, 1982.
Barth, Karl. *Church Dogmatics.* Translated by G. W. Bromiley. Translated and edited by G. W. Bromiley and T. F. Torrance. London: T&T Clark, 2009.
Barton, John. *The Nature of Biblical Criticism.* Louisville; London: Westminster John Knox, 2007.
Bauckham, Richard. *God Crucified: Monotheism and Christology in the New Testament.* The Didsbury Lecture Series. Carlisle: Paternoster, 1998.
Bauer, Hans, and Pontus Leander. *Historische Grammatik der hebräischen Sprache I.* Halle: M. Niemeyer, 1922.
Baumgartner, Walter, Otto Eissfeldt, Karl Elliger and Leonhard Rost, eds. *Festschrift Alfred Bertholet zum 80 Geburtstag.* Tübingen: Mohr Siebeck, 1950.
Beach-Verhey, Kathy. "Exodus 3:1-12." *Int* (2005): 180-82.
Beer, G. *Hebräische Grammatik.* Edited by R. Meyer. 2nd Rev. ed. Berlin: de Gruyter, 1952.
Beitzel, B. J. "Exodus 3:14 and the Divine Name: A Case of Biblical Paronomasia." *TJ* 1 (1980): 5-20.
Berlejung, Angelika. "History and Religion of 'Israel': Basic Information." Translated by Thomas Riplinger. In Jan Christian Gertz et al., *T&T Clark Handbook of the Old Testament*, 61-94.
Black, C. Clifton. "Trinity and Exegesis." *ProEccl* 19, no. 2 (2010): 151-80.
Blenkinsopp, Joseph. "The Midianite-Kenite Hypothesis Revisited and the Origins of Judah." *JSOT* 33, no. 2 (2008): 131-53.
———. *Prophecy and Canon: A Contribution to the Study of Jewish Origins.* SJCA 3. Notre Dame: Notre Dame University, 1977.
Bogaert, Pierre-Maurice. "La Bible latine des origines au moyen âge." *RTL* 19 (1988): 137-59.
Boman, Thorleif. *Hebrew Thought Compared with Greek.* Translated by Jules L. Moreau. Library of History and Doctrine. Westminster, 1960. 1st ed. 1954.
Botterweck, G. J. and H. Ringgren, eds. *TDOT.* Translated by J. T. Willis, G. W. Bromiley, and D. E. Green. 15 vols. Grand Rapids: Eerdmans, 1974-2006.
Brachtendorf, Johannes. *Die Struktur des menschlichen Geistes nach Augustinus: Selbstreflexion und Erkenntnis Gottes in "De Trinitate".* Hamburg: Meiner Verlag, 2000.
Brekelmans, Chr. H. W. "Exodus XVIII and the Origins of Yahwism in Israel." *OtSt* 10 (1954): 215-24.
Brett, Mark. *Biblical Criticism in Crisis? The Impact of the Canonical Approach on Old Testament Studies.* Cambridge: Cambridge University, 1991.
Brichto, Herbert Chanan. *Toward a Grammar of Biblical Poetics: Tales of the Prophets.* New York; Oxford: Oxford University, 1992.
Briggs, Richard S. and Joel N. Lohr, eds. *A Theological Introduction to the Pentateuch: Interpreting the Torah as Christian Scripture.* Grand Rapids: Baker, 2012.

Briggs, Richard S. *The Virtuous Reader: Old Testament Narrative and Interpretive Virtue.* Studies in Theological Interpretation. Grand Rapids: Baker Academic, 2010.

Brongers, H. A. "Der Eifer des Herrn Zebaoth." *VT* 13, no. 3 (1963): 269-84.

Brueggemann, Walter. "The Crisis and Promise of Presence in Israel." *HBT* 1, no. 1 (1979): 47-86.

———. *Deuteronomy.* AOTC. Nashville: Abingdom, 2001.

———. *Theology of the Old Testament: Testimony, Dispute, Advocacy.* 9th ed. Minneapolis: Fortress, 2005.

Brunn, Emilie zum. *St. Augustine: Being and Nothingness.* Translated by Ruth Namad. New York: Paragon House, 1988.

Buber, Martin. *Kingship of God.* 3rd ed. Translated by Richard Scheimann. New York: Harper & Row, 1967.

———. *Moses.* Oxford; London: East & West Library, 1944.

Cameron, Michael. "Augustine and Scripture." In *A Companion to Augustine*, edited by Mark Vessey, 200-14. Blackwell Companions to the Ancient World. Malden, MA; Oxford: Wiley-Blackwell, 2012.

———. *Christ Meets Me Everywhere: Augustine's Early Figurative Exegesis.* Oxford; New York: Oxford University, 2012.

Casanowicz, Immanuel M. "Paronomasia in the Old Testament." *JBL* 12, no. 2 (1893): 105-67.

Cassuto, Umberto. *A Commentary on the Book of Exodus.* Jerusalem: Magnes, 1967.

Cavadini, John C. "The Sweetness of the Word: Salvation and Rhetoric in Augustine's *De Doctrina Christiana.*" In Arnold and Bright, eds., *De doctrina christiana*, 164-81.

Chapman, Stephen B. *The Law and the Prophets: A Study in Old Testament Canon Formation.* FAT 27. Tübingen: Mohr Siebeck, 2000.

Childs, Brevard S. *Biblical Theology of the Old and New Testaments: Theological Reflection on the Christian Bible.* London: SCM, 1992.

———. *Biblical Theology in Crisis.* Philadelphia: Westminster, 1970.

———. *The Book of Exodus: A Critical, Theological Commentary.* Louisville: Westminster, 1974.

———. "Does the Old Testament Witness to Jesus Christ?" In *Evangelium, Schriftauslegung, Kirche: Festschrift für Peter Stuhlmacher zum 65. Geburtstag*, edited by Jostein Ådna, S. J. Hafemann and O. Hofius, 57-64. Göttingen: Vandenhoeck & Ruprecht, 1997.

———. "Interpretation in Faith: The Theological Responsibility of an Old Testament Commentary." *Int* 18, no. 4 (1964): 432-49.

———. *Introduction to the Old Testament as Scripture.* Minneapolis: Fortress, 1979.

———. *Isaiah: A Commentary.* OTL. Louisville: Westminster John Knox, 2001.

———. "Karl Barth as Interpreter of Scripture." In *Karl Barth and the Future of Theology: A Memorial Colloquium Held at Yale Divinity School January 28, 1969*, edited by D. L. Dickerman, 30-39. New Haven, CT: Yale Divinity School Association, 1969.

———. *Old Testament Theology in a Canonical Context.* London: SCM, 1985.

———. "The *Sensus Literalis* of Scripture: An Ancient and Modern Problem." In *Beiträge zur Alttestamentlichen Theologie: Festschrift für Walther Zimmerli zum 70. Geburtstag*,

edited by Walther Zimmerli, Herbert Donner, Robert Hanhart and Rudolf Smend, 80-93. Göttingen: Vandenhoeck & Ruprecht, 1977.
———. "Toward Recovering Theological Exegesis." *ProEccl* 6, no. 1 (1997): 16-26.
Christensen, D. L. *Deuteronomy 1:1-21:9*. 2nd ed. WBC. Nashville: Thomas Nelson, 2001.
Clements, Ronald E. *The Book of Deuteronomy: A Preacher's Commentary*. London: Epworth, 2001.
Coats, George W. *Exodus 1-18*. FOTL. Grand Rapids: Eerdmans, 1999.
———. "Humility and Honor: A Moses Legend in Numbers 12." In *The Moses Tradition*, 88-98. Sheffield: JSOT, 1993.
———. "Self-Abasement and Insult Formulas." *JBL* 89, no. 1 (1970): 14-26.
Craigie, Peter C. *The Book of Deuteronomy*. NICOT. Grand Rapids: Eerdmans, 1976.
———. *The Problem of War in the Old Testament*. Grand Rapids: Eerdmans, 1978.
Cross, Frank Moore. *Canaanite Myth and Hebrew Epic: Essays in the History of the Religion of Israel*. Cambridge; London: Harvard University, 1973.
———. "Yahweh and the God of the Patriarchs." *HTR* 55, no. 4 (1962): 225-59.
Daley, Brian E., SJ. "A Humble Mediator: The Distinctive Elements in Saint Augustine's Christology." *WS* 9 (1987): 100-17.
Davies, Graham I. "The Exegesis of the Divine Name in Exodus." In *The God of Israel*, edited by Robert P. Gordon, 139-53. Cambridge: Cambridge University, 2007.
Davis, Dale Ralph. "Rebellion, Presence, and Covenant: A Study in Exodus 32-34." *WTJ* 44 (1982): 71-87.
Davis, Ellen F., and Richard B. Hays. *The Art of Reading Scripture*. Grand Rapids: Eerdmans, 2003.
Davis, Ellen F. *Scripture, Culture, and Agriculture: An Agrarian Reading of the Bible*. Cambridge: Cambridge University, 2009.
Dawson, John David. *Christian Figural Reading and the Fashioning of Identity*. Berkeley; Los Angeles; London: University of California, 2002.
Dentan, Robert C. "The Literary Affinities of Exodus 34:6f." *VT* 13, no. 1 (1963): 34-51.
Dijkstra, Meindert, Bob Becking, Marjo C. A. Korpel, and Karel J. H. Vriezen. *Only One God? Monotheism in Ancient Israel and the Veneration of the Goddess Asherah*. London: Sheffield Academic, 2001.
Dijkstra, Meindert. "El, the God of Israel—Israel, the People of YHWH: On the Origins of Ancient Israelite Yahwism." In *Only One God?*, 81-126.
Dozeman, Thomas B. *Commentary on Exodus*. Grand Rapids: Eerdmans, 2009.
———. *God at War: Power in the Exodus Tradition*. New York; Oxford: Oxford University, 1996.
Driver, Daniel R. *Brevard Childs, Biblical Theologian: For the Church's One Bible*. FAT II 46. Tübingen: Mohr Siebeck, 2010.
Driver, G. R. *Canaanite Myths and Legends*. OTS 3. T&T Clark, 1956.
———. "The Original Form of the Name 'Yahweh': Evidence and Conclusions." *ZAW* (1928): 7-25.
———. "Reflections on Recent Articles." *JBL* 73, no. 3 (1954): 125-36.
Driver, S. R. *The Book of Exodus*. Cambridge: Cambridge University, 1918.

———. *Notes on the Hebrew Text of the Books of Samuel.* 2nd ed. Oxford: Oxford University, 1913.
Dubarle, Dominique. "Essai sur l'ontologie théologale de Saint Augustin." *RechAug* 16 (1981): 197–288.
Duhm, Bernhard. *Israels Propheten.* Tübingen: J. C. B. Mohr (Paul Seibeck), 1916.
Durham, John I. *Exodus.* WBC 3. Nashville: Thomas Nelson, 1987.
Eden, Kathy. *Hermeneutics and the Rhetorical Tradition: Chapters in the Ancient Legacy & Its Humanist Reception.* New Haven; London: Yale University, 1997.
Elliger, Karl. "Ich bin der Herr—euer Gott." In *Theologie als Glaubenswagnis, Festschrift K. Heim,* 9–34. Hamburg: Furche-Verlag, 1954.
Esau, Ken. "Divine Deception in the Exodus Event?" *Direction* 35, no. 1 (2006): 4–17.
Eslinger, Lyle. "Freedom or Knowledge? Perspective and Purpose in the Exodus Narrative (Exodus 1–15)." *JSOT* 16, no. 52 (1991): 43–60.
Fischer, Georg. *Jahwe unser Gott: Sprache, Aufbau und Erzähltechnik in der Berufung des Mose (Ex 3–4).* Orbis Biblicus et Orientalis. Göttingen: Vandenhoeck & Ruprecht, 1989.
Fleteren, Frederick, van. "Principles of Augustine's Hermeneutic: An Overview." In van Fleteren and Schnaubelt, *Augustine: Biblical Exegete,* 1–32.
Fleteren, Frederick van and Joseph C. Schnaubelt, OSA, eds. *Augustine: Biblical Exegete.* New York: Peter Lang, 2001.
Ford, William A. *God, Pharaoh and Moses: Explaining the Lord's Actions in the Exodus Plagues Narrative.* Milton Keynes; Waynesboro, GA: Paternoster, 2006.
Fowl, Stephen E. *Engaging Scripture.* Oxford; Malden, MA: Wiley-Blackwell, 1998.
———. "The Importance of Multivoiced Literal Sense of Scripture: The Example of Thomas Aquinas." In *Reading Scripture with the Church: Toward a Hermeneutic for Theological Interpretation,* edited by Kevin J. Vanhoozer, A. K. M. Adam and Stephen Fowl, 35–50. Grand Rapids: Baker Academic, 2006.
———. *The Theological Interpretation of Scripture: Classic and Contemporary Readings.* Blackwell readings in modern theology. Malden, MA: Wiley-Blackwell, 1997.
Fox, Everett. *The Five Books of Moses: A New Translation with Introduction, Commentary and Notes.* New York: Schocken Books, 1983.
Freedman, David Noel. "The Aaronite Benediction (Numbers 6:24–26)." In *Pottery, Poetry and Prophecy: Studies in Early Hebrew Poetry,* 229–42. Winona Lake, IN: Eisenbrauns, 1980.
———. "The Name of the God of Moses." *JBL* 79, no. 2 (1960): 151–56.
———. "'Who Is Like Thee Among the Gods?' the Religion of Early Israel." In *Ancient Israelite Religion: Essays in Honor of Frank Moore Cross,* edited by Patrick D. Miller, Jr., Paul D. Hanson and S. Dean McBride, 315–35. Philadelphia: Fortress, 1987.
Frei, Hans W. *The Eclipse of Biblical Narrative.* London: Yale University, 1980.
———. *The Identity of Jesus Christ: The Hermeneutical Bases of Dogmatic Theology.* Philadelphia: Fortress, 1975.
———. *Types of Christian Theology.* Edited by George Hunsinger and William C. Placher. New Haven; London: Yale University, 1992.

Frei, Hans W. "The 'Literal Reading' of Biblical Narrative in the Christian Tradition: Does It Stretch or Will It Break?" In *Theology and Narrative: Selected Essays*, edited by George Hunsinger, and William C. Placher, 117-52. New York; Oxford: Oxford University, 1993.
Fretheim, Terence E. *Exodus*. IBC. Louisville: Westminster John Knox, 1991.
———. "The Plagues as Ecological Signs of Historical Disaster." *JBL* (1991): 385-96.
———. "Suffering God and Sovereign God in Exodus: A Collision of Images." *HBT* 11, no. 1 (1989): 31-56.
Geljon, Albert C. "Philo of Alexandria and Gregory of Nyssa on Moses at the Burning Bush." In van Kooten, ed., *The Revelation of the Name YHWH to Moses*, 225-37.
Gertz, Jan Christian, Angelika Berlejung, Konrad Schmid, and Markus Witte. *T&T Clark Handbook of the Old Testament: An Introduction to the Literature, Religion and History of the Old Testament*. London; New York: T&T Clark, 2012.
Gertz, Jan Christian. "The Overall Context of Genesis-2 Kings," trans. Peter Altmann, in Gertz et al., *T&T Clark Handbook of the Old Testament*, 237-71.
Gilson, Etienne. *The Spirit of Mediæval Philosophy: Gifford Lectures 1931-1932*. Translated by A. H. C. Downes. London: Sheed & Ward, 1936.
Gnuse, Robert Karl. *No Other Gods: Emergent Monotheism in Israel*. Sheffield: Continuum, 1997.
Goitein, S. D. "YHWH the Passionate: The Monotheistic Meaning and Origin of the Name YHWH." *VT* 6 (1956): 1-9.
Gorday, Peter. *Principles of Patristic Exegesis: Romans 9-11 in Origen, John Chrysostom, and Augustine*. Studies in the Bible and Early Christianity. New York; Toronto: Edwin Mellen, 1983.
Gorringe, Tim. "Three Texts About Moses: Numbers 12, 16, and 20." *ExpTim* 118, no. 4 (2007): 177-79.
Gowan, Donald E. *Theology in Exodus: Biblical Theology in the Form of a Commentary*. Louisville: Westminster John Knox, 1994.
Grabbe, Lester L. *Ancient Israel: What Do We Know and How Do We Know It?* London; New York: T&T Clark, 2007.
Gray, George Buchanan. *A Critical and Exegetical Commentary on Numbers*. Edinburgh: T&T Clark, 1903.
Greenberg, Moshe. "The Thematic Unity of Exodus III-XI." In *Fourth World Congress of Jewish Studies I*, 151-54. Jerusalem: Magnes. 1967.
———. *Understanding Exodus*. Heritage of Biblical Israel. New York: Behrman House, 1969.
Greene-McCreight, K. E. *Ad Litteram: How Augustine, Calvin, and Barth Read the "Plain Sense" of Genesis 1-3*. Issues in Systematic Theology. New York: Peter Lang, 1999.
Grenz, Stanley J. *The Named God and the Question of Being: A Trinitarian Theo-Ontology*. Louisville: Westminster John Knox, 2005.
Greßmann, Hugo. *Mose und seine Zeit: ein Kommentar zu den Mose-sagen*. FRLANT 18. Göttingen: Vandenhoeck & Ruprecht, 1913.
Guillaume, A. "Magical Terms in the Old Testament." *JRASGBI* (1942): 111-31.
———. "Paronomasia in the Old Testament." *JSS* 9, no. 2 (1964): 282-90.

Gunn, David M. "The 'Hardening of Pharaoh's Heart': Plot, Character and Theology in Exodus 1–14." In *Art and Meaning: Rhetoric in Biblical Literature*, edited by David J. A. Clines and Alan J. Hauser, 72–96. JSOT. Sheffield: JSOT, 1982.

Habel, N. "The Form and Significance of the Call Narratives." *ZAW* 77 (1965): 297–323.

Hadot, Pierre. "Dieu comme acte d'être dans le Néoplatonisme. a propos des théories d'E. Gilson sur la métaphysique de l'Exode." In *Dieu et l'être: Exegeses d'Exode 3,14 et Coran 20,11–24*, 57–63. Paris: Etudes Augustiniennes, 1978.

Hamilton, Victor P. *Exodus: An Exegetical Commentary*. Grand Rapids: Baker, 2011.

Hamori, Esther J. *When Gods Were Men: The Embodied God in Biblical and Near Eastern Literature*. Berlin: de Gruyter, 2008.

Harnack, Adolph. *History of Dogma*. 3rd ed. Translated by N. Buchanan, J. Millar, E. B. Speirs and W. M'Gilchrist. 7 vols. London: Williams & Norgate, 1894.

Hauge, Martin Ravndal. *The Descent From the Mountain: Narrative Patterns in Exodus 19–40*. Sheffield: Continuum, 2001.

Haupt, Paul von. "Der Name Jahwe." *OLZ* 12, no. 5 (1909): 212–13.

Hepner, Gershon. "Moses' Cushite Wife Echoes Hosea's Woman of Harlotries: Exposure of Unfaithfulness in the Wilderness." *SJOT* 23, no. 2 (2009): 233–42.

Hertog, Cornelis den. *The Other Face of God: "I Am That I Am" Reconsidered*. HBM 32. Sheffield: Sheffield Phoenix, 2012.

Hess, Richard S. "The Divine Name Yahweh in Late Bronze Age Sources?" *UF* 23 (1991): 181–88.

Higton, Mike. *Christ, Providence and History: Hans W. Frei's Public Theology*. London; New York: T&T Clark, 2004.

Hollander, Harm W. "Seeing God 'In a Riddle' or 'Face to Face': An Analysis of 1 Corinthians 13.12." *JSNT* 32, no. 4 (2010): 395–403.

Holter, Knut. *Deuteronomy 4 and the Second Commandment*. StBL 60. New York: Peter Lang, 2003.

Houtman, Cornelis. *Exodus*. Historical Commentary on the Old Testament. 4 vols. Translated by Johan Rebel and Sierd Woudstra. Kampen: Peeters, 1993–2002.

Houtman, C., and R. Roukema. *The Interpretation of Exodus: Studies in Honour of Cornelis Houtman*. Leuven: Peeters, 2006.

Humbert, Paul. "'Qânâ' en Hébreu biblique." In Baumgartner et al., eds., *Festschrift Alfred Bertholet*, 259–66.

Hyatt, J. Philip. *Commentary on Exodus*. NCB. Illustrated ed. Edinburgh: Oliphants, 1971.

———. "Was Yahweh Originally a Creator Deity?" *JBL* 86, no. 4 (1967): 369–77.

Jacob, Benno. *The Second Book of the Bible: Exodus*. Translated by Walter Jacob and Yaakov Elman. Hoboken, NJ: Ktav, 1992.

Janzen, J. Gerald. "And the Bush Was Not Consumed." *Enc* 63, no. 1/2 (2002): 119–28.

———. "The Most Important Word in the Shema (Deuteronomy VI 4–5)." *VT* 37, no. 3 (1987): 280–300.

Janzen, Waldemar. *Exodus*. BCBC. Waterloo, ON; Scottdale, PA: Herald, 2000.

Jeppensen, Knud. "Is Deuteronomy Hostile Towards Prophets?" *SJOT* 8, no. 2 (1994): 252–56.

Joüon, Paul, and T. Muraoka. *A Grammar of Biblical Hebrew*. 2nd rev. ed. *SubBi* 27. Rome: Editrice Pontificio Histituto Biblico, 2006. First published in French in 1923; first English edition, 1991.
Kalimi, Isaac. "Three Assumptions About the Kenites." *ZAW* 100, no. 3 (1988): 386–93.
Kalisch, Moritz Markus. *A Historical and Critical Commentary on the Old Testament: Exodus*. London: Longman, Brown, Green and Longmans, 1855.
Kaufmann, Y. *The Religion of Israel from its Beginning to the Babylonian Exile*, trans. M. Greenberg. New York: Schocken, 1960.
Kearney, R. *The God Who May Be*. Indianapolis: Indiana University, 2001.
Keil, C. F., and F. Delitzsch. *Biblical Commentary on the Old Testament*. Edinburgh: T&T Clark, 1854.
Kerr, Fergus. *After Aquinas: Versions of Thomism*. Oxford: Wiley-Blackwell, 2002.
Kinyongo, Jean. *Origine et signification du nom divín Yahvé à la lumière de récents travaux et de traditions Sémitico-bibliques (Ex 3,13–15 Et 6,2–8)*. BBB. Bonn: P. Hanstein, 1970.
Kloos, Kari. "Seeing the Invisible God: Augustine's Reconfiguration of Theophany Narrative Exegesis." *AugStud* 36, no. 2 (2005): 397–420.
Knauf, Ernst A. *Midian: Untersuchungen zur Geschichte Palästinas und Nordarabiens am Ende des 2. Jahrtausends V. Chr*. Abhandlungen des Deutschen Palästinavereins. Wiesbaden: Otto Harrassowitz, 1988.
———. "Yahwe." *VT* 34, no. 4 (1984): 467–70.
Knight, George A. F. *Theology as Narration: A Commentary on the Book of Exodus*. Edinburgh: Handsel, 1976.
Knoppers, Gary N. "'There Was None Like Him': Incomparability in the Books of Kings." *CBQ* 54 (1992): 411–31.
Koehler, L., W. Baumgartner, and J. J. Stamm. *HALOT*. Translated and edited under the supervision of M. E. J. Richardson. 4 vols. Leiden: Brill, 1994–1997.
Koehler, Ludwig. *Old Testament Theology*. Translated by A. S. Todd. London: Lutterworth, 1953.
Kooten, George H. van. "Moses/Musaeus/Mochos and His God Yahweh, Iao, and Sabaoth, Seen From a Graeco-Roman Perspective." In van Kooten, ed., *The Revelation of the Name YHWH to Moses*, 107–38.
———, ed. *The Revelation of the Name YHWH to Moses: Perspectives From Judaism, the Pagan Graeco-Roman World, and Early Christianity*. Themes in Biblical Narrative: Jewish and Christian Traditions. Leiden; Boston: Brill, 2006.
Krašovec, Jože. "Unifying Themes in Ex 7,8–11,10." In *Pentateuchal and Deuteronomistic Studies*, edited by C. Brekelmans and J. Lust, 47–66. Leuven: Leuven University, 1990.
Kselman, J S. "A Note on Numbers XII 6–8." *VT* 26, no. 4 (1976): 500–5.
Labuschagne, C J. *The Incomparability of Yahweh in the Old Testament*. POS 5. Leiden: Brill, 1966.
LaCocque, André. "The Revelation of Revelations." In LaCocque and Ricoeur, *Thinking Biblically*, 307–29.

LaCocque, André and Paul Ricoeur. *Thinking Biblically: Exegetical and Hermeneutical Studies*. Translated by David Pellauer. Chicago; London: University of Chicago, 1998.
Lagarde, Paul Anton de. *Erklärung hebräischer Wörter*. Göttingen: Dieterischsche, 1880.
Lane, Nathan C. *The Compassionate, but Punishing God: A Canonical Analysis of Exodus 34: 6-7*. Eugene: Wipf & Stock, 2010.
Larsson, Göran. *Bound for Freedom: The Book of Exodus in Jewish and Christian Traditions*. Peabody, MA: Hendrickson, 1999.
Levenson, Jon D. "Exodus and Liberation." *HBT* 13, no. 1 (1991): 134-74.
Levering, Matthew. *Scripture and Metaphysics: Aquinas and the Renewal of Trinitarian Theology*. Illustrated ed. Malden, MA: Wiley-Blackwell, 2004.
Lewy, J. "Influences hurrites en Israel." *RES* (1938): 49-75.
Lienhard, Joseph T., SJ. *Exodus, Leviticus, Numbers, Deuteronomy*. Ancient Christian Commentary on Scripture. Vol. 3. Downers Grove: IVP, 2001.
Lind, Millard. *Yahweh is a Warrior*. Scottdale, PA: Herald, 1980.
Lindblom, Johannes. "Noch einmal die Deutung des Jahwe-Namens in Ex 3, 14." *ASTI* 3 (1964): 4-15.
Lipiński, Edward. Review of *Book of Exodus: A Critical, Theological Commentary*, by Brevard S. Childs. *VT* 26, no. 3 (1976): 378-83.
Lipton, Diana. "God's Back! What Did Moses See on Sinai?" In *The Significance of Sinai: Traditions About Sinai and Divine Revelation in Judaism and Christianity*, edited by George J. Brooke, Hindy Najman and Loren T. Stuckenbruck, 287-312. Leiden: Brill, 2008.
Littmann, E. Review of *Le Inscrizioni Antico-Ebraiche Palestinesi, raccotte e illustrate* by David Diringer. *AfO* 11 (1936): 162.
Liverani, Mario. *Israel's History and the History of Israel*. Translated by Chiara Peri and Philip R. Davies. BibleWorld. London; Oakville: Equinox, 2005.
Loewe, Raphael. "The 'Plain' Meaning of Scripture in Early Jewish Exegesis." In *Papers of the Institute of Jewish Studies London*, 140-85. Edited by Joseph George Weiss. Jerusalem: Magnes, Hebrew University, 1964.
Lof, L. J. van der. "L'exégèse exacte et objective des théophanies de l'Ancien Testament dans le 'De Triniate'." *Augustiniana* 14 (1964): 485-99.
Long, D. Stephen. *Speaking of God: Theology, Language, and Truth*. The Eerdmans Ekklesia Series. Grand Rapids: Eerdmans, 2009.
Longman, Tremper, III, and Daniel G Reid. *God Is a Warrior*. Carlisle: Paternoster, 1995.
Louth, Andrew. *Discerning the Mystery: An Essay on the Nature of Theology*. Reprint ed. Oxford: Clarendon, 1983.
Lubac, Henri de, SJ. *Medieval Exegesis: The Four Senses of Scripture*. Translated by Mark Sebanc. Grand Rapids: Eerdmans, 1998.
———. "Spiritual Understanding." Translated by Luke O'Neill. In Fowl, ed., *The Theological Interpretation of Scripture*, 3-25.
MacDonald, Nathan. *Deuteronomy and the Meaning of "Monotheism."* FAT II 1. Tübingen: Mohr Siebeck, 2003.

MacLaurin, E. C. B. "YHWH, the Origin of the Tetragrammaton." *VT* 12, no. 4 (1962): 439-63.
Mann, Thomas W. *The Book of the Torah: The Narrative Integrity of the Pentateuch.* Louisville: Westminster John Knox, 1988.
———. *Divine Presence and Guidance in Israelite Traditions: The Typology of Exaltation.* The Johns Hopkins Near Eastern Studies. Baltimore: Johns Hopkins University, 1977.
Marion, Jean-Luc. "God Without Being, Trans." In *God Without Being; Hors-Texte.* Translated by Thomas A. Carlson. Chicago; London: University of Chicago, 1991.
———. "*Idipsum*: The Name of God According to Augustine." In *Orthodox Readings of Augustine*, edited by Aristotle Papanikolaou and George E. Demacopoulos, 167-89. Crestwood, NY: St. Vladimir's Seminary, 2008.
Marshall, Bruce D. "Absorbing the Word: Christianity and the Universe of Truths." In *Theology and Dialogue: Essays in Conversation with George Lindbeck*, 69-102. Notre Dame: Notre Dame University, 1990.
Mayes, A. D. H. *Deuteronomy.* NCB. Edinburgh: Oliphants, 1979.
McCabe, Herbert. *God Still Matters.* London; New York: Continuum, 2005.
McCarthy, Dennis J. "Exod 3:14: History, Philology and Theology." *CBQ* 40 (1978): 311-22.
———. "Moses' Dealings with Pharaoh: Exod 7:8-10:27." *CBQ* 27, no. 4 (1965): 336-47.
———. "Plagues and Sea of Reeds: Exodus 5-14." *JBL* 85, no. 2 (1966): 137-58.
McConville, J. G. *Deuteronomy.* Apollos Old Testament Commentary 5. Leicester; Downers Grove: Apollos; IVP, 2002.
Meek, Theophile James. *Hebrew Origins.* Revised ed. New York: Harper & Brothers, 1950.
Mettinger, Tryggve N. D. "The Elusive Essence: YHWH, El and Baal and the Distinctiveness of Israelite Faith." In *Die hebräische Bibel und ihre zweifach Nachgeschichte (Festscrift Rendtorff).* Edited by Erhard Blum, Christian Macholz and Ekkehard W. Stegemann, 393-413. Neukirchen-Vluyn: Neukirkchener Verlag, 1990.
———. *In Search of God: The Meaning and Message of the Everlasting Names.* Translated by Frederick H. Cryer. Philadelphia: Fortress, 2006.
———. *Reports from a Scholar's Life: Select Papers on the Hebrew Bible.* Edited by Andrew Knapp. Winona Lake, IN: Eisenbrauns, 2015.
Meyers, Carol L. *Exodus.* New Cambridge Bible Commentary. Cambridge; New York: Cambridge University, 2005.
Milgrom, Jacob. *JPS Torah Commentary: Numbers.* Philadelphia: JPS, 1990.
———. "Magic, Monotheism and the Sin of Moses." In *The Quest for the Kingdom of God: Studies in Honor of George E. Mendenhall.* Edited by H. Herbert Bardwell Huffmon, Frank A. Spina and Alberto Ravinell Whitney Green, 251-66. Winona Lake, IN: Eisenbrauns, 1983.
Miller, Patrick D. *Deuteronomy.* IBC. Louisville: Westminster John Knox, 1990.
———. *The Divine Warrior in Early Israel.* Cambridge, MA: Harvard University, 1973.
———. "God the Warrior: A Problem in Biblical Interpretation and Apologetics." *Int* 19 (1965): 39-46.

———. "Israelite Religion." In *The Hebrew Bible and Its Modern Interpreters,* 3rd ed, edited by Douglas A. Knight and Gene M. Tucker, 201-37. Minneapolis: Fortress, 1985.

———. "Moses My Servant: The Deuteronomic Portrait of Moses." *Int* 41, no. 3 (1987): 245-55.

Moberly, R. W. L. *At the Mountain of God: Story and Theology in Exodus 32-34.* JSOTSup 22. Sheffield: JSOT, 1983.

———. "How May We Speak of God? A Reconsideration of the Nature of Biblical Theology." *TynBul* 53, no. 2 (2002): 177-202.

———. *The Old Testament of the Old Testament: Patriarchal Narratives and Mosaic Yahwism.* Minneapolis: Fortress, 1992.

———. *Prophecy and Discernment.* CSCD. Cambridge: Cambridge University, 2006.

———. "Toward An Interpretation of the Shema." In Seitz and Greene-McCreight, *Theological Exegesis,* 124-44.

———. "The Use of the Old Testament in Pope Benedict XVI's *Jesus of Nazareth.*" In *The Pope and Jesus of Nazareth,* edited by Angus Paddison and Adrian Pabst, 97-108. London: SCM, 2009.

———. "'Yahweh Is One': The Translation of the Shema." In *Studies in the Pentateuch.* Edited by John Adney Emerton, 209-16. VT.S. Leiden: Brill, 1990.

Montgomery, James A. "The Hebrew Divine Name and the Personal Pronoun Hū." *JBL* 63, no. 2 (1944): 161-63.

Moor, Johannes C. de. *The Rise of Yahwism: The Roots of Israelite Monotheism.* 2nd, Rev. ed. Leuven: Leuven University, 1997.

Mowinckel, Sigmund. "The Name of the God of Moses." *HUCA* 32 (1961): 121-33.

Murtonen, A. *A Philological and Literary Treatise on the Old Testament Divine Names.* Helsinki: Soumalaisen Kirjallisuuden Seuran Kirjapainon Oy, 1952.

Nicholson, E. W. *Exodus and Sinai in History and Tradition.* Growing Points in Theology. Oxford: Basil Blackwell, 1973.

Niehr, Herbert. "'Israelite' Religion and 'Canaanite' Religion." In *Religious Diversity in Ancient Israel and Judah,* edited by John Barton and Francesca Stavrakopoulou, 23-36. London; New York: T&T Clark, 2010.

Noble, Paul R. *The Canonical Approach: A Critical Reconstruction of the Hermeneutics of Brevard S. Childs.* Biblical Interpretation Series. Leiden; New York: Brill, 1995.

Noth, Martin. *Exodus: A Commentary.* Reprint ed. OTL. Philadelphia: Westminster, 1974.

———. *Numbers: A Commentary.* Translated by James D. Martin. OTL 7. Philadelphia: Westminster, 1968.

Obermann, J. "The Divine Name YHWH in the Light of Recent Discoveries." *JBL* 68, no. 4 (1949): 301-23.

Oesterley, W. O. E., and T. H. Robinson. *Hebrew Religion, Its Origin and Development.* 2nd ed. London: Society for Promoting Christian Knowledge, 1937.

Olson, Dennis T. *Deuteronomy and the Death of Moses: A Theological Reading.* OBT. Minneapolis: Fortress, 1994.

———. *Numbers.* IBC. Louisville: Westminster John Knox, 1996.

Oxford Dictionaries Online. Oxford: Oxford, 2012. http://oxforddictionaries.com

Pannell, R. J. "I Would Be Who I Would Be! A Proposal for Reading Exodus 3:11-14." *BBR* 16, no. 2 (2006): 351.
Parke-Taylor, Geoffrey H. יהוה = *Yahweh: The Divine Name in the Bible*. Waterloo, ON: Wilfrid Laurier University, 1975.
Pattison, George. *God and Being: An Enquiry*. Oxford: Oxford University, 2011.
Perkins, Larry. "'The Lord Is a Warrior'—'The Lord Who Shatters Wars': Exod 15:3 and Jdt 9:7; 16:2." *BIOSCS* 40 (2007): 121-38.
Philo. *The Works of Philo: Complete and Unabridged*. Translated by Charles Duke Yonge. Peabody, MA: Hendrickson, 1993.
Pietersma, Albert, and Benjamin G. Wright, eds. *NETS*. New York; Oxford: Oxford University, 2007.
Polak, Frank. "Theophany and Mediator: The Unfolding of a Theme in the Book of Exodus." In *Studies in the Book of Exodus: Redaction, Reception, Interpretation*, edited by Marc Vervenne, 113-48. BETL 126. Leuven: Leuven University, 1996.
Preus, James Samuel. *From Shadow to Promise: Old Testament Interpretation From Augustine to the Young Luther*. Cambridge, MA: Harvard University, 1969.
Propp, William H. C. *Exodus: A New Translation with Introduction and Commentary*. 2 vols. New York: Doubleday, 1999-2006.
Rad, Gerhard von. *Deuteronomy: A Commentary*. Translated by Dorothea Barton. OTL. London: SCM, 1966.
———. *Old Testament Theology: The Theology of Israel's Historical Traditions*. Translated by D. M. G. Stalker. 2 vols. London: SCM, 1975.
Radner, Ephraim. "Taking the Lord's Name in Vain." In *I Am the Lord Your God: Christian Reflections on the Ten Commandments*, edited by Carl E. Braaten and Christopher R. Seitz, 77-94. Grand Rapids: Eerdmans, 2005.
Rahlfs, Alfred and Robert Hanart, eds. *Septuaginta*. 2nd ed. Stuttgart: Deutsche Bibelgesellschaft, 2006.
Reisel, M. *The Mysterious Name of YHWH: The Tetragrammaton in Connection with the Names of EHYEH Ašer EHYEH—Hūhā—Šem Hammephôraš*. Studia Semitica Neerlandica. Assen: Van Gorcum, 1957.
Renaud, Bernard. *Je suis un Dieu jaloux: évolution sémantique et signification théologique de qine'ah*. Paris: Éditions du Cerf, 1963.
———. *La théophanie du Sinaï: Ex 19-24: exégèse et théologie*. Cahiers de la Revue Biblique 30. Paris: J. Gabalda, 1991.
Rendtorff, Rolf. *The Canonical Hebrew Bible: A Theology of the Old Testament*. Translated by David E. Orton. Leiderdorp: Deo, 2005.
Reno, R. R. "'You Who Once Were Far Off Have Been Brought Near': Reflections in the Aid of Theological Exegesis." *ExAud* 16 (2000): 169-82.
Revell, E. J. "The Repetition of Introductions to Speech as a Feature of Biblical Hebrew," *VT* 47 (1997), 91-110.
Ricoeur, Paul. "From Interpretation to Translation." In LaCocque and Ricoeur, *Thinking Biblically*, 331-61.
Robinson, Bernard P. "The Jealousy of Miriam: A Note on Num 12." *ZAW* 101, no. 3 (1989): 428-32.

Rofé, Alexander. "The Monotheistic Argumentation in Deuteronomy IV 32-40: Contents, Composition and Text." *VT* 35, no. 4 (1985): 434-45.

Rogers, Cleon. "Moses: Meek or Miserable?" *JETS* 29, no. 3 (1986): 257-63.

Römer, Thomas, and Albert de Pury. "Deuteronomistic Historiography (DH): History of Research and Debated Issues." In *Israël Constructs Its History: Deuteronomistic Historiography in Recent Research*, edited by Albert de Pury, Thomas Römer and Jean-Daniel Macchi, 24-144. Sheffield: Sheffield Academic, 2000.

Rowe, C. Kavin. "Biblical Pressure and Trinitarian Hermeneutics." *ProEccl* 11, no. 3 (2002): 295-312.

Rowley, H. H. *From Joseph to Joshua: Biblical Traditions in the Light of Archaeology*. The Schweich Lectures of the British Academy. Oxford: Oxford University, 1950.

Rylaarsdam, J. Coert, and J. Edgar Park. *The Book of Exodus*. IB. New York; Nashville: Abingdon, 1952.

Sæbø, Magne. "God's Name in Exodus 3.13-15: An Expression of Revelation or of Veiling?" In *On the Way to Canon: Creative Tradition History in the Old Testament*, 78-92. JSOTSup Sheffield: Continuum, 1998.

Sailhamer, John H. *The Pentateuch as Narrative: A Biblical Theological Commentary*. Grand Rapids: Zondervan, 1992.

Sakenfeld, Katharine Doob. Review of *Book of Exodus: A Critical, Theological Commentary*, by Brevard S. Childs. *ThTo* 31, no. 3 (1974): 275-78.

Sanders, James A. Review of *Book of Exodus: A Critical, Theological Commentary*, by Brevard S. Childs. *JBL* 95, no. 2 (1976): 286-87.

Sarna, Nahum M. *Exodus = [Shemot]: The Traditional Hebrew Text with the New JPS Translation*. JPS Torah Commentary. Philadelphia: JPS, 1991.

———. *Exploring Exodus: The Origins of Biblical Israel*. Illustrated ed. New York: Schocken Books, 1986.

Savran, George W. *Encountering the Divine: Theophany in Biblical Narrative*. London; New York: Continuum, 2005.

Schild, E. "On Exodus III 14: 'I Am That I Am'." *VT* 4, no. 3 (1954): 296-302.

Schmid, Konrad. *Genesis and the Moses Story: Israel's Dual Origins in the Hebrew Bible*. Translated by James Nogalski. Winona Lake, IN: Eisenbrauns, 2010.

Schneiders, Sandra M. "Faith, Hermeneutics, and the Literal Sense of Scripture." *TS* 39, no. 4 (1978): 719-36.

Scruton, Roger. *The Face of God*. London; New York: Continuum, 2012.

Seitz, Christopher R. and Kathryn Greene-McCreight, eds. *Theological Exegesis: Essays in Honor of Brevard S. Childs*. Grand Rapids: Eerdmans, 1999.

Seitz, Christopher. "The Call of Moses and the 'Revelation' of the Divine Name: Source-Critical Logic and Its Legacy." In Seitz and Greene-McCreight, *Theological Exegesis*, 145-61.

———, ed. *Nicene Christianity: The Future for a New Ecumenism*. Grand Rapids: Brazos, 2001.

———. "The Trinity in the Old Testament." In *The Oxford Handbook of the Trinity*, edited by Giles Emery, OP and Matthew Levering, 28-40. Oxford: Oxford University, 2011.

———. *Word Without End: The Old Testament as Abiding Theological Witness*. Grand Rapids: Eerdmans, 1998.
Simon, U. *Reading Prophetic Narratives*. Bloomington: Indiana University, 1997.
Smith, Mark S. *The Early History of God: Yahweh and the Other Deities in Ancient Israel*. 2nd ed. Grand Rapids: Eerdmans, 2002.
———. *The Origins of Biblical Monotheism: Israel's Polytheistic Background and the Ugaritic Texts*. New York; Oxford: Oxford University, 2001.
Smith, Ronald Gregor. *The Doctrine of God*. London: Collins, 1970.
Soden, Wolfram von. "Jahwe 'Er ist, er erweist sich'." *WO* 3, no. 3 (1966): 177–87.
Soskice, Janet Martin. "Athens and Jerusalem, Alexandria and Edessa: Is There a Metaphysics of Scripture?" *IJST* 8, no. 2 (2006): 149–62.
———. "*Creatio ex Nihilo*: Its Jewish and Christian Foundations." In *Creation and the God of Abraham*, edited by David Burrell, 24–39. Cambridge: Cambridge University, 2010.
———. *Metaphor and Religious Language*. Oxford: Clarendon, 1985.
Soulen, R. Kendall. *The Divine Name(s) and the Holy Trinity: Distinguishing the Voices*. Louisville: Westminster John Knox, 2011.
———. "YHWH the Triune God." *MT* 15, no. 1 (1999): 25–54.
Strauss, H. "Das Meerlied Des Moses—ein 'Siegeslied' Israels?" *ZAW* 97 (1985): 103–9.
Strawn, Brent A. "And These Three Are One: A Trinitarian Critique of Christological Approaches to the Old Testament." *PRS* 31, no. 2 (2004): 191–210.
Stubbs, David L. *Numbers*. BTCB. Grand Rapids: Brazos, 2009.
Studer, Basil, OSB. *The Grace of Christ and the Grace of God in Augustine of Hippo: Christocentrism or Theocentrism?* Translated by Matthew J. O'Connell. Collegeville, MN: Liturgical, 1997.
Sumner, George R. and Ephraim Radner, eds. *The Rule of Faith: Scripture, Canon, and Creed in a Critical Age*. New York: Church Publishing, 1998.
Suomala, Karla R. *Moses and God in Dialogue: Exodus 32–34 in Postbiblical Literature*. StBL. New York: Peter Lang, 2004.
Talmon, Shemaryahu. "The Concept of Revelation in Biblical Times." In *Literary Studies in the Hebrew Bible: Form and Content*, 192–215. Jerusalem; Leiden: Magnes; Brill, 1993.
Tanner, Kathryn E. "Theology and the Plain Sense." In *Scriptural Authority and Narrative Interpretation*. Edited by Garrett Green, 59–78. Philadelphia: Fortress, 1987.
Tengström, Sven. "Moses and the Prophets in the Deuteronomistic History." *SJOT* 8, no. 2 (1994): 257–66.
Terrien, Samuel L. *The Elusive Presence: Toward a New Biblical Theology*. Eugene: Wipf & Stock, 2000.
Thompson, Thomas L. "How Yahweh Became God: Exodus 3 and 6 and the Heart of the Pentateuch." *JSOT* 20, no. 68 (1995): 57–74.
Tiele, Cornelis. *Vergerlijkende Geschiedenis van der egyptische en mesopotamische Godsdiensten*. Amsterdam: Van Kampen, 1872.
Tigay, Jeffrey H. *Deuteronomy*. JPS Torah Commentary. Philadelphia: JPS, 1996.

———. "The Significance of the End of Deuteronomy (Deuteronomy 34:10-12)." In *Texts, Temples and Traditions: A Tribute to Menahem Haran*. Edited by Michael V. Fox, Victor Avigdor Hurowitz, Avi Hurvitz, Michael L. Klein, Baruch J. Schwartz and Nili Shupak, 137–43. Winona Lake, IN: Eisenbrauns, 1996.

———. *You Shall Have No Other Gods: Israelite Religion in the Light of Hebrew Inscriptions*. HSS 31. Atlanta: Scholars, 1986.

Toorn, K. van der, B. Becking, and P. W. van der Horst, eds. *Dictionary of Deities and Demons in the Bible*. 2nd, rev. ed. Leiden: Brill, 1999.

Toorn, K. van der. "Yahweh." In van der Toorn, Becking and van der Horst, eds., *DDD*, 910–19.

VanGemeren, W. A., ed. *NIDOTTE*. 5 vols. Grand Rapids: Zondervan, 1997.

Vaux, Roland de. "Sur l'origine Kénite ou Madianite du Yahvisme." *ErIsr* 9 (1969): 28–32.

———. "The Revelation of the Divine name YHWH." In *Proclamation and Presence: Old Testament Essays in Honor of Gwynne Henton Davies*, edited by John I. Durham and J. Roy Porter, 48–75. London: SCM, 1970.

Vergote, J. "Une théorie sur l'origine Égyptienne du nom de Yahweh." *ETL* 39 (1963): 447–52.

Vriezen, Th. C. "'EHJE 'AŠER 'EHJE." In Baumgartner et al., eds., *Festschrift Alfred Bertolet*, 489–510.

Walker, Norman. "Concerning Ex 34:6." *JBL* 79 (1960): 277.

———. "Concerning Hû' and 'ani Hû'." *ZAW* 74 (1962): 205–6.

———. "The Riddle of the Ass's Head, and the Question of a Trigram." *ZAW* 75 (1963): 226.

———. *The Tetragrammaton, Its Origin, Meaning and Interpretation*. The Author, 1948.

———. "Yahwism and the Divine Name 'YHWH'." *ZAW* 70 (1958): 262–65.

Watson, Francis. *Paul and the Hermeneutics of Faith*. London; New York: T&T Clark, 2004.

Watts, James W. "The Legal Characterization of Moses in the Rhetoric of the Pentateuch." *JBL* 117, no. 3 (1998): 415–26.

Weinandy, Thomas G. *Does God Suffer?* Edinburgh: T&T Clark, 2000.

Wellhausen, Julius. *Israelitische und jüdische Geschichte*. 8th ed. Berlin; Leipzig: de Gruyter, 1921.

———. *Prolegomena to the History of Israel*. Translated by J. Sutherland Black and Allan Menzies. Edinburgh: A. & C. Black, 1885.

Westphal, M. "The God Who Will Be: Hermeneutics and the God of Promise." *Faith and Philosophy* 20, no. 3 (2003): 328–44.

Wette, Wilhelm M. L. de. *Über Religion und Theologie: Erläuterungen zu seinem Lehrbuche der Dogmatik*. Berlin: Realschulbuchhandlung, 1815.

———. *Beiträge zur Einleitung in das Alte Testament*. 2 vols. Hildesheim; New York: G. Olms, 1971. 1st ed. 1806–1807.

Widmer, Gabriel-Philippe. "L'interprétation Barthienne d'Exode 3,14." In *Celui qui est: Interprétations Juives et Chrétiennes d'Exode 3-14*, edited by Alain de Libera and Emilie zum Brunn, 277–301. Marbourg; Paris: Patrimoines, 1986.

Williams, Catrin H. *I Am He: The Interpretation of 'Anî Hû' in Jewish and Early Christian Literature.* WUNT 2. Reihe. Tübingen: Mohr Siebeck, 2000.
Williams, Rowan. *On Christian Theology.* Challenges in Contemporary Theology. Oxford: Blackwell, 2000.
Williams, Thomas. "Biblical Interpretation." In *The Cambridge Companion to Augustine.* Reprint ed., edited by Eleonore Stump and Norman Kretzmann, 59-70. Cambridge; New York: Cambridge University, 2001.
Wilson, Ian. *Out of the Midst of the Fire: Divine Presence in Deuteronomy.* SBLDS 151. Atlanta: Scholars, 1995.
Wilson, Robert R. "The Hardening of Pharaoh's Heart." *CBQ* 41 (1979): 18-36.
Yeago, David S. "The New Testament and the Nicene Dogma: A Contribution to the Recovery of Theological Exegesis." *ProEccl* 3, no. 2 (1994): 152-64.
Young, Frances M. *Biblical Exegesis and the Formation of Christian Culture.* Cambridge: Cambridge University, 1997.
Zannoni, Arthur E. "Review of *Book of Exodus: A Critical, Theological Commentary*." *AThR* 58, no. 2 (1976): 231-32.
Zevit, Z. "The Priestly Redaction and Interpretation of the Plague Narrative in Exodus." *JQR* 66, no. 4 (1976): 193-211.
Zimmerli, Walther *Ezekiel I.* Translated by R. E. Clements. Hermeneia. Philadelphia: Fortress, 1979.
———. *I Am Yahweh.* Edited by Walter Brueggemann. Translated by Douglas W. Stott. Atlanta: John Knox, 1982.
———. *Old Testament Theology in Outline.* Translated by David E. Green. Edinburgh: T&T Clark, 1978.

Index of Scripture

Genesis
1   142–43
1:31   72
2:23   111
3:18   64
4:26   133–34
15:7   135
18   148
22:1   117
22:11   117, 161
23:6   17
24:2   184
27:29   20
31:29   17
32   148
32:22–32   201
32:28   201
32:30   127–28, 172, 174, 201
39:4–5   184

Exodus
2:3   168
2:10   111
2:23–25   214
3   1, 3, 30–31, 34, 63, 103, 112, 121, 133–35, 138, 165–66, 194–95, 203–4, 220, 229
3:1   194
3:1–6   33
3:1–4:17   9, 32, 35, 110, 117, 129, 165, 168, 187, 191, 194, 197,

Exodus (cont.)
198–99, 202–3, 207
3:2   64–65, 117, 185, 194–96
3:2–3   185, 196
3:2–4   33, 194
3:3   117, 131, 185, 195–96, 203
3:4   117, 161, 195–96
3:5   33, 191, 196, 203
3:6   33, 82, 118, 127–29, 134, 196, 214
3:6–10   197
3:7   143, 197
3:7–8   33, 34
3:7–10   118
3:8   197
3:9   197
3:9–12   34
3:9–15   33
3:10   194
3:11   118–19, 131, 157, 199
3:12   116, 119, 120–21, 123, 129, 157, 199, 200, 231
3:13   34–35, 84, 112, 118, 121–22, 126–27, 136, 157–58, 199, 200–2, 204
3:13ff.   34
3:13–15   2–6, 8–9, 13–14, 26–27, 30–35, 40,

Exodus (cont.)
45, 57–60, 68, 104–5, 109–13, 121, 124, 126–30, 134, 137, 153, 164–65, 167, 191, 194, 199–200, 203, 206–8, 211, 214, 219, 228–29, 230–35
3:14   4–6, 8, 14–15, 18–19, 24, 28–29, 34–38, 57, 59–60, 64, 68–69, 71, 78–81, 88–92, 98, 102–3, 105, 109–16, 123–29, 136, 159, 161, 164, 199–200, 202–5, 207, 213, 215–19, 224–26, 228–29, 231
3:14–15   1–2, 4, 8–9, 14–15, 34–35, 59–60, 64, 68–69, 75–76, 80, 84–85, 87–88, 102–4, 110, 112, 122–23, 125–26, 164, 200, 202, 214, 219, 224–27
3:14–17   194
3:15   57–58, 60, 80–83, 85, 88, 122, 125–29, 136, 162, 194, 199–200, 202–5, 214, 225–27
3:16   128
3:16–22   33
3:16–24   22, 129

Exodus (cont.)
- 3:18   130
- 3–4   110
- 3–15   119, 145
- 4:1   118–22, 130, 198
- 4:1ff.   198
- 4:1–9   188, 194
- 4:1–16   33
- 4:3–8   120
- 4:9   120
- 4:10   118, 120, 198
- 4:10ff.   198
- 4:10–17   4
- 4:11   120
- 4:12   120, 123, 198
- 4:13   120, 198
- 4:13ff.   145
- 4:14–17   120
- 4:15   129
- 4:15–16   198
- 4:17   33, 143, 198
- 4:18   121
- 4:21   143
- 4:27ff.   130
- 4:30   120, 130
- 4:30–31   120
- 4:31   130
- 4–5   130
- 5   130–31
- 5:1   130
- 5:2   110, 130–32, 139
- 5:6–21   132
- 5:22–23   132
- 5–6   137
- 5–14   155
- 5–15   129, 149
- 5–40   164
- 6   3, 132–35
- 6:1   132
- 6:2   131–32, 134
- 6:2–3   3, 14, 25–27
- 6:2–5   132

Exodus (cont.)
- 6:2–8   134
- 6:3   110, 133, 137
- 6:3–8   137
- 6:6   132
- 6:6ff.   132
- 6:7   132, 135–36, 154
- 6:8   132
- 7:1   168, 198
- 7:3   143, 193
- 7:5   110, 138, 140
- 7:8–13   120
- 7:9   143
- 7:14ff.   120
- 7:17   110, 138–39
- 7:25   139
- 7–14   138, 142
- 7–15   119
- 8:4[8]   144
- 8:6[10]   110, 138, 140–41
- 8:11[15]   144
- 8:15[19]   146
- 8:16[20]   139
- 8:17[23]   143
- 8:18[22]   110, 138, 140–41
- 8:18–19[22–23]   141
- 9:1   140
- 9:3   114
- 9:13   140
- 9:14   110, 138, 140–41
- 9:14–16   140
- 9:16   110, 139–41
- 9:20   144, 146
- 9:24–25   142
- 9:27   144
- 9:28–29   141
- 9:29   110, 139–41
- 9:30   144
- 10:1–2   143
- 10:2   110, 139

Exodus (cont.)
- 10:3   140
- 10:6   142
- 10:7   145
- 10:24ff.   145
- 11:9–10   143
- 12:12   110, 139, 142
- 14   147, 148, 202
- 14:4   110, 139–40
- 14:13–14   145
- 14:15   145
- 14:18   110, 139–40
- 14:25   146
- 14:27   146
- 14:31   146–47
- 14–15   138, 143, 153
- 15   146
- 15–16   153
- 15:1   147–48
- 15:3   110, 146–49, 162
- 15:4   148
- 15:6   146
- 15:11   110, 146
- 15:13   146
- 15:14   146
- 15:18   146–47
- 15:20   179
- 15:26   110
- 16:6–7   186
- 16:7   154
- 16:7–8   118–19
- 16:10   154, 186
- 16:12   110
- 19:8   156
- 19:12–13   191
- 19:16–20:21   189
- 19:18   196
- 19:19   198
- 19:21   185
- 19–20   64, 173
- 20   110, 149–153

Index of Scripture

Exodus (cont.)
20:2   110, 135–36, 149–50, 201
20:3   149–50
20:3–12   149
20:4   185
20:4–5   150
20:5   110, 150, 162
20:5–6   151, 162
20:5–7   153
20:7   110, 152–53
20:13–17   150
20:15–18   198
20:18ff.   174
20:18–21   168, 174
20–23   153
23:20ff.   156
23:21   110
23:21–22   156
24:17   154, 196
25   157
25–31   153
29:42–43   153
29:43   154
29:44   154
29:45   153
29:45–46   110
29:46   154
32   151, 154–55, 162, 177
32:1   155
32:1–6   155
32:9–14   156
32:11–14   177
32:25–29   156
32:30   156
32:32   177
32:33   177
32:34   156
32–34   110, 151, 153–63, 213
33   178, 179

Exodus (cont.)
33:2–3   156
33:3   156
33:4   155, 157
33:7–11   177
33:11   172, 178–79, 184, 191, 196
33:12   157
33:12ff.   157
33:13   157–58
33:14   158
33:15–16   158
33:17   158
33:18   81, 83, 140–41, 158
33:18ff.   172, 186
33:18–22   177–78
33:18–23   151, 185
33:18–34:9   118
33:19   19, 110, 123, 153, 155, 158–59, 161–62
33:19–34:7   83
33:20   160, 172, 177, 196
33:20ff.   158
33:20–23   160, 172, 191, 203
33:22   160
33:22–24   155
33:23   160, 161
33–34   153
34   160, 162–63
34:1–4   161
34:5   161
34:5–7   110, 155, 178
34:6   161–62
34:6–7   153, 159, 161–62
34:7   162
34:8   118
34:14   151, 162
40:34   154

Exodus (cont.)
40:34–35   141
40:34–38   186
40:38   196
Leviticus
19:12   152
Numbers
5   150
11   179, 183
11:16–20   179
11:29   179
12   180, 182
12:1   179–80
12:1–2   179
12:2   179–81
12:3   180–82, 186–87, 193
12:4   180, 183
12:5   183
12:6   184–85
12:6–8   179, 181, 183, 185, 187, 188
12:7   183–84
12:7–8   166
12:8   172, 184–87, 191, 196, 204–5
12:9–10   181
12:11–15   181
12:13   182, 184, 186
14:10–12   159
16:19ff.   159
20:12   176
33:4   142
Deuteronomy
1–4   173
1:37   176–77
3:24   120
4   174, 190, 211, 215
4:1–4   190
4:5–8   189
4:7   189–90
4:8   190

Deuteronomy (cont.)
4:12   185, 195–96
4:15   195–96
4:15–16   174–75, 185
4:23   185
4:25   185
4:32–39   190
4:32–40   189–91, 217
4:33   189–91, 196, 203
4:33–35   189
4:34   189–90
4:34–35   90
4:35   189, 214–15, 217
4:36   189–91, 196
4:36–40   189
4:37   189, 214
4:37–38   190
4:37–39   215
4:39   189, 214–15, 217
4:40   189
4–5   64
5   173–74, 176, 186, 189, 195, 203
5:1–5   173
5:1–21   174
5:3   173
5:4   172–74
5:4–5   196
5:5   173–74
5:6   173
5:7–21   173
5:8   185
5:21   190
5:22–26   196
5:22–27   172
5:22–28   174
5:22–31   168–69, 173, 186
5:23   190
5:23–26   174
5:23–27   170
5:24–26   174

Deuteronomy (cont.)
5:25–26   174–75, 179
5:25–31   199
5:26   175, 203
5:27   175
5:28   175
5:28–31   177
5:29   175
5:32–33   173, 175
5–28   173
6   215
6:4   209–14, 216, 218–19, 228
6:4–9   208
6:9   210
6:13   152
6:22   189
7:19   189
9   177
9:9   178
9:10   196
9:18   177–78
9:19   178
9–10   213
10:4   196
11:3   189
13:2–3[1–2]   188–89, 192, 198
13:3[2]   188
18   199
18:9–14   170
18:15   169–70
18:15–18   169–70
18:16   170, 175, 196
26:8   189
28:32   17
28:46   189
29:2–4   189
29–31   173
32:4   215
32:8–9   25
32:15   215

Deuteronomy (cont.)
32:18   215
32:29   215
32:30   215
32:31   215
32:37   215
32:39   36–37
32:51   176
33:1   166
33–34   173
34   171, 176, 187, 192
34:10   167–68, 171–73, 179–80, 187–88, 191–92, 205
34:10–12   165–67, 170–71, 179, 183, 187, 191, 193, 200, 203
34:11   168, 171, 187–88
34:11–12   187–89, 191–93, 205
34:12   188

Joshua
2:11   168
5:1   168
5:12   168
22:22   25

Judges
2:14   168
6   165
6:12   195
6:15   118
6:22   172, 174
6:22–24   190
13   128
13:3   195
17   151

1 Samuel
1:18   20, 168
3:4   117
3:10   117, 161
3:20   183
9:21   118

Index of Scripture

1 Samuel (cont.)
18:18   118
23:13   123
2 Samuel
3:11   168
7:8   118
9:8   118
11:23   20
14:10   168
15:20   114, 123
1 Kings
3:12   168
10:5   168
10:10   168
11:15   20
12   151
13   189
18   150, 214
18:9   118
18:21   150, 214
2 Kings
2:12   168
4–5   189
8:1   123
18:5   168
18:35   131
23:25   168
25:19   184
1 Chronicles
19:19   168
21:17   113
2 Chronicles
2:5   118
9:4   168
13:20   168
Nehemiah
6:6   20
Job
1–2   142–43
3:12   118
4:16   185
6:11   118

Job (cont.)
7:17   118
15:14   118
21:15   118, 131
22:17   131
23:13   212–13
24:4   181
31   212–13
31:15   212–13
37:6   20
38–39   120
41:17   17
Psalms
8:5   118
9:13   181
9:19   181
10:2   181
17:15   185–86
22:27   182
36:7   17
50:19   73
68   97–98
68:3   95
77:14   146
77:16   146
86:5–7   159
89:14   146
89:15   146
89:47[46]   118
90:13   73
93:1ff.   146
95:3   146
96:5   146
96:7ff.   146
98:2   146
100:5   159
101[102]   89–93, 95
101[102]:25[24]   90
101[102]:25–28[24–27]   103
101[102]:27[26]   89–90
105:26–27   192

Psalms (cont.)
106:1–2   159
106:20–21   156
107:1ff.   159
114:3   118
118:1   159
118:29   159
121[122]   76–80, 84, 89
121[122]:3   76–77, 103
121[122]:1–4   76–77
134   84
135:9   192
145:9   159
Proverbs
3:14   181
3:27   17
6:34   150
14:21   181
14:35   20
15:33   182
16:19   181
18:12   182
30:4   120
30:9   131
Ecclesiastes
2:22   20
11:3   20
Song of Songs
6:8–9   209–10
Isaiah
6   165
6:3   93
6:8   117
8   189
8:11   189
16:4   20
20   189
32:7   181
40:12–14   120
40:26   120
40–55   36–37
44:6   36

Isaiah (cont.)
  53   118
Jeremiah
  1   165
  1:6   120
  1:9   189
  13   189
  15:17   189
  28:9   188, 198
  44:22   168
  46:25   142
Ezekiel
  1   165
  1:3   189
  3:14   189
  4   189
  12   189
  12:25   123
  16:38   150
  16:42   150
  20:35   172
  23:25   150
  24   189
  31:11   17
  32:21   17
  33:22   168
  37:1   189
  40:1   189

Daniel
  3   151
Hosea
  1:9   31, 126
Joel
  3:3[2:30]   189
Amos
  8:4   181
Micah
  2:1   17
Habakkuk
  3:7   180
Zechariah
  3:8   189
Judith
  9:7   148
  16:2   148
Matthew
  11:29   70
  22:32   35, 194
  28:19   220
Mark
  12:26   35, 194
Luke
  20:37   35, 194
John
  1   85–86, 103
  1:10   70
  1:13   70

John (cont.)
  1:14   70, 79
  8:28   87, 103
Acts
  2   64, 220
  17:27–28   84
Romans
  1:20   69, 71–72, 103
  7:22–33   73
  13:13–14   75
1 Corinthians
  1:24   100–2
  4:5   205
  13   205
  13:12   204
  15:28   90
2 Corinthians
  5:5   73
  8:9   96
Philippians
  2:6   79, 96
  2:6–8   59
1 John
  4:8   227
  4:16   227
Revelation
  1:8   36
  4:8   93
  21:5   73

Index of Authors and Subjects

Aaron   120-21, 130-32, 179-83, 198
Albrektson, B.   113-14
Albright, W. F.   3, 18, 19, 21, 24, 29
Allen, M.   2, 4, 76, 202
Alm, R. von der   21
Alt, A.   3
Alter, R.   166, 194
Amzallag, N.   2
Anderson, J. F.   79
Aquinas, T.   2, 38, 46, 204
Ashley, T. R.   180, 184-85
Auerbach, E.   234
Augustine   2, 8-9, 38, 56-57, 59-105, 109-10, 113, 115-16, 125, 127-28, 163, 167, 177, 200-5, 210, 213, 216-17, 219, 226-27, 231-34
Ayres, L.   56, 94, 100

Babcock, W. S.   66-67
Barnes, M. R.   56, 94, 100
Barr, J.   8, 27-28, 37, 46
Barth, K.   41-42, 124-25
Bauer, H.   15, 20, 29
Beach-Verhey, K. 2
Beer, G.   18, 21
Beitzel, B. J.   111
Berlejung, A.   23-24
biblical theology   8, 33, 40, 43-44, 219
Biblical Theology Movement   7-8, 33, 37-39
Black, C. C.   2
Blenkinsopp, J.   2, 21, 167-68, 172, 192
Bogaert, P-M.   64

Boman, T.   8
Boulding, M.   77
Brekelmans, Ch. H. W.   21
Brett, M.   31
Brichto, H. C.   155, 157-59
Briggs, R.   4, 176, 181-82, 186, 193
Brongers, H. A.   150
Brunn, E. zum   3, 68-69, 76, 79, 87
Buber, M.   21, 33, 133
Bultmann, R.   40-41

call narrative   165-66, 197-98
Cameron, M.   60, 62, 69, 87
Canaanite religion   14, 20-24, 27
canon   8, 32, 40-41, 44, 50-51, 53-54, 57, 68, 109, 151, 164, 167, 222, 226, 232-33
Casanowicz, I. M.   111, 112
Cassuto, U.   6, 131, 133, 144, 152, 154-55, 160, 161
Cavadini, J. C.   61
Chadwick, H.   69
Chapman, S. B.   166-69, 171-73, 187-89, 192-93
Childs, B. S.   8, 13, 21, 31-46, 52-55, 58, 68, 105, 110, 115-16, 118-19, 123, 126, 130-31, 138, 145-46, 149-52, 155-57, 161, 173, 178, 232, 234-35
Coats, G. W.   118, 181-82
contemplation   68, 74, 77-78, 80-81, 88, 104, 186, 204
Craigie, P. C.   170-71, 174

creation   9, 39, 59, 61, 68, 70–72, 74–76, 81–82, 84, 88–89, 93–99, 103–4, 109, 120, 142–43, 146–47, 151, 218, 222, 231, 233, 235
Cross, F. M., Jr.   3, 18–19, 24–25

Davies, G. I.   2, 137
Davis, D. R.   155, 158, 163
Davis, E. F.   4, 186
Dawson, J. D.   46–47, 60, 61
Denton, R. C.   161–62
Dijkstra, M.   25
divine name   *see* "God, name of" and "'YHWH' (name)"
Dozeman, T. B.   6, 110, 116, 147–50, 152, 162
Driver, D. R.   40–41, 44, 53–54
Driver, G. R.   17–18
Driver, S. R.   19, 123
Dubarle, D.   69
Duhm, B.   15
Durham, J. I.   6, 126, 130, 148, 155–59, 161

Eden, K.   61, 65
Eslinger, L.   146
etymology   6, 8, 13, 14–20, 24–30, 57–59, 104, 109–13, 124, 164, 224, 229, 231
Eusebius   38

Ford, W. A.   138, 140
form criticism   33–35, 119, 165–66, 197
Fowl, S. E.   234
Freedman, D. N.   18–19, 29, 124, 184–185
Frei, H.   8, 45–58, 60, 68, 105, 114, 232, 235
Fretheim, T. E.   131, 138, 143

Gertz, J. C.   3, 26
Gilson, E.   2, 38, 218
Ghillany, F. W.   21

God
  action of   3, 6–7, 30, 39, 59, 109–110, 116, 124, 138, 143, 147, 149, 162, 164, 189–93, 197, 205, 210–12, 215, 217, 226–30
  as subject matter of Scripture   57, 232
  attributes of   59–60, 69–71, 75–84, 88–89, 91–94, 98–100, 102–4, 110, 115–16, 125, 127, 137, 140, 145–47, 149–53, 157–65, 177, 179, 203–4, 211–15, 217–18, 225, 227, 229–31
    simplicity   93, 100, 102
  being of   6–9, 37–39, 59, 63, 69, 71, 77–79, 81, 86, 88–105, 109–10, 124, 152, 161, 202, 207–10, 212–14, 216–18, 223–28, 231, 234–35
  identity of   3, 7, 47, 59, 82, 109, 122, 137, 148–49, 163–64, 202, 206–8, 212, 214, 217, 222, 226–31
  knowledge of   4, 6, 8–10, 39, 59–60, 65, 81, 83–84, 88, 104, 110, 124–25, 127, 129–30, 132–33, 135–39, 141, 143–45, 148–49, 152, 154, 156–59, 162–65, 170, 174, 176, 183, 185, 202–5, 207, 213, 216, 218–19, 226–31, 233
  name of   2–3, 6–7, 13–20, 24–25, 27–31, 34, 38, 80–84, 88, 105, 109–13, 115–16, 121–38, 141, 149–50, 152–54, 159, 161–64, 178, 194, 199–203, 206–7, 214, 218–32   *see also* "YHWH"
  perception of (seeing and hearing God)   118, 132, 140–41, 154, 158–60, 165, 174–76, 178–79, 183–88, 191, 194–98, 203–7
  revelation of   *see* "knowledge of"
  Trinity   3, 7, 8–9, 13, 40, 45, 55–58, 60, 68–69, 76, 87–88, 94–105, 109, 207, 219–24, 226–30, 232–35
    inseparable operations   55-58
  word of   168–71, 173, 178, 183, 187, 199

God *(cont.)*
    Word of   see *"Jesus Christ"*
Gowan, D. E.   144, 150–151, 157, 160
Grabbe, L. L.   26–27
Gray, G. B.   182, 185
Greek mentality   7–8, 36–37, 45, 69
Greenberg, M.   118–20, 133, 195
Greene-McCreight, K. E.   63
Guillaume, A.   111–12
Gunn, D. M.   138, 144–45, 155
Gunneweg, A. H. J.   21

Habel, N.   33, 165, 197
Hamilton, V. P.   6
Hamori, E. J.   148, 160
Harnack, A.   5
Haupt, P. von   18, 24
Hays, R. B.   4
Hebrew mentality   7–8, 37, 45
Hepner, G.   180
Hertog, C. den   2, 5, 31, 79, 111–12, 116, 121, 123–28, 148, 201
Hill, E.   80
Hollander, H. W.   204–5
Houtman, C.   117, 126, 148

idem per idem   19, 123–25, 200, 202
interpretation   14, 32, 41–44, 46, 48–49, 52–55, 62, 104, 234–35
    canonical   31–32, 40–41, 45, 51, 57–58, 104–5, 163–64
    christological   48, 50–52, 55–58, 84, 88
    figural   46, 49, 51, 53–54, 60–61, 76
    history of   4–5, 8–9, 35, 39, 45, 233–34
    narrative   6, 8–9, 33, 47–55, 58, 61, 65, 80, 109, 117, 129, 131, 140, 152–53, 155, 157, 160–61, 163–64, 194, 198, 201, 219, 228, 230, 233–34
    ontological   5, 9, 33, 36–37, 40, 44, 176, 206–8, 210–11, 213, 215, 217–18, 228, 230, 233, 235

    theological   4–5, 7, 9, 13, 59, 105, 133, 207, 232, 235
    Trinitarian   9, 45, 55–58, 60, 68, 76, 88–89, 94–105, 109, 219–20, 224–30, 232–35
Israelite religion   14, 16–18, 133–36, 165, 171
    historical reconstruction of   3, 13–14, 20–28, 30, 35, 37, 104, 208, 231

Jacob, B.   116, 133
Janzen, J. G.   2, 209, 212–15
Jerome   79
Jesus Christ   39, 41, 43–45, 48–51, 54–55, 57–59, 61, 68, 72–76, 80, 82, 84–87, 96–97, 100, 169, 194, 211, 220, 222–23, 230, 232
Joüon, P.   19, 123
Jowett, B.   53
Justin Martyr   2

Kaufmann, Y.   21
Kearney, R.   2, 6, 116
Kenite hypothesis   20–21, 23
Kerr, F.   2
Kinyongo, J.   15, 19–20
Knauf, E. A.   15, 16, 19, 29
Knight, G. A. F.   150, 152, 159–60
Knoppers, G. N.   168, 171
Koehler, L.   28
Kooten, G. H. van   2
Krašovec, J.   140, 144
Kselman, J. S.   185

Labuschagne, C. J.   118, 120, 141
Lagarde, P. A. de   18
Larsson, G.   6, 7
Leander, P.   15, 20, 29
Levenson, J. D.   144
Levering, M.   2, 201, 204, 224
Lind, M.   147
Lindblom, J.   113–14

Lipiński, E. 32
Lipton, D. 160
literal sense   *see "senses of Scripture, literal"*
Liverani, M. 26-27
Lohr, J. N. 4
Long, D. S. 228
Louth, A. 30
love 49, 62, 65-67, 70-71, 204, 216-18, 227
Lubac, H. de 4, 63

MacDonald, N. 207-19, 228
MacLaurin, E. C. B. 15
Manichaeism 71-72, 87
Marion, J-L. 77-79, 91
Marshall, B. 46, 229
Masoretic text 5-7, 24, 69, 76-79, 81, 113-15, 128, 148, 184, 186, 230-31, 233
Mayes, A. D. H. 169
McCabe, H. 218
McCarthy, D. J. 140
Meek, T. J. 15-17
Mettinger, T. N. D. 23-24
Milgrom, J. 176-77, 180-81, 183-84
Miller, P. D. 23, 147, 171, 214-15
Miriam 179-83
Moberly, R. W. L. 4, 6, 110, 117, 121-22, 124, 126, 133-37, 155-63, 165, 168-70, 174-76, 195, 200, 209
monotheism 21-23, 25, 207-8, 211-12, 214-17, 219
Moor, J. C. de 3, 25
Moses 1, 9, 22, 25-26, 34-35, 38, 63-65, 80-81, 83-84, 88, 110, 117-19, 121-23, 125-26, 128-29, 131-35, 137, 139, 141, 145-46, 151, 153, 155-61, 163, 165-85, 187, 189, 191-206, 219, 228-29, 231
   covenant mediator 165, 170, 172-79, 191, 193-94, 196, 199, 201-2, 204, 206, 219, 228-29
   Moses' wife 179-81
   proximity to YHWH 165, 175-79, 187, 194-97, 205-6
Mowinckel, S. 29
Muraoka, T. 19, 123
Murtonen, A. 15

Niehr, H. 22
Noble, P. 31, 43
Noth, M. 21, 123, 166, 179-81

Obermann, J. 17-18
Oesterley, W. O. E. 3, 15
Olson, D. T. 166, 170, 173-74, 176, 179-80, 185, 189-90, 192
ontology 37, 39, 45, 53, 69, 71, 81, 208, 210-11, 213, 215-19
Origen 50

Pannell, R. J. 2
Parke-Taylor, G. H. 21
paronomasia   *see "wordplay"*
Pattison, G. 2
Pedersen, J. 114
Perkins, L. 148
Pharaoh 117-21, 130-32, 137-46, 149, 187, 193, 198
Philo 2, 36, 81
Platonism 70-75, 85
   Neoplatonism 61, 79, 226
Polak, F. 197, 199-200, 202
Preus, J. S. 62
prophecy 128, 165, 167-71, 175, 179, 183-84, 187-89, 192-94, 198, 201, 204-5
Propp, W. H. C. 22-23, 123

Rad, G. von 6, 13-14, 21, 31, 59, 109, 113, 151, 169-70, 178, 208

Radner, E.   4
religio-historical approaches   *see "Israelite religion, history of"*
Renaud, B.   151
Rendtorff, R.   142
Reno, R. R.   4
Revell, E. J.   123
Ricoeur, P.   4, 5, 129
Robinson, B. P.   179-81
Robinson, T. H.   3, 15
Rofé, A.   190-91
Rogers, C.   182
Rowe, C. K.   7
Rowley, H. H.   21
Rule of Faith   62, 65

Sæbø, M.   124
Sailhamer, J. H.   6, 8
Sakenfeld, K. D.   32
Sanders, J. A.   32
Sarna, N. M.   64, 116, 126, 131, 140, 142-44, 153, 159, 162
Savran, G. W.   166, 195-98
Schild, E.   113-14
Schmid, K.   3, 116, 122
Scruton, R.   210
Seitz, C. R.   4, 6-7, 52, 116, 126, 134-37, 221-22
senses of Scripture   46-47, 63
  allegorical/figurative (Augustine)   63, 65, 67, 76, 203, 232
  historical   41-42, 52-53, 63
  literal   3, 8-9, 13, 40, 45-58, 60, 65-69, 76, 103-5, 109-10, 206, 229, 232, 235
  literal/proper (Augustine)   63, 65-67, 76, 232
  literal/corporeal (Augustine)   65-66
  plain   47-48, 50
  spiritual (Augustine)   65, 67-68, 232

Septuagint   5-7, 36, 76-77, 81, 113, 115, 128, 148, 178-79, 184-86, 229, 231-32
Simon, U.   166
Sinai/Horeb   22, 33, 119, 134, 155, 156, 178, 196, 199-201
Smith, M. S.   22-23, 25-26
Soden, W. von   18
Soulen, R. K.   2, 207, 219-28
source criticism   3-4, 33-35, 122, 133, 137, 142
Strawn, B.   55-58, 232
Stubbs, D. L.   180
Studer, B.   85
substance   96-99, 101, 103
Sumner, G. R.   4

tabernacle   141, 153-54, 156-58, 183
Targums   36-37, 178-79
tent of meeting   *see "tabernacle"*
Terrien, S. L.   137
Tetragrammaton   *see "God, name of, 'YHWH'"*
theological interpretation   *see "interpretation, theological"*
theophany   80, 103, 117, 148, 161, 174, 178-79, 185, 196-97
Tiele, C.   21
Tigay, J.   21, 166-68, 170, 175-77, 188
tradition, Christian   3-5, 7-9, 29-31, 38-39, 49-50, 59, 223, 229, 231, 235
translation   4-5, 7, 113-16, 148, 182-85, 209
Toorn, K. van der   18, 21, 24

Vaux, R. de   15, 17-18, 20-21, 113
Vetus Latina   64, 78-79, 81-82, 115, 125, 128, 229, 231-32
Vriezen, T. C.   110-12, 123
Vulgate   78-79, 81, 128, 184-85, 229, 232

Walker, N.   215

Watson, F. 58
Weinandy, T. G. 7
Weinfeld, M. 21
Weippert, M. 21
Wellhausen, J. 5, 15–16
Westphal, M. 2
Wette, W. M. L. de 5
Williams, C. H. 215
Wilson, R. R. 138
wordplay 14, 110–13, 164, 224–25, 229, 232

Yahwism see "Israelite religion"

Yeago, D. S. 7, 37, 103, 216
"YHWH" (name) 2–3, 6–7, 13–20, 25–30, 34, 110–13, 121–23, 125–29, 131–36, 138–42, 146, 149–50, 152–54, 159, 161–64, 199–202, 206–7, 214–15, 218–22, 224–33 see also "God, name of"
Young, F. M. 46

Zevit, Z. 142
Zimmerli, W. 132, 138, 149–51, 165–66, 169

www.ingramcontent.com/pod-product-compliance
Lightning Source LLC
Chambersburg PA
CBHW030513080526
44586CB00011B/174